MW00638581

C. HALE SIPE, A. B

The Indian Wars of Pennsylvania

An Account of the Indian Events, in Pennsylvania, of the French and Indian War, Pontiac's War, Lord Dunmore's War, the Revolutionary War and the Indian Uprisings from 1789 to 1795

Book One

C. Hale Sipe

HERITAGE BOOKS
2008

HERITAGE BOOKS
AN IMPRINT OF HERITAGE BOOKS, INC.

Books, CDs, and more—Worldwide

For our listing of thousands of titles see our website
at
www.HeritageBooks.com

A Facsimile Reprint
Published 2008 by
HERITAGE BOOKS, INC.
Publishing Division
100 Railroad Ave. #104
Westminster, Maryland 21157

— Publisher's Notice —
In reprints such as this, it is often not possible to remove blemishes from the original. We feel the contents of this book warrant its reissue despite these blemishes and hope you will agree and read it with pleasure.

International Standard Book Numbers
Paperbound: 978-0-7884-4666-5
Clothbound: 978-0-7884-7675-4

To the Memory of his Sainted Mother,
from Whom he Inherited a Love for
the History of Pennsylvania,
this Book is Reverently
Dedicated by The
Author

Principal Sources Utilized in the Preparation of this Work

Archives of Pennsylvania.

Colonial Records of Pennsylvania.

Egle's History of Pennsylvania.

Gordon's History of Pennsylvania.

Day's Historical Collections.

Frontier Forts of Pennsylvania.

Pennypacker's Pennsylvania, the Keystone.

Loudon's Indian Narratives.

Rupp's County Histories.

Magazines of the Historical Society of Pennsylvania.

Egle's Notes and Queries.

Miner's History of Wyoming.

Jenkin's Pennsylvania, Colonial and Federal.

Lossing's Field Book of the Revolution.

On the Frontier with Colonel Antes.

Meginness' Otzinachson.

Linn's Annals of Buffalo Valley.

Hassler's Old Westmoreland.

Fisher's Making of Pennsylvania.

McClure's Old Time Notes.

Parkman's Works.

Jones' Juniata Valley.

Hanna's Wilderness Trail.

March's History of Pennsylvania.

Smith's History of Armstrong County.

Veech's Monongahela of Old.

McKnight's Pioneer History of Northwestern Pennsylvania.

Conover's Journal of the Military Expedition of Major-General Sullivan against the Six Nations of New York in 1779.

Craig's The Olden Time.

Darlington's Fort Pitt and Letters from the Frontier.

Darlington's Christopher Gist's Journals.

Hodge's Handbook of American Indians.

Sylvester's Indian Wars of New England.

Hulbert's Historic Highways of America.

Rupp's Early History of Western Pennsylvania and the West.

Thwaites' Early Western Travels.

Thwaites' Documentary History of Lord Dunmore's War.

Walton's Conrad Weiser and the Indian Policy of Colonial Pennsylvania.

Withers' Chronicles of Border Warfare.

Craig's History of Pittsburgh.

Cort's Henry Bouquet.

Keith's Chronicles of Pennsylvania.

Boucher's History of Westmoreland County.

Albert's History of Westmoreland County.

Donehoo's Pennsylvania—A History.

DeSchweinitz's Life of David Zeisberger.

Espenshade's Pennsylvania Place Names.

Heckewelder's Works.

Mann's Life of Henry Melchior Muhlenberg.

Father Lambing's Works.

Butterfield's Washington-Irvine Correspondence.

Washington's Journal.

Celeron's Journal.

Colden's History of the Five Nations.

Volwiler's George Croghan.

Johnson's Swedish Settlements on the Delaware.

Loskiel's History of the Mission of the United Brethren Among the Indians of North America.

Patterson's History of the Backwoods.

Doddridge's Settlement and Indian Wars of Virginia and Pennsylvania.

Godcharles' Daily Stories of Pennsylvania.

Sawvel's Logan, the Mingo.

And many others.

INTRODUCTION

IT affords me much pleasure to write these few words of introduction to "The Indian Wars of Pennsylvania," of which I have read the manuscript.

Mr. Sipe has wisely followed the same scientific method in the collection of his data for this work which he did in his "Indian Chiefs of Pennsylvania." As a consequence the two books give a thoroughly accurate picture of the thrillingly romantic period of Pennsylvania history from 1755 to 1795, during which the mountains and the valleys of the frontiers of Pennsylvania were literally drenched with blood.

For nearly three quarters of a century after the Treaty of William Penn with the Indians on the Delaware, the settlements of the European races had spread peacefully westward to the Blue Mountains. Even though there were occasional rumblings of a threatening storm, the sky was still clear and peace dwelt in the far-flung settlements, which stretched westward to the foothills of the Alleghenies.

The struggle between France and Great Britain for the possession of the Ohio valley and the consequent effort on the part of both of these rivals for the friendship of the Indian was the final cause for the conflict between the Indian and the English settler. The French had traded with the Delaware and the Shawnee, but had not taken his lands for settlement. On the other hand, the English had driven the Delaware from his ancestral habitat on the river which bears his name to the Susquehanna and then to the Ohio by his land purchases, just and unjust, and the same fact applies to the Shawnee. The English had, in their spreading settlements, taken up Indian lands, until practically nothing was left of their lands east of the mountain ridges. Even their last place of refuge on the waters of the Ohio, which they were occupying by permission of the Iroquois, was sought for by the "land hungry" English.

This land hunger was, so far as the English were concerned, a hunger for homes by these people of the British Empire, who had never known what it was to own lands of their own. It was the real motive in all of the migrations of these peoples from the lands across the seas. And yet, it caused as serious consequences to the Indian as did the Spanish search for gold.

INTRODUCTION

After the defeat of the army of General Edward Braddock by the French and Indians in 1755, the storm which had been slowly gathering along the waters of the upper Ohio, broke in all of its mad fury along the eastern foothills of the Alleghenies and for a period of forty years it raged with but few slight intermissions.

After the Conspiracy of Pontiac, 1763–4, the scene of action for the worst Indian wars was shifted west of the Alleghenies. The Purchase of 1768 opened the lands west of the mountains to the settlers who poured over the mountain ridges in an ever increasing tide. The occupation of these lands along the Ohio by the white settlers from Pennsylvania and Virginia met with the armed opposition of the Indians. As a consequence, there was the long series of Border Wars, expeditions into the "Indian country" west of the Ohio, and later the union of the British with the Indians against all of the settlements in western Pennsylvania. These wars did not end until the final overthrow of the Indian and British by General Anthony Wayne, at Fallen Timbers, and the Treaty at Greenville, which resulted, in 1795.

The hardships and sufferings of the pioneer settlers of Pennsylvania during these long, weary years of border wars was, however, the foundation upon which a new nation was to be builded. Without the training and the discipline in hardship of those years the War of the American Revolution, which followed so closely upon these Indian wars, would have been doomed to failure. These frontiers-men were trained in the use of the rifle and in the methods of warfare. The generation of young men, which made up the very backbone of Washington's army had known nothing but warfare and strife from their earliest infancy. The war-whoop of the Indian and the whistle of rifle bullets were the familiar sounds of childhood.

Germantown, Valley Forge, Monmouth, Trenton, Saratoga and Yorktown could not have been without these years of bitter training, in the making of Morgan's Riflemen, Proctor's Brigade, the Eighth Pennsylvania, the Thirteenth Virginia and the other bodies making up the Continental Army from the frontiers of Pennsylvania.

Not only the enlisted men, but also the great majority of the most effective officers of the Army of Washington were trained for war on the frontiers of Pennsylvania. Washington, Wayne, Mercer, Morgan, Armstrong, Proctor, Burd, Clapham, Shippen, Brodhead, St. Clair, Irvine, Crawford and Sullivan are but a few of the graduates of this "West Point" of the frontiers of Pennsylvania.

Mr. Sipe in his "Indian Chiefs of Pennsylvania" has given a critical, and romantic picture of the Indian chiefs who played such vital parts upon the stage of history during this period. In the present work, "The Indian Wars of Pennsylvania," he tells what these chiefs did to make the pioneer history of the frontiers of Pennsylvania one of the most thrilling chapters in American history. He fully and accurately covers the events of these Border Wars, which had so much to do with the Birth of a Nation.

GEORGE P. DONEHOO.

PREFACE

"THE Indian Wars of Pennsylvania" has been written in response to the requests of many historians and educators, not only in Pennsylvania but in other parts of the United States, who were well pleased with the author's "Indian Chiefs of Pennsylvania." Until the appearance of "The Indian Chiefs of Pennsylvania," in April, 1927, the author was unknown to the lovers of the history of the Keystone State; and he believes that the fine reception given this book was due, in large measure, to the fact that it was highly endorsed by that eminent authority on Pennsylvania history, Dr. George P. Donehoo, whose "History of the Indian Place Names in Pennsylvania" and forthcoming "History of the Indian Trails of Pennsylvania" should find a place in the library of every lover of the history of the Pennsylvania Indians.

"The Indian Wars of Pennsylvania" is based primarily on the Pennsylvania Archives and the Pennsylvania Colonial Records. No effort has been spared to make the book a trustworthy and authoritative work on the great Indian wars and uprisings which crimsoned the soil of Pennsylvania with the blood of both the Indian and the white man during the long period from 1755 to 1795. Throughout the book will be found many references to the Pennsylvania Archives and the Pennsylvania Colonial Records and many quotations from these and other trustworthy sources.

The need for the present volume is apparent. There is no more thrilling and tragic chapter in American History than the period of the Indian wars and uprisings in Pennsylvania. Pennsylvania suffered more than did any other Colony during this period. Yet how few are familiar with this important period in the history of Pennsylvania! And the reason is that historical writers have not given the Indian wars and uprisings in Pennsylvania the attention that their importance deserves.

We read the history of Greece, of Rome, of England. Why should we neglect the history of the great race that roamed the hills and vales of Pennsylvania and left its sounding names on the Pennsylvania mountains, valleys and streams?

The reader will note that more than one hundred and seventy-five pages of the present volume deal with the Indian events in

Pennsylvania during the Revolutionary War. The author believes that students of the Revolutionary struggle will appreciate this fact. Few historians seem to realize how largely the Revolutionary War was fought on the frontiers of Pennsylvania.

Perhaps a few words should be said concerning the plan of "The Indian Wars of Pennsylvania." The author thought it well not to have the book begin abruptly with the account of the first conflict between the Indian and the white man in Pennsylvania. Hence, the opening chapters are devoted to the Indian's religion and character; to a view of the Indian tribes that inhabited Pennsylvania; to a discussion of the Indian policy of the Swedes on the Delaware and of William Penn; and to the leading events in the Indian history of Pennsylvania before the bloody warfare between the two races began. This plan, the author believes, will enable the reader to make a more intelligent and satisfactory study of the many years of bloody conflict between the two races in Pennsylvania. The volume is thus much more than a history of the Indian wars and uprisings in the state bearing the name of Penn, the apostle.

C. HALE SIPE.

Butler, Pennsylvania,
February 2, 1929.

ACKNOWLEDGMENTS

THE author desires to thank the hundreds of Pennsylvanians and others who subscribed for "The Indian Wars of Pennsylvania" before the manuscript was handed to the printer. He especially thanks the following persons for substantial subscriptions:

Governor John S. Fisher and State Librarian Frederick A. Godcharles of Pennsylvania; Prof. John A. Anthony, Pittsburgh, Penna., Jos. A. Beck, Esq., Pittsburgh, Penna.; G. H. Blakeley, Bethlehem, Penna.; Hon. Marshall Brown, Pittsburgh, Penna.; Capt. W. R. Furlong, Washington, D. C.; Earle R. Forrest, Washington, Penna.; John Gribbel and W. Griffin Gribbel, Wyncote, Penna.; Jos. F. Guffey, Pittsburgh, Penna.; Hon. D. B. Heiner, Kittanning, Penna.; Dr. C. G. Hughes, Pittsburgh, Penna.; E. H. Hutchison, Harmony, Penna.; Dr. C. E. Imbrie, Butler, Penna.; Prof. V. K. Irvine, Butler, Penna.; Mrs. Cecelia R. Jamison, Greensburg, Penna.; Hon. J. W. King, Kittanning, Penna.; Hon. Richard H. Koch, Pottsville, Penna.; H. K. Landis, Lancaster, Penna.; J. B. Landis, Butler, Penna.; Rachel R. Lowe, Pittsburgh, Penna.; Hon. W. Frank Mathues, Philadelphia, Penna.; Hon. Geo. W. Maxey, Scranton, Penna.; W. H. McClane, Washington, Penna.; Harry A. Neeb, Jr., Pittsburgh, Penna.; H. R. Pratt, Baltimore, Md.; W. L. Riggs, Esq., McKeesport, Penna.; A. C. Robinson, Sewickley, Penna.; J. V. Scaife, Pittsburgh, Penna.; Samuel Shoemaker, Philadelphia, Penna.; Homer H. Swaney, Esq., Beaver Falls, Penna.; Vernon F. Taylor, Indiana, Penna.; Hon. Henry W. Temple, Washington, Penna.; Hon. Theo. L. Wilson, Clarion, Penna; Henry Wittmer, Pittsburgh, Penna.; J. E. Henretta, Kane, Penna.; J. B. Warriner, Lansford, Penna.; W. M. Laverty, Philadelphia, Penna.; and M. Wilson Stewart, Esq., Pittsburgh, Penna.

The author is under great obligation to Dr. George P. Donehoo for his careful reading of the proofs and making many suggestions.

Additional thanks are due State Librarian Frederick A. Godcharles for many courtesies extended the author in the use of rare volumes in the Pennsylvania State Library. Finally, the author thanks the many educators and historians in Pennsylvania and other parts of the United States, who suggested to him the writing of this specialized history, and he hopes the book will come up to their expectations.

C. HALE SIPE.

Butler, Pennsylvania,
February 2, 1929.

LIST OF ILLUSTRATIONS

CONTENTS

CHAPTER I

The Pennsylvania Indians—Their Religion and Character

GO where we may, in Pennsylvania, we are put in remembrance of the American Indian by the beautiful names he gave to the valleys, streams and mountains where he roamed for untold generations, never dreaming that from afar would come a stronger race which would plant amid the wilderness the hamlet and the town and cause cities to rise where the forest waved over the home of his heart. The Wyoming Valley; the Tuscarora Valley; the winding Susquehanna; the blue Juniata; the broad Ohio; the Kittatinny Mountain; the Allegheny Mountains—these are but a few of the everlasting reminders of the Pennsylvania Indians. Until the new heavens arch themselves and until the new earth comes, our Pennsylvania valleys will lie smiling in the sunlight, our Pennsylvania streams will go singing to the sea, and our Pennsylvania mountains will lift their summits to the sky; and throughout the ages may succeeding generations of Pennsylvanians realize that the Indian loved these valleys, these streams, these mountains, with a love as strong as that hallowing passion which touched the Grecian mountain-pass of Thermopylae more than twenty-four hundred years ago, and has caused it to glow with never-dying lustre through the long night of centuries. It was love for the land of his fathers that caused the Indian to fight to the death for his home and hunting grounds.

A child of nature, the Indian knew not the God of revelation; but the God of the universe and nature he acknowledged in all things around him,—the sun, the moon, the stars, the flowers, the singing birds, the mighty oaks and sighing pines of the forest, the pleasant valleys, the babbling brooks, the dashing water-falls, the rushing rivers, the lofty mountains. Reverently he worshipped the Great Spirit, who created him, who governed the world, who taught the streams to flow and the bird to build her nest, who caused day and night and the changing seasons, who stocked the streams with fish and the forests with game for his Red Children. To the Great Spirit went up many a pure prayer from the Indian's dark bosom. He prayed when he went on the chase; he prayed when he sat down to partake of the fruits of the chase; he prayed when he went to war. And when he closed his eyes in death, it was in the firm belief that death was mere transition to the Happy Hunting Ground, where, with care and sorrow removed, he would pursue the deer throughout the endless ages of eternity.

The Testimony of Heckewelder

The Moravian missionary, Rev. John Heckewelder, who labored for many years among the Delawares of Pennsylvania and Ohio, beginning his work in 1762, makes the following statements concerning the Indian's religion and character, in his "Indian Nations", published in 1818:

"The Indian considers himself as being created by an all-powerful, wise, and benevolent Mannito (Manitou); all that he possesses, all that he enjoys, he looks upon as given to him or allotted for his use by the Great Spirit who gave him life. He therefore believes it to be his duty to adore and worship his Creator and benefactor; to acknowledge with gratitude his past favours, thank him for present blessings, and solicit the continuation of his good will. An old Indian told me, about fifty years ago, that when he was young, he still followed the custom of his father and ancestors, in climbing upon a high mountain or pinnacle, to thank the Great Spirit for all the benefits before bestowed, and to pray for a continuance of his favor; that they were sure their prayers were heard, and acceptable to the Great Spirit, although he did not himself appear unto them.

"They think that he, the Great Spirit, made the earth and all that it contains for the common good of mankind; when he stocked the country that he gave them with plenty of game, it was not for the benefit of a few, but of all. Every thing was given in common for the sons of men . . . From this principle, hospitality flows as from its source. With them, it is not a virtue, but a strict duty. Hence they are never in search of excuses to avoid giving, but freely supply their neighbour's wants from the stock prepared for their own use. They give and are hospitable to all, without exception, and will always share with each other and often with the stranger, even to their last morsel. They rather would lie down themselves on an empty stomach, than have it laid to their charge that they had neglected their duty by not satisfying the wants of the stranger, the sick or the needy. . .

"They treat each other with civility, and show much affection on meeting after an absence . . . They are not quarrelsome, and are always on their guard, so as not to offend each other. They do not fight with each other; they say that fighting is only for dogs and beasts. They are, however, fond of play, yet very careful that they do not offend. They are remarkable for the particular respect which they pay to old age. In all their meetings, whether public or private, they pay the greatest attention to the observations and advice of the aged; no one will attempt to contradict them, nor to interfere in any manner or even to speak, unless he is specially called upon."

Heckewelder says that, while marriages among the Indians were not contracted for life, it being understood that the parties were not to live together longer than they should be pleased with each other, yet both parties, sensible of this understanding, did every thing in their power to please each other. The husband built the home, and considered himself bound to support the wife and family by his exertions as hunter, fisher and trapper, while the wife took upon herself the labor of planting and raising corn and other products of the soil. The wife, he says, considered her labor much lighter than that of the husband, "for they themselves say that, while their field labour employs them at most six weeks in the year, that of the men continues the whole year round. Neither creeks nor rivers, whether shallow or deep, frozen or free from ice, must be an obstacle to the hunter, when in pursuit of a wounded deer, bear, or other animal, as is often the case. Nor has he then leisure to think on the state of his body, and to consider whether his blood is not too much heated to plunge without danger into the cold stream, since the game he is in pursuit of is running off from him with full speed. Many dangerous accidents often befall him, both as a hunter and a warrior (for he is both), and are seldom unattended with painful consequences, such as rheumatism, or comsumption of the lungs, for which the sweat-house, on which they so much depend, and to which they often resort for relief, especially after a fatiguing hunt or warlike expedition, is not always a sure preservative or an effectual remedy."

Heckewelder also says that, if the sick squaw longed for an article of food, be it what it may or however difficult to procure, the husband would at once endeavor to get it for her, and that he knew of instances where the husband would go forty or fifty miles for a mess of cranberries to satisfy his wife's longing.

Speaking of the Indians' cruelty to their enemies, Heckewelder says:

"The Indians are cruel to their enemies! In some cases they are, but perhaps not more so than white men have sometimes shewn themselves. There have been instances of white men flaying or taking off the skin of Indians who had fallen into their hands, and then tanning those skins, or cutting them in pieces, making them up into razor-straps, and exposing those for sale, as was done at or near Pittsburg, sometime during the Revolutionary War. Those things are abominations in the eyes of the Indians, who, indeed, when strongly excited, inflict torments on their prisoners and put them to death by cruel tortures, but never are guilty of acts of barbarity in cold blood. Neither do the Delawares, and some other Indian nations, ever, on any account, disturb the ashes of the dead."

Contrary to the general supposition, the Indian was not cruel by nature. His cruelty was confined to the times when he was on the war path; and even then, there is no record of his having committed a deed as disgusting, revolting and horrible as the murder of the ninety-six Christian Delawares, at Gnadenhuetten, Ohio, on the 8th of March, 1782, by Colonel David Williamson and his band of Scotch-Irish settlers from Washington County, Pennsylvania.

During the long Indian wars, in Pennsylvania, from 1755 to 1795, hundreds of white persons, captured by the Indians, were adopted into Indian families, to take the places mostly of warriors who had fallen on the field of the slain. These captives, so adopted, were treated with great kindness, and were looked upon by the Indians as their own flesh and blood. Many, indeed, were the instances of captives, recovered by the whites, who later returned to the forest homes of their Indian friends and adopted Indian relatives. Heckewelder speaks of the humanity and delicacy with which the Indians treated female prisoners whom they intended to adopt. The early Indian never captured women, white or red, for immoral purposes. (Page 381.)

The fiercest passion in the Indian's wild heart was the love of revenge, but, on the other hand, he would give his life for the protection of a friend. There was none more constant and steadfast as a friend. He would share his last morsel with the stranger within his gates. He was the noblest type of primitive man that ever trod the earth.

Among the children of men there were none who could equal him in power of endurance and capacity for suffering. He could travel on foot for days without food. He could be tortured to death by fire without a groan escaping his lips, and he chanted his death song with his latest breath.

The Indian's Pride

Says, Heckewelder, speaking of the Delawares or Lenni-Lenape; "They will not admit that the whites are superior beings. They say that the hair of their heads, their features, the various colours of their eyes, evince that they are not like themselves Lenni Lenape, an *Original People*, a race of men that has existed unchanged from the beginning of time; but they are a *mixed* race, and therefore a troublesome one. Wherever they may be, the Great Spirit, knowing the wickedness of their disposition, found it necessary to give them a great Book, and taught them how to read it, that they might know and observe what he wished them to do and to abstain from. But they, the Indians, have no need of any such book to let them know the will of their Maker; they find it engraved on their own hearts; they have had sufficient discernment given to them to distinguish good from evil, and by following that guide, they are sure not to err.

"It is true, they confess, that when they first saw the whites, they took them for beings of a superior kind. They did not know but that they had been sent to them from the abode of the Great Spirit for some great and important purpose. They therefore welcomed them, hoping to be made happier by their company. It was not long, however, before they discovered their mistake, having found them an ungrateful, insatiable people, who, though the Indians had given them as much land as was necessary to raise provisions for themselves and their families, and pasture for their cattle, wanted still to have more, and at last would not be contented with less than the *whole country*. 'And yet,' say those injured people, 'these white men would always be telling us of their great Book which God had given to them; they would persuade us that every man was good who believed in what the Book said, and every man was bad who did not believe in it. They told us a great many things, which, they said, were written in the good Book, and wanted us to believe it all. We would probably have done so, if we had seen them practise what they pretended to believe, and act according to the good words which they told us. But no! While they held their big Book in one hand, in the other, they had murderous weapons, guns and swords wherewith to kill us, poor Indians. Ah! and they did so, too; they killed those who believed in their Book, as well as those who did not. They made no distinction!"

Effects of the White Man's Rum and Vices

Having seen that the Indian had many virtues, it is but fair to add that many of these virtues were broken down by the white man. We refer particularly to the ruin wrought among the Indians by the white man's rum and vices. The Indian knew neither rum nor shameful diseases until his contact with the white man. Hear Heckewelder:

"So late as about the middle of the last century (the eighteenth century), the Indians were yet a hardy and healthy people, and many very aged men and women were seen among them, some of whom thought they had lived about one hundred years. They frequently told me and others that, when they were young men, their people did not marry so early as they did since, that even at twenty they were called boys, and durst not wear a breech-clout, as the men did at that time, but had only a small bit of skin hanging before them. Neither, did they say, were they subject to so many disorders as in later times, and many of them calculated on dying of old age. But since that time, a great change has taken place in the constitution of those Indians who live nearest to the whites. By the introduction of ardent spirits among them, they have been led into vices which have brought on disorders which, they say, were unknown before; their blood became corrupted by a shameful complaint, which, they say, they had never known or heard of until the Europeans came among them. Now the Indians are affected with it to a great degree; children frequently inherit it from their parents, and after lingering for a few years, at last die victims to this poison. *Our vices have destroyed them more than our swords.*

"The general prevalence of drunkenness among the Indians is, in a great degree, owing to the unprincipled white traders, who persuade them to become intoxicated that they may cheat them the more easily, and obtain their lands or pelfries for a mere trifle. Within the last fifty years, some instances have even come to my knowledge of white men having enticed Indians to drink, and when they were drunk, murdered them. The effects which intoxication produces upon the Indians are dreadful. It has been the cause of an infinite number of murders among them. I cannot say how many have died of colds and other disorders, which they have caught by lying upon the cold ground, and remaining exposed to the elements, when drunk; others have lingered out their lives in excruciating rheumatic pains and in wasting consumptions until death came to relieve them of their sufferings. I once asked an Indian at Pittsburgh, whom I had not seen before, who he was. He answered in broken English: 'My name is Blackfish; when at home with my nation, I am a clever fellow, and when here, a *hog*.' He meant that by means of the liquor which the white people gave him, he was sunk to the level of that beast."

Heckewelder says that reflecting Indians keenly remarked "that it was strange that a people who professed themselves believers in a religion, revealed to them by the Great Spirit himself; who say that they have in their houses the Word of God and his laws and commandments textually written, could think of making a beson (liquor), calculated to bewitch people and make them destroy one another."

Heckewelder's observations concerning the English traders are the sad truth. They took advantage of the Indians' inordinate appetite for rum; they cheated them out of their skins and furs; they debauched their women. The Pennsylvania Assembly, in a letter to Governor Hamilton, February 27th, 1754, characterized the traders as "the vilest of our own inhabitants and convicts imported from Great Britain and Ireland." The traders of other Colonies, many of whom entered Pennsylvania, were no better than the Pennsylvania traders. Said Governor Dinwiddie, of Virginia, in a letter to Governor Hamilton, of Pennsylvania, May 21st, 1753: "The Indian traders, in general, appear to me to be a set of abandoned wretches." In a word, the English traders, with few exceptions, were a vile and infamous horde, who, instead of contributing to the betterment of the Indian, corrupted and debauched him.

Protests Against the Rum Traffic

Rum was the curse of the Red Man, and the leading Indian chiefs recognized it as such. Hence, from the very beginning of the rum traffic among the Pennsylvania Indians, we find a series of protests by their chiefs to the Pennsylvania Authorities. When the Conestoga or Susquehanna chief, Oretyagh, with a number of other chiefs of the Conestogas and Shawnees, bade farewell to William Penn, on October 7th, 1701, just a short time before Penn left his Province never to return, this sachem, in the name of the rest, told him that the Indians had long suffered from the ravages of the rum traffic, and Penn informed Oretyagh and associate chiefs that the Assembly was at that time enacting a law, according to their desire, to prevent their being abused by the selling of rum among them. (Pa. Col. Rec., Vol. 2, pages 45-46.) Penn early saw the degredation which the Indians' unquenchable thirst for strong drink wrought among them, and he did all in his power to remedy this matter. But the law was no sooner enacted than it was disregarded by the traders. Then, in the minutes of a council held at Philadelphia, on May 16th, 1704, we read the last reference to Oretyagh in recorded history, a protest against the rum traffic, as follows:

"Oretyagh, the chief now of Conestoga, requested him [Nicole Godin, a trader] to complain to the Governor [John Evans] of the great quantities of rum continually brought to their town, insomuch that they [the Conestogas] are ruined by it, having nothing left, but have laid out all, even their clothes for rum, and may now, when threatened with war, be surprised by their enemies, when besides themselves with drink, and so utterly be destroyed." (Pa. Col. Rec., Vol. 2, page 141.)

The great Shikellamy, the most renowned Indian that ever lived in Pennsylvania, shortly after taking up his residence on the Susquehanna, as vice-gerent of the Six Nations over the Delawares, Shawnees and other Indians in the eastern part of Pennsylvania, served notice on the Colonial Authorities that, if the rum traffic among the Indians were not better regulated, friendly relations between the Six Nations and the Colony of Pennsylvania would cease.

As we shall see in the next chapter, the Shawnees, who entered eastern Pennsylvania as early as 1694, began, about 1724 to 1727, to migrate to the valleys of the Ohio and Allegheny. One of the reasons why they migrated to the western part of the state, was to escape the ruinous effects of strong liquor. But the trader with his rum followed them into the forests of their western homes.

Then the Shawnee on the Conemaugh, Kiskiminetas, and Allegheny took steps, in 1738, to restrain this pernicious traffic. On March 20th of that year, three of their chiefs in this region, namely; "Loyporcowah (Opessah's Son), Newcheconneh (Deputy

King), and Coycacolenne, or Coracolenne (Chief Counsellor)," wrote a letter to Thomas Penn and James Logan, Secretary of the Provincial Council, in which they acknowledged the receipt of a present from Penn and Logan of powder, lead, and tobacco, delivered to them by the trader, George Miranda; in which they say they have a good understanding with the French, the Five Nations, the Ottawas, and all the French Indians; that the tract of land reserved for them by the Proprietory Government on the west side of the Susquehanna does not suit them at present; and that they desire to remain in the region of the Allegheny and Kiskiminetas, make a strong town there, and keep their warriors from making war upon other nations at a distance. They then add:

"After we heard your letter read, and all our people being gathered together, we held a council together, to leave off drinking for the space of four years . . . There was not many of our traders at home at the time of our council, but our friends, Peter Chartier and George Miranda; but the proposal of stopping the rum and all strong liquors was made to the rest in the winter, and they were all willing. As soon as it was concluded of, all the rum that was in the towns was staved and spilled, belonging both to Indians and white people, which in quantity consisted of about forty gallons, that was thrown in the street; and we have appointed four men to stave all the rum or strong liquors that is brought to the towns hereafter, either by Indians or white men, during the four years." A pledge signed by ninety-eight Shawnees and the two traders above named accompanied this letter, agreeing that all rum should be destroyed, and four men appointed in every town to see that no strong liquor should be brought into the Shawnee towns for the term of four years. (Pa. Archives, Vol. 1, pages 549-551.)

Previous to this action on part of Loyparcowah and other chiefs of the Shawnees, the Delawares at Kittanning made complaints concerning the rum traffic. In 1732, the trader, Edmund Cartlidge, wrote the Governor from Kittanning that the chiefs there made reflections on the Government for permitting such large quantities of rum to be carried to the Allegheny and sold to the Indians at that place, contrary to law. Also, in 1733, the Shawnee chiefs in the Allegheny region wrote the Governor requesting that he send them an order permitting them "to break in pieces all kegs of rum so brought yearly and monthly by some new upstart of a trader without a license, who comes amongst us and brings nothing but rum, no powder, nor lead, nor clothing, but takes away with him those skins which the old licensed traders who bring us everything necessary, ought to have in return for their goods sold us some years since." Also in 1734, the Shawnee chiefs at Allegheny wrote the Governor and requested that none of the licensed traders be allowed to bring them more than thirty gallons of rum twice in a year, except Peter Chartier, who "trades further than ye rest."

Also, the able Indian orator and wise counselor, Scarouady, later successor to Tanacharison, the Half King, protested to the Pennsylvania Commissioners at the Carlisle Conference of October, 1753, as follows:

"Your traders now bring scarce any thing but Rum and Flour . . . The Rum ruins us. We beg you would prevent its coming in such quantities by regulating the traders . . . When these Whiskey Traders come, they bring thirty or forty Caggs (kegs) and put them down before Us and make Us drink, and get all the Skins that should go to pay the Debts We have contracted for Goods bought of the Fair Traders, and by these means we not only ruin Ourselves but them too. These wicked Whiskey Sellers, when they have once got the Indians in Liquor, make them sell the very Clothes from their Backs. In short, if this Practice be continued, We must inevitably be ruined. We most earnestly, therefore, beseech You to remedy it." (Pa. Col. Rec., Vol. 5, page 676.)

The whiskey traders were not checked. They continued their work unabated, in spite of the solemn protestations of the Indian chiefs and in spite of the protestations of such good white men as Conrad Weiser, who, on November 28th, 1747, wrote the Provincial Council of Pennsylvania characterizing the havoc wrought among the Pennsylvania Indians as "an abomination before God and man." (Pa. Col. Rec., Vol. 5, page 167.)

The Testimony of Adario

The foregoing statements relate principally to the Pennsylvania Indians. Let us, at this point, hear the testimony of a great Indian chief whose tribe did not inhabit Pennsylvania, the brave and sagacious Huron chief, Adario, who was gathered to his fathers in 1701. Out of the past comes the voice of Adario:

"As for the maple-water that we drink, 'tis sweet, well tasted, healthful, and friendly to the stomach, whereas your wine and brandy destroy the natural heat, pall the stomach, inflame the blood, intoxicate, and create a thousand disorders. A man in drink loses his reason before he is aware, or, at least, his reason is so drowned that he is not capable of distinguishing what he ought to do." When told that God had sent the Europeans to America to save the souls of the Indians, this great Huron replied that it was more likely that God had sent the Europeans to this continent to learn to be good; "for", said he, "the innocence of our lives, the love we tender to our brethren, and the tranquility of mind which we enjoy in contemplating business to our interest, these, I say, are the three great things that the Great Spirit requires of all men in general. We practice all these things in our villages naturally; while the Europeans defame, kill, rob, and pull one another to pieces, in their towns. Your money is the father of luxury, lasciviousness, intrigues, tricks, lying, treachery, falseness, and, in a word, all the mischief in the world . . . Consider this and tell me if we are not right in refusing to finger it, or so much as look upon the cursed metal, since all these evils caused by it are unknown to us . . . All our actions are guided by justice, equity, charity, sincerity and true faith . . . Using bad language and cursing the Great Spirit were never heard among us."

The Author's Purpose

The author's purpose in writing this chapter and the three which follow before the wars between the Pennsylvania Indians and the white man are treated, is to give the reader and student that background which any fair minded student of the Indian wars of Pennsylvania should have. As the reader proceeds, he will find many things that reflect no honor on the whites. But it is the author's duty to record the wrongs committed upon the Indian as well as the wrongs committed by him. History must not hide the truth.

CHAPTER II

The Pennsylvania Indian Tribes

We shall devote this chapter to a brief view of the Indian tribes that inhabited Pennsylvania within the historic period.

The Susquehannas, Minquas, or Conestogas

THE Susquehannas is the general term applied to the Indians living on both sides of the Susquehanna River and its tributaries, in Pennsylvania, at the beginning of the historic period. Racially and linguistically, they were of Iroquoian stock, but were never taken into the league of the Iroquois, except as subjects. These related tribes were known by various names. Captain John Smith, the Virginia pioneer, who met them while exploring Chesapeake Bay and its tributaries in 1608, called them the "Susquehannocks." The French called them the Andastes, while the Dutch and Swedes called them Minquas. In the latter days of their history as a tribe, they were called the Conestogas.

To Captain John Smith, of the Colony of Virginia, belongs the distinction of being the first white man to see the Indians of Pennsylvania, though he never set foot on Pennsylvania soil; and the Indians meeting him and his companions, beheld for the first time the race that was coming to drive them from their streams and hunting grounds. These Indians were the Susquehannas. Smith held a conference with sixty of the Susquehannocks, near the head of Chesapeake Bay, about August 1, 1608, as he and twelve companions were making an exploring expedition. The sixty Susquehannocks had come from one of their principal towns in what is now Lancaster County, Pennsylvania. Smith gives the following interesting description of these Indians:

"Such great and well proportioned men are seldom seen, for they seemed like giants to the English, yea, and to their neighbors, yet seemed of an honest and simple disposition. They were with much ado restrained from adoring us as gods. These are the

CAPTAIN JOHN SMITH'S SKETCH OF A SUSQUEHANNA OR CONESTOGA CHIEF.

strangest people of all these countries, both in language and attire; for their language it may well become their proportions, sounding from them as a voice in the vault. Their attire is the skins of bears and wolves; some have cossacks made of bears' heads and skins, that a man's head goes through the skin's neck, and the ears of the bear fastened to his shoulders, the nose and teeth hanging down his breast, another bear's face split behind him, and at the end of the nose hung a paw, the half sleeves coming to the elbows were the necks of bears, and the arms through the mouth with paws hanging at their noses. One had the head of a wolfe hanging in a chain for a jewel, his tobacco pipe three quarters of a yard long, prettily carved with a bird, a deer, or some such device at the great end, sufficient to beat out one's brains; with bows, arrows, and clubs, suitable to their greatness. Five of their chief Werowances came aboard us and crossed the bay in the barge. The picture of the greatest of them is signified in the map. The calf of whose leg was three-quarters of a yard about, and all the rest of his limbs so answerable to that proportion that he seemed the goodliest man we ever beheld. His hair, the one side was long, the other shorn close with a ridge over his crown like a cock's comb. His arrows were five quarters long, headed with the splinters of a white christall-like stone, in form of a heart, an inch broad, an inch and a half or more long. These he wore in a wolf's skin at his back for his quiver, his bow in the one hand and his club in the other, as is described."

Smith goes on to say that these Susquehannas were scarce known to Powhatan, the great Virginia chief, but that they were a powerful tribe living in palisaded towns to defend them from the Massawomeks, or Iroquois, and having six hundred warriors. During the ceremonies connected with the visit of this band of Susquehannas, Smith says that they first sang "a most fearful song," and then, "with a most strange, furious action and a hellish voice began an oration." When the oration was ended, they decorated Smith with a chain of large white beads, and laid presents of skins and arrows at his feet, meanwhile stroking their hands about his neck. They told him about their enemies, the Iroquois, who, they said, lived beyond the mountains far to the north and received their hatchets and other weapons from the French in Canada. They implored Smith to remain with them as their protector, which, of course, he could not do. "We left them at Tockwogh," he says, "sorrowing for our departure."

Smith's account of the large stature of the Susquehannas has been corroborated by subsequent discoveries, when burying grounds of this tribe, in Lancaster County, were opened and very large human skeletons found.

The Susquehannas, in the early part of the seventeenth century, carried on war with the "River Indians," as the Delawares, or Lenape then living along the Delaware River, were called. The Susquehannas were friendly with both the Swedes and the Dutch, and shortly after the Swedes arrived on the Delaware in 1638, they sold part of their lands to them. The Swedes equipped these Indians with guns, and trained their warriors in European tactics. When the Hurons were being worsted by the Iroquois in 1647, the Susquehannas offered the friendly Hurons military assistance, "backed by 1300 warriors in a single palisaded town, who had been trained by Swedish soldiers." They were also friendly with the colony of Maryland in the early days of its history, selling part of their lands to the Marylanders, and receiving military supplies from them.

The Swedes, during their occupancy of the lower Delaware, carried on trade with the Susquehannas, the extent of which is seen in the report of Governor-General John Printz, of New Sweden, for 1647, in which he states that, because of the conflict of his colonists with the Dutch, he had suffered a loss of "8,000 or 9,000 beavers which have passed out of our hands" and which, but for the Dutch, would have been gotten from "the great traders, the Minquas."

The French explorer, Champlain, says that, in 1615, the Carantouannais, as he calls the Susquehannas, had many villages on the upper part of the Susquehanna, and that their town, Carantouan, alone, could muster more than eight hundred warriors. The exact location of Carantouan has been a matter of much conjecture, but the weight of authority places it on or near the top of Spanish Hill, in Athens Township, Bradford County, Pennsylvania, and within sight of the town of Waverly, New York

In the summer of 1615, Champlain was assisting the Hurons in their war against the Iroquois, and when he was at the lower end of Lake Simcoe, making preparations for advance against the Iroquois town located most likely near the present town of Fenner, in Madison County, New York, he learned from the Hurons that there was a certain nation of their allies dwelling three days journey beyond the Onondagas, who desired to assist the Hurons in this expedition with five hundred of their warriors. These allies were none other than that portion of the Susquehannas, living along the Susquehanna River, near the boundary between the states of Pennsylvania and New York. Accordingly, Champlain sent his interpreter, Estienne Brule, with twelve Huron companions, to visit Carantouan, the chief town of the Susquehannas in that region, for the purpose of hastening the coming of the five hundred warriors.

Brule and his five hundred allies from Carantouan arrived before the Onondaga fortress too late to be of any assistance to Champlain, who had already made two attacks upon the town, had been wounded twice by the Onondagas, and, despairing of the arrival of the promised assistance of five hundred warriors, had already retreated toward Canada several days before the arrival of Brule and his Indians. Brule then returned with his five hundred warriors to the town of Carantouan.

Brule spent the autumn and winter of 1615 and 1616 in a tour of exploration into the very heart of Pennsylvania, visiting the various clans of the Susquehannas and, some authorities say, the Eries. He followed the Susquehanna River to its mouth, and returned to Carantouan. This intrepid Frenchman thus gained, by actual observation, a knowledge of a large section of the state and of its primitive inhabitants almost one hundred years before any other white man set foot within the same region.

Another town of the Susquehannas was the one, later called Gahontoto, at the mouth of Wyalusing Creek, Bradford County. The Moravian missionaries, Bishop Commerhoff and David Zeisberger, visited the site of this town in the summer of 1750.

Another of the towns of the Susquehannas is believed to have been at the mouth of Sugar Creek, in Bradford County, above the present town of Towanda. Still another of their towns, this one fortified, was near the mouth of Octorara Creek, on the east side of the Susquehanna River, in Maryland, about ten miles south of the line between Pennsylvania and Maryland. One of their forts was in Manor Township, Lancaster County, near the Susquehanna River, between Turkey Hill and Blue Rock. Another was on Wolf Run near Muncy, Lycoming County. The location of their principal fort was long a matter of dispute, and, at one time, actual warfare, between the heirs of Lord Baltimore and the heirs of William Penn, for the reason that the southern boundary of Penn's colony was supposed to be marked by it. The weight of authority seems to place its location on the west side of the Susquehanna River, in York County, Pennsylvania, opposite Washington Borough.

The Iroquois, the mortal enemies of the Susquehannas, attacked them at one of their principal towns, in either York or Lancaster County, Pennsylvania, in 1663, sending down the Susquehanna River, in April of that year, an expedition of eight hundred Onondagas, Cayugas, and Senecas. On their arrival, they found the town defended on one side by the river and on the other by tree trunks; it was flanked by two bastions, constructed after the European method, and had also several pieces of artillery. The Iroquois decided not to make an assault, but to attempt to outwit the Susquehannas by a ruse. Twenty-five Iroquois were admitted into the fort, but these were seized, placed on high scaffolds, and burned to death in sight of their comrades. The humiliated Iroquois now returned to their home in New York.

After this defeat of the Iroquois, the war was carried on by small parties, and now and then a Susquehanna was captured and carried to the villages of the Iroquois, and tortured to death. In 1669, the Susquehannas defeated the Cayugas, and offered peace; but their ambassador was put to death, and the war went on. At this time, the Susquehannas had a great chief named Hochitqgete, or Barefoot; and the medicine men of the Iroquois assured the warriors of the confederacy that, if they would make another attack on the Susquehannas, their efforts would be rewarded by the capture of Barefoot and his execution at the stake. So, in the summer of 1672, a band of forty Cayugas descended the Susquehanna in canoes, and twenty Senecas marched overland to attack the enemy in the fields; but a band of sixty Susquehanna boys, none over sixteen, routed the Senecas, killing one and capturing another. The band of youthful warriors then pressed on against the Cayugas, and defeated them, killing eight and wounding fifteen or sixteen more, but losing half of their own gallant band. At this time, it is said, the Susquehannas were so reduced by war and pestilence that their fighting force consisted of only three hundred warriors.

Finally, in 1675, according to the Jesuit Relation and Colden in his "History of the Five Nations", the Susquehannas fell before the arms of the Iroquois; but the details of the defeat are sadly lacking. It seems that the Iroquois, about this time, had driven them down upon the tribes of the South who were then allies of the English, and that this involved them in war with Maryland and Virginia. Finding themselves surrounded by enemies on all sides, a portion of the Susquehannas left the land of their forefathers and the beautiful river bearing their name, and took up their abode in the western part of Maryland, near the Piscataways.

In the summer of 1675, a white man was murdered by some Indians, most probably Senecas, on the Virginia side of the Potomac; whereupon, a party of Virginia militia killed fourteen of the Susquehannocks and Doeg Indians in retaliation. Shortly afterwards several other whites were murdered on both sides of the Potomac. The colony of Virginia then organized several companies, led by Colonel John Washington, great-grandfather of George Washington, to co-operate with a Maryland force of two hundred and fifty troops, led by Major Thomas Truman. The Susquehannocks claimed that they were entirely innocent of any of these murders and sent four of their chiefs as an embassy to Major Truman, who were knocked on the head by his soldiers. This so enraged the Susquehannocks that a long border warfare ensued which was kept up until they became lost to history.

Another portion of the Susquehannocks remained near their old home at Conestoga, Lancaster County, where they were later joined by a third portion which had been taken by the Iroquois to the Oneida country in New York, and there retained until they lost their language, when they were permitted to join their brethren at Conestoga. Here William Penn and his son, William, visited the Conestogas during his last stay in his province in 1701. Here, also, the Conestogas lived until the descendants of this remnant of a once powerful tribe were killed in December, 1763, by a band of Scotch-Irish settlers from Donegal and Paxtang,—the last melancholy chapter in the history of the Susquehannas, or Conestogas. Conestoga, for generations the central seat of this tribe in the lower Susquehanna region, was about four miles southwest of Millersville, Lancaster County. A monument marks the site of this historic Indian town. It was erected in 1924 by the Lancaster County Historical Society and the Pennsylvania Historical Commission.

The Delawares or Lenape

At the dawn of the historic period of Pennsylvania, we find the basin of the Delaware River inhabited by an Indian tribe called the Delawares, or Lenape. The English called them Delawares from the fact that, upon their arrival in this region, they found the council-fires of this tribe on the banks of the Delaware River. The French called them Loups, "wolves", a term probably first applied to the Mohicans, a kindred tribe, on the Hudson River in New York. However, in their own language, they were called Lenape, or Lenni-Lenape, meaning "real men", or "original men."

The Lenape belonged to the great Algonquin family—by far the greatest Indian family in North America, measured by the extent of territory occupied. This family surrounded on all sides the Iroquoian family, of which we shall hereafter speak, and extended from Labrador westward through Canada to the Rocky Mountains and southward to South Carolina. It also extended westward through the Mississippi Valley to the RockyMountains. The most important tribes of this family were the Mohican, Massachuset, Miami, Sac and Fox, Ojibwa, Blackfoot, Illinois, Shawnee, and Lenape; and among the great personages of the Algonquins were King Philip, Pocahontas, Pontiac, Tecumseh, and Tamenend, the last of whom made the historic treaty with William Penn described in Chapter III.

Traditional History of the Lenape

The early traditional history of the Lenape is contained in their national legend, the Walum Olum. According to this sacred tribal history, the Lenape, in long ages past, lived in the vast region west of the Mississippi. For some reason not known, they left their western home, and, after many years of wandering eastward, reached the Namaesi Sipu, or Mississippi, where they fell in with the Mengwe, or Iroquois, who had likewise emigrated from the distant West in search of a new home, and had arrived at this river at a point somewhat higher up. The spies sent forward by the Lenape for the purpose of reconnoitering, had discovered, before the arrival of the main body, that the region east of the Mississippi was inhabited by a powerful nation called the Talligewi, or Alligewi, whose domain reached eastward to the Allegheny Mountains, which together with the beautiful Allegheny River, are named for this ancient race. The Alligewi had many large towns on the rivers of the Mississippi and Ohio valleys, and had built innumerable mounds, fortifications and intrenchments, hundreds of which still remain, and are called the works of the "Mound Builders". Says Schoolcraft: "The banks of the Allegheny were, in ancient times, occupied by an important tribe, now unknown, who preceded the Delawares and Iroquois. They were called Alleghans (Alligewi) by Colden." It is related that the Alligewi were tall and stout, and that there were giants among them.

When the Lenape arrived at the Mississippi, they sent a message to the Alligewi requesting that they be permitted to settle among them. This request was refused, but the Lenape obtained permission to pass through the territory of the Alligewi and seek a settlement farther to the eastward. They accordingly began to cross the Mississippi; but the Alligewi, seeing that their numbers were vastly greater than they had supposed, made a furious attack upon those who had crossed, and threatened the whole tribe with destruction, if they dared to persist in crossing to the eastern side of the river.

Angered by the treachery of the Alligewi and not being prepared for conflict, the Lenape consulted together as to whether they should make a trial of strength, and were convinced that the enemy were too powerful for them. Then the Mengwe, who had hitherto been spectators from a distance, offered to join the Lenape, on condition that, after conquering the Alligewi, they should be entitled to share in the fruits of the conquest.

Having united their forces, the Lenape and the Mengwe declared war against the Alligewi, and started on their onward march eastward across the continent, gradually driving out the Alligewi, who fled down the Mississippi Valley never to return. This conquest lasted many years, during which the Lenape lost great numbers of their best warriors, while the Mengwe would always lag back in the rear leaving them to bear the brunt of battle. At the end, the conquerors divided the possessions of the defeated race; the Mengwe taking the country in the vicinity of the Great Lakes and their tributary streams, and the Lenape taking the land to the south. There has been much conjecture as to who the ancient Alligewi were, some historians believing them to have been the "Mound Builders," but most modern authorities believe them to have been identical with the Cherokees.

For a long period, possibly many centuries, according to the Walum Olum, the Mengwe and Lenape resided peacefully in this country, and increased rapidly in population. Some of their hunters and warriors crossed the Allegheny Mountains, and, arriving at the streams flowing eastward, followed them to the Susquehanna River, and this stream to the ocean. Other enterprising pathfinders penetrated the wilderness to the Delaware River, and exploring still eastward, arrived at the Hudson. Some of these explorers returned to their nation and reported the discoveries they had made, describing the country as abounding in game and the streams as having an abundance of water-fowl and fish, with no enemy to be dreaded.

The Lenape considered these discoveries as fortunate for them, and believed the newly found region to be the country destined for them by the Great Spirit as their permanent abode. Consequently they began to migrate thither, settling on the four great rivers,—the Susquehanna, the Potomac, the Delaware, and the Hudson. The Walum Olum states, however, that not all of the Lenape reached the eastern part of the United States, many of them having remained behind to assist a great body of their people who had not crossed the Mississippi, but had retreated into the interior of the country on the other side, on being informed of the treacherous attack of the Alligewi upon those who had attempted to cross this stream. It is further stated that another part of the Lenape remained near the eastern bank of the Mississippi.

According to this traditional history, therefore, the Lenape nation finally became divided into three separate bodies; the part that had not crossed the Mississippi; the part that remained near the eastern bank of the Mississippi; and the part that settled on the four great eastern rivers above named.

That branch of the Delawares which settled in the eastern part of the country divided into three divisions, or clans,—the Munsee, (later corrupted to Monsey), the Unami, and the Unalachitgo. These were called the Wolf, the Turtle, and the Turkey clans respectively, from their respective animal types of totems. With these creatures which they had adopted as their symbols, they believed themselves connected by a mystic and powerful tie.

The Munsee (Wolf Clan), at the dawn of the historic period, were living in the mountain country, from about the mouth of the Lehigh River northward into New York and New Jersey, embracing the territory between the Blue or Kittatinny Mountains and the sources of the Susquehanna and Delaware Rivers. A part of the tribe, also, dwelt on the Susquehanna, and still another part had a village and peach orchard near Nazareth in Northampton County, in the triangle between the Delaware and Lehigh. However, their chief village was Minisink, in Sussex County, New Jersey. The Munsee were the most warlike of the Delawares; they took a prominent part in the Indian wars of Colonial

Pennsylvania. Being defrauded out of their lands by the notorious "Walking Purchase" of 1737, which obliged them to move, first to the Susquehanna and then to the Ohio, they became the bitter enemies of the white man, and drenched the frontier settlements with the blood of the pioneers. The Munsee have frequently been considered a separate tribe, inasmuch as they differed greatly from the other clans of the Lenape, and spoke a different dialect.

The Unami (Turtle Clan), "down river people," at the opening of the historic period dwelt on both sides of the Delaware from the mouth of the Lehigh to the line dividing the states of Pennsylvania and Delaware. Their chief village was Shackamaxon, which was probably the capital of the Lenape nation, and it stood on about the site of Germantown, a suburb of Philadelphia. The principal chief of the Unami was the "King" of the united Lenape nation, by immemorial custom presiding at all the councils of the tribe.

The Unalachtigo (Turkey Clan) "people living near the sea," at the opening of the historic period, occupied the land on the lower reach of the Delaware River and Delaware Bay. Their villages were on both sides of the river; and their chief village, or capital of the clan, was Chikoki, on the site of Burlington, New Jersey.

From these three clans, or tribes, comprising the great body of the Delawares, have sprung many others, who, for their own convenience, chose distant parts in which to settle. Among these were the Mahicans, or Mohicans, who by intermarriage became a detached body, and crossing the Hudson River, dwelt in eastern New York and western Connecticut; and the Nanticokes, who had proceeded to the South, and settled in Maryland and Virginia.

It is to be noted, too, that the Delawares, by reason of priority of political rank and of occupying the central home territory from which the kindred tribes had diverged, were assigned special dignity and authority. It is said that forty tribes looked up to them with respect, and that, in the great councils of the Algonquins, they took first place as "grandfathers" of the race, while others were called by them "children," "grandchildren," and "nephews." It is not certain that this precedence of the Delawares had any importance within the period of white settlement, but it no doubt had in the far dim past. And it seems true that the Algonquin tribes refrained from war with one another.

The Iroquois Form a Great Confederation and Subjugate the Lenape

It will be remembered that, when the Lenape, or Delawares, and the Mengwe, or Iroquois, divided the country of the Alligewi between them, the Mengwe took the part in the vicinity of the Great Lakes and their tributary streams, north of the part taken by the Lenape. The Mengwe later proceeded farther and settled below the Great Lakes and along the St. Lawrence River, so that when the Lenape had moved to the eastern part of the United States, the Mengwe became their northern neighbors. The Mengwe now became jealous of the growing power of the Lenape, and finally assumed dominion over them.

To the Moravian Missionary, Rev. John Heckewelder, who had lived among the Delawares for more than thirty years, they related how this dominion came about. The great chiefs of the Delawares stated to Heckewelder that the Mengwe clandestinely sought to start quarrels between the Lenape and distant tribes, hoping thus to break the might of the Lenape. Each nation had a particular mark on its war clubs, different from that of any other nation. So the Mengwe, having stolen into the Cherokee country and secretly murdered a Cherokee and left beside the victim a war club, such as the Lenape used, the Cherokees naturally concluded that the Lenape committed the murder, and fell suddenly upon them, and a long and bloody war ensued between the two nations. The treachery of the Mengwe having been at length discovered, the Lenape resolved upon the extermination of this deceitful tribe. War was declared against the Mengwe, and carried on with vigor, when the Mengwe, finding that they were no match for the powerful Lenape and their kindred tribes, resolved upon uniting their clans into a confederacy. Up until this time, each tribe of the Mengwe had acted independently of the others, and they had not been inclined to come under any supreme authority. Accordingly, about the year 1570, the Mengwe formed the great confederacy of their five kindred tribes, the Mohawks, the Oneidas, the Onondagas, the Cayugas, and the Senecas, known as the Five (later Six) Nations.

Thus the Delawares claimed that the Iroquois Confederacy was formed for the purpose of preventing the extermination of the Mengwe by the Lenape. Other authorities say that the purpose was to end inter-tribal feud and war among the Mengwe, themselves; to enable the allied tribes to make mutual offense and defense, and to advance their general welfare. Thannawage, it is claimed, was the aged Mohawk chief who first proposed the alliance. Other authorities say that Dekanawida, the Iroquois statesman, prophet and law giver, planned and formed the historic confederation; and that he was assisted in this work by his disciple and co-adjutor, Hiawatha, whose name has been immortalized by the poet, Longfellow, in his charming poem. It is to be noted, however, that, while in "Hiawatha", Longfellow gave the English language one of its finest poems; yet, due to his adopting the error of Schoolcraft in applying to Hiawatha the myths and legends relating to the Chippewa deity, Manabozho, this poem does not contain a single fact or fiction relating to the great chieftain of the Iroquois.

The following chiefs, also, assisted in forming the confederacy: Toganawita, representing the Onondagas; Togahayon, representing the Cayugas; and Ganiatario and Satagaruyes, representing the Senecas. This confederacy is known in history as the Five Nations, until the Tuscaroras, a tribe having been expelled from North Carolina and Virginia in 1712 or 1713, and having sought an asylum among the Iroquois of Pennsylvania and New York, were formally admitted to the alliance in 1722, after which time the confederacy is known as the Six Nations. The French gave the Indians of the confederacy the name of Iroquois, while the Delawares continued to call them Mengwe, later corrupted to Mingo. The Mohicans and the Dutch called them Maquas, while Powhatan called them Massawomekes.

But, to resume the story which the Delawares told Heckewelder. They said that, after the forming of the confederacy, very bloody wars were carried on between the Iroquois and themselves in which they were generally successful, and while these wars were in progress, the French landed in Canada and combined against the Iroquois, inasmuch as the Five Nations were not willing that these Europeans should establish themselves in that country. At last the Mengwe, or Iroquois, seeing themselves between two fires, and not seeing any prospect of conquering the Lenape by arms, resorted to a stratagem to secure dominion over them.

The plan was to persuade the Lenape to abstain from the use of arms, and to assume the station of mediators and umpires among their warlike neighbors. In the language of the Indians, the Lenape were to be made "women." As explaining the significance of this expression, the Delawares said that wars among the

Indians in those days were never brought to an end, but by the interference of the weaker sex. It was not considered becoming for a warrior to ask for peace. He must fight to the end. "With these dispositions, war would never have ceased among Indians, until the extermination of one or the other party, if the tender and compassionate sex had not come forward, and by their moving speeches, persuaded the enraged combatants to bury their hatchets, and make peace. On these occasions they were very eloquent . . . They would describe the sorrows of widowed wives, and, above all, of bereaved mothers. The pangs of childbirth, they had willingly suffered. They had carefully reared their sons to manhood. Then how cruel it was to see these promising youths fall victims to the rage of war,—to see them slaughtered on the field, or burned at the stake. The thought of such scenes made them curse their own existence and shudder at the thought of bearing children." Speeches like these generally had the desired effect, and the women, by the honorable function of peace-makers, held a very dignified position. Therefore, it would be a magnanimous and honorable act for a powerful nation like the Lenape to assume that station by which they would be the means of saving the Indian race from extinction.

Such, according to Heckewelder, were the arguments used by the artful Iroquois to ensnare the Lenape. Unfortunately the Delawares listened to the voice of their enemies, and consented to become the "woman nation" among the Indians. With elaborate ceremonies, they were installed in their new function. Eloquent speeches were made, accompanied with belts of wampum. The place of the ceremony of "taking the hatchet out of the hand of the Lenape" and of placing them in the situation of "the woman" was at Nordman's Kill, about four miles south of Albany, New York. The year of the alleged occurrence is unknown, but it is said to have been somewhere between 1609 and 1620. Both the Delawares and the Mohicans told Heckewelder that the Dutch were present at this ceremony and had no inconsiderable part in the intrigue, the Mohicans explaining that it was fear that caused the Dutch of New York to conspire with the Mengwe against the Lenape. It appears that, at the place where the Dutch were then making their settlement, great bodies of warriors would pass and repass, interrupting their undertakings; so that they thought it well to have an alliance with the Iroquois. Furthermore, the Delawares told Heckewelder that, when the

English took New York from the Dutch, they stepped into the same alliance with the Iroquois that their predecessors had made.

The Iroquois denied that such an intrigue as related above ever took place. They alleged, on the other hand, that they had conquered the Lenape in battle and had thus compelled them to become "women,"—to submit to the greatest humiliation a spirited and warlike nation can suffer. Many historians believe that the Delawares imposed upon the venerable Rev. Heckewelder by inventing a cunning tale in explanation of the humiliation under which they were smarting. Also, President William Henry Harrison, in his "Aborigines of the Ohio Valley", gives the story of the Delawares little credence. He says that the Delawares were too sagacious a race to fall into such a snare as they allege the Iroquois laid for them. Rev. Heckewelder, the staunch friend of the Delawares, calls attention to the fact that, while the Iroquois claim they conquered the Delawares by force of arms and not by stratagem, yet the Iroquois have no tradition among them of the particulars of the conquest.

So much for the story which the Delawares told Heckewelder. Many authorities state, however, that the time of the subjugation of the Delawares was much later than the date given Heckewelder. Some have stated that the Delawares were not made tributaries of the Iroquois until after the coming of William Penn; but the celebrated Delaware chief, King Beaver, told Conrad Weiser at Aughwick on September 4, 1754, that the subjugation took place before Penn's arrival. It has been contended that, when the Iroquois finally conquered the Susquehannas, in 1675, the Delawares were allies of the Susquehannas, and that therefore the overcoming of the Susquehannas included the subjugation of the Delawares. At the first extended conference between the Pennsylvania Authorities and the Indians, of which a record has been preserved, held at Philadelphia on July 6, 1694, the Delaware chief, Hithquoquean, or Idquoquequoan, advised the Colonial Authorities that he and his associate chiefs had shortly before this time received a message from the Onondagas and Senecas containing the following statement: "You Delaware Indians do nothing but stay at home and boil your pots, and are like women; while we Onondagas and Senecas go ahead and fight the enemy." We, therefore, conclude that it cannot be stated with exactness, just when the subjugation of the Delawares took place; and, inasmuch as there is no record of any conquest after the time of Penn's arrival, it may be that the subjugation took place through fear and intimidation rather than by war.

Whatever may be the facts as to how the Iroquois reduced the Delawares to a state of vassalage—whether by artifice, intimidation, or warfare—the fact remains that about the year 1720, this powerful northern confederacy assumed active dominion over them, forbidding them to make war or sales of lands,—a condition that existed until the time of the French and Indian War. During the summer of 1755, the Delawares declared that they were no longer subjects of the Six Nations, and, at Tioga, in the year 1756, their great chieftain, Teedyuscung, extorted from the chiefs of the Iroquois an acknowledgment of Delaware independence. However, from time to time, after 1756, the Iroquois persisted in claiming the Delawares were their vassals, until shortly before the treaty of Greenville, Darke County, Ohio, in August, 1795, when they formally declared the Delaware nation to be no longer "women," but MEN.

Westward Migration of the Delawares

As early as 1724, Delawares of the Turtle and Turkey clans began, by permission of the Six Nations, to migrate from the region near the Forks of the Susquehanna to the valleys of the Allegheny and Ohio, coming chiefly from the country to the east and southeast of Shamokin (Sunbury). They proceeded up the east side of the West Branch of the Susquehanna as far as Lock Haven, where they crossed this stream, and ascended the valley of Bald Eagle Creek to a point near where Milesburg, Center County, now stands. From there, they went in a westerly direction along Marsh Creek, over or near Indian Grave Hill, near Snowshoe and Moshanon, Center County, crossing Moshanon Creek; and from there through Morris, Graham, Bradford, and Lawrence Townships, Clearfield County, reaching the West Branch of the Susquehanna again at Chinklacamoose on the site of the present town of Clearfield, Clearfield County. From this point, they ascended the West Branch of the Susquehanna for a few miles; thence up Anderson's Creek, crossing the divide between this stream and the Mahoning, in Brady Township, Clearfield County; thence down the Mahoning Valley through Punxsutawney, Jefferson County, to a point on the Allegheny River, about ten miles below the mouth of the Mahoning, where they built their first town in the course of their westward migration, which they called Kittanning,—a town famous in the Indian annals of Pennsylvania. Other Delaware towns were soon established in the Allegheny Valley and other places in the western part of the state to which the migration continued until the outbreak of the French and Indian War. The "Walking Purchase" of 1737 caused the westward migration of the Delawares of the Wolf clan. Thus it is seen that the Delawares retraced their steps across Pennsylvania. By the outbreak of the Revolutionary War, nearly all the Delawares had been pressed westward into Ohio.

Domain of the Iroquois

When the historic period of Pennsylvania begins, we find the domain of the Five Nations extending from the borders of Vermont to Lake Erie, and from Lake Ontario to the headwaters of the Delaware, Susquehanna, and Allegheny. This territory they called their "long house." The Senecas, who lived on the headwaters of the Allegheny, and many of whose settlements were in Pennsylvania, guarded the western door of the house, the Mohawks, the eastern, and the Cayugas, the southern, or that which opened on the Susquehanna.

The principal village and capital of these "Romans of America," as DeWitt Clinton called them, was called Onondaga, later Onondaga Castle, and was situated from before 1654 to 1681, on Indian Hill, in the present town of Pompey, near Onondaga Lake, in central New York. In 1677 it contained 140 cabins. Afterward it was removed to Butternut Creek, where the castle was burned in 1696, in the war between the Five Nations and the French. In 1720, it was again removed to Onondaga Creek, a few miles south of Lake Onondaga.

The Smithsonian Institution, in its "Handbook of American Indians," says the following of the Iroquois: "Around the Great Council Fire of the League of the Iroquois at Onondaga, with punctilious observance of the parliamentary proprieties recognized in Indian diplomacy and statescraft, and with a decorum that would add grace to many legislative assemblies of the white man, the federal senators of the Iroquois tribes devised plans, formulated policies, and defined principles of government and political action, which not only strengthened their state and promoted their common welfare, but also deeply affected the contemporary history of the whites in North America. To this body of half-clad federal chieftains were repeatedly made overtures of peace and friendship by two of the most powerful kingdoms of Europe, whose statesmen often awaited with apprehension the decisions of this senate of North American Savages." And Colden in his "History of the Five Nations," says: "The Five Nations are a poor and, generally called barbarious people; and yet a bright and noble genius shines through these black clouds. None of the greatest Roman heroes discovered a greater love to their country, or a greater contempt of death, than these people called barbarians have done, when liberty came in competition . . . They carried their arms as far southward as Carolina, to the northward of New England, and as far west as the River Mississippi, over a vast country, which extends twelve hundred miles in length, and about six hundred miles in breadth; where they entirely destroyed many nations, of whom there are now no accounts remaining among the English . . . Their great men, both Sachems and Captains, are generally poorer than the common people; for they affect to give away and distribute all the presents and plunder they get in their treaties or in war, so as to leave nothing to themselves . . . There is not the least salary or any sort of profit annexed to any office, to tempt the covetous or sordid; but, on the contrary, every unworthy action is unavoidably attended with the forfeiture of their commission; for their authority is only the esteem of the people, and ceases the moment that esteem is lost."

Says Governor DeWitt Clinton in his discourse on the Iroquois: "All their proceedings were conducted with great deliberation, and were distinguished for order, decorum and solemnity. In eloquence, in dignity, and in all the characteristics of profound policy, they surpassed an assembly of feudal barons, and were perhaps not far inferior to the great Amphyctionic Council of Greece."

So great was the scourge of the Iroquois that, during the closing decades of the seventeenth century and the first two decades of the eighteenth century, the region south of Lake Erie on both sides of the upper Ohio and Allegheny contained practically no Indian population; and the Iroquois looked upon this vast territory as their great hunting ground.

Speaking of the warfare of the Iroquois, DeWitt Clinton said: "They reduced war to a science, and all their movements were directed by system and policy. They never attacked a hostile country until they had sent out spies to explore and designate its vulnerable points, and when they encamped, they observed the greatest circumspection to guard against spies. Whatever superiority of force they might have, they never neglected the use of stratagem, employing all the crafty wiles of the Carthagenians."

The Iroquois commenced their conquests of all the tribes to the south and west of them, soon after these "Romans of America" acquired firearms from the Dutch on the Hudson River. Tribes that were not utterly destroyed or absorbed by them, were held in subjugation and ruled by Iroquois deputies or vice-gerents. The greatest of these vice-gerents was the renowned Shikellamy, who, in 1727 or 1728, was sent by the Great Council at Onondaga to rule over the Delawares, Shawnees and other tribes in the valley of the Susquehanna, taking up his residence first near Milton and later at Shamokin (Sunbury), Pennsylvania. Two other vice-gerents sent by the Iroquois to rule over subjugated tribes in Pennsylvania were Tanacharison, the Half King, and Scarouady, his successor. The former ruled over the Delawares and Mohicans of the Ohio Valley, with his residence at Logstown, on the north bank of the Ohio, about eighteen miles below Pittsburgh; and the latter ruled over the Shawnees of the Ohio Valley, with his residence also at Logstown. Tanacharison and Scarouady took up their duties as vice-regents in the year 1747. As we shall see, the Iroquois Confederation played an important part in the Indian history of Pennsylvania.

The Shawnees

The Shawnees, too, occupied parts of Pennsylvania during the historic period. The name means "Southerners." They were a branch of the Algonquin family, and are believed to have lived in the Ohio Valley in remote ages, and to have built many of the mounds and earthworks found there. Some have attempted to identify them with the Eries of the early Jesuits, the Massawomecks of Smith, and the Andaste, but without success. The traditional history of the Lenape, the Walum Olum, connects them, the Lenape, and Nanticokes as one people, the separation having taken place after the Alligewi, (Cherokees) were driven from the Ohio Valley by the Lenape and the Mengwe (Iroquois) on their onward march eastward across the continent. Then the Shawnees went south. Their real history begins in 1669-70, when they were living in two bodies a great distance apart,—one body being in South Carolina and the other in the Cumberland basin in Tennessee. Between these two bodies were the then friendly Cherokees, who claimed the land vacated by the Shawnees when the latter subsequently migrated to the North. The Shawnees living in South Carolina were called Savannahs by the early settlers.

As we shall see, later in this chapter, the Iroquois destroyed the Eries about 1655 or 1656. Shortly thereafter, these northern conquerors began a conquest of the Shawnees, which, according to Charlevoix, they completed in 1672.

On account, probably, of dissatisfaction with the early settlers, the Shawnees of South Carolina began a general movement to the north in 1690, and continued it at intervals for thirty years. The first reference to this tribe to be found in the Provincial records of Pennsylvania is probably a deposition made before the Provincial Council, December 19, 1693, by Polycarpus Rose. In this deposition there is a reference to "strange Indians" called "Shallnarooners." These strange Indians appear to have made a temporary stop in Chester County in migrating possibly from Maryland to the Forks of the Delaware or to Pequea Creek. Many authorities believe these "strange Indians" mentioned in the affidavit of Polycarpus Rose to have been Shawnees. This is conjecture.

But, leaving the realm of conjecture and entering the realm of historical truth, we find that the first Shawnees to enter Pennsylvania were a party who settled on the Delaware at Pechoquealin near the Water Gap, in the summer of 1694, or shortly thereafter. These came from the Shawnee villages on the lower Ohio. Arnold Viele, a Dutch trader, from Albany, New York, spent the winter of 1692-1693 with the Shawnees on the lower Ohio, returning in the summer of 1694, and bringing with him a number of this tribe who settled at Pechoquealin. Pechoquealin was a regional name whose center seems to have been the mouth of Shawnee Run in Lower Smithfield Township, Monroe County, and which included the surrounding territory on both sides of the Delaware, above the Delaware Water Gap. Viele was probably the first white man to explore the region between the valleys of the Susquehanna and the Ohio.

About four years later, or in 1697 or 1698, about seventy families of Shawnees came from Cecil County, Maryland, and settled on the Susquehanna River, near the Conestoga Indians, in Lancaster County. Probably at about the same time others migrated to the Ohio Valley. At the mouth of Pequea Creek, Lancaster County, the seventy families come from Maryland, built their village, also called Pequea. Their chief was Wapatha, or Opessah. They secured permission from the Colonial Government to reside near the Conestogas, and the latter became security for their good behavior, under the authority of the Iroquois Confederation. By invitation of the Delawares, a party of seven hundred Shawnees came soon after and settled with the Munsee Clan on the Delaware River, the main body taking up their abode at the mouth of the Lehigh, near Easton, while others went as far south as the mouth of the Schuylkill. Those who had settled on the Delaware afterwards removed to the Wyoming Valley near the present town of Plymouth, Luzerne County, on a broad plain still called Shawnee Flats. This band under Kakowatcheky removed from Pechoquealin to the Wyoming Valley in 1728; and it is probable that they were joined there by those who had settled at Pequea, which was abandoned about 1730.

The Shawnees also had a village on the flats at the mouth of Fishing Creek, near Bloomsburg, and another at Catawissa,—both being in Columbia County. They had other villages in the eastern part of the state on the Swatara, Paxtang, Susquehanna, and Delaware. Several villages were scattered along the west side of the Susquehanna, between the mouth of Yellow Breeches Creek and the Conodoguinet, in Cumberland County. Another of their villages, called Chenastry, was at the mouth of Chillisquaque Creek on the east side of the West Branch of the Susquehanna, in Northumberland County.

The Shawnees from Tennessee migrated to the Ohio Valley, finally collecting along the north bank of the Ohio in Pennsylvania as far as the mouth of the Monongahela, about the year 1730. Sauconk and Logstown were villages on the Ohio which they established possibly as early as that time. The former was at the mouth of the Beaver, and the latter on the north bank of the Ohio, about eighteen miles below Pittsburgh.

Another clan of Shawnees, called the Sewickleys, Asswikales, Shaweygila, and Hathawekela, came from South Carolina prior to 1730 by way of Old Town, Maryland and Bedford, Pa., and settled in different parts of Southwestern Pennsylvania. Their principal village called Sewickley Town was at the junction of this creek and the Youghiogheny River, in Westmoreland County. They were probably the first Shawnees to settle in Western Pennsylvania.

The Shawnees of the eastern part of Pennsylvania eventually went to the Ohio and Allegheny Valleys. In the report of the Albany congress of 1754, it is found that some of the tribe had moved from the eastern part of the state to the Ohio about thirty years previously; and, in 1734, another Shawnee band consisting of about forty families and described as living on the Allegheny, refused to return to the Susquehanna at the solicitation of the Delawares and Iroquois. During their westward migration, they established villages on the Juniata and Conemaugh. About the year 1755 or 1756, practically all the Shawnees abandoned the Susquehanna and other parts of eastern Pennsylvania, and joined their brethren on the Ohio, where they became allies of the French in the French and Indian War. By the outbreak of the Revolutionary War, nearly all the Shawnees had been pressed westward into Ohio.

There is something mysterious in the wanderings of the Shawnees. As we have seen, their home, in remote times, was in the Ohio Valley; then we later hear of them in the South; and still later they came to Pennsylvania. There is good evidence, however, tending to show that that body of the Shawnees which entered Lancaster County, Pennsylvania, in 1697 or 1698, came originally from as far west as the region of Fort St. Louis, near the town of Utica, LaSalle County, Illinois, leaving that place in 1683 and being accompanied in their wanderings to Maryland by Martin Chartier, a French Canadian, who had spent some eight or nine years among them. At any rate, this band reached Maryland near the mouth of the Susquehanna in 1692, and such is the story they told. They gradually moved up the Susquehanna to Lancaster County, as we have seen, where Chartier became a trader at their village of Pequea, on the east side of the Susquehanna near the mouth of Pequea Creek, and only a few miles from Conestoga, which was on the north side of Conestoga Creek.

The Shawnees who settled at Paxtang, on or near the site of Harrisburg, most likely came from Pequea.* Before 1727, many of this tribe from Paxtang and Pequea had settled on the west side of the Susquehanna River at what is now New Cumberland, near the mouth of Yellow Breeches Creek and as far north as the mouth of the Conodoquinet. These dwellers on the west side of the Susquehanna, about the year 1727, crossed the mountains to the valleys of the Ohio and Allegheny. Some, however, had gone to Big Island (Lock Haven) before going to the Ohio region.

Opessah, the chief of the Shawnees on the lower Susquehanna, did not remove to the Ohio or Allegheny Valley. He remained at Pequea until 1711, when he abandoned both his chieftainship and his tribe, and sought a home among the Delawares of Sassoonan's clan. It is not clear why he abandoned his people. There is a

*There were never many Shawnees at Paxtang, their larger settlements in this region being on the west side of the Susquehanna.

traditionary account that he left because he became enamoured of a Delaware squaw, who refused to leave her own people. Later, in 1722, he removed to what was called Opessah's town on the Potomac, now Old Town, Maryland.

Neither the Pennsylvania Archives nor the Colonial Records show the name of the chief of those Shawnees who settled at Pechoquealin until 1728, when their head man was Kakowatchey. Some of Kakowatchey's clan removed directly to the Ohio before 1732, but a majority seem to have gone only as far as the Wyoming Valley in Luzerne County, where, as we have seen, they took up their abode on the west side of the North Branch of the Susquehanna at a place subsequently known as Shawnee Flats, just below the site of the present town of Plymouth. Their town at this place was called Skehandowana (Iroquois for "Great Flats"), and it remained a town of considerable importance until 1743. Some time after April of that year, Kakowatchey himself, with a number of his followers removed from Skehandowana and settled at Logstown on the Ohio.

After Kakowatchey left Wyoming, Paxinosa became chief of the Shawnees who still remained at that place. He said that he was born "at Ohio", and possibly he was one of the company of Shawnees who accompanied Arnold Viele to the Pechoquealin territory.

A number of the Shawnees at Chenastry, on the West Branch of the Susquehanna, near the mouth of Chillisquaque Creek, went to the valleys of the Ohio and Allegheny prior to the autumn of 1727 to hunt, and no doubt some of them made their permanent homes or took up their abode in this western region, during or prior to the summer of 1727.

But some of the Shawnees went directly from Maryland to the Ohio and Allegheny. Two chiefs of the Potomac Shawnees, Opaketchwa and Opakeita, by name, came from the Ohio Valley to Philadelphia in September, 1732, after they had abandoned their town on the north branch of the Potomac. Governor Gordon asked them why they had gone "so far back into the woods as Allegheny," and they replied that "formerly they had lived at 'Patawmack' [Potomac], where their king died; that, having lost him, they knew not what to do; that they then took their wives and children and went over the mountains (to Allegheny) to live."

In concluding this sketch of the Shawnees, we state that one of their reasons for migrating from Eastern Pennsylvania to the

Ohio Valley was to escape the ruinous effects of the rum traffic. The Colony of Pennsylvania made many attempts to persuade them to return to their eastern homes, fearing that they would yield to French influence if they remained in the valleys of the Ohio and Allegheny. The powerful Iroquois were asked to join in the attempt to persuade them to return. The Iroquois, at the Treaty of 1732, promised the Pennsylvania Authorities to use their influence with the Shawnees, and kept their promise. But all efforts to persuade them to return nearer the eastern settlements of the Colony were without avail.

The Tuscaroras

Another Indian tribe inhabiting portions of Pennsylvania within the historic period was the Tuscaroras. They were of the Iroquoian linguistic group. It will be recalled that this tribe, after being expelled from North Carolina and Virginia, sought an asylum with the Five Nations, and was later, in 1722, admitted formally as an addition to the Iroquois Confederacy, making the Six Nations. The Tuscaroras had suffered greatly in wars with the people of North Carolina and Virginia, before they were expelled in 1712. Their women were debauched by the whites, and both men and women were kidnapped and sold into slavery. Some were brought as far north as Pennsylvania, and sold as slaves.

Surveyor-General Lawson, of North Carolina, who, in September, 1711, was captured and executed by the Tuscaroras, says the following of these Indians:

"They have really been better to us [the people of North Carolina] than we have been to them, as they always freely give us of their victuals at their quarters, while we let them walk by our doors hungry, and do not often relieve them. We look upon them with disdain and scorn, and think them little better than beasts in human form; while, with all our religion and education, we possess more moral deformities and vices than these people do."

Moreover, the colonists of North Carolina, like the Puritans of New England, did not recognize in the Indian any right to the soil; and so the lands of the Tuscaroras were appropriated without any thought of purchase. They had suffered these and similar wrongs for many years, and, as early as 1710, sent a petition to the Government of Pennsylvania reciting their wrongs and stating that they desired to remove to a more just and friendly government. Governor Charles Gookin and the Provincial Council of Pennsylvania dispatched two commissioners to meet the embassy which brought the petition, at Conestoga, Lancaster County, on June 8, 1710, where they found not only the Tuscarora embassy, but Civility and four other Conestoga chiefs, as well as Opessah, head chief of the Shawnees.

The names of the Tuscarora ambassadors were: Iwaagenst, Terrutawanaren and Teonnotein. The account of their meeting with the Pennsylvania commissioners is contained in Pa. Archives, Vol. 2, pages 511 and 512.

In the presence of the Pennsylvania officials, the Tuscarora ambassadors delivered their proposals, which were attested by eight belts of wampum. This petition was a very lucid and condensed statement of the wrongs suffered by the Tuscaroras in their southern home.

By the first belt, the aged women and mothers of the tribe besought the friendship of the Christian people and the Indians and Government of Pennsylvania, so that they might bring wood and water without danger. By the second, the children, born and unborn, implored that they might be permitted to play without danger of slavery. By the third, the young men sought the privilege of leaving their towns to pursue the game in the forest for the sustenance of the aged, without fear of death or slavery. By the fourth, the old men sought the privilege of spending their declining days in peace. By the fifth, the entire Tuscarora nation sought a firm and lasting peace with all the blessings attached thereto. By the sixth, the chiefs and sachems sought the establishment of lasting peace with the Government and Indians of Pennsylvania, so that they would be relieved from "those fearful apprehensions which they have these several years felt." By the seventh, the Tuscaroras implored a "cessation from murdering and taking them," so that they might not be in terror upon every rustling of the leaves of the forest by the winds. By the eighth, the entire Tuscarora tribe, being hitherto strangers to the colony of Pennsylvania, implored that the sons of "Brother Onas" might take them by the hand and lead them, so that they might lift up their heads in the wilderness without fear of slavery or death.

This petition, it is seen, was couched in the metaphorical language of the Indian; but its plain meaning proves it to be a statement of a tribe at bay, who, on account of the large numbers of their people killed, kidnapped, or sold into slavery by the settlers of North Carolina, were endeavoring to defend their offspring, friends, and kindred, and were seeking a more friendly dwelling place in the North, within the domain of the just government of Penn, the apostle.

The Provincial Council of Pennsylvania advised the Tuscarora ambassadors that, before they could consent to the Tuscaroras taking up their abode within the bounds of Penn's Province, they should first be required to produce a certificate from the colonial authorities of North Carolina as to their good behavior in that colony. This, of course, the Tuscaroras were unable to do. Then, the Conestoga chiefs, by the advice of their council, determined to send the wampum belts, or petition, of the Tuscaroras to the Five Nations of New York. This was done, and it was the reception of these belts, setting forth the pitiful message of the Tuscaroras, that moved the Five Nations to take steps to shield and protect the Tuscaroras, and eventually receive them, in 1722, as an additional member of the Iroquois Confederation.

In their migration northward, the Tuscaroras did not all leave their ancient southern homes at once. Some sought an asylum among other southern tribes, and lost their identity. However, the major portion came north, and many of them resided for a number of years in Pennsylvania, before going to New York, the seat of the Five Nations. In fact, the Tuscaroras were ninety years in making their exodus from their North Carolina home to more friendly dwelling places in the North.

One body of the Tuscaroras, on their way north, tarried in the Juniata Valley in Juniata County, Pennsylvania, for many years, giving their name to the Tuscarora Mountain. There is evidence of their having been there as late as 1755. Another band settled about two miles west of Tamaqua, in Schuylkill County, where they planted an orchard and lived for a number of years. Also, in May, 1766, a band of Tuscaroras halted at the Moravian mission at Friedenshuetten, on the Susquehanna in Bradford County, and remained there several weeks. Some remained at the mission, and these had planted their crops in 1766, at the mouth of Tuscarora Creek, Wyoming County.

In a word, the residence places of the Tuscaroras in Pennsylvania during their migration to New York, were those localities where their name has been preserved ever since, such as: Tuscarora Mountain dividing Franklin and Perry Counties from Huntingdon and Juniata; Tuscarora Path Valley (now Path Valley) in the western part of Franklin County at the eastern base of Tuscarora Mountain; Tuscarora Creek running through the valley between Tuscarora and Shade mountains, which valley forms the greater part of Juniata County; and also the stream called Tuscarora Creek running down through the southeastern part of Bradford County and joining the North Branch of the Susquehanna in the northwestern part of Wyoming County. The Tuscarora Path marks the route followed by the Tuscaroras during their migration to New York and of their subsequent journeyings to and fro between New York and Pennsylvania on the north and Virginia and North Carolina on the south.

The Conoy, Ganawese or Piscataway

The Conoy, also called the Ganawese and the Piscataway, inhabited parts of Pennsylvania during the historic period. They were an Algonquin tribe, closely related to the Delawares, whom they called "grandfathers," and from whose ancestral stem they no doubt sprang. Heckewelder, an authority on the history of the Delawares and kindred tribes, believed them to be identical with the Kanawha, for whom the chief river of West Virginia is named; and it seems that the names, Conoy and Ganawese, are simply different forms of the name Kanawha, though it is difficult to explain the application of the same name to the Piscataway tribe of Maryland, except on the theory that this tribe once lived on the Kanawha.

As stated formerly, the Conestogas, when defeated by the Iroquois in 1675, invaded the territory of the Piscataways in western Maryland. This, it is believed, caused the northward migration of the Piscataways. At any rate, they shortly thereafter retired slowly up the Potomac, some entering Pennsylvania about 1698 or 1699, and the rest a few years later. The Iroquois assigned them lands at Conejoholo, also called Connejaghera and Dekanoagah, on the east side of the Susquehanna at the present town of Washington Borough, Lancaster County. Later they removed higher up the Susquehanna to what was called Conoy Town, at the mouth of Conoy Creek, in Lancaster County. Still later they gradually made their way up the Susquehanna, stopping at Harrisburg, Shamokin (Sunbury), Catawissa, and Wyoming; and in 1765, were living in southern New York. After their arrival in Pennsylvania, they were generally called Conoy. During their residence in Pennsylvania, their villages, especially those on the lower Susquehanna, were stopping places for war parties of the Iroquois on their way to and return from attacks upon the Catawbas in the South; and this fact made considerable trouble for the Colonial Authorities as well as the Conoy.

The Nanticokes

The Nanticokes, also, dwelt within the bounds of Pennsylvania during the historic period. These were an Algonquin tribe, formerly living on the Nanticoke River on the eastern shore of Maryland, where Captain John Smith, in 1608, located their principal village called Nanticoke. They were of the same parent stem as the Delawares. The tenth verse of the fifth song of the Walum Olum, the sacred tribal history of the Lenape, contains the statement that "the Nanticokes and the Shawnees went to the Southlands." It is not clear, however, where the separation of the Nanticokes from the Lenape took place, but Heckewelder states that they separated from the Lenape after these had reached the eastern part of the United States, and that the Nanticokes then went southward in search of hunting and trapping grounds, they being great hunters and trappers.

A short time after the settlement of Maryland, they had difficulties with the settlers of that colony. They were formally declared enemies in 1642, and the strife was not ended until a treaty entered into in 1678. A renewal of hostilities was threatened in 1687, but happily prevented, and peace was once more reaffirmed. In 1698, and from that time forward as long as they remained within the bounds of Lord Baltimore's colony, reservations were set aside for them. At this early day they began a gradual migration northward, though a small part remained in Maryland. The migration to the North covered many years. On their way they stopped for a time on the Susquehanna as guests of the Conoy; later at the mouth of the Juniata; and still later, in 1748 the greater part of this tribe went up the Susquehanna, halting at various points and finally settling, during the French and Indian War, under the protection of the Iroquois, at Chenango, Chugnut, and Owego, on the east branch of the Susquehanna in southern New York. For a number of years, their principal seat in Pennsylvania was on the east bank of the Susquehanna below the mouth of the Lackawanna, not far from Pittston, Luzerne County. Other villages of this tribe were on Nanticoke Creek and at or near the site of the present town of Nanticoke, Luzerne County.

As late as 1766 and 1767, bands of Nanticokes passed through the Moravian mission at Wyalusing (Friedenshuetten), Bradford County, on their way to what is now the state of New York.

Many marvelous stories were told concerning this tribe. One was that they were said to have been the inventors of a poisonous substance by which they could destroy a whole settlement at once. They were also accused of being skilled in the art of witchcraft, and, on this account they were greatly feared by the neighboring tribes. Heckewelder states that he knew Indians who firmly believed that the Nanticokes had men among them who, if they wished, could destroy a whole army by merely blowing their breath toward them.

They had the singular custom of removing the bones of their dead from place to place during their migrations, and this they would do even in cases where the dead had not been buried long enough to be reduced to a skeleton. In cases where the dead had not been buried long, they would scrape the flesh from the bones, reinter it, and then take the skeleton with them. Heckewelder relates that between the years 1750 and 1760 he saw several bands of Nanticokes go through the Moravian town of Bethlehem, Pennsylvania, on their migration northward, loaded with the bones of their relatives and friends. At this time Heckewelder was a boy, having been born in 1743.

The Tutelo

The Tutelo were a Siouan tribe, related to the Sioux, of Dakota of the far Northwest. For some time before their entering Pennsylvania soon after 1722, they had been living in North Carolina and Virginia. They were first mentioned by Captain John Smith, of Virginia, in 1609, as occupying the upper waters of the James and Rappahannock, and were described by him as being very barbarous. Their first seat in Pennsylvania was at Shamokin (Sunbury) where they resided under Iroquois protection. At this place, the Rev. David Brainerd found them in 1745. Later they moved up the Susquehanna to Skogari. In 1771, the Tutelo were settled on the east side of Cayuga inlet about three miles from the south end of the lake of that name in New York. How this tribe became so widely separated from the western Sioux still remains unknown.

The Conoy, the Nanticoke, and the Tutelo were not large tribes. In 1763, according to Sir William Johnson, the three tribes numbered about one thousand souls.

As has been stated, the Shawnees, the Conoy, and the Nanticokes, belonged to the Algonquin parent stem; the Tutelo to the Siouan; and the Tuscarora to the Iroquoian. These three groups were widely separated. It is thus seen that, at the time when the English, the Germans and the Scotch-Irish, and other European races were coming to Pennsylvania, as widely separated races of North American Indians were coming from the South to make their homes in its wilderness and along its streams. Of these incoming tribes, the one to figure most prominently in the history of Pennsylvania was the Shawnee. Following Braddock's defeat, July 9th, 1755, Pennsylvania suffered the bloodiest Indian invasion in American history,—the invasion of the Shawnees and Delawares, brought about in part, by the fact that the Shawnees yielded to French influence. However, as we shall see, the fraudulent "Walking Purchase" of 1737 and the Purchase of 1754 had much to do with causing these two powerful Indian tribes to take up arms against Pennsylvania.

The Eries

The Eries, also known as the Erieehronons, were populous sedentary tribe of Iroquoian stock, which, in the seventeenth century, inhabited that part of Pennsylvania extending from Lake Erie to the Allegheny River, possibly as far south as the Ohio River, and eastward to the lands of the Susquehannas. They are also known as the Cat Nation, from the abundance of wild cats and panthers in their territory. Recorded history gives only glimpses of them; but it appears that they had many towns and villages, and that their town, Rique, had, in 1654, between 3,000 and 4,000 combatants, exclusive of women and children. Rique was located, as nearly as can be determined, at or near where the city of Erie, Pennsylvania, now stands.

In the Jesuit Relation of 1653, it is stated that the Eries were forced to proceed farther inland in order to escape their enemies dwelling west of them. Who these enemies were is not positively known. Finally, about 1655 or 1656, they were conquered by the Iroquois. The conquerors entered their palisaded town of Rique, and there "wrought such carnage among the women and children that the blood was knee-deep in places." However, this victory at Rique was dearly bought by the Iroquois, who were compelled to remain in the country of the Eries two months to care for the wounded and bury the dead. The Erie power now being broken, the people were either destroyed, dispersed, or led into captivity. Six hundred Eries, who had surrendered at one time, were taken to the Iroquois country and adopted. There is a tradition that, some years after the defeat of the Eries, a band of their descendants came from the West, ascended the Allegheny River, and attacked the Senecas, and were slain to a man.

According to the Jesuit Relation of 1655-56, the cause of the war between the Iroquois and the Eries was the accidental killing of a Seneca by one of thirty Erie ambassadors who had gone to the Seneca capital, Sonontouan, to renew the then existing peace between these two tribes. The Senecas then put all the Erie ambassadors to death, except five, and determined to exterminate the tribe. However, before being utterly defeated at Rique, the Eries were successful in burning a Seneca town and in defeating a body of Senecas, which events aroused the Senecas to savage wrath, causing them to invade the Erie country with eighteen hundred warriors and to destroy the town of Rique.

The estimated population of the Eries in 1654 was 14,500. Besides Rique, they had another large town, Gentaienton, located, it seems, in the southern part of Erie County, New York.

The Wenro

The Wenro, a tribe of Iroquoian stock, also known as the Ahouenrochrhonons, are mentioned in the Jesuit Relation as having dwelt some time prior to 1639, "beyond the Erie," or Cat Nation; and it is probable that their habitat was on the upper territory of the Allegheny, and, part of it at least, within the bounds of the State of Pennsylvania. This tribe, too, fell before the arms of the Iroquois. A notation on Captain John Smith's map of his explorations, says that they traded with the whites on the Delaware River.

The Black Minquas

The Wenro seem to have been allied with the Black Minquas who, according to Herrmann's map of 1670, are placed in the region west of the Allegheny Mountains, and on the Ohio, or "Black Minquas River." The Jesuit Relation states that both the Wenro and the Black Minquas traded with the people on the upper Delaware, some going by way of the West Branch of the Susquehanna, down to Sunbury (Shamokin), up to Wyoming, and then across to the Delaware River, near the Water Gap; and others reaching the Delaware by way of the Conemaugh, Juniata, and Susquehanna. The Black Minquas were so called because "they carried a black badge on their breast." About all that is known of the fate of this tribe is the legend on Herrmann's map, which reads: "A very great river called Black Minquas River—where formerly those Black Minquas came over the Susquehanna, as far as the Delaware to trade; but the Sasquhana and the Sinnicus Indians went over and destroyed that very great nation."

The Akansea

A Siouan tribe, the Akansea, in remote times, occupied the upper Ohio Valley, according to many historians, and were driven out by the Iroquois. This stream was called the "River of the Akansea," because this tribe lived upon its shores. When or how long this river valley was their habitat, is not known.

No other rivers in Pennsylvania, or on the continent, have seen more changes in the races of Indians living in their valleys than have the Ohio and the Allegheny,—the dwelling place of the Alligewi; the Delawares, or Lenape, in the course of their migration eastward; the Akansea; the Shawnees; the Black Minquas; the Eries; the Wenro; the Senecas; then once more the Shawnees and Delawares in their march toward the setting sun before the great tide of white immigration. What battles and conquests, all untold, took place in the valleys of these historic streams before the white man set foot upon their shores! Who would not seek to draw aside the curtain, which, it seems, must forever hide this unrecorded history from our view?

Having given this survey of thc Indian tribes that inhabited Pennsylvania, we shall devote the next chapter to a brief treatment of the Indian policy of the Swedes on the Delaware and William Penn.

CHAPTER III

The Swedes and William Penn

Founding of New Sweden

AS early as 1624, Sweden's most famous king, Gustavus Adolphus, one of the heroic and admirable characters of all time, proposed to found a free state in the New World, "where the laborer should reap the fruits of his toil, where the rights of conscience should be inviolate," and which should be an asylum for the persecuted of every nation and every clime. At that time, the awful Thirty Years War was raging in Europe, and amid its fire and blood and desolation, the Swedish King had a vision of such a "Holy Experiment" as William Penn started more than half a century later. Before he could carry out his plans of colonization, the noble Gustavus Adolphus laid down his life on the bloody battle-field of Lutzen, Germany, on November 16th, 1632. According to Bancroft and others, the King, just a few days before his death, recommended his noble enterprise to the people of Germany, as he had before to the people of his beloved Sweden.

Christina, the daughter of Gustavus Adolphus, succeeded her father to the throne of Sweden, and was destined to play a vital part in the development of the plans of her illustrious parent. Late in the autumn of 1737, two ships left Sweden carrying a small band of resolute emigrants purposing to establish a Swedish colony in the New World under the patronage of Queen Christina. These ships, commanded by Peter Minuit, who had been the Dutch Company's director at Manhattan from 1626 to 1632, arrived on the west bank of the Delaware River, in the middle of March, 1638. Charmed by the beauty of the region, the Swedes gave the name of Paradisudden (Paradise Point) to a particularly beautiful spot where they landed temporarily. Passing on up the river, their ships arrived at the Minquas Kill of the Dutch (White Clay and Christina Creeks), which enters the Delaware from the west. The ships then sailed up the Minquas Kill some distance, and cast anchor at a place where some Indians had pitched their wigwams.

Peter Minuit then fired a salute of two guns and went ashore with some of his men to reconnoiter and establish connection with the Indians. They also went some distance into the country. Minuit then returned to his ship. The roar of his cannon had the desired effect; several Indian chiefs made their appearance, and Minuit at once arranged a conference with them for the sale of land. The leader of these chiefs was Mattahorn. Possibly Minuit from his acquaintance with the Dutch trade on the Delaware River during his administration at Manhattan, had some previous knowledge of this chieftain. Minuit and the chiefs had no difficulty in coming to an agreement. He explained to the Indians that he wanted ground on which to build a "house," and other ground on which to plant. For the former he offered a "kettle and other articles," and for the latter, half of the tobacco raised upon it. On the same, or following day, Mattahorn and five other chiefs went aboard one of the ships of the Swedes and sold as much "of the land on all parts and places of the river, up the river, and on both sides, as Minuit requested."

The merchandise specified in the deeds being given to them, the chiefs traced their totem marks on the documents, and Peter Minuit, Mans Kling, and others signed their names below. The extent of this purchase embraced the territory lying below the Minquas Kill to Duck Creek, a distance of forty miles and up the river to the Schuylkill, a distance of twenty-seven miles along the bank of the Delaware, in both cases stretching an indefinite distance to the westward. The purchase being concluded, Minuit with his officers and soldiers went ashore. A pole was then erected with the Coat of Arms of Sweden upon it; "and with the report of cannon, followed by other solemn ceremonies, the land was called New Sweden."

To be specific, the lands purchased by the Swedes from the Indians extended along the west bank of the Delaware from the mouth of Minquas Creek to a point opposite Trenton, New Jersey. Near the mouth of Minquas Creek, so named by them because it was one of the main trails to the land of the Minquas or Susquehannas, they erected Fort Christina, named in honor of the Swedish Queen. As stated in Chapter II, the Swedes also purchased lands from the Susquehanna tribe. It is probable that a large part of this purchase was a confirmation of the purchase from the Delawares.

The first Indians with whom the Swedes dealt in making the first settlements within the bounds of Pennsylvania, were the Delawares or Lenape of the Unalachtigo or Turkey Clan. At that time, the Delawares on the lower reaches of the river of the same name were called "River Indians," and it seems true that they were subject to the authority of the Minquas or Susquehannas. It has been contended, as pointed out in Chapter II, that the conquering of the Susquehannas by the Iroquois, in 1675, carried with it the subjugation of the Delawares. Soon after the founding of their first settlements on Pennsylvania soil, the Swedes dealt also with the Minquas or Susquehannas, carrying on a vast fur trade with them and thereby incurring the jealousy and enmity of the Dutch at Manhattan, a fact which led to the overthrow of New Sweden by the Dutch, in 1655. It is said that the Swedes exported 30,000 skins during the first year of their occupancy of Fort Christina, and, as was stated in Chapter II, Governor-General John Printz, of New Sweden, in his report for the year 1647, says that, because of the conflict of his colonists with the Dutch, he had suffered a loss of "8,000 or 9,000 beavers which have passed out of our hands" and which, but for the Dutch, would have been gotten from "the great traders, the Minquas." As was stated in Chapter II, the Swedes assisted the Susquehannas in their struggle against the might of the Iroquois, furnishing them arms for their warriors after the manner of European soldiers.

Indian Policy of the Swedes

The principles on which New Sweden was founded and the benevolent intentions of the Swedes towards the Indians are thus set forth in the letter granting the privileges to the colonists, signed by Chancellor Axel Oxenstierna, of Sweden, dated January 24th, 1640, and directed to the Commandant and inhabitants of Fort Christina.

"As regards religion, we are willing to permit that, besides the Augsburg Confession, [of the Lutheran Church], the exercise of the pretended reformed religion may be established and observed in that country, in such manner, however, that those who profess the one or the other religion live in peace, abstaining from every useless dispute, from all scandal and all abuse. The patrons of this colony shall be obliged to support, at all times, as many ministers and school masters as the number of inhabitants shall seem to require, *and to choose, moreover, for this purpose, persons who have at heart the conversion of the pagan inhabitants to Christianity.*"

The policy of the Swedes towards the Indians is more specifically set forth in the "Instructions to Governor John Printz," dated at Stockholm, August 15th, 1642, as follows:

"The wild nations, bordering on all sides, the Governor shall treat with all humanity and respect, and so that no violence or wrong be done to them by Her Royal Majesty or her subjects aforesaid; but he shall rather . . . exert himself that the same wild people may be gradually instructed in the truths and worship of the Christian religion, and in other ways brought to civilization and good government, and in this manner properly guided. Especially shall he seek to gain their confidence, and impress upon their minds that neither he, the Governor, nor his people and subordinates are come into these parts to do them any wrong, or injury, but much more for the purpose of furnishing them with such things as they may need for the ordinary wants of life."

These "Instructions" further admonished the Governor that he "must bear in mind that the wild inhabitants of the country" are "its rightful lords."

There is no sublimer chapter in American history than the story of the relations between the Swedes on the Delaware and the aborigines of Pennsylvania. The Swede treated the Indian with justice. He recognized that there was a title in the Indian to the land which he loved with an undying love, the land where he was born and where his fathers were born for countless generations. Furthermore, the Swede labored with success in converting the Indians to the Christian faith. The Swedish Lutheran clergyman, the Reverend John Campanius, who accompanied Governor John Printz to New Sweden in 1643, was active as a missionary among the Delawares and translated Martin Luther's Catechism into the Delaware tongue,—the first book to be translated into the language of the North American Indians. The petition, "Give us this day our daily bread," Campanius translated, "Give us this day a plentiful supply of venison and corn." This Lutheran clergyman was the first missionary of the Christian religion to labor among the Indians of Pennsylvania; and the Swedish Lutheran church at Tinicum, which he dedicated on September 4th, 1646, and of which he was pastor, "was the first regularly dedicated church building within the limits of Pennsylvania." The Rev. Campanius is sometimes referred to as Campanius Holm. "Holm" indicates that he was from Stockholm.

The year 1644 was the only year in which Indian troubles threatened New Sweden. The cause of this trouble was the fact that the Dutch at Manhattan adopted a course of "extermination" of the Indians on the lower reaches of the Hudson, and during the years 1644 and 1645, had killed sixteen hundred of the natives at Manhattan and in its neighborhood. They slaughtered all ages and both sexes; and the word of these shocking and unpardonable cruelties spread along the Atlantic Ocean, causing the Indians of the Delaware to feel bitter towards all newcomers. In the spring of 1644, a Swedish woman and her husband, an Englishman, were killed not far from the site of Chester, Pennsylvania,—the first white blood shed in Pennsylvania by the Indians. Governor John Printz of the Swedish colony then assembled his people for the defense of Chester; but the Indian chiefs of that region came to him disowning the act and desiring peace. He then made a treaty of peace with them, distributing presents and restoring friendly relations. During this year there was a great Indian council held, which has been described by Rev. John Campanius, over which the Delaware Chief, Mattahorn, presided and in which the destruction of the Swedes was considered. Mattahorn is said to have presented the question for the consideration of the council; but the decision was that the Swedes should not be molested. The warriors said that the Swedes should be considered "good friends," and that the Indians had "no complaint to make of them."

On June 17th, 1654, a great council of the Delawares was held at Printz Hall, at Tinicum, for the purpose of renewing the ancient bond of friendship that existed between the Indians and the Swedes. At this council the Delaware, (some say Minquas or Susquehanna) chief, Naaman, whose name is preserved in Naaman's Creek, near the Delaware line, praised the virtues of the Swedes. Campanius thus describes the occasion:

"The 17th June, 1654, was gathered together at Printz Hall at Tinicum, ten of the sachemans of the Indian chiefs, and there at that time was spoken to them in the behalf of the great Queen of Sweedland for to renew the old league of friendship that was betwixt them, and that the Sweeds had bought and purchased land of them. They complained that the Sweeds they should have brought in with them much evil, because so many of them since are dead and expired. Then there was given unto them considerable presents and parted amongst them. When they had received the presents they went out, and had a conference amongst them a pretty while, and came in again, and then spoke one of the chiefs, by name Noaman [Naaman], rebuked the rest, and that they had spoken evil of the Sweeds and done them harm, and that they should do so no more, for they were good people. Look, said he, pointing upon the presents, what they have brought us, and they desire our friendship, and then he stroked himself three times down his arm, which was an especial token of friendship. Afterwards he thanked for the presents they had received, which he did in all their behalfs, and said that there should hereafter be observed and kept a more strict friendship amongst them than there hath been hitherto. That, as they had been in Governor Printz his time, one body and one heart, (beating and knocking upon his breast), they should henceforward be as one head. For a token waving with both his hands, and made as if he would tye a strong knot; and then he made this comparison, that as the callibash is of growth round without any crack, also they from henceforth hereafter as one body without any separation, and if they heard or understood that any one would do them or any of theirs any harm, we should give them timely notice thereof, and likewise if they heard any mischief plotting against the Christians, they would give them notice thereof, if it was at midnight. And then answer was made unto them, that that would be a true and lasting friendship, if everyone would consent to it. Then the great guns were fired, which pleased them exceedingly well, saying, 'Pu-hu-hu! mo ki-rick pickon.' That is, 'Hear! now believe! The great guns are fired.' And then they were treated with wine and brandy. Then stood up another of the Indians and spoke, and admonished all in general that they should keep the league and friendship with the Christians that was made, and in no manner or way violate the same, and do them no manner of injury, not to their hogs or their cattle, and if any one should be found guilty thereof, they should be severely punished, others to an example. They advised that we should settle some Sweeds upon Passaiunck, where then there lived a power of Indians for to observe if they did any mischief, they should be confirmed, the copies of the agreements were then punctually read unto them. But the originals were at Stockholm, and when their names (were read) that had signed, they seemed when they heard it rejoiced, but when anyone's name was read that was dead, they hung their heads down and seemed to be sorrowful. And then there was set upon the floor in the great hall two great kettles, and a great many other vessels with sappan, that is, mush, made of Indian corn or Indian wheat, as groweth there in abundance. But the sachemans they sate by themselves, but the common sort of Indians they fed heartily, and were satisfied. The above mentioned treaty and friendship that then was made betwixt the Sweeds and the Indians, hath been ever since kept and observed, and that the Sweeds have not been by them molested."

As stated earlier in this chapter, New Sweden was overthrown by the Dutch in 1655. However, the Swedes were permitted to remain on their lands. The Indian's love for the Swede never abated, and when William Penn came to his Province in 1682, he used Swedes as his interpreters in getting in touch with the Indians. Indeed, the just and kindly treatment of the Delawares by the Swedish settlers caused that friendly reception which these children of the forest William Penn, when, with open heart and open hand, they welcomed him to the shores of the Western World.

Dr. William M. Reynolds, in the introduction to his translation of Acrelius' "History of New Sweden," emphasizes a great historical truth when he says:

"The Swedes inaugurated the policy of William Penn, for which he has been deservedly praised, in his purchase of the soil from the Indians, and his uniformly friendly intercourse with them."

A Contrast

The Indian policy of the Swedes on the Delaware stands out in strong contrast with the Indian policy of many other colonies, especially with the Indian policy of early New England. At this point, let us raise the curtain and take a view of what was happening on the shores of New England while the sublime things we have just related were happening on the shores of the Delaware, on Pennsylvania soil. The "Pilgrim Fathers" came to New England in 1620. They were kindly welcomed and kindly treated by the Indians. Not long after the landing at Plymouth, the Indian, Samoset, entered the town, exclaiming, "Welcome, Englishmen!" He was a member of the Wampanoag tribe, and, in the name of his nation, invited the Pilgrims to possess the soil. In a few days, he returned with another of his tribe, Squanto by name, who became a benefactor of the infant colony, teaching the white men many things about fishing and raising corn.

Soon the aborigines of New England were given the white man's rum, the curse of the Red man. Soon troubles came on apace between the Indian and the New Englander, caused, in large measure, by the New Englander's trickery and failure to recognize in the Indian a title to the land of himself and his fathers. Soon we see the Puritan antagonizing the Indian and deliberately planning his utter extinction. Soon we see Captain Miles Standish disturbing and despoiling the resting places of the Indian dead, to the horror and rage of the Indians. Soon we see Standish stabbing the Indian, Pecksuot, to death and Standish's men killing many of Pecksuot's companions, which caused the Rev. John Robinson, father of the Plymouth church, to exclaim: "It would have been happy if they had converted some before they killed any."

Time passes, and we see the Puritan hunting the Indian through the forests and swamps of New England like a wild beast. We see the Puritan trafficking in Indian women and children, and selling them into slavery. Many were shipped to the slave markets of the West Indies. At one time, as many as fifty Indian women and children were captured for the purpose of selling them as slaves.

The intolerance of the Puritan found a natural vent in the extinction of the Indian. The Puritan lauded his treacheries and inhumanities towards the unsophisticated children of the forest. Puritan malignity reached a climax in the offering of a reward for Indian scalps, irrespective of sex or age. And then, there rise up in history the grim and grisly features of those Puritan clergymen who gloried in the extinction of the Indian, especially the Mathers. The New Englanders shot and burned to death six hundred men, women and children of the Pequot tribe in one day. Concerning this horrible affair, the "learned and pious Rev. Cotton Mather" wrote: "Many of them were broiled unto death in the avenging flames;" while Increase Mather wrote exultingly concerning the same slaughter of women and children: "It was supposed that no less than 500 or 600 Pequot souls were brought down to hell that day." Thus did these "great New England divines and theologians" glory in the slaughter of the Indians, irrespective of age or sex. Thus were these clergymen "inspired to prayers of thankfulness and praise." (For the Puritan's Indian policy, see

Sylvester's "Indian Wars of New England," Vol. 1, pages 97 to 99, 156 to 162, 169 and 170, 293 and 313.)

Many school books contain pictures of the Puritans going to church with guns on their shoulders to defend themselves from the Indians. These pictures tell only a half truth, which is often as misleading as a downright falsehood. There should be explanatory notes at the bottom of the pictures telling why it was necessary for the Puritans to carry guns as they went to worship the Prince of Peace.

New England historians and New England poets have thrown a glamour around the early history of New England which the facts do not justify. The Puritan, by his barbarous treatment of the Indian, has left a stain on the early history of New England which no New England historian and no New England poet, however friendly or however gifted, can ever efface.

In addition to its just Indian policy, New Sweden had many other excellencies that stand out in strong contrast with the early history of New England. With her, liberty of conscience was a historical fact, and not a mockery or a myth, as with the "Pilgrim Fathers" of New England. She laid down the principles of liberty of conscience and education of the people, as the foundation of her political structure, before William Penn was born; and she steadfastly adhered to these principles to the end of her separate and independent existence, giving them an impetus that contributed very largely to their adoption as the most cherished and sacred principles in the structure of our American Commonwealth. No man had his ears cut off, no man had his tongue bored through, no man was hanged for not adhering to the Lutheran Church of New Sweden—all this in striking contrast with the way the "Pilgrim Fathers" of New England persecuted those who did not accept the Puritan type of religion. The Lutheran Swedes who landed on the shores of the Delaware and made the first settlements in Pennsylvania, had far more to do with molding American history than had the "Pilgrim Fathers" of New England. "America," says Woodrow Wilson, "did not come out of New England." Well for us that America did not take on the stamp of the bigotry and intolerance of the "Pilgrim Fathers" of New England, but took on the stamp of liberty of conscience of the Lutheran Swedes of Pennsylvania.

The history of the beginnings in Pennsylvania is as much more glorious than the history of the beginnings in New England as the light of the sun is more glorious than the light of a candle. The

Swedes on the Delaware deserve monuments of marble and bronze, medals of silver and gold; but their best monument is the best love of the best American hearts, and the truest impression of their image is in the improved condition of mankind, which came about as the fruits of the immortal principles to which they adhered.

The Coming of William Penn

After the conquest of New Sweden, in the autumn of 1655, the Dutch continued their rule on the Delaware until the autumn of 1664, when English rule began on this stream. Charles II granted to his brother James, Duke of York, the territory embracing the states of New York and New Jersey, and, by a later grant, the state of Delaware. The Dutch colony on the Delaware yielded to the Duke of York without bloodshed. On March 4th, 1681, Charles II affixed his signature to William Penn's charter for the Province of Pennsylvania. As the great founder of the Province was on his way to the shores of this Western World to treat the Red Man with justice and to establish an asylum for the persecuted of every sect and every creed, the following letter was written by the "great New England divine and theologian," Cotton Mather:

"September ye 15, 1682.

To ye aged and beloved Mr. John Higginson:

There is now at sea a ship called the Welcome, which has on board an hundred or more of the heretics and malignants called Quakers, W. Penn, who is the chief scamp, at the head of them.

The general court has accordingly given secret orders to Master Malachi Huscott of the brig Porpoise to waylay the said Welcome slyly, as near the Cape of Cod as may be, and make captive the said Penn and his ungodly crew, so that the Lord may be glorified and not mocked on the soil of this new country with the heathen worship of these people. Much spoil can be made by selling the whole lot to Barbados, where slaves fetch good prices in rum and sugar, and we shall not only do the Lord great service by punishing the wicked but we shall make great good for his Minister and people.

Master Huscott feels hopeful and I will set down the news when the ship comes back.

Yours in ye bowels of Christ,

COTTON MATHER."

The Indian Policy of William Penn

William Penn did not set foot upon the soil of his Province until the 29th day of October, 1682; but, after maturing his plans for the new colony during the summer of 1681, he appointed his cousin, William Markham, to be his deputy governor. Markham left England in the spring of 1682, and arrived at New York about the middle of June of that year. He then proceeded to Upland, or Chester, Pennsylvania, and, no doubt, presented his credentials to the justices and announced to them and the settlers that once more a change of government had been decreed.

William Penn decided to follow the advice of the Bishop of London and the example of the Swedes, and purchase from the Indians inhabiting his Province whatever lands, within the bounds of the same, might from time to time, become occupied by his colonists. The first Indian deed of record was a purchase of lands in Bucks County, made by Deputy Governor Markham for William Penn, dated the 15th day of July, 1682. The native grantors were fourteen Delaware chiefs or "sachemakers," bearing the following names: Idauahon, Ieanottowe, Idquoquequon, Sahoppe for himself and Okonikon, Merkekowon, Orecton for Nannacussey, Shaurwawghon, Swanpisse, Nahoosey, Tomakhickon, Westkekitt and Tohawsis.

Markham paid the Indians for this purchase: 350 fathoms of wampum, 20 fathoms of "stroudwaters," 20 white blankets, 20 guns, 20 coats, 40 shirts, 40 pairs of stockings, 40 hose, 40 axes, 2 barrels of powder, 60 fathoms of "duffields," 20 kettles, 200 bars of lead, 200 knives, 200 small glasses, 12 pairs of shoes, 40 copper boxes, 40 tobacco tongs, 2 small barrels of pipes; 40 pairs of scissors, 40 combs, 20 pounds of red lead, 100 awls, two handfuls of fish hooks, two handfuls of needles, 40 pounds of shot, 10 bundles of beads, 10 small saws, 12 drawing knives, 2 ankers of tobacco, 2 ankers of rum, 2 ankers of cider, 2 ankers of beer, and 300 guilders in money,—a formidable list, indeed, and all very acceptable to the Indians.

William Penn Purchases Land from Tamanend

On June 23rd, 1683, William Penn, at a meeting with Tamanend and a number of other Delaware chiefs at Shakamaxon, within the limits of Philadelphia, purchased two different tracts of land from the Indians. The first deed was from Tamanend, who made "his mark" to the same, being a snake coiled. This deed conveyed all of Tamanend's lands "lying betwixt the Pemmapecka [Pennypack] and Nessaminehs [Neshaminy] Creeks, and all along Nessaminehs Creek." The consideration was "so many guns, shoes, stockings, looking glasses, blankets, and other goods as the said William Penn shall please to give."

On the same date, (June 23, 1683), William Penn purchased a second tract of land from Tamanend, the deed being signed by Tamanend and Metamequan. It conveyed all the grantors' lands "lying betwixt and about Pemmapecka and Nessaminehs Creeks, and all along Nessaminehs Creek." The consideration was "so much wampum and other goods as he, the said William Penn, shall be pleased to give unto us." However, there is a receipt attached to this deed for the following articles: 5 pairs of stockings, 20 bars of lead, 10 tobacco boxes, 6 coats, 2 guns, 8 shirts, 2 kettles, 12 awls, 5 hats, 25 pounds of powder, 1 peck of pipes, 38 yards of "duffields," 16 knives, 100 needles, 10 glasses, 5 caps, 15 combs, 5 hoes, 9 gimlets, 20 fish hooks, 10 tobacco tongs, 10 pairs of scissors, 7 half-gills, 6 axes, 2 blankets, 4 handfuls of bells, 4 yards of "stroudswaters" and 20 handfuls of wampum.

Also, on the 5th day of July 1697, "King Taminy [Tamanend], and Weheeland, my Brother and Weheequeckhon alias Andrew, who is to be king after my death, Yaqueekhon alias Nicholas, and Quenameckquid alias Charles, my Sons," granted to William Penn, who was then in England, all the lands "between the Creek called Pemmapeck [Pennypack] and the Creek called Neshaminy, in the said province extending in length from the River Delaware so far as a horse can travel in two summer dayes, and to carry its breadth according as the several courses of the said two Creeks will admit, and when the said Creeks do so branch that the main branches or bodies thereof cannot be discovered, then the Tract of Land hereby granted, shall stretch forth upon a direct course on each side and so carry on the full breadth to the extent of the length thereof." For copies of Tamanend's deeds of June 23d, 1683 and July 5th, 1697, see Penna. Archives First Series, Vol. I, pages 62, 64 and 124.

It is to be noted that in the list of articles which Penn gave in exchange for the various tracts of land purchased from Tamanend and his associate chiefs, no brandy or other strong liquor appeared It will be recalled that in Markham's purchase in Bucks County on the 15th of July, 1682, he gave the contracting sachems, rum, cider and beer as part of the purchase price. Penn, however, was more scrupulous than his deputy governor, doubtless having realized more strongly than Markham, the injury done the Indians by liquor. Indeed, in the "Great Law" which Penn drew up shortly after his arrival, there was a provision for punishing any person by fine of five pounds who should "presume to sell or exchange any rum or brandy or any strong liquors at any time to any Indian, within this province." Later the Indians found their appetite for strong liquor to be so strong that they agreed, if the colonists would sell them liquor, to submit to punishment by the civil magistrates "the same as white persons."

Penn's Treaty with Tamanend

Penn's memorable treaty with Tamanend and other Delaware chiefs, of the Turtle Clan, under the great elm at Shakamaxon, within the limits of Philadelphia, is full of romantic interest. Unarmed, clad in his sombre Quaker garb, he addressed the Indians assembled there, uttering the following words, which will be admired throughout the ages: "We meet on the broad pathway of good faith and good-will; no advantage shall be taken on either side, but all shall be openness and love. We are the same as if one man's body was to be divided into two parts; we are of one flesh and one blood." The reply of Tamanend, is equally noble: "We will live in love with William Penn and his children as long as the creeks and rivers run, and while the sun, moon, and stars endure."

No authentic record has been preserved of the "Great Treaty," made familiar by Benjamin West's painting and Voltaire's allusion to it "as the only treaty never sworn to and never broken;" and there has been a lack of agreement among historians as to the time when it took place. Many authorities claim that the time was in the November days, shortly after Penn arrived in his Province. "Under the shelter of the forest," says Bancroft, "now leafless by the frosts of autumn, Penn proclaimed to the men of the Algonquin race, from both banks of the Delaware, from the borders of the Schuylkill, and, it may have been, even from the Susquehanna, the same simple message of peace and love which George Fox had professed before Cromwell, and Mary Fisher had borne to the Grand Turk."

Other authorities, in recent times, fix the time of the treaty as on the 23rd day of June, 1683, when Penn, as has been seen, purchased the two tracts of land from Tamanend and his associates; in other words, that the purchase of land and the "Great Treaty" took place at the same time and at the same place. Moreover, a study of West's painting of the treaty scene shows the trees to be in full foliage, thus not suggesting a late autumn or winter day, as contended by Bancroft, but rather a day in the leafy month of June. Even if we should not grant the purchase of the two tracts of land from Tamanend and others on the 23rd of June, 1683, the distinction of being the "Great Treaty," it was most certainly *a treaty* of great importance and entitled to a prominent place in the Indian history of Pennsylvania and the Nation.

Says Jenkins, in his "Pennsylvania, Colonial and Federal": "In the years following 1683, far down into the next century, the Indians preserved the tradition of an agreement of peace made with Penn, and it was many times recalled in the meetings held with him and his successors. Some of these allusions are very definite. In 1715, for example, an important delegation of the Lenape chiefs came to Philadelphia to visit the Governor. Sassoonan—afterward called Allummapees, and for many years the principal chief of his people—was at the head, and Opessah, a Shawnee chief, accompanied him. There was 'great ceremony,' says the Council record, over the 'opening of the calumet.' Rattles were shaken, and songs were chanted. Then Sassoonan spoke, offering the calumet to Governor Gookin, who in his speech spoke of 'that firm Peace that was settled between William Penn, the founder and chief governor of this country, at his first coming into it,' to which Sassoonan replied that they had come 'to renew the former bond of friendship; that William Penn had at his first coming made a clear and open road all the way to the Indians, and they desired the same might be kept open and that all obstructions might be removed,' etc. In 1720, Governor Keith, writing to the Iroquois chiefs of New York, said: 'When Governor Penn first settled this country he made it his first care to cultivate a strict alliance and friendship with all the Indians, and condescended so far as to purchase his lands from them.' And in March, 1722, the Colonial Authorities, sending a message to the Senecas, said: 'William Penn made a firm peace and league with the Indians in these parts near forty years ago, which league has often been repeated and never broken.' " In fact, the "Great Treaty" was never broken until the Penn's Creek Massacre of October 16, 1755.

Unhappily, then, historians are not able to agree in stating the exact date of the "Great Treaty" under the historic elm on the banks of the Delaware,—a treaty that occupies a high and glorious place in the Indian history and traditions of Pennsylvania and the Nation. Though the historian labors in vain to establish the date, the *fact* of the treaty remains as inspiring to us of the present day as it was to the historians, painters, and poets of the past.

On August 16th, 1683, William Penn wrote a long letter to the Free Society of Traders, in which he describes a council that he had with the Indians,—possibly the "Great Treaty":

"I have had occasion to be in council with them (the Indians) upon treaties for land, and to adjust the terms of trade. Their order is thus: The King sits in the middle of an half moon, and hath his council, the old and wise, on each hand; behind them or at a little distance, sit the younger fry in the same figure . . . When the purchase was agreed, great promises passed between us of kindness and good neighborhood, and that the Indians and English must live in love as long as the sun and moon give light; which done, another made a speech to the Indians in the name of all the Sachamakers or Kings, first to tell them what was done; next to charge and command them to love the Christians, and particularly live in peace with me, and the people under my Government; that many Governors had been on the River, but that no Governor had come himself to live and stay here before; and having now such an one that treated them well, they should never do him or his any wrong. At every sentence of which they shouted and said Amen in their way."

The "Great Treaty" was preserved by the head chiefs of the Turtle Clan of Delawares for generations. Chief Killbuck is said to have lost the historic document when, on March 24th, 1782, he fled to Fort Pitt to escape death at the hands of the Scotch-Irish settlers who attacked him and other friendly Delawares on Smoky Island, also called Killbuck's Island, in the Ohio River, near the fort.

Tamanend

The great Delaware chief, Tamanend, (Tammany, etc.) from whom William Penn and his agents purchased lands and with whom Penn made the "Great Treaty," was head chief of the Unami or Turtle Clan of Delawares from before 1683 until 1697 and, perhaps, later. He is referred to in the Colonial Records of Pennsylvania as "King" of the Delawares, owing to the fact that the head chief of the Turtle Clan always presided at the councils of the three clans composing the Delaware nation. Heckewelder thus describes Tamanend:

"The name of Tamanend is held in the highest veneration by all the Indians. Of all the chiefs and great men which the Lenape nation ever had, he stands foremost on the list. But, although many fabulous stories are circulated about him among the whites, but little of his real history is known. The misfortunes which have befallen some of the most beloved and esteemed personages among the Indians since the Europeans came among them, prevent the survivors from indulging in the pleasure of recalling to mind the memory of their virtues. No white man who regards their feeling, will introduce such subjects in conversation with them. All we know, therefore, of Tamanend is that he was an ancient Delaware chief who never had an equal. He was, in the highest degree, endowed with wisdom, virtue, prudence, charity, affability, meekness, hospitality; in short with every good and noble qualification that a human being may possess. He was supposed to have had intercourse with the great and good Spirit; for he was a stranger to everything that is bad. The fame of this great man extended even among the whites, who fabricated numerous legends concerning him, which I never heard, however, from the mouth of an Indian, and, therefore, believe to be fabulous. In the Revolutionary War, his enthusiastic admirers dubbed him a saint and he was established under the name of Saint Tammany, the Patron Saint of America. His name was inserted in some calendars and his festival celebrated on the first day of May in every year."

Heckewelder then describes the celebrations in honor of Saint Tammany. They were conducted along Indian lines, and included the smoking of the calumet and Indian dances in the open air. "Tammany Societies" in the early part of our history as a nation, were organized in several American cities.

Tamanend's last appearance in recorded history was when he, his brother and sons, conveyed the lands to William Penn on July 5th, 1697. But three years prior thereto, or on July 6th, 1694, he appeared at a council at Philadelphia, a number of other Delaware chiefs accompanying the venerable sachem. At this council, he thus expressed his friendly feelings for the colonists, in a speech addressed to Lieutenant-Governor Markham: "We and the Christians of this river [Delaware] have always had a free roadway to one another, and although sometimes a tree has fallen across the road, yet we have still removed it again, and kept the path clean; and we design to continue the old friendship that has been between us and you."

Tamanend died before July, 1701, but the date of his death is not known. All that is mortal of this great and good chieftain reposes in the soil of the beautiful valley of the Neshamminy,— the region which he and his associate chiefs conveyed to "Miquon," or "Brother Onas," as the Indians affectionately called William Penn. His grave is believed to be in "Tammany Burial Ground," near Chalfonte, Bucks County.

Penn's Two Sojourns in his Province

William Penn remained in his Province until June 12th, 1684, on which date he sailed for England. Before leaving, he provided for the administration of the government of the Province, lodging the executive power with the Provincial Council. During the spring or summer of 1683, he had visited the interior of the Province, going as far as the Susquehanna and holding many friendly conferences with the Indians of the interior.

William Penn returned to Pennsylvania in December, 1699, after an absence of fifteen years; and he remained in his Province until the autumn of 1701, when he left finally, arriving in England about the middle of December of that year. During his second sojourn in Pennsylvania, he made his home in his commodious Manor House, at Pennsbury, in Falls Township, Bucks County, about twenty miles from Philadelphia. The erection of the mansion had been started during his absence and was completed by him after his return. Here he received many visits from different Indian chiefs, a room in the mansion having been set apart for Indian conferences.

During Penn's second sojourn in his Province, he endeavored to obtain additional legislation placing restrictions on the intercourse with the Indians, in order to protect them from the arts of the whites and the ravages of the rum traffic. He also endeavored to have the natives instructed in the doctrines of Christianity. In order to improve the temporal condition of the natives, he held frequent conferences at his manor house with various sachems; and frequently visited them in their forest homes, participating in their festivals. When they visited him at Pennsbury, it is said that he joined with them in their sports and games, ate hominy, venison, and roasted acorns with them, and matched them in strength and agility. It is recorded that nineteen Indian treaties were concluded and conferences held at Pennsbury.

Penn's Treaty with the Susquehannas, Shawnees, Conoys and Five Nations

After the close of King William's war, the governor of New York made a treaty of peace with the Five Nations; and at William Penn's suggestion it was extended to the other English colonies. On April 23rd, 1701, Penn entered into "Articles of Agreement," or a treaty at Philadelphia, with the Susquehannas, Minquas, or Conestogas, the Shawnees, the Ganawese, Conoys, or Piscataways, the latter then dwelling on the northern bank of the Potomac, and the Five Nations. In this treaty the Susquehannas were represented by Connodaghtoh, their "King," and three chiefs of the same; the Shawnees were represented by Opessah, or Wopaththa, their "King," and two other chiefs; the Conoys, Ganawese, or Piscataways, were represented by four of their chiefs; and the Five Nations were represented by Ahoakassongh, "brother to the emperor or great king of the Onondagas."

We are now ready to state the provisions of the treaty. After first reciting the good understanding that had prevailed between William Penn and his lieutenants, on the one hand, and the various Indian nations inhabiting his Province, on the other hand, since his first arrival in Pennsylvania, and expressing that there should be forever a firm and lasting peace between Penn and his successors and the various Indian chiefs of his Province, the treaty provided as follows:

First. That the said "kings and chiefs" and the various Indians under their authority should, at no time, hurt, injure or defraud any inhabitants of the Colony of Penn; and that Penn and his successors should not suffer any injury to be done the Indians by any of his colonists.

Second. That the Indians should, at all times, behave themselves in a sober manner according to the laws of the Colony where they lived near or among the Christian Inhabitants thereof; and that they should have the full and free privileges and immunities of the laws of the Colony of Penn in the same manner as the whites, and acknowledge the authority of the crown of England in the Province.

Third. That none of the Indians should, at any time, aid,

assist or abet any other nation, whether of Indians or others, that would at any time not be in amity with the king of England.

Fourth. That, if at any time, the Indians should hear from evil-minded persons or sowers of sedition any unkind reports of the English, representing that the English had evil designs against the Indians, in such case the Indians should send notice thereof to Penn or his successors, and not give credence to such reports until fully satisfied concerning the truth of the same. Penn agreed that he and his successors should at all times act in the same manner toward the Indians.

Fifth. That the Indians should not suffer any strange nations of Indians to settle on the farther side of the Susquehanna or about the Potomac, except those that were already seated there, nor bring any other Indians into any part of the Province without the permission of Penn or his successors.

Sixth. Penn, for the purpose of correcting abuses that were too frequently connected with the fur trade with the Indians, agreed on the part of himself and his successors, that no one should be permitted to trade with the Indians without first securing a license under the Governor's hand and seal; and the Indians agreed, on their part, not to permit any person whatsoever to buy or sell, or have any trade with them, without first having a license so to do.

Seventh. The Indians agreed not to sell or dispose of any of their skins or furs to any person whatsoever outside of the Province; and Penn bound himself and his successors to furnish the Indians with all kinds of necessary goods for their use, at reasonable rates.

Eighth. The Conoys, Ganawese, or Piscataways, should have leave of Penn and his successors to settle on any part of the Potomac River within the bounds of Penn's Province. (At this time, the vexed question as to the boundary line between Pennsylvania and Maryland was unsettled.)

Ninth. The Susquehannas, or Conestogas, as a part of these articles of agreement, absolutely ratified and confirmed the sale of lands lying near and about the Susquehanna, formerly conveyed to William Penn, by deed of Governor Dongan of New York, and later confirmed by the deed of the Conestogas, dated the 13th day of September, in the year 1700. The Susquehannas also agreed to be, at all times, ready further to confirm and make good the said sale, according to the tenor of the same, and that they would be answerable to Penn and his successors for the good behavior of the Conoys or Ganawese, and for their performing of their several agreements which were a part of this treaty.

Tenth. In the last item of the agreement, Penn promised, for himself and his successors, that they would, at all times, show themselves true friends and brothers to all of the Indians by assisting them with the best of their "advices, directions and counsel," and would, in all things just and reasonable, befriend them; and the chiefs promised, for themselves and their successors, to behave themselves according to the tenor of the agreement, and to submit to the laws of the Province in the same manner as "the English and other Christians therein do." The agreement was then concluded by the exchange of skins and furs, on the part of the Indians, and goods and merchandise, on the part of Penn.

At about the time of making this historic treaty of peace with the Indians on the Susquehanna, William Penn had journied into the interior of his Province, and conferred with the Conestogas at Conestoga, their principal town, in Lancaster County, the Conestogas being responsible for the good behavior of the Shawnees in their vicinity, as was pointed out in Chapter II. Penn wrote to James Logan, in June, 1701, of his visit to the Conestoga region, as follows: "We were entertained right nobly at the Indian King's palace at Conestoga." At that time, Penn intended the founding of a "great city" in the Conestoga region, on the Susquehanna.

At the time of this treaty, most of the Conoy were living on the north bank of the Potomac, though some had already entered Pennsylvania as early as 1698 or 1699, as stated in Chapter II. Some years after the treaty, or in the summer of 1705, the Delaware chief, Manangy, living on the Schuylkill, interviewed Governor John Evans, at Philadelphia, explaining that the Conoy, "settled in this Province near the head of the Potomac, being now reduced by sickness to a small number, and desirous to quit their present habitation where they settled about five years ago with the Proprietor's consent, the Conestoga Indians then becoming guarantees of a treaty of friendship, made between them, and showing a belt of wampum they had sent to the Schuylkill Indians to engage their friendship and consent that they might settle amongst them near Tulpehocken, request of the Governor that they may be permitted to settle in the said place." The Governor then permitted the Conoy to settle in the valley of the Tulpehocken, Manangy and his band on the Schuylkill guaranteeing their good behavior.

The historic Treaty or Articles of Agreement of April 23d, 1701 should have a high and glorious place in the history of Pennsylvania. The articles are recorded in Pa. Col. Rec., Vol. 2, pages 15 to 18; also in Pa. Archives, Vol. 1, pages 144 to 147. The treaty was carefully preserved by the Shawnees for many decades. On November 12th, 1764, when Colonel Henry Bouquet was holding conferences with Nimwha, Red Hawk, Cornstalk and other Shawnee chiefs, on the Muskingum, relative to the part this tribe had taken in Pontiac's War, Red Hawk produced this historic document and three messages or letters from the Governor of Pennsylvania of different dates, and said:

"Now, Brother, I beg we, who are warriors, may forget our disputes, and renew the friendship which appears by these papers to have subsisted between our fathers."

Indians Bid Farewell to William Penn

Shortly before embarking for England, in the autumn of 1701, William Penn assembled a large company of the Delawares at his manor house at Pennsbury to review and confirm the covenants of peace and good will, which he had formerly made with them. The meeting was held in the great hall of the manor house. The sachems assured him that they had never broken a covenant "made with their hearts and not with their heads." After the business of the conference had been transacted, Penn made them many presents of coats and other articles, and then the Indians retired into the courtyard of the mansion to complete their ceremonies.

By some authorities it is said that Queen Allaquippa, of the Senecas, with her husband and infant visited William Penn at New Castle, Delaware, shortly before he sailed for England the last time. These authorities say that Queen Allaquippa's infant was Canachquasy, the great peace apostle among the Delawares during the early days of the French and Indian War. In this connection, we point out that, in the minutes of a meeting of the Provincial Council, August 22nd, 1755, (Pa. Col. Rec., Vol. 6, pages 588 and 589), Canachquasy is referred to as "the son of old Allaguipas, whose mother was now alive and living near Ray's Town"; also that George Croghan wrote from Aughwick, December 23d, 1754, (Pa. Archives, Vol. 2, page 218), that, "Alequeapy, ye old quine, is dead and Left several children." It seems quite likely, therefore, that Canachquasy was the son of the Iroquois chief, Allaguipas, whose name was similar in sound to that of Queen Allaquippa.

Likewise, Oretyagh, with a number of the sachems of the Conestogas and Shawnees, came to Philadelphia shortly before Penn's final departure for England, to take leave of their beloved "Brother Onas." At this conference, which was held on October 7th, 1701, Penn informed the chiefs that it was likely the last interview that he would ever have with them; that he had ever loved and been kind to them and ever would continue so to be, not through political designs or for a selfish interest, but out of real affection. He desired them, in his absence to cultivate friendship with those whom he would leave in authority, so that the bond of friendship already formed might grow the stronger throughout the passing years. He also informed them that the Assembly was at that time enacting a law, according to their desire, to prevent their being abused by the selling of rum among them, with which Oretyagh, in the name of the rest, expressed great satisfaction, and desired that the law might speedily and effectually be put into execution. Oretyagh said that his people had long suffered from the ravages of the rum traffic, and that he now hoped for redress, believing that they would have no reason for complaint of this matter in the future.

Penn early saw the degradation which the Indians' unquenchable thirst for strong drink wrought among them, and he did all in his power to remedy this matter. He said that it made his heart sick to note the deterioration of character and the degradation which the strong liquor and vices of the white man wrought among the Indians during his short stay in the Province.

Finally, at this leavetaking, Penn requested the Indians that, if any of his colonists should ever transgress the law and agreement, which he and his governor had entered into with them, they should at once inform the government of his Province, so that the offenders might be prosecuted. This they promised to observe faithfully, and that, if any rum were brought among them, they would not buy it, but send the person who brought it back with it again. Then, informing the chiefs that he had charged the members of his Council that they should, in all respects, be kind and just to the Indians in every manner as he had been, and making them presents, he bade them adieu never to meet them again.

Well would it have been for the Colony of Pennsylvania, if Penn's successors had always emulated his example, and the example of the Swedes, in dealing with the Indians—if his successors had been imbued with his kindly spirit, and had treated the natives with justice. He died on the 30th of July, 1718, at Ruscombe, near Tywford, in Buckinghamshire, England, at the age of seventy-four; and when his great heart was cold and still in death, the Red Man of the Pennsylvania forests lost his truest friend. During Penn's life there were no serious troubles between his colony and the Indian, and no actual warfare, as we shall see, for some years thereafter; but, less than a generation after this great apostle of the rights of man was gathered to his fathers, the Delawares, who had welcomed him so kindly, and the Shawnees, rose in revolt, after a long series of wrongs, and spread terror, devastation, and death throughout the Pennsylvania settlements.

Says Dr. George P. Donehoo: "The memory of William Penn lingered in the wigwams of the Susquehanna and the Ohio until the last red man of this generation had passed away; and then the tradition of him was handed down to the generations which followed until today, when it still lingers, like a peaceful benediction, among the Delaware and Shawnee on the sweeping plains of Oklahoma."

CHAPTER IV

Principal Indian Events From 1701 to 1754

AS stated in the preceding chapter, William Penn left his Province in the autumn of 1701 never to return. For many years after his departure, there was much uneasiness among the Indians of the lower Susquehanna due to the following facts: (1) The Iroquois regarded the Shawnees as enemies because of the latter's alliance with the Susquehannas or Conestogas. (2) The Iroquois made the villages of the Conoys on the lower Susquehanna their stopping places while going to and returning from the Carolinas in their war against the Catawbas and Cherokees. (3) The boundary dispute between Pennsylvania and Maryland caused friction between the white traders of the Conestoga region, and led to open hostility of the people of Maryland to the Susquehannas, Shawnees, Conoys and other Indians of this region.

At a meeting of the Provincial Council, held on May 9, 1704 and reported in Pennsylvania Colonial Records, Vol. 2, page 138, Edward Farmer reported to Governor John Evans that "Carolina Indians" (most likely Catawbas), to the number of forty, had recently made a raid into the Conestoga region in revenge for the capture of one of their number by the Iroquois the year before. Farmer, who had received his information from Nicole Godin, a trader at Conestoga, further advised the Governor that the "Carolina Indians" declared that for many years they had been attacked by Indians from the northward, "whom they had always hitherto taken to be those of Canada, but now found who they were, viz: ye Senecas & those Potomock & Conestogoe, & that they were Resolved to be Revenged, & to that end three nations had Joyned & would shortly come up & either destroy or be destroyed by them." Two weeks later Peter Bezallion, a French trader in the Conestoga region, reported to the Provincial Council that he had heard that the Five Nations were coming into the Province to carry off the Shawnees settled near Conestoga and those settled at the mouth of the Lehigh, "they being colonies of a nation that were their enemies."

Council with Conestogas, Shawnees, and Conoys

On the sixth and seventh of June, 1706, a council was held at Philadelphia between Governor John Evans and "the chiefs of the Conestogas, Shawnees, and Ganawese, or Conoys," concerning public affairs relating to these tribes. Indian Harry, of the Conestogas, was the interpreter. In the minutes of the council, the Colonial Records do not specifically state that Opessah was present, but, being the head of the Shawnees at Pequea, there is no doubt that he attended the council. This council opened with Secretary James Logan's account of his journey to the Conestogas and Conoy during the preceding October and the treaty which was then held with the Conoy at their town (Connejaghera, Conejoholo, Dekanoagah) near the site of Washington Borough, Lancaster County, by the terms of which treaty, the Conoy were assured that they would be safe in Penn's Province. The Conoy explained to James Logan, at the time of his visit, that they had had much trouble with the Virginians, and, considering it not safe to dwell in their old abode on the Potomac, had come within the bounds of Pennsylvania, where they hoped to dwell in peace.

At the meeting at Conestoga, in October, 1705, Secretary Logan reminded the assembled chiefs that "Governor W. Penn, since first he came into this Countrey, with all those under him, had always inviolably maintain'd a perfect Friendship with all the natives of this Countrey, that he found Possess'd of it at his first arrival" and that "when he was last in the Countrey he visited those of that place Conestoga, and his son upon his arrival did the same, in order to cultivate the ancient friendship:" and complaint was also made that John Hans Steelman was building a trading house at Conestoga, much to the annoyance of Pennsylvania, as Steelman was represented to be a Marylander, and had no license to trade with the Indians of Penn's Province. The chiefs informed Logan that they did not encourage Steelman's activities.

During this council at Philadelphia, Andaggy-Junguagh, chief of the Conestogas, laid before Governor Evans a very large belt of wampum, which he said was a pledge of peace formerly delivered by the Onondagas to the Nanticokes when the Onondagas had subjugated this tribe. He explained that the Nanticokes, being lately under some apprehension of danger from the Five Nations, some of them had, in the spring of 1706, come to the region of the Conestogas, and had brought this belt with them, as well as another belt, which, the chief explained, he left at his village in Lancaster County. He further advised the Governor that the Five Nations, of whom the Onondagas, as has been seen, were a member, were presently expected to send deputies to receive the tribute of the Nanticokes; that he had brought this belt to Philadelphia in order that the Colonial Authorities might be able to show it to any of the Five Nations, who might come to Philadelphia, as evidence to them that peace had been made. The Provincial Council, after considering the matter, concluded to keep the belt according to the proposal of the Conestogas; and the Conestogas promised to retain the other belt at their chief town, to be shown to the Five Nations if any of their deputies should come to Conestoga.

The remaining time of the council was taken up by explaining to the chiefs of these three nations the laws which had been recently enacted regulating the intercourse between the Province and these Indians. Evans explained to the chiefs that a law had recently been enacted providing that no person should trade with them but such as should first have a license from the Governor under his hand and seal. The chiefs requested the Governor that only two traders be licensed, but Evans explained that the fewer the number of traders the more likely it would be that the Indians would be imposed upon. They then desired of the Governor that he would not permit the traders to go beyond their towns and meet the Indians returning from hunting, explaining that it had been the traders' custom to meet the Indians returning from their hunt, when they were loaded with furs and peltries, make them drunk, and get all of the fruits of their hunt before they returned to their wives and families. The Governor agreed to this proposal and told the chiefs that their people should have no dealings with the traders, except at their own villages, and that he would instruct the traders not to go any farther into the Susquehanna region than the principal Indian towns, and to do no trading whatever, except in those places. Liberal presents were then given the chiefs, and the council adjourned.

The minutes of this important council are found in the Pennsylvania Colonial Records, Vol. 2, pages 244 to 248.

At a meeting of the Provincial Council on the 31st of August, 1706, it was decided that Governor Evans should visit Conestoga and the region round about it, for the purpose of further strengthening the bond of friendship between the Indians and the Colony. The Governor accordingly journeyed to this region early in September, where he was well received by the Conestogas, Shawnees and Conoys; but his visit was the cause of much scandal on account of his actions while there.

Governor Evans' Journey to the Susquehanna Region

The French, as early as 1707, had their emissaries among the Conestogas under the guise of traders, miners or colonists in an effort to draw them away from their allegiance to the English. Likewise, the colony of Maryland was pushing her pioneers over the boundary, in an effort to forestall the claims of William Penn by actual settlement.

In the month of June, 1707, Governor Evans, accompanied by Colonel John French, William Tonge, and several other Friends, and four servants, made a journey among the Susquehanna Indians, upon receiving a message from the Conestogas that the Nanticokes, who now had been tributaries of the Five Nations for twenty-seven years, intended journeying to the Onondagas in New York. He visited the following places: Pequea, Dekanoagah Conestoga, and Paxtang, near Harrisburg.

At Pequea, the Governor and his party were received by the Shawnees with a discharge of firearms, and a conference was held, on June 30th, with Opessah, in which the chief told the Governor that he and his people were "happy to live in a country at peace, and not as in those parts where we formerly lived, for then, upon returning from hunting, we found our town surprised, and our women and children taken prisoners by our enemies." While the Governor was at Pequea, several Shawnees from the South came to settle there, and were permitted to do so by Opessah, with the Governor's consent.

At Dekanoagah, the Governor was present at a meeting of the Shawnees, Conoys, and Nanticokes from seven of the surrounding towns. After having satisfied himself that the Nanticokes were a well meaning people, the Governor guaranteed them the protection of the Colony of Pennsylvania.

The Governor, having received information at Pequea that a Frenchman, named Nicole, was holding forth among the Indians at Paxtang, about whom he had received many complaints, and having advised the chief at Paxtang of his intention to seize this

French trader, captured Nicole, after much difficulty, and, having mounted him on a horse with his legs tied, conveyed him through Tulpehocken and Manatawney, to Philadelphia, and lodged him in jail.

The report of Governor Evans' trip is recorded in the Pennsylvania Colonial Records, Vol. 2, pages 386 to 390.

Troubles Between the Northern and the Southern Indians Continue—Great Conferences at Conestoga

As was pointed out in Chapter II, the Tuscaroras began their migration from the Carolinas and Virginia to the territory of the Five Nations in New York, in 1712 or 1713, and were formally admitted, in 1722, as a constituent part of the Iroquois Confederation. While the Tuscaroras were still living in their southern home, they were bitter enemies of the Catawbas, and their hatred did not abate upon their removing to New York. Almost every summer after 1713, roving bands of the Tuscaroras and other members of the Five Nations, followed the mountain valleys through Pennsylvania to the South, on their way to attack the Catawbas and Cherokees; and many Conestogas joined these war parties. Some destruction was done by these bands within the Province of Pennsylvania, but presently the Colonial Authorities adopted the method of having the farmers, whose crops were injured, place their bill in the hands of the nearest justice of the peace, who would, in turn, forward it to the Provincial Council; and, at the next conference with the Indians, the Council would deduct the amount of the bill from the present given to the Indians at that conference. This method made Pennsylvania practically free from ravages wrought by these bands. The colony of Virginia, however, did not fare so well, and both lives and property were destroyed by these bands of warriors from the North.

These war parties of the Iroquois frequently made Conestoga their stopping place on their way to and return from the territory of the Catawbas and Cherokees, and many a captive Catawba and Cherokee was tortured to death at Conestoga. Finally a treaty of peace was made between the Conestogas and Catawbas, on August 31st, 1715, but this did not put a stop to the expeditions of the Iroquois against the Southern Indians.

In June, 1717, Governor William Keith received a message from the Conestoga chief, Civility, and several other chiefs of the

Conestoga region, desiring him to visit them without delay to consult about affairs of great importance. The Governor, accordingly, journeyed to Conestoga, in July, where he met the chiefs of the Conestogas, Delawares, Shawnees, and Conoys, and inquired of them the cause of their alarm. He ascertained that about two months previously a young Delaware, son of a chief, had been killed on one of the branches of the Potomac by a party of Virginians accompanied by some Indians. These latter were no doubt Catawbas, who, at that time, were at peace with Virginia. At this meeting at Conestoga, Governor Keith brought to the attention of the Indians that many complaints had been made by the inhabitants of Virginia concerning the destruction caused by the war parties of the Iroquois against the Catawbas; and he reminded them of the fact that, although divided into different colonies, the English were one people; that to injure or make war upon one body of them was to make war upon all, and that the Indians, therefore, must never molest or trouble any of the English colonists, nor make war upon any Indians who were in friendship with, or under the protection of, the English.

At this conference, Keith stressed the fact that recently a band of Senecas had attacked some Catawbas near Fort Christian, in the colony of Virginia, killing six and capturing a woman; and he called upon the Indians of the Conestoga region to explain their connection with this insult to Virginia. The Shawnee chief told the Governor that six young men of this tribe had accompanied the party of Senecas who made the attack upon the Catawbas, but explained that none of the six were present at the time and place of this conference, "their settlements being much higher up the Susquehanna River." The chief further stated that the six Shawnees declared, upon their return, that they had nothing to do with the attack upon the Catawbas.

Governor Keith closed the conference with the following stipulations, quoted from the minutes of the conference:

"1st. That he expected their strict observance of all former contracts of friendship made between them and the Government of Pennsylvania.

"2dly. That they must never molest or disturb any of the English Governments, nor make war upon any Indians whatsoever who are in friendship with and under the protection of the English.

"3dly. That, in all cases of suspicion or danger, they must

advise and consult with this Government before they undertook or determined any thing.

"4thly. That, if through accident any mischief of any sort should happen to be done by the Indians to the English, or by the English to them, then both parties should meet with hearty intention of good will to obtain an acknowledgment of the mistake, as well as to give or receive reasonable satisfaction.

"5thly. That, upon these terms and conditions, the Governor did, in the name of their great and good friend, William Penn, take them and their people under the same protection, and in the same friendship with this Government, as William Penn himself had formerly done, or could do now if he was here present.

"And the Governor hereupon did promise, on his part, to encourage them in peace, and to nourish and support them like a true friend and brother.

"To all which the several chiefs and their great men presently assented, it being agreed, that, in testimony thereof, they should rise up and take the Governor by the hand, which accordingly they did with all possible marks of friendship in their countenance and behaviour."

The chiefs taking part in these councils at Conestoga, in July, 1717, represented the Conestogas or Susquehannas, the Delawares, the Shawnees and the Conoys. Peter Bezallion was the interpreter. For a detailed account of the conferences, the reader is referred to the Pennsylvania Colonial Records, Vol. 3, pages 19 to 25.

In 1719, great difficulties arose concerning the hunting grounds of the Northern and the Southern Indians. The Iroquois sent out many war parties, which stopped at Conestoga on their way south, and were joined by many of the Conestogas. These raids into the Shenandoah Valley brought many white settlers of Virginia and the Carolinas into hostility to the Iroquois; for these colonies were then on friendly terms with the Catawbas and Cherokees, against whom the raids were directed. In fact, a general uprising of the settlers of Virginia and the Carolinas was imminent. The Iroquois conducted their warfare on the Southern Indians with great brutality, torturing many captives to death at Conestoga and villages on the Susquehanna.

On receiving a letter from Civility and other chiefs at Conestoga advising that some of their Indians had been killed by the Southern Indians, Governor Keith sent Colonel John French to Conestoga, where a council was held on June 28th, 1719, with

Civility and Queen Canatowa of the Conestogas, "Wightomina, King of the Delawares, Sevana, King of the Shawnees," who succeeded Opessah at Pequea, and "Winninchack, King of the Canawages" [Conoys]. In the name of Governor Keith, Colonel French made the following demands of Civility and the other chiefs: That they should not receive the war parties of the Tuscaroras, or any other tribes of the Five Nations, if coming to their towns on their way to or return from the South; and that they would have to answer to the Colonial Authorities, if any prisoner were tortured by them. It appeared, however, that the warriors of the Five Nations, on their way southward, practically forced the young men of the Conestogas, Shawnees, and Conoy to accompany them. As the conquerors of these tribes, the Iroquois demanded their allegiance and help. The chiefs promised faithfully to obey the commands of Governor Keith, but the war went on.

James Logan, Secretary of the Provincial Council, on June 27, 1720, held a conference at Conestoga with Civility and chiefs of the Shawnees, Delawares, and Conoy, in an attempt to dissuade these Indians from making raids into Virginia. Not long before, ten Iroquois and two Shawnees had been killed by the Southern Indians about one hundred and sixty miles from Conestoga. At this conference, Logan learned that the Pequea Shawnees could not be restrained from assisting the Iroquois, inasmuch as since the departure of Opessah, no one could control them. True, the Conestogas were answerable for the behavior of these Shawnees, but Civility advised Logan that he "had only the name without any authority, and could do nothing." Moreover, it was difficult for Logan to impress upon the minds of these Indians the fact that the English of Virginia and Maryland were not at war with the English of Pennsylvania. They could not see why the Indians in friendship with Pennsylvania should not go to war against the Virginians, just as the Iroquois went to war against the Indians of Virginia and the Carolinas.

At the close of the conference, Civility told Logan privately that the Five Nations, especially the Cayugas, were much dissatisfied because of the large settlements the English were making on the Susquehanna, and that the Iroquois claimed a property right in those lands. As to the Iroquois' claim to a property right in the Susquehanna lands, Logan told Civility that the Indians well knew that the Iroquois had long before conveyed those lands to the Governor of New York, and that William Penn had pruchased this right, as will be pointed out later in this chapter. Civility acknowledged this fact.

Realizing the awful consequences of a general war between the Iroquois and their allies, on the one side, and the Southern Indians on the other, involving the settlers of the South, Governor Keith, in the spring of 1721, visited Governor Spotswood of Virginia with whom he framed an agreement, by the terms of which the tributary Indians of Virginia would not, in the future, pass the Potomac nor "the high ridge of mountains extending along the back of Virginia; provided that the Indians to the northward of the Potomac and to the westward of those mountains" would observe the same limits.

Governor Keith, accompanied by seventy armed horsemen, visited Conestoga on July 5th, 1721, where he conferred, at Civility's lodge, not only with the Conestogas but also with four deputies of the Five Nations, who had recently arrived there, telling the spokesman of the Five Nations, Ghesoant, that, "whereas the English from a very small beginning had now become a great people in the Western World, far exceeding the number of all the Indians, which increase was the fruit of peace among themselves, the Indians continued to make war upon one another and were destroying one another, as if it was their purpose that none of them should be left alive." He called attention to the suffering that their wars caused to the women and children at home, and, in various ways, tried to mollify their warlike passions, but stated that, if they were determined to continue warfare, they must, in journeying to and from the South, take another path lying farther to the west, and not pass through the settled parts of the Province. The result of the conference was the ratifying by the Conestogas and Five Nations of the agreement arranged by Governor Keith and Governor Spotswood as to the limits of the hunting grounds of the Virginia and the Pennsylvania Indians. Keith closed the conference by giving Ghesoant a gold coronation medal of George, the First, which he asked him to take as a token of friendship to the greatest chief of the Five Nations, Kannygoodk. Thus, happily, the immediate danger of a general Indian uprising was averted.

This was the most important Indian treaty ever held at Conestoga. Its details are recorded in the Pennsylvania Colonial Records, Vol. 3, pages 121 to 130. Later, troubles came on apace between the Iroquois and the Southern Indians, but the Iroquois abandoned the Susquehanna route to the South, taking the

Warrior's Path, which crossed the Potomac at Old Town (Opessah's Town), and, still later, when white settlers occupied the valley along Warrior Ridge, a trail farther westward, crossing the counties of Westmoreland and Fayette.

Sassoonan's Deed of Release

In the autumn of 1718, Sassoonan and several other chiefs of the Delawares came to Philadelphia, claiming that they had not been paid for their lands. Then, James Logan, secretary of the Provincial Council, produced to them, in the presence of the Council, a number of deeds, and convinced Sassoonan and his brother chiefs that they were mistaken in their contention. Accordingly, Sassoonan and six other chiefs executed a release on the 17th day of September, 1718, by the terms of which they acknowledged that their ancestors had conveyed to William Penn, in fee, all the land and had been paid for the same. By the same instrument these Indians released all the land "between the Delaware and the Susquehanna from Duck Creek [in Delaware] to the mountains [the South Mountain] on this side of Lechay [by the Lehigh River]."

At the time of executing this deed of release, Sassoonan was living at Paxtang, and adjacent parts; but it is probable that shortly thereafter he took up his abode at Shamokin (Sunbury), which became his home for the remainder of his life.

Tawena and Springettsbury Manor

Tawena, a chief of the Conestogas, claims our remembrance on account of his connection with the survey of Springettsbury Manor, in June, 1722. At that time, the boundary line between Pennsylvania and Maryland was still in dispute, and Maryland settlers were encroaching on territory claimed by Pennsylvania. In order to secure a right and title to the lands, in Pennsylvania upon which these settlers had encroached, Governor William Keith, before he went to attend the Albany treaty, or conference, of September, 1722, conceived the idea of obtaining permission of the Indians along the lower Susquehanna to lay off a large manor, and accordingly went to Conestoga, where, on June 15th and 16th of that year, he held a conference with the Conestoga, Shawnee and Conoy chiefs, telling them of the encroachments of the Marylanders in what is now York County, and suggesting the plan to take up a large tract of land on the west side of the Susquehanna for Springett Penn, grandson of the founder of the Province. Keith spoke at great length and with great earnestness. He told the Indians that the grandson had the same kind of heart as his grandfather had, and that he would be glad to give the Indians a part of the land for their use and occupation. He further said that the land should be marked with Springett Penn's name upon the trees, so that the Maryland people would then keep off, and that such marking would prevent all white persons from settling near enough the Indians to disturb them.

Owing to the love of these Indians for William Penn, Governor Keith won his point. They replied through Tawena, agreeing to give up the land, but requesting that the Governor take up the matter further with the Cayugas when he would attend the Albany conference. However, they requested that the land be surveyed at once. The warrant was made out, and John French, Francis Worley and James Mitchell surveyed the tract on June 20th and 21st. It was named Springettsbury Manor, and contained 75,520 acres, according to the survey. The boundary line began opposite the mouth of Conestoga Creek, and ran southwest ten miles, thence northwest twelve miles to a point north of the present city of York, thence northeast to the Susquehanna River, thence along this stream to the place of beginning. The Marylanders paid no attention to the survey. The Manor was surveyed again, in 1768.

The warrant and survey were not returned to the land office, and the entire transaction appears to have been done under the private seal of Governor Keith. Nor was any actual purchase made from the Indians, at the conference of June 15th and 16th, 1722. Springett Penn held whatever title he had in trust for the proprietaries.

The Threatened Uprising of 1728

On May 6, 1728, Governor Gordon advised the Provincial Council that he had recently received a letter from John Wright, a trader, at Conestoga, stating that two Conestogas had been murdered by several of the Shawnees in that neighborhood, and that the Conestogas seemed to be preparing to declare war on the Shawnees, in retaliation. The Governor also advised the Council, at this time, that he had received a petition signed by a great number of the settlers in the back parts of Lancaster County, setting forth that they were under great apprehension of being attacked by the Indians, and that many families had left their homes through fear of an Indian uprising. Wright further informed the Governor, in his letter, that the Shawnees had brought the Shawnee murders as far as Peter Chartier's house, at which place the party engaged in much drinking, and, through the connivance of Chartier, the two Shawnee murderers escaped. It is not surprising that Chartier let the murderers escape, as he himself was a half blood Shawnee. He was at that time trading at Pequea Creek. His action so incensed the Conestogas that they threatened to destroy all the Shawnees in that region.

Almost at the same time that the murder of the Conestogas occurred, the settlers along the valley of the Schuylkill became much alarmed for their safety from another quarter. Kakowatcheky, who was the head of the Shawnees living at Pechoquealin, in what is now lower Smithfield Township, Monroe County, claimed that he had learned that the Flatheads, or Catawbas, from North Carolina, had entered Pennsylvania with the intention of striking the Indians along the Susquehanna; and he, accordingly, led eleven warriors to ascertain the truth of this rumor, who, when they came into the neighborhood of the Durham Iron Works, near Manatawny, in the northern part of Berks County, their provisions failed, and they forced the settlers to give them food and drink. The settlers did not know these Indians, and believing the chief of the band to be a Spanish Indian, they were in great terror; families fled from their plantations and women and children suffered greatly from exposure, as the weather was raw and cold. There seems to be little doubt that Kakowatcheky was leading this band to Paxtang to assist the Shawnees of that place, who had been threatened by the Conestogas on account of the above mentioned murder of the two Conestogas.

A band of about twenty settlers took up arms and approached the invaders, sending two of their number to treat with the chief, who, instead of receiving them civilly, brandished his sword, and commanded his men to fire, which they did, and wounded two of the settlers. The settlers thereupon returned the fire, upon which the chief fell, but afterwards got up and ran into the woods, leaving his gun behind him. The identity of this Indian band was not known until May 20th, when two traders from Pechoquealin, John Smith and Nicholas Schonhoven, came to Governor Gordon and delivered to him a message from Kakowatcheky, explaining the unfortunate affair, sending his regrets, and asking the Governor for the return of the gun which he dropped when wounded. The Governor, then, accompanied by many citizens of Philadelphia, went to the troubled district, and personally pleaded with those settlers who had left their plantations to return. He found them so excited that they seemed ready to kill Indians of both sexes, but finally succeeded in pacifying them.

The Governor was about ready to return home when he received the melancholy news from Samuel Nut that an Indian man and two women were cruelly murdered, on May 20th, at Cucussea, then in Chester County, by John and Walter Winters, without any provocation whatever, and two Indian girls badly wounded; upon which a hue was immediately issued in an effort to apprehend the murderers. It appeared from investigation that, on the day of this murder, an Indian man, two women, and two girls, appeared at John Roberts' house, and that their neighbors noticing this, rallied to their defense, shot the man and one of the women, beat out the brains of the other woman, and wounded the girls, their excuse being that the Indian had put an arrow into his bow, and that they, having heard reports that some settlers had been killed by Indians, believed that the settlers might lawfully kill any Indian they could find.

The murderers were apprehended and placed in jail at Chester, for trial. A message was then sent to Sassoonan, Opekasset, and Manawkyhickon, acquainting them with the unhappy affair and requesting them to come to Conestoga, where a treaty would be held with Chief Civility and the other Indians at that place. The Provincial Council being apprehensive that this barbarous murder would stir up the Indians to take revenge on the settlers, a commission was appointed to get the inhabitants together and put them in a state to defend themselves. This commission consisted of John Pawling, Marcus Hulings, and Mordecai Lincoln, the great-great-grandfather of Abraham Lincoln, whose home was about ten miles east of the present town of Reading. Having sent Kakowatcheky the gun he had dropped, as well as the tomahawks dropped by his eleven warriors when they fled from the band of twenty settlers, as related above, together with a request that he warn the Indians under his authority to be more careful in the future, the Governor, accompanied by thirty residents of Philadelphia, met the Indians at a council at Conestoga on the 26th of May, where he conferred with Civility and other Conestoga, Shawnee, Conoy, and Delaware chiefs, made them many presents, and promised to punish the two murderers, if found guilty. John and Walter Winters were subsequently tried, found guilty, and hanged for the murder of the Indian man and two women.

At this point, the author desires to say that, in no work on Abraham Lincoln or his ancestry, has he been able to find a reference to the fact that the Great Emancipator's ancestor, Mordecai Lincoln, was a man of such ability and prominence as to be appointed by the Governor and Provincial Council of Pennsylvania as one of the three members of the important commission whose duty it was to place the Province in a state of defense during the threatened Indian uprising in 1728. For the account of Mordecai Lincoln's appointment, the reader is referred to the Pennsylvania Colonial Records, Vol. 3, page 304.

Sassoonan and the Tulpehocken Lands

At a meeting of the Provincial Council, held on June 5th, 1728 and reported in the Pennsylvania Colonial Records, Vol. 3, pages 318 to 321, the great Delaware chief, Sassoonan, or Allummapees, then residing at Shamokin (Sunbury), complained that the Palatines (immigrants from Germany) were settling on lands in the valley of the Tulpehocken, in Berks and Lebanon Counties, which, he claimed, had not been purchased from the Indians. These particular Palatines had first settled in the Schoharie Valley in New York, where they endured much suffering. When Governor Keith attended the Albany Conference, the hardships of these Germans were brought to his attention; whereupon his interest and sympathy were aroused, and he offered them a home in Pennsylvania. The next year (1723) some of these Palatines emigrated from New York to the Tulpehocken Valley, but a much greater number, about fifty families, came in 1727. They descended the Susquehanna to the mouth of Swatara Creek, in Dauphin County. Ascending this stream and crossing the divide between the Susquehanna and the Schuylkill, they entered the fertile and charming valley of the Tulpehocken. They had scarcely erected their rude cabins and commenced to plant their little patches of corn in the clearings in the wilderness, when the Indians of the neighborhood informed them that this land had never been purchased by the Pennsylvania Government. The Indians were much surprised that these settlers should be permitted to take up their abode on unpurchased land.

"Surely," said they, "if Brother Onas were living, such things would never happen."

At this conference, Sassoonan said that he could not have believed that these lands were settled upon, if he had not gone there and seen the settlements with his own eyes. In the minutes of the conference, we read: "He (Sassoonan) said he was grown old and was troubled to see the Christians settle on lands that the Indians had never been paid for; they had settled on his lands for which he had never received anything. That he is now an old man, and must soon die; that his children may wonder to see all their father's lands gone from them without his receiving anything for them; that the Christians now make their settlements very near them (the Indians); and they shall have no place of their own left to live on; that this may occasion a difference between their children and us, and he would willingly prevent any misunderstanding that may happen."

Governor Gordon suggested to Sassoonan that possibly the lands in dispute had been included in some of the other purchases; but Sassoonan and his brother chiefs replied that no lands had ever been sold northwest of the Blue Ridge, then called the Lehigh Hills. This conference did not succeed in settling the matter of these settlements in the Tulpehocken Valley. The matter dragged along until 1732, when Sassoonan, Elalapis, Ohopamen, Pesqueetamen, Mayemoe, Partridge, and Tepakoasset, on behalf of themselves and all other Indians having a right in the lands, in consideration of 20 brass kettles, 20 fine guns, 50 tomahawks, 60 pairs of scissors, 24 looking glasses, 20 gallons of rum, and various other articles so acceptable to the Indians, conveyed unto John Penn, Thomas Penn, and Richard Penn, proprietors of the Province, all those lands "situate, lying and being on the River Schuylkill and the branches thereof, between the mountains called Lechaig (Lehigh) to the south, and the hills or mountains, called Keekachtanemin, on the north, and between the branches of the Delaware River on the east, and the waters falling into the Susquehanna River on the west,"—a grant which embraced the valley of the Tulpehocken. (Pa. Archives, Vol. 1, pages 344 to 346.)

Sassoonan was head chief of the Turtle Clan of Delawares from a date prior to June 14th, 1715 until his death in the autumn of 1747. By some very high authorities, it is claimed that he was a son of Tamanend and, as a little boy, was with his father at the "Great Treaty" at Shackamaxon. These authorities make

Sassoonan identical with "Weheequeckhon, alias Andrew," who as stated in Chapter II, joined with his father, Tamanend, his two brothers, and his uncle, in conveying to William Penn, on the fifth day of July, 1697, certain lands between the Pennypack and Neshaminy Creeks, and whom Tamanend describes in the deed, as, "my son who is to be king after my death."

At a meeting of the Provincial Council, held in August, 1731, and reported in the Pennsylvania Colonial Records, Vol. 3, pages 404 to 406, the frequent complaints made by the Indians on account of the large quantities of rum being carried to them by the traders, were taken up. The Council's attention was called to the fact that the pernicious liquor traffic had recently caused a very unhappy incident in the family of Sassoonan. In a fit of drunkenness, he had killed his nephew, (some authorities say his cousin) Shackatawlin, at their dwelling place at Shamokin, now Sunbury. Sassoonan's grief over the unhappy incident was so great that it almost cost him his life. It was at this meeting of the Provincial Council that the great Shikellamy, who accompanied Sassoonan, issued an ultimatum to the Colonial Authorities that, if the liquor traffic among the Indians were not better regulated, friendly relations between Pennsylvania and the powerful Confederation of the Six Nations would cease.

At Shamokin, on the banks of the beautiful Susquehanna, in the autumnal days of 1747, the aged Sassoonan, who had done so much to preserve the friendship that William Penn established with the Indians, yielded up his soul to the Great Spirit. Great changes in the relations between the Delawares and the Colony had taken place during the span of his life, and still greater changes were destined to come. In life's morning and noontide, he beheld the Delawares contented and happy in the bond of affection between them and "Onas;" yet, before the night had come, his dim eyes saw on the horizon the gathering clouds of the storm that, in the autumn of 1755, broke with fury upon the land of his birth.

Efforts to Have the Shawnees Return and the Treaty of 1732

As has been seen in a former chapter, the abuses of the liquor traffic among the Shawnees were among the causes which forced a large number of this tribe to migrate from the Susquehanna to the Ohio and Allegheny valleys several years prior to 1730, when

French emissaries, coming from Canada, seized upon this opportunity to alienate the Shawnees from the English interest. Therefore, Governor Gordon at a council held at Philadelphia on August 16th, 1731, decided to adopt the suggestion of Secretary James Logan that a treaty be arranged with the Six Nations "to renew and maintain the same good-will and friendship for the Five Nations which the Honorable William Penn always expressed to them in his lifetime," and to prevail upon the Six Nations to assist in holding the Shawnees in their allegiance to the English. Accordingly, at this same conference, it was decided to send Shikellamy, "a trusty, good man and a great lover of the English" to Onondaga, the capital of the Six Nations, to invite them to send deputies to Philadelphia to arrange a treaty.

In keeping with Pennsylvania's efforts to retain the friendship of the Shawnees on the Allegheny, Governor Gordon sent them a message in December, 1731, reminding them of the benefits they had received from William Penn and his successors, while they lived in the eastern part of the Province, to which message Neucheconneh and other Shawnee chiefs on the Allegheny, replied in their letter to the Governor, of June, 1732, giving the reasons why they had removed from the Susquehanna.

In the autumn of 1731, a tract of land, called the "Manor of Conodoguinet" and located on the west side of the Susquehanna between Conodoguinet and Yellow Breeches Creeks, was set aside for the Shawnees in an effort to induce those of this tribe who had gone to the Ohio and Allegheny, to return to the Susquehanna. Peter Chartier conveyed this information to the Shawnees on the Ohio, but they still refused to return to the eastern part of the Province.

Shikellamy returned to Philadelphia from his journey to Onondaga, on December 10th, 1731, accompanied by a Cayuga chief named Cehachquely, and Conrad Weiser and John Scull as interpreters. He reported that the Six Nations were very much pleased to hear from the Governor of Pennsylvania, but that, as winter was now coming on and their chiefs were too old to make such a fatiguing journey in the winter time, they would come to Philadelphia in the spring to meet the Governor and enter into a treaty.

On his way to meet the Governor at this time, Shikellamy stopped at the home of Conrad Weiser, near Womelsdorf, in the present county of Berks, took him along to Philadelphia and introduced him to Governor Gordon as "an adopted son of the

Mohawk Nation;" and as this conference (December 10, 1731,) is Weiser's first connection with the Indian affairs of Pennsylvania, it will be well to pause long enough, at this point, to give a short sketch of the history of this noted man of the frontier, who later had so much to do with bringing about the ascendency of the Anglo-Saxon in the Western World.

This sturdy German was born at Afsteadt, in Herrenberg, near Wurtemberg, Germany, in 1696. At the age of thirteen, he accompanied his father to America, and, for several years, assisted him in making tar and raising hemp on Livingston Manor, New York. The Weiser family spent the winter of 1713 and 1714 with several of the Iroquois at Schenectady, New York, where Conrad doubtless secured his first lessons in the Iroquois tongue. In the spring of 1714, he accompanied his father to the Schoharie Valley, where they endured much hardship in company with the other Palatines in that valley. When he was seventeen years old, young Weiser went to live with Quagnant, a prominent Iroquois chief, who, taking a great fancy to Conrad, requested the father that the young man might dwell with him for a time. He remained with the Iroquois chief for eight months, learning the Iroquois language and customs thoroughly, and was adopted by them.

In 1729, Conrad Weiser and his young wife went from New York to the Tulpehocken Valley, Pennsylvania, where, as has been related, a number of Palatines from the Schoharie Valley had settled, in 1727. The young couple built their home about one mile east of Womelsdorf, Berks County, where Weiser continued to reside until a few years before his death, when he removed to Reading. It is said that while on a hunting trip he met the great Iroquois chief, Shikellamy, the vice-gerent of the Six Nations, who was well pleased with Weiser on account of his being able to speak the Iroquois tongue, and they became fast friends.

While visiting his old home near Womelsdorf, he died July 13, 1760, much lamented by the Colony of Pennsylvania as well as by the Indians. Said a great Iroquois chieftain, commenting on the death of Weiser: "We are at a loss, and sit in darkness."

If all white men had been as just to the Indians as was this sturdy German, the history of the advance of civilization in America undoubtedly would not contain so many bloody chapters. Conrad Weiser's home is still standing, and in the orchard above the house, rests all that is mortal of this distinguished frontiersman; while beside him are the graves of several Indian chiefs.

Having loved him in life, they wished to repose beside him in death. A beautiful monument has been erected to his memory in the "Conrad Weiser Memorial Park," near Womelsdorf, having thereon the words which George Washington uttered concerning him, while standing at his grave, in 1793:

"Posterity Will Not Forget His Services."*

The Six Nations, no doubt mistrusting the motives of the English, failed to send deputies to Philadelphia in the spring of 1732, as they had promised Shikellamy. In the meantime, traders in the valleys of the Ohio and Allegheny reported that the French were rapidly gaining the friendship of the Shawnees in the Ohio Valley; that these Indians complained bitterly about the great quantities of rum brought to them by the English traders; and that they would have declared war against the English, on this account, save for the influence of Peter Chartier. The Shawnees said, furthermore, that it had been only five years since the Six Nations themselves had endeavored to persuade the Ohio Indians to declare war on the English. In view of these facts, there was much anxiety on the part of the Provincial Council of Pennsylvania, over the failure of the deputies of the Six Nations to make their appearance in Philadelphia in the spring of 1732.

Finally, on August 18th, 1732 the deputies of the Six Nations arrived, consisting of a number of Oneida, Cayuga, and Onondaga chiefs, among whom was the celebrated Shikellamy. A few days' time being given the chiefs in which to refresh themselves after their long and toilsome journey, the famous treaty of August 23rd to September 2nd, 1732, was entered into between the Six Nations and the Colony of Pennsylvania.

We have stated that Secretary James Logan suggested this treaty; but Logan's knowledge of the influence and importance of the Six Nations and their power over the Shawnees, Delawares and other tributary tribes, was gotten from Conrad Weiser. Not until the coming of Weiser did the Colony fully realize the importance of this powerful confederation.

The deputies of the Six Nations, who arrived in Philadelphia some days before the opening of the conference, as we have seen, were chiefs of only the Oneida, Cayuga, and Onondaga tribes; but they claimed that they were authorized to speak for the other members of the Iroquois Confederation. In the early stages of the conference, complaints were made, possibly by members of the Assembly, against the private nature of the council; and Conrad Weiser, the interpreter, was selected to interview the

*Weiser was the grandfather of the Lutheran clergyman and noted Revolutionary General, Peter Muhlenberg, about whom the poet, Read, wrote "The Rising of 1776."

ABOVE—Monument to Conrad Weiser, Indian Interpreter of the Colony of Pennsylvania, in Conrad Weiser Memorial Park, near Womelsdorf, Berks County, Pa.

BELOW—Home of Conrad Weiser, in Conrad Weiser Memorial Park, erected about 1732. Here the famous clergyman, Rev. Henry Melchior Muhlenberg, D. D., founder of the Lutheran Church in America, for whom Muhlenberg College, at Allentown, Pa., is named, wooed and won Weiser's daughter, Anna.

Iroquois deputies to learn their pleasure in the matter. The chiefs replied that they were content to continue in secret session, but were willing to deal in a more public manner, if such was desired. Thomas Penn, son of the founder of the Colony, having lately arrived in Philadelphia, spoke for the Province. He called the attention of the chiefs to the policy which his father had pursued in dealing with the Indians, and assured them that he came to the Province with a desire and design to follow in the footsteps of his parent. He then asked the Iroquois deputies how their Confederation stood toward the French, their former enemies. He inquired how the French behaved toward the Six Nations, and how all the other nations of Indians to the northward or the westward were affected toward the Iroquois.

The Iroquois deputies replied through their speaker, Hetaquantagechty, that they had no great faith in the governor of Canada, or the French, who had deceived them. "The Six Nations," said they, "are not afraid of the French. They are always willing to go and hear what they have to propose. Peace had been made with the French. A tree had been planted big enough to shelter them both. Under this tree, a hole had been dug, and the hatchets had been buried therein. Nevertheless, the chiefs of the Six Nations thought that the French charged too much for their goods, and, for this reason, they recommended their people to trade with the English, who would sell cheaper than the French." The deputies confided to the Governor that, when representatives of the Six Nations were at Montreal, in 1727, the governor of Canada told them that he intended to make war upon Corlear (the term applied to the governors of New York), and that he desired the Six Nations to remain neutral. On this occasion, one of the chiefs answered, saying: "Onontejo [the Indian name for the governor of Canada], you are very proud. You are not wise to make war with Corlear, and to propose neutrality to us. Corlear is our brother; he came to us when he was very little and a child. We suckled him at our breasts; we have nursed him and taken care of him till he is grown up to be a man. He is our brother and of the same blood. He and we have but one ear to hear with, one eye to see with, and one mouth to speak with. We will not forsake him nor see any man make war upon him without assisting. We shall join him, and, if we fight with you, we may have our own father, Onontejo, to bury in the ground. We would not have you force us to this, but be wise and live in peace."

The Iroquois deputies were told, through Conrad Weiser, that the Shawnees who were settled to the southward, being made uneasy by their neighbors, had come up to Conestoga about thirty-five years before, and desired leave of the Conestoga Indians located at that place, to settle in the neighborhood; that the Conestogas applied to the Government of Pennsylvania that the Shawnees might be permitted to settle there, and that they would become answerable for their good behavior; that William Penn, shortly after the arrival of the Shawnees, agreed to their settlement, and the Shawnees thereupon came under the protection of the Pennsylvania Colony; that, from that time, greater numbers of the Shawnee Indians followed, settling upon the Susquehanna and the Delaware. The deputies were further told that the Colony of Pennsylvania had held several treaties with the Shawnets, treating them from their first coming as "our own Indians," but that some of their young men, four or five years previously, being afraid of the Six Nations, had removed to the Allegheny Valley, and put themselves under the protection of the French, who had received them as children; that the Colony had sent a message asking them to return, and to encourage them, had laid out a large tract of land on the west side of the Susquehanna near Paxtang, and desired, by all means, that they would return to that place.

The Iroquois answered that they never had intended to harm the Shawnees, and that, as they were coming on their way to Philadelphia, they had spoken with Kakowatcheky, their (the Shawnees') old chief, then at Wyoming, and told him that he should not "look to Ohio, but turn his face to us." They had met Sassoonan, too, the old chief of the Delawares, then at Shamokin, and told him that the Delawares, too, should not settle in the Ohio and Allegheny valleys, upon which Sassoonan had sent messengers to the Delawares lately gone to the Ohio and Allegheny Valleys, requiring them to return. It will be remembered that, in the times of which we are writing, and for a long period thereafter, the Allegheny River was considered simply as a continuation of the Ohio, and was generally called the Ohio.

The deputies were then told that, as they were the chiefs of all the northern Indians in the Province, and the Shawnees had been under their protection, they should oblige them to return nearer the Pennsylvania settlements; whereupon the chiefs asked if the Six Nations should do this themselves, or join with the Authorities of Pennsylvania. They were told that it was the desire of the Pennsylvania Colony that the Six Nations should join with the Colonial Authorities in efforts to have the Shawnees return.

The representatives of the Six Nations told the Governor that they believed that they could bring the Shawnees back, if Pennsylvania would prohibit her traders from going to the Allegheny Valley, explaining that, as long as the Shawnees were supplied at that place with such goods as they needed, they would be more unwilling to remove. It was finally agreed that Pennsylvania would remove such traders, and that the Six Nations would see that the French traders in the Ohio region were also removed.

The main purpose of this treaty was to secure the aid of the Six Nations in efforts to bring the Shawnees from the Allegheny Valley; but it contained other provisions, notably the one obligating the Six Nations to "forbid all their warriors, who are often too unruly, to come amongst or near the English settlements, and especially that they never, on any account, rob, hurt, or molest any English subjects whatsoever, either to the Southward or elsewhere."

The Iroquois delegation having requested that, in their future dealings with Pennsylvania, Conrad Weiser should continue to be the interpreter, this request was granted, and the conference came to an end by the giving of many presents to the deputies, among which were six japanned and gilt guns, which were to be delivered one to each chief of the Six Nations. These guns were the gift of Thomas Penn, which he had brought with him from England for this purpose.

A full account of the Treaty of 1732, the first treaty to bring the powerful Confederation of the Six Nations into definite relations with Pennsylvania, is found in the Pennsylvania Colonial Records, Vol. 3, pages 435 to 452. The Six Nations were faithful to their promise, in this treaty, to induce the Shawnees of the Allegheny Valley to take up their abode in the Valley of the Susquehanna. They used every means short of war, to accomplish this result, but in vain.

One of the efforts of the Six Nations to induce the Shawnees of the Ohio and Allegheny valleys to return to the eastern part of the Province is recorded in Pa. Col. Rec., Vol. 3, pages 607 to 609. At a meeting of the Provincial Council, September 10th, 1735, Hetaquantagechty, a Seneca chief, and Shikellamy gave the Council a report concerning a mission the Six Nations had sent to the Hathawekela or Asswikales Clan of Shawnees, urging them to take up their abode near the Susquehanna. Hetaquantagechty said that a great chief of the Iroquois, named Sagohandechty, who lived on the Allegheny went with other chiefs of the Six Nations in 1734 to prevail upon the Shawnees to return. Sagohandechty pressed the Shawnees so closely to return that they took a great dislike to him, and some months after the other chiefs had returned, they cruelly murdered him. Hetaquantagetchty said that this murder had been committed by the Asswikales, who then fled southward, and as he supposed had returned "to the place from whence they first came, which is below Carolina." Hetaquantagechty described them as "one tribe of those Shawnees who had never behaved themselves as they ought." The Asswikales were probably the first Shawnees to settle in Western Pennsylvania within historic times, coming by way of Old Town, Maryland, to Bedford, and then westward. Sewickley Creek, in Westmoreland County, Sewickley Town, at the mouth of that creek, and another placed called Sewickley Old Town, which some authorities locate on the Allegheny River some miles below Chartier's Old Town, (Tarentum), were their places of residence.

The Treaty of 1736

At the instigation of Shikellamy and Conrad Weiser, the Colonial Authorities of Pennsylvania were very anxious to have the treaty of August, 1732, confirmed by deputies representing all the members of the Iroquois Confederation, and Conrad Weiser was directed to employ his influence with Shikellamy to the end that these two mediators between the Colony of Pennsylvania and Great Council of the Six Nations might bring about a conference that would represent every member of that great Confederation. The summers came and went, and still the promised visit of the Iroquois was deferred. Finally, at a conference of Delaware and Conestoga chiefs, among whom were Sassoonan, representing the Delawares, and Civility, representing the Conestogas, held at Philadelphia on August 20, 1736, an appeal was made to them to explain why the Iroquois did not send deputies to Philadelphia, as they had promised. Sassoonan said that he knew nothing particularly of the Iroquois; that he had been in expectation to see them for three years past, but understood that they had been detained by nations that came to treat with them. He further stated that he expected that they would be on hand the next spring. The Provincial Council made a very liberal present to the Delawares and Conestogas on the occasion of this conference, accompanying it with the special request that they make an effort to ascertain from the Six Nations why they had not sent their deputies as they promised the preceding year, or at least to send a message stating the reasons for their delay.

This present to the Delawares had the desired effect, and in less than six weeks thereafter, Conrad Weiser sent word to the Provincial Council from his home near Womelsdorf, in the Tulpehocken Valley, that he had received intelligence that one hundred chiefs, representing all members of the Iroquois Confederation, had arrived at Shamokin (Sunbury) on their way to Philadelphia. On the 27th of September, Weiser arrived at Philadelphia, accompanied by this delegation of one hundred Iroquois. At this time, smallpox was raging in Philadelphia, on account of which Weiser took the Indians to James Logan's mansion at Stenton, a few miles from the city (now in the Twenty-second Ward, Philadelphia), and invited the provincial officers and proprietors out to meet them. The Indians were greatly pleased with Weiser's care for their health, and the esteem in which they held him increased by this act of solicitation on his part. The Iroquois had told the Colonial Authorities at the treaty of 1732 that Weiser and Shikellamy were the proper persons "to go between the Six Nations and this government." They said that their bodies were to be equally divided between "the Sons of Onas and the Red Men, half to the Indian and half to the white man." Weiser, said they, was faithful, honest, good, and true; that he had spoken their words for them and not his own.

The Iroquois delegation, by far the largest that ever appeared at Philadelphia at a treaty, was entertained for three nights at Stenton. The sessions of the different conferences connected with the making of this treaty lasted until the 25th of October. They were held in the great meeting house at Fifth and Arch Streets. The Iroquois deputies reported that, following the suggestion of the Provincial Council at the treaty of 1732, they had strengthened their confederation by entering into firm leagues of friendship and alliance with other nations around them, to-wit: Onichkaryagoes, Sissaghees, Troumurtihagas, Attawantenies, Twechtwese, and Oachtaumghs. All these tribes, said the deputies, had promised to acknowledge the Iroquois as their elder brother and to act in concert with them.

The Iroquois deputies made the request that the Pennsylvania traders be removed from the Ohio and Allegheny country, but the

Provincial Council politely refused this request, arguing that its Indians there could not live without being supplied with goods, and that, if the Pennsylvania traders did not supply them with goods others from Maryland and Virginia would. The Iroquois also asked that no strong drink be sold at Allegheny by the traders. This petition was evaded. James Logan, President of the Council, upon which the administration of the government devolved since the death of Governor Gordon, on August 5th, 1736, rebuked the Indians for not controlling their appetite for rum. "All of us here," said he, "and all you see of any credit in this place, can every day have as much rum of their own to drink as they please, and yet scarce one of us will take a dram, at least not one man will, on any account, be drunk, no, not if he were hired to it with great sums of money."

But the most important part of this treaty was the execution and delivery of two deeds by the Iroquois to the Proprietaries of the Province of Pennsylvania—a momentous transaction brought about by that astute Iroquois statesman, Shikellamy, assisted by Conrad Weiser.

The first was a deed to all the lands on both sides of the Susquehanna, extending as far east as the heads of the streams running into the Susquehanna, as far west "as the setting of the sun" (afterwards interpreted by the Indians to mean as far as the crest of the Allegheny Mountains), as far south as the mouth of the Susquehanna, and as far north as the Blue, Kittatinny, or Endless Mountains.

The following is the interesting history of these Susquehanna lands:

By deed dated September 10th, 1683, the Conestoga or Susquehanna chief, Kekelappan, conveyed to William Penn "that half of all my lands betwixt the Susquehanna and Delaware, which lieth on the Susquehanna side." Then, on October 18th, 1683, the Conestoga chief, Machaloha, who claimed to exercise authority over the Indians "on the Delaware River, Chesapeake Bay and up to ye falls of ye Susquehanna River," conveyed to Penn his right in his lands. Penn thought it advisable to get the consent of the Five Nations to his possession of these lands, no doubt knowing that the Five Nations had conquered the Susquehannas. Accordingly he sent agents to confer with the Iroquois chiefs in New York, and also wrote acting Governor Brockholls of New York, "about some Susquehanna land on ye back of us, where I intend a colony forthwith." About the time of his writing Governor Brockholls, Governor Thomas Dongan displaced Brockholls. Governor Dongan persuaded some of the Iroquois chiefs to give him a deed for these same lands. This he did, in order to get the matter in his own hands. Then, in the late autumn of 1683, he wrote Penn, advising him of the purchase and saying that he and Penn would not "fall out" over the matter. Thus the matter stood until January 13th, 1696, on which date Penn got a deed of lease and release from Dongan for the lands. In order to get indisputable title to these lands, Penn, on September 13th, 1700, concluded a treaty with Oretyagh and Andaggy-Junkquagh, chiefs of the Susquehannas or Conestogas, by the terms of which they ratified Dongan's deed to Penn. This sale was further confirmed in the "Articles of Agreement" of April 23d, 1701, between Penn and the Five Nations, Susquehannas, Shawnees and Conoys. However, the Iroquois contended that they had deeded the Susquehanna lands to Dongan simply in trust and did not release any control over or rights in the same. At the time of this treaty of 1736, the Colonial Authorities of Pennsylvania were impressed by Conrad Weiser with the power and influence of the Six Nations, and, accordingly, did not dispute with their deputies when they claimed indemnity for all the Susquehanna lands south and east of the Blue Mountains.

The consideration of the deed for these lands, dated October 11th, 1736, was 500 pounds of powder, 600 pounds of lead, 45 guns, 100 blankets, 200 yards of cloth, 100 shirts, 40 hats, 40 pairs of shoes and buckles, 40 pairs of stockings, 100 hatchets, 500 knives, 100 hoes, 100 tobacco tongs, 100 scissors, 500 awls, 120 combs 2000 needles, 1000 flints, 20 looking glasses, 2 pounds of vermillion, 100 tin pots, 25 gallons of rum, 200 pounds of tobacco, 1000 pipes, and 24 dozens of garters. That part of these goods which represented the consideration for the lands on the east side of the Susquehanna, was delivered, but that which represented the consideration for the lands on the west side of the river, was, at the Indians' desire, retained, and was finally delivered in 1742.

Shikellamy and twenty-two other chiefs of the Onondagas, Senecas, Oneidas, Tuscaroras and Cayugas, all the allied tribes of the great Iroquois Confederation, except the Mohawks, signed this deed, a copy of which is recorded in the Pennsylvania Archives, Vol. 1, pages 494 to 498.

The sale of the Susquehanna lands greatly offended the Shawnees. When this tribe came to Pennsylvania, they were given permission by the Iroquois to live on these lands. Therefore, when the Shawnees learned of the treaty of 1736, they sent one hundred and thirty of their leaders with a belt to the French, saying; "Our lands have been sold from under our feet; may we come and live with you?" The French readily consented, and offered to come and meet them with provisions. This information came from the Mohawks, who received no share of the articles given for the lands. Indeed, this sale of the Susquehanna lands had much to do with bringing about finally the total alienation of the Shawnees from the English cause. Conrad Weiser, the advisor of the Pennsylvania authorities, had a great love and admiration for the Iroquois, but little or no respect for the Shawnees, and it was his opinion that the Province would establish a dangerous precedent, if it were to recognize the claims of the Shawnees to these lands, inasmuch as they were only sojourners on the same.

But the sale of the Susquehanna lands involved Maryland and Virginia, which colonies had never paid the Iroquois for the lands in their dominions to which the Iroquois claimed title as the conquerors of the tribes formerly owing them. As we shall see, this matter was adjusted at the Lancaster Treaty of 1744 by the purchase of these lands by Maryland and Virginia.

On October 25th, just two weeks after the signing of the deed of the Susquehanna lands, when most of the influential deputies of the Iroquois had left Philadelphia, and after those who remained had been drinking heavily, another deed was drawn up embracing all the Six Nations' claim to lands within Pennsylvania "beginning eastward on the River Delaware, as far northward as the ridge or chain of Endless Mountains as they cross ye country of Pennsylvania, from eastward to the West." This deed established a precedent for an Iroquois claim to all the lands owned by the Delaware Indians, and was the cause, as we shall see, of greatly embittering the Delawares.

Shikellamy was one of the signers of this deed to the Delaware lands, which, in addition to conveying the lands of the Delawares, contained the solemn promise that at no time would the Six Nations sell any lands within the Province of Pennsylvania to any person or persons, Indians or white men, except to "the said Wm. Penn's Children." For copy of the deed, see Pennsylvania Archives, Vol. 1, pages 498 and 499.

It is clear that, while William Penn recognized the claim of the Six Nations to the lands of the Susquehannas or Conestogas, yet he never recognized any claim on the part of the Six Nations to the lands of the Delawares; and, prior to this treaty of 1736, it cannot be found that the Iroquois themselves ever made any claim to the lands of the Delawares, although of course, they had exercised an overlordship over them, "declaring them women and forbidding them to make war." It is very probable that, at the time of making the Iroquois deed for the Delaware lands, no one realized what the outcome of such a deed would be. It was an indirect way of denying to the Delaware Indians all title to their lands. The Iroquois had promised that in the future they would never sell any land within the limits of Pennsylvania to anyone except Penn's heirs, and, probably, the chief purpose in securing this deed was to place this promise of the Six Nations permanently in writing.

This action in purchasing the Delaware lands from the Iroquois marked a great change in the Indian policy of Pennsylvania —a change brought about by Shikellamy and Conrad Weiser. Weiser interpreted the deed to the Iroquois, and they were evidently aware that they had gained a most important point; that, henceforth, the Colony of Pennsylvania would be a sponsor for their claims on the Delaware River; and that all the ancient disputes with the Delawares in this matter were settled. Furthermore, by this action, the Colony of Pennsylvania had taken sides in the age-long quarrel between the Iroquois on the one hand and the Delawares on the other. William Penn had refused to take sides in any Indian differences, but his sons were more bent on personal profit than on public justice and public security.

From the date of this purchase, it was no longer possible for the Colony of Pennsylvania to treat the Delawares as formerly. The Six Nations had been recognized as the favorite people and the Delawares, the affectionate friends of William Penn, as underlings. The Delawares had already been offended through the long delay in purchasing from them the Tulpehocken lands, which had been settled many years before the Colony got an Indian title for the same. Now, in purchasing their lands from the Iroquois, the Colony started that long series of events with the Delawares, which resulted in the bloodiest invasion in colonial history—an invasion which drenched Pennsylvania in blood from 1755 to 1764; but at the same time, while thus bringing upon herself a Delaware and Shawnee war, she escaped a Six Nation war, which no doubt would have been much more serious in its consequences.

The two deeds gotten from the Iroquois at the Treaty of 1736 embraced the counties of York, Adams, and Cumberland, that part of Franklin, Dauphin, and Lebanon southeast of the Blue or Kittatinny Mountains, and that part of Berks, Lehigh, and Northampton not already possessed.

For a full account of the Treaty of 1736, the reader is referred to the Pennsylvania Colonial Records, Vol. 4, pages 79 to 95.

During the spring following the treaty of 1736, Conrad Weiser, at the solicitation of Governor Gooch of Virginia, was sent by the Colonial Authorities of Pennsylvania to the central seat of the Six Nations at Onondaga, New York, in an effort to arrange a peace between the Iroquois and the Catawbas, Cherokees and allied tribes of the South. On this terrible journey through the deep snows of Pennsylvania and New York, Weiser was accompanied by a neighbor, named Stoffel Stump, Shikellamy and an Onondaga Indian, named Owisgera. The Iroquois agreed to an armistice of one year. Weiser's account of his mission is found in Vol. 1 of the Collections of the Historical Society of Pennsylvania, and is one of the most interesting and valuable documents relating to the early history of the Keystone State.

"The Walking Purchase"

While the Six Nations at the treaty held at Philadelphia in October, 1736, just described, went on record in declaring that the Delaware nation had no lands to sell, yet the Colonial Authorities of Pennsylvania depended for quiet enjoyment upon the old deeds from the Delawares to William Penn and his heirs, mentioned in an earlier chapter. In 1734, Thomas Penn, son of the founder of the Colony, claimed to have found a copy of a certain deed from the Delaware chiefs, Mayhkeerickkishsho, Taughhoughsey, and Sayhoppy, to his father, dated August 30, 1686, calling for a dimension "as far as a man can go in a day and a half" and thence to the Delaware River and down the courses of the same. The original of this deed, Thomas Penn claimed, had been lost for many years. The alleged description set forth in the original deed was as follows:

"All those lands lying and being in the province of Pennsylvania, beginning upon a line formerly laid out from a corner spruce tree, by the river Delaware, and from thence running along the ledge or the foot of the mountains west northwest (west southwest) to a corner white oak marked with the letter P. standing by the Indian path that leadeth to an Indian town called Playwiskey, and from thence extending westward to Neshaminy Creek, from which said line, the said tract or tracts thereby granted doth extend itself back into the woods, as far as a man can go in one day and a half, and bounded on the westerly side with the creek called Neshaminy, or the most westerly branch thereof, and from thence by a line to the utmost extent of said creek one day and a half's journey to the aforesaid river Delaware, and thence down the several courses of the said river to the first mentioned spruce tree."

The Delaware town, Playwiskey, or Playwickey, was the residence of the great Delaware chief, Tamanend, or Tammany, and was located about two and a half miles west of the present town of Langhorne, Bucks County. A monument now marks its site.

The dimension set forth in the foregoing alleged deed was never "walked" in the lifetime of William Penn. Thomas Penn and the other Colonial Authorities were anxious that the lands described in the alleged deed should be measured without further delay. Some of the Delawares did not wish the line measured, but, on August 25, 1737, the more influential chiefs of the Munsee Clan, among whom were "King Nutimus" and Manawkyhickon, entered into a treaty with Thomas Penn by the terms of which they agreed that the land should be measured by a walk according to the provisions of the deed. This agreement of August 25th was virtually a deed of release of the lands claimed to have been granted by the deed of August 30, 1686. We shall now see how well Thomas Penn and his associates were prepared for the "walk" and how it was accomplished:

The 19th day of September, 1737, was the day appointed for the "walk." It was agreed that the starting point should be a chestnut tree standing a little above the present site of Wrightstown, Bucks County. Timothy Smith, the sheriff of Bucks County, and Benjamin Eastburn, the surveyor-general, supervised the so-called walk. The persons employed by the Colonial Authorities to perform the walk, after the Proprietaries had advertised for the most expert walkers in the Province, were athletes famous for their abilities as fast walkers; and, as an inducement for their making this walk a supreme test of their abilities, a compensation of five pounds in money and 500 acres of land was offered the one who could go the longest distance in the allotted time. Their names were Edward Marshall, a native of Bucks County, a noted chain carrier, hunter and backwoodsman; James Yates, a native of the same county, a tall and agile man, with much speed of foot;

and Solomon Jennings also a man of remarkable physique. These men had been hunted out by the Proprietaries' agents as the fastest backwoodsmen in the Province, and as a preliminary measure, they had been taken over the ground before, spending some nine days, during which their route was marked off by blazing the trees and clearing away the brush.

At sunrise on the day appointed, these three athletes, accompanied by a number of Indians and some white persons, some of whom carried refreshments for them, started from the chestnut tree above Wrightstown; and, at first, they walked moderately, but before long they set such a pace that the Indians frequently called upon them to walk and not run. The remonstrance of the Indians producing no effect, most of them left in anger and disgust, asserting that they were basely cheated. By previous arrangement, a number of white people were collected about twenty miles from the starting point, to see the "walkers" pass. Yates was much in the lead, and was accompanied by several persons on horseback; next came Jennings, but out of sight; and lastly, Marshall, proceeding in an apparently careless manner, eating a biscuit and swinging a hatchet from hand to hand, evidently to balance the motion of his body. The above mentioned body of whites bet strongly in favor of Yates. Jennings and two of the Indians who accompanied him were exhausted before the end of the first day, and were unable to keep up with the other two. Jennings never thereafter recovered his health. However, Yates and Marshall kept on, and, at sunset, had arrived at the north side of the Blue Mountains.

At sunrise of the next day, Yates and Marshall started again, but, when crossing a stream at the foot of the mountain, Yates fell into the water, and Marshall turned back and supported him until some of the attendants came up, and then continued on his way alone. Yates was stricken with blindness and lived only three days. At noon Marshall threw himself full length upon the ground and grasped a sapling which stood on a spur of the Second or Broad Mountain, near Mauch Chunk, Carbon County, which was then declared to mark the distance that a man could travel on foot in a day and a half—estimated to be about sixty-five miles from the starting point. Thus, one man out of three covered this distance, and lived.

In the agreement with Thomas Penn to have the bounds of the alleged deed made by a walk, the Delawares believed that as far as a man could go in a day and a half would not extend beyond the Lehigh Hills, or about thirty miles from the place of beginning; but the crafty and unprincipled Colonial Authorities had laid their plans to extend the walk to such a point as to include the land in the Forks of the Delaware and also farther up that river, it being their desire to obtain, if possible, the possession of that desirable tract of land along the Delaware River above the Blue Mountains, called the "Minisink Lands." Having, as we have seen, reached a point more than thirty miles farther to the northwestward than the Delawares had anticipated, the Colonial Authorities now proceeded to draw a line from the end of the walk to the Delaware River. The alleged deed did not describe the course that the line should take from the end of the walk to the river; but any fair-minded person would assume that it should follow the shortest distance between these two places. However, the agent of the Proprietaries, instead of running the line by the nearest course to the Delaware, ran it northeastward across the country so as to strike the river near the mouth of the Lackawaxen, which flows into the Delaware River in the northern part of Pike County. The extent of this line was sixty-six miles. The territory as thus measured was in the shape of a great triangle whose base was the Delaware River and whose apex was the end of the walk, and included the northern part of Bucks, almost all of Northampton, and a portion of Pike, Carbon, and Monroe Counties. This fraudulent measurement thus took in all the Minisink Lands and many thousand acres more than if the line had been run by the nearest course from the end of the walk to the Delaware.

Delawares Driven from Lands of "Walking Purchase"

When the settlers began to move upon the lands covered by the Walking Purchase of 1737, which they did soon after the "walk" was made, King Nutimus and several of the other Delaware chiefs who had signed the treaty or deed of release of 1737, were not willing to quit the lands or to permit the new settlers to remain in quiet possession. Indeed, they remonstrated freely and declared their intention to remain in possession, even if they should have to use force of arms.

In the spring of 1741, a message was sent by the Colonial Authorities to the Six Nations, requesting them to come down and force the Delawares of the Munsee Clan to quit these lands. The Six Nations complied and sent their deputies to Philadelphia, where this and other matters were taken up in the treaty of July, 1742, to be described presently. At this treaty, Governor Thomas called the attention of Canassatego, the speaker of the Iroquois delegation, to the fact that a number of the Delaware Indians, residing on the Minisink lands above the mouth of the Lehigh River, had refused to surrender peaceful possession of the territory secured to the Colony by the Walking Purchase. However, the Governor did not tell Canassatego that, when John and Thomas Penn were persuading the Delawares to confirm the deeds covered by the Walking Purchase, they had promised these Indians that the said papers "would not cause the removal of any Indians then living on the Minisink Lands." These Delawares had requested that they be permitted to remain on their settlements, though within the bounds of the Walking Purchase, without being molested, and their request was granted. Later, on August 24, 1737, just the day before the Delaware chiefs signed the deed, or treaty, confirming the alleged deed of August 30, 1786, the assurances given the Delawares by John and Thomas Penn were repeated and confirmed at a meeting of the Provincial Council at Philadelphia.

Canassatego, unaware of the assurances given the Delawares, replied as follows:

"You informed us of the misbehavior of our cousins, the Delawares, with respect to their continuing to claim and refusing to remove from some land on the River Delaware, notwithstanding their ancestors had sold it by deed under their hands and seals to the Proprietors for a valuable consideration, upwards of fifty years ago, and notwithstanding that they themselves had about five years ago, after a long and full examination, ratified that deed of their ancestors, and given a fresh one under their hands and seals; and then you requested us to remove them, enforcing your request with a string of wampum. Afterwards you laid on the table, by Conrad Weiser, our own letters, some of our cousins' letters, and the several writings to prove the charge against our cousins, with a draught of the land in dispute. We now tell you that we have perused all these several papers. We see with our own eyes that they [the Delawares] have been a very unruly people, and are altogether in the wrong in their dealings with you. We have concluded to remove them, and oblige them to go over the River Delaware, and to quit all claim to any lands on this side for the future, since they have received pay for them, and it has gone through their guts long ago. To confirm to you that we will see your request executed, we lay down this string of wampum in return for yours."

Attending the treaty were some Delawares from the Sunbury region, headed by Sassoonan, and a delegation from the Forks of the Delaware, headed by Nutimus. As soon as Canassatego finished the foregoing speech, taking a belt of wampum in his hand, he turned to the Delawares, and delivered the following humiliating address:

"COUSINS:—Let this belt of wampum serve to chastise you; you ought to be taken by the hair of the head and shaked severely till you recover your senses and become sober; you don't know what ground you are standing on, or what you are doing. Our Brother Onas' case is very just and plain, and his intentions to preserve friendship; on the other hand your cause is bad; your head far from being upright, you are maliciously bent to break the chain of friendship with our Brother Onas. We have seen with our eyes a deed signed by nine of your ancestors above fifty years ago for this very land, and a release signed not many years since by some of yourselves and chiefs now living to the number of fifteen or upwards.

"But how came you to take upon you to sell land at all? We conquered you; we made women of you; you know you are women and can no more sell land than women. Nor is it fit that you should have the power of selling land, since you would abuse it. This land that you claim is gone through your guts. You have been furnished with clothes and meat and drink by the goods paid you for it, and now you want it again like children, as you are. But what makes you sell land in the dark? Did you ever tell us that you had sold this land? Did we ever receive any part, even the value of a pipe shank for it?

"You have told us a blind story that you sent a messenger to inform us of the sale, but he never came amongst us, nor we never heard anything about it. This is acting in the dark, and very different from the conduct which our Six Nations observe in their sales of land. On such occasions, they give public notice and invite all the Indians of their united nations, but we find that you are none of our blood. You act a dishonest part, not only in this, but in other matters. Your ears are ever open to slanderous reports about our brethren . . . And for all these reasons we charge you to remove instantly; we don't give you liberty to think about it. You are women; take the advice of a wise man, and remove immediately. You may return to the other side of the Delaware, where you came from, but we don't know whether, considering how you have demeaned yourselves, you will be permitted to live there, or whether you have not swallowed that land down your throats, as well as the land on this side. We, therefore, assign you two places to go,—either to Wyoming or Shamokin. You may go to either of these places, and then we shall have you more under our eye, and shall see how you behave. Don't deliberate, but remove away, and take this belt of wampum."

Canassatego spoke with the air of a conqueror and one having authority; and both the manner of the delivery of his speech and the manner in which it was received by the trembling Delawares, would indicate that the Six Nations must have been right in their contention that they gained the ascendency over the Delawares, not by artifice, as the Delawares told Heckewelder, but by force of arms, some authorities asserting that, when the Iroquois conquered the Susquehannas in 1675, this conquest carried with it the subjugation of the Delawares, inasmuch as the Susquehannas were overlords of the Delawares. "When this terrible sentence was ended," says Watson, "it is said that the unfeeling political philosopher [Canassatego] walked forward, and, taking strong hold of the long hair of King Nutimus, of the Delawares, led him to the door and forcibly sent him out of the room, and stood there while all the trembling inferiors followed him. He then walked back to his place like another Cato, and calmly proceeded to another subject as if nothing happened. The poor fellows [Nutimus and his company], in great and silent grief, went directly home, collected their families and goods, and, burning their cabins to signify they were never to return, marched reluctantly to their new homes."

Shortly after the treaty of 1742, the Delawares of the Munsee Clan left the bounds of the "Walking Purchase" and the beautiful river bearing their name, and began their march toward the setting sun. The greater part of them, under Nutimus settled on the site of Wilkes-Barre, opposite Wyoming Town, and at "Niskebeckon," on the left bank of the North Branch of the Susquehanna, not far from the mouth of Nescopeck Creek, in Luzerne County. The town which they established near the mouth of Nescopeck Creek was called "Nutimy's Town." Others went to the region around Sunbury; and others took up their abode on the Juniata, near Lewistown, Mifflin County. Later all went to the valleys of the Ohio and Allegheny with their wrongs rankling in their bosoms. Furthermore, these Delawares of the Munsee or Wolf Clan went to the valleys of the Allegheny and Ohio at a critical time,—when the French were coming into the same valleys, asserting their claim to the region drained by these beautiful rivers, a claim based on the explorations of La Salle and the heroic Jesuit Missionaries, those true Knights of the Cross, to whom any one who correctly writes the early history of the region between the Mississippi River and the Allegheny Mountains must needs pay a high tribute of esteem. The French sympathized with the wronged Delawares. It is no wonder, then, that the Delawares joined the French in the French and Indian War, and brought upon defenseless Pennsylvania the bloodiest Indian invasion in American history.

The term "Walking Purchase" is a term of derision. This fraudulent purchase has been called "the disgrace of the Colonies." It was the subject of much discussion between the Quaker and Proprietary parties as being one of the chief causes of the alienation of the Delawares and of their taking up arms against the Colony during the French and Indian War, until the charge of "fraud" was withdrawn and the Delawares were reconciled through the influence of the Moravian missionary, Christian Frederick Post, at the treaty at Easton, in the summer of 1758. Says Dr. George P. Donehoo, in his recent great work, "Pennsylvania—A History": "It matters little whether the Delaware were influenced by the Quakers to complain of the 'fraud,' or whether they themselves felt that they had been cheated, the fact still remains that the 'Walking Purchase' directly and indirectly, led to the gravest of consequences, so far as the warlike Munsee Clan of the Delaware was concerned."

In connection with the removal of the Delawares from the bounds of the Walking Purchase, is the case of Captain John and Tatemy, two worthy Delaware chiefs who had always been warm friends of the white man. In November, 1742, they petitioned Governor Thomas, setting forth that they had embraced Christianity, and desired to live where they were, near the English. The Governor sent for them, and they appeared before the Provincial Council. Captain John did not own any ground, but advised the Governor, if permitted to live among the English, he would buy some. Tatemy owned three hundred acres of land, granted him by the Proprietaries; and he said he simply wanted to spend the remaining years of his life on his own plantation in peace with all men. The Governor ordered that Canassatego's speech be read to these poor Indians, refused their petition, and told them they would have to secure the consent of the Six Nations, the conquerors of the Delawares. Evidently the Six Nations made no objections, as Tatemy continued to live on his tract near Stockertown, Northampton County, until his death, which took place about 1761. His house was one of the landmarks of the region. Here he was visited by Count Zinzendorf, in 1742. He attended many important councils with the Colonial Authorities. As we shall see later in this volume, his son, William, was mortally wounded while on his way to attend the Easton conference of July and August, 1757.

The Shawnee Treaty of 1739

The Colonial Authorities of Pennsylvania, realizing that the Shawnees were rapidly being won over by the French, induced Kakowatcheky, of Wyoming, Kishacoquillas of the Juniata, and Neucheconneh and Tamenebuck, of the Allegheny, and other Shawnee chiefs, whose settlements were scattered from Wyoming and Great Island (Lock Haven) to the Allegheny, to come to a conference, or treaty, at Philadelphia on July 27th to August 1st, 1739. At this conference the Conestoga and Shawnee agreement with William Penn, dated April 23rd, 1701, was brought to the attention of the chiefs; and they were told that the Colonial Authorities thought it proper to remind them of this solemn engagement which their ancestors had entered into with Penn, inasmuch as the said Authorities knew that the emissaries of the French were endeavoring to prevail upon the Shawnees to renounce their agreement with the Colony. In other words, the Governor and Provincial Council put the plain question of the Shawnees' loyalty to past agreements with Pennsylvania. The chiefs desired that their reply be postponed until the following day, explaining that "it was their custom to speak or transact business of importance only whilst the sun was rising, and not when it was declining." In the morning, they showed that all past agreements had been kept by them quite as faithfully as by the white men. And since Pennsylvania had, about a year previously, promised to issue an order forbidding the sale of any more rum among them, they had sent one of their young men to the French, as an agent to induce them 'for all time, to put a stop to the sale of rum, brandy, and wine.' " The result of the conference was that the Shawnees, with the full understanding that the rum traffic was to be stopped, promised not to join any other nation, and confirmed the old Conestoga and Shawnee agreement or treaty of April 23rd, 1701. (Pa. Col. Rec., Vol. 4, pages 336 to 347.)

The Treaty of 1742

Reference has been made to the Treaty of 1742 in connection with Canassatego's ordering the Delawares of the Munsee Clan from the bounds of the Walking Purchase. For a full account of this treaty, see the Pennsylvania Colonial Records, Vol. 4, pages 559 to 586.

This treaty of July, 1742, was called for the purpose of paying the Iroquois for that part of the land purchased from them by Pennsylvania at the treaty of 1736 which lay west of the Susquehanna River. Shikellamy and the other deputies of the Six Nations were expected to arrive in Philadelphia in May, 1742, but it was not until June 30th that the deputies, representing all tribes of the Confederation, except the Senecas and the Mohawks, arrived at Philadelphia, empowered to receive the pay for the lands west of the Susquehanna. The Senecas were not present at this treaty, because of a great famine among them; nor were the Mohawks, because they were not considered to have any claims upon the Susquehanna lands. The sessions of the treaty began on July 2nd. The three remaining nations of the Iroquois confederacy, early in the conference, received the goods in payment of that part of the Susquehanna lands lying west of the Susquehanna River, comprising the counties of York, Cumberland, Adams, and most of Franklin.

Soon after the goods in payment of the Susquehanna lands were divided, the Iroquois deputies expressed their dissatisfaction with the amount, although admitting that it was as agreed upon. They said they felt sure that, if the sons of William Penn, who were then in England, were present, they would agree to giving a large amount out of pity for the Indians on account of their poverty and wretchedness. Through their chief speaker, Canassatego an Onondago chieftain, they begged Governor Thomas, inasmuch as he had the keys to the Proprietors' chest, to open the same and take out a little more for them. Governor Thomas replied that the Proprietors had gone to England and taken the keys with them; whereupon, the Indians, as an additional reason for their request, called attention to the increasing value of the lands sold, and also to the fact that the whites were daily settling on Indian lands that had not been sold. They called attention to the fact that, at the last treaty with the Colony, the Iroquois had complained about the whites settling on unsold lands, and that the Governor, at that time, agreed to remedy this wrong.

Said Canassatego: "Land is everlasting, and the few things we receive for it are soon worn out and gone; for the future, we will sell no lands but when Brother Onas [meaning the sons of William Penn] is in the country, and we will know beforehand the quality of goods we are to receive. Besides, we are not well used with respect to the lands still unsold by us. Your people daily settle on these lands and spoil our hunting. We must insist on your removing them, as you know they have no right to the northward of the Kittochtinny Hills [Kittatinny, or Blue Mountains]. In particular, we renew our complaints against some people who are settled at Juniata, a branch of the Susquehanna, and all along the banks of that river as far as Mahaniay, and desire that they be forwith made to go off the land, for they do great damage to our cousins, the Delawares."

Canassatego further called attention to the fact that Maryland and Virginia had not paid the Iroquois for lands within their bounds upon which the whites were settling, and that, at the treaty of 1736, the Governor of Pennsylvania had promised to use his influence with Maryland and Virginia in their behalf in regard to this matter. "This affair," said Canassatego, "was recommended to you by our chiefs at our last treaty and you then, at our earnest desire, promised to write a letter to that person who has authority over those people, and to procure us an answer. As we have never heard from you on this head, we want to know what you have done in it. If you have not done anything, we now renew our request, and desire you will inform the person whose people are seated on our lands that that country [western Maryland and Virginia] belongs to us by right of conquest, we having bought it with our blood, and taken it from our enemies in fair war." Canassatego threatened that, if Maryland and Virginia did not pay for these lands, the Iroquois would enforce payment in their own way.

Governor Thomas replied that he had ordered the magistrates of Lancaster County to drive off the squatters from the Juniata lands, and was not aware that any had stayed. The Indians interrupted, and said that the persons who had been sent to remove the squatters, did not do their duty; that, instead of removing them from the Juniata lands, they were in league with the squatters, and had made large surveys for themselves. The earnest arguments of Canassatego had the desired effect. The Provincial Council decided to add to the value of the goods a present of three hundred pounds.

The Governor advised Canassatego that, shortly after the treaty of 1736, James Logan, President of the Council, had written the Governor of Maryland about the lands, but received no reply. Now the Governor promised to intercede with Maryland and Virginia, and, if possible, to secure payment for the lands of the Iroquois upon which the whites of those colonies were settling. He also renewed his promise to remove the squatters from the Juniata Valley.

The squatters in the Juniata Valley were Germans. True to his promise to Canassatego, Governor Thomas had these persons removed the following year. But the squatters in the Big Cove, Little Cove, Big Connoloways, Little Connoloways, and the majority of those in Path Valley and Sherman's Valley were Scotch-Irish. These dwellers on lands not yet purchased from the Indians were not removed until May 1750, when Lieutenant-Governor Morris, after the organization of Cumberland County, in that year, sent Richard Peters, George Croghan, Conrad Weiser, James Galbraith and others with the under-sheriff of Cumberland County, to remove all persons who had settled north of the Blue or Kittatinny Mountains. Some of the cabins of these intruders were burned after the families had moved out, so as to prevent settlements in the future. It is thus that Burnt Cabins, in the north eastern part of Fulton County, got its name. Among the settlers removed on this occasion was Simon Girty, the elder, father of Simon, Jr., Thomas, George and James Girty. A sketch of the Girtys will appear later in this volume. In 1752, Governor Hamilton directed Andrew Montour to take up his residence in what is now Perry County for the purpose of preventing settlements being made on lands not purchased from the Indians.

The Lancaster Treaty of 1744

Hardly had the Iroquois deputies returned home from the treaty of 1742 when fresh troubles started between the Confederation of the Six Nations and the Catawbas and Cherokees of the South. These troubles involved Virginia, as some Iroquois were killed by Virginia settlers while on their way to attack the Catawbas. Learning of these matters, the Provincial Council of Pennsylvania sent Conrad Weiser to Shamokin to interview

Shikellamy. Weiser held conferences with this great Iroquois vice-gerent on February 4th and April 9th, 1743. About this time, Governor Gooch of Virginia sent word to Governor Thomas of Pennsylvania that Virginia would accept the latter's mediation with the Six Nations. The Pennsylvania Authorities then sent Weiser and Shikellamy to Onondaga to arrange for a time and place of holding a treaty or conference between the Six Nations and Virginia. The Great Council at Onondaga accepted the offer of Governor Thomas of Pennsylvania and Governor Gooch of Virginia for a conference or treaty at Harris Ferry (Harrisburg) the next spring. Later, on account of the inconvenience of meeting at Harrisburg, it was decided to hold the treaty at Lancaster, a small town then sixteen years old.

At Onondaga, the Iroquois chief, Zillawallie, gave the cause of the war between the Six Nations and the Catawbas. Addressing Weiser, he said; "We are engaged in a great war with the Catawbas, which will last to the end of the world; for they molest us, and speak contemptuously of us, which our warriors will not bear, and they will soon go to war against them again. It will be in vain for us to dissaude them from it."

On this mission to Onondaga, Conrad Weiser prevented a war between Virginia and the Six Nations—a war which would eventually have involved the other colonies.

Before describing the Lancaster Treaty, we call attention to the fact that, scarcely had the treaty of 1742 been concluded, when the Colonial Authorities of Pennsylvania were asked by the Governor of Maryland for advice and assistance in that Colony's trouble with the Six Nations. It appeared that, in the early part of the summer of 1742, some Nanticokes in Maryland were imprisoned, and that their friends, the Shawnees and Senecas, threatened to make trouble unless they were released. Governor Thomas of Pennsylvania engaged Conrad Weiser to accompany the Maryland messenger to the region of the Six Nations, as interpreter, for the purpose of inviting the Six Nations to a treaty to be held at Harris' Ferry (Harrisburg) in the spring of 1743. It does not appear that the Iroquois did any more than simply deliberate on this matter; but Maryland's advances at least had the virtue of opening negotiations at the Great Council of the Six Nations on the part of that Colony.

On Friday, June 22nd, 1744, the long expected delegation of the Six Nations arrived at Lancaster for the purpose of entering into a treaty with Pennsylvania, Maryland, and Virginia. The delegation consisted of two hundred and forty-two, and was headed by Canassatego. There were many squaws and children mounted on horseback. Arriving in front of the Court House, the leaders of the delegation saluted the commissioners from Pennsylvania, Maryland, and Virginia, with a song. This was an invitation to the whites to renew former treaties and to make good the one now proposed.

When the Maryland commissioners came to the Lancaster treaty, they had no intention whatever of recognizing any Iroquois claims to lands within the bounds of their province, basing their position upon the following facts: (1) Maryland had bought from the Minquas, or Susquehannas, in 1652, all their claims on both sides of the Chesapeake Bay as far north as the mouth of the Susquehanna River. (2) The Minquas, aided by troops from Maryland, had, in 1663, defeated eight hundred Senecas and Cayugas of the Iroquois Confederation.

But the Iroquois never abandoned their war on the Minquas until they overwhelmingly defeated this tribe in 1675, when they were reduced by famine and Maryland had withdrawn her alliance. Now, in view of their conquest of the Minquas, the Six Nations claimed a right to the Susquehanna lands to the head of Chesapeake Bay.

The Maryland commissioners receded from their position. The release for the Maryland lands was signed, on Monday, July 2nd, at George Sanderson's Inn, instead of at the Court House. Conrad Weiser signed in behalf of the absent member of the Iroquois Confederation, (Mohawk), both with his Indian name of Tarach-a-wa-gon, and that of Weiser. By his dexterous management, the lands released were so described as not to give Maryland a title to lands claimed by Pennsylvania, the boundary dispute between Maryland and Pennsylvania being at the time still pending. The release was for all "lands lying two miles above the uppermost forks of Patowmack or Cohongoruton River, near which Thomas Cresap has his hunting or trading cabin, [at Old Town fourteen miles east of Cumberland, Maryland,] by a line north to the bounds of Pennsylvania. But, in case such limits shall not include every settlement or inhabitant of Maryland, then such other lines and courses from the said two miles above the forks to the outermost inhabitants or settlements, as shall include every settlement and inhabitant in Maryland, and from thence by a north line to the bounds of Pennsylvania, shall be the limits. And, further, if any people already have or shall settle beyond the lands now described and bounded, they shall enjoy the same free from any disturbance of us in any manner whatsoever, and we do and shall accept these people for our Brethren, and as such will always treat them." Thus was the purchase happily affected.

However, Shikellamy refused to sign the deed of the Maryland lands, being determined not to recognize that Maryland had any land claims north of the disputed boundary line between herself and Pennsylvania.

The Virginia commissioners had their negotiations with the Iroquois deputies in progress at the same time as Maryland. They found the Iroquois very determined not to yield any part of their claim to the Virginia lands. Said Tachanoontia, an Onondaga chieftain: "We have the right of conquest—a right too dearly purchased, and which cost us too much blood to give up without any reason at all." Finally, after much oratory, the Six Nations released all their land claims in Virginia for a consideration of two hundred pounds in goods and two hundred pounds in gold, with a written promise to be given additional remuneration as the settlements increased to the westward; and the Virginia commissioners guaranteed the Indians an open road to the Catawba country, promising that the people of Virginia would do their part if the Iroquois would perform theirs. The Iroquois understood this to mean that the Virginians would feed their war parties, if they (the Iroquois) would not shoot the farmers' cattle, chickens, etc., when passing to and from the Catawba country.

"When the treaty was over, the Indians believed that they had established land claims in Virginia, that the open road was guaranteed, that their warriors were to be fed while passing through the state, and that they had sold land only to the head-waters of the streams feeding the Ohio River. The Virginians, on the other hand, believed that they had extinguished all Iroquois land claims forever within the charter limits of their colony." The western bounds of the Virginia purchase were set forth as "the setting sun," leading Virginia to believe that the purchase included the Ohio Valley, but the Iroquois afterwards explained that by "the setting sun" was meant the crest of the Allegheny Mountains. It was after the treaty that large tracts of land were granted the Ohio Company; and it was not until the year 1768 that the Six Nations, by the treaty of Fort Stanwix, New York, relinquished all their rights to the region on the east and south side of the Ohio, from the Cherokee River, in Tennessee, to Kittanning, Pennsylvania.

Pennsylvania, the Peacemaker

In the Lancaster Treaty, Pennsylvania was the mediator and peacemaker, inducing Maryland and Virginia to lay aside their opposition to Iroquois land claims, and settle in such a manner as to secure the friendship of the Six Nations. Thus the French were thwarted, and the English frontier from New England to the Carolinas was protected. Pennsylvania also confirmed her former treaties with the Iroquois.

But while Pennsylvania was acting as peacemaker, she had trouble of her own to adjust with the Iroquois deputies. On April 9th, 1744, John (Jack) Armstrong, a trader on his way to the Allegheny, and his two servants, James Smith and Woodward Arnold, were murdered at Jacks Narrows (named for "Jack" Armstrong), on the Juniata, in Huntingdon County, by a Delaware Indian named Musemeelin. It appeared that Musemeelin owed Armstrong some skins, and Armstrong seized a horse and rifle belonging to the Indian in lieu of the skins. Later Musemeelin met Armstrong near the Juniata and paid him all his indebtedness except twenty shillings, and demanded his horse, but Armstrong refused to give the animal up until the entire debt was paid. Shortly after this, Armstrong and his servants passed the cabin of Musemeelin on their way to the Allegheny, and Musemeelin's wife demanded the horse, but by this time Armstrong had sold it to James Berry. Musemeelin was away on a hunting trip at the time his wife made the demand on Armstrong, and, when he returned, she told him about it. This angered him and he determined on revenge. Taking two young Indians with him, Musemeelin went to the camp of Armstrong, shot Smith who was there alone and Arnold whom they found returning to camp, and, meeting Armstrong, who was sitting on an old log, he demanded his horse. Armstrong replied: "He will come by and by." "I want him now," said Musemeelin. "You shall have him. Come to the fire and let us smoke and talk together," said Armstrong. As they proceeded, Musemeelin shot and tomahawked him.

The matter was placed by Governor Thomas in the hands of Shikellamy at Shamokin, who caused the murderers to be apprehended, and, after a hearing, ordered two of them to be sent to the Lancaster jail to await trial. Conrad Weiser was the bearer of the Governor's message to Shikellamy and Sassoonan. While

Shikellamy's sons were conveying the prisoners to Lancaster, the friends of Musemeelin, who was related to some important Delaware chiefs, induced Shikellamy's sons to allow Musemeelin to escape. The other Indian was locked in jail.

At the Lancaster treaty, Governor Thomas demanded of the Iroquois that they command their subjects, the Delawares, to surrender Musemeelin to the Provincial Authorities, and the Indians were invited to Lancaster to witness the trial. The Iroquois deputies replied that the Provincial Authorities should not be too much concerned; that three Indians had been killed at different times on the Ohio by the whites, and the Iroquois had never mentioned anything concerning them to the Colony. However, they stated that they had severely reproved the Delawares, and would see that the goods which the murderers had stolen from Armstrong be restored to his relatives, and Musemeelin be returned for trial, but not as a prisoner. Later on August 21st, 1744, Shikellamy brought the two prisoners to the Provincial Authorities at Philadelphia. Musemeelin was not convicted. He returned to his wigwam.

No Delawares, the friends of William Penn, were present at the Lancaster Treaty, the Iroquois having forbidden them to attend.

It is difficult to overstate the importance of the Lancaster Treaty—in many respects the most important Indian Council ever held in Pennsylvania up to this time. War between England and France, King George's War, was then raging. At the opening of this conflict, the question uppermost in the minds, not only of the Governors of Pennsylvania, Maryland, and Virginia, but of all the colonies, was, "What will be the attitude of the powerful Six Nations?" The successful settling of the disputed land claims of the Iroquois in Maryland and Virginia, by this treaty, through the mediation of Pennsylvania, with Weiser as mentor, had much to do with making possible the success of Weiser's future negotiations with the Onondaga Council, negotiations that resulted in the neutrality of the Iroquois during King George's War. Had not the Iroquois deputies, at the Treaty of Lancaster, promised to inform the Governor of Pennsylvania as to the movements of the French? Had this great Confederation sided with the French, the English colonies would have been swept into the sea.

A full account of the Lancaster Treaty of 1744 is found in the Pennsylvania Colonial Records, Vol. 4, pages 698 to 737.

Peter Chartier Deserts to the French

Peter Chartier was the only son of Martin Chartier, who accompanied the Shawnees, under Opessah, to Pequea, Lancaster County, in 1697 or 1698, and his mother was a Shawnee squaw. The father was a Frenchman, who had lived among this band of Shawnees for many years prior to their entering Pennsylvania, and accompanied them in their wanderings. He set up a trading house at Pequea a few years after the Shawnees took up their abode there. At least, he traded at Pequea as early as 1707. Some years later, he removed his trading post to Dekanoagah, which we have seen was located on or near the present site of Washington Borough, Lancaster County. Here he died in 1718.

Peter Chartier is said to have followed his father's example by marrying a Shawnee squaw. In 1718, he secured a warrant for three hundred acres of land "where his father is settled, on Susquehanna river." For some years he traded with the Shawnees who had left Pequea and settled near the site of Washington Borough and at Paxtang. Later he traded with those members of this tribe who had settled on the west side of the Susquehanna, at the mouth of Shawnee (now Yellow Breeches) Creek, on the site of the present town of New Cumberland, Cumberland County. We have already seen how he, in 1728, aided in the escape of the Shawnees who had murdered the two Conestogas. Still later, he is said to have removed to the valley of the Conococheague. About 1730, he commenced trading with the Shawnees on the Conemaugh, and Kiskiminetas, and a little later, on the Allegheny.

Chartier's principal seat on the Allegheny was Chartier's, Town, sometimes called Chartier's Old Town and Neucheconneh's Town, located near the site of Tarentum, Allegheny County. No doubt he and the Shawnee chief, Neucheconneh founded Chartier's Town, about 1734. Chartier carried on a large trade with the Shawnees, and was the trusted interpreter in many councils between the Shawnees and the Colonial Authorities. However, he yielded to French influence, and, in the summer of 1745, with about four hundred Shawnees, deserted to the French. He and his followers went from his seat on the Allegheny, thence down the Allegheny and Ohio, robbing English traders as they descended the rivers. At Logstown, they made an unsuccessful attempt to have the aged Shawnee chief, Kakowatcheky, join them. They proceeded on down the Ohio to the mouth of the Scioto, at which place another Shawnee settlement had been made possibly a decade before, and known for many years afterwards as the Lower Shawnee Town. From the Lower Shawnee Town, Chartier and his Shawnees proceeded southward along the Catawba Trail, and established a town about twelve miles east of the site of the present town of Winchester, Kentucky. Their object was to be nearer the French settlements on the Mississippi.

Some time after Chartier's desertion, many of his followers returned, among these being Neucheconneh and his band. In 1747, the Council of the Six Nations placed the Oneida chief, Scarouady, in charge of Shawnee affairs, with his central seat at Logstown. Shortly thereafter, Neucheconneh, with Kakowatcheky, applied submissively to Scarouady to intercede for the returned Shawnees with the Colonial Authorities. Then, at a meeting on July 21st, 1748, at Lancaster, with the commissioners appointed by the Colony to hold a conference with the Six Nations, Twightwees and other Indians, the apology of the former deserters was received. At this meeting, the Shawnee chief, Tamenebuck, the famous Cornstalk of later years, eloquently pled that the misled Shawnees be forgiven. Said he: "We produce to you a certificate of the renewal of our friendship in the year 1739, by the Proprietor and Governor. Be pleased to sign it afresh, that it may appear to the world we are now admitted into your friendship, and all former crimes are buried and entirely forgotten."

The request of Tamenebuck was rejected. The commissioners refused to sign the certificate, and the Shawnees were told that it was enough for them to know that they were forgiven on condition of future good behavior, and that when that condition was performed, it would be time enough for them to apply for such testimonials. It is not known whether Weiser advised this course or not, but it is certain that he could have prevented it, and induced the Colonial Authorities to make a valuable peace with the Shawnees now when they were so submissive and humble. Other tribes received presents at this Lancaster conference, but the Shawnees only had their guns mended. They went away in disgrace, brooding over such treatment. Arriving at their forest homes in the valleys of the Ohio and Allegheny, they were met by the sympathizing French, and, in a few short years, became allies of the French, in the French and Indian War, and spread terror, devastation and death throughout the Pennsylvania settlements. (Pa. Col. Rec., Vol. 4, page 757; Vol. 5, pages 311 to 315.)

Efforts to make Peace Between the Iroquois and the Southern Indians

As early as 1744, many Shawnees of the upper part of the Ohio began to move down this stream to the mouth of the Scioto, and it was believed that the Catawbas were the instigators of this action. Fearing that, not only the Catawbas, but the whole Muskokee Confederation would join the French, Virginia and Carolina renewed their efforts to bring about a peace between the Catawbas and Iroquois; and Governor Gooch of Virginia wrote Governor Thomas of Pennsylvania in November of that year advising that the Catawbas were willing to make peace and requesting that Conrad Weiser get in touch with the Six Nations in the matter.

Accordingly Weiser was sent once more to Onondaga on a peace mission. On May 19th, 1745, in company with Shikellamy, Shikellamy's son, Andrew Montour (son of Madam Montour), Bishop Spangenberg of the Moravian Church and two other Moravian missionaries, this veteran Indian Agent of the Colony of Pennsylvania set out from Shamokin for Onondaga, at which place he arrived on the 6th day of June. Weiser urged the Onondaga Council to enter into peace negotiations with the Catawbas for the sake of the Governors of Virginia and Pennsylvania, if for no other reason. The Black Prince of the Onondagas, the speaker of the Iroquois, replied that the Great Council would be willing to send deputies to Philadelphia to meet the deputies of the Catawbas, but that they could not be sent until the summer of 1746.

At this point we call attention to the fact that, at the Albany Treaty, held in October, 1745, between the Six Nations and New York, Connecticut, Massachusetts and Pennsylvania, in an unsuccessful attempt to persuade the Iroquois to take up arms against the French in King George's War, the matter of the Catawba war again came up, but was not pressed. On that occasion, Canassatego explained to Thomas Laurence, John Kinsey, and Isaac Norris, the Commissioners from Pennsylvania, that the chiefs of the Six Nations were not able to restrain their young warriors from making raids into the Catawba country until peace was declared. The Great Council of the Six Nations had all it could do, at that time, to preserve neutrality in the struggle between the French and English, known as King George's War. In fact the Iroquois and Catawba War went on intermittently until 1769.

Shikellamy and Weiser found the Great Council at Onondaga very much incensed at the conduct of Peter Chartier, in deserting to the French and leading a band of Shawnees down the Ohio. They asked why Pennsylvania did not declare war against him at once.

The reason why Bishop Spangenberg and the other Moravian missionaries accompanied Shikellamy and Weiser on this journey, was that the Moravians at that time had a project on foot to transfer their mission at Shekomeko, New York, to the Wyoming Valley, on the North Branch of the Susquehanna, in Pennsylvania; and this necessitated negotiations with the Great Council at Onondaga to whose dependencies Wyoming belonged. Count Zinzindorf had held a conference with the great Iroquois chieftain, Canassatego, at Weiser's home near Womelsdorf, in August, 1742, when the Iroquois deputies were returning from the treaty of 1742, at which conference the Moravians were given permission by the Iroquois to establish their missions in Pennsylvania. Now the Onondaga Council replied to the request of Bishop Spangenberg that they were glad to renew their contract with Count Zinzindorf and the Moravians, and they gave their consent to the proposed Moravian settlement at Wyoming.

The Moravians founded the town of Bethlehem in December, 1741, which has ever since been the central seat of the Moravian Church in America. Later, they established a mission at Friedensheutten, near Bethlehem, another called Friedensheutten, (Tents of peace), the Indian town of Wyalusing, Bradford County, another at Gnadenhuetten (Tents of grace), near Weissport, in Carbon County, another at Shamokin, the great Indian capital, and another at Wyoming, Luzerne County. They also established missions in the western part of the state. These were at and in the vicinity of the Munsee Delaware town of Goschgoschunk, near Tionesta, Forest County, and Friedensstadt (City of peace) on the Beaver, in Lawrence County. In 1772, the Moravian missionaries, John Etwein and John Roth, conducted the congregation from Wyalusing to Friedensstadt on the Beaver. The efforts of the Moravian Church to convert the Delawares and other Indians of Pennsylvania to the Christian faith is one of the most delightful chapters in the history of the Commonwealth.

The First Embassy to the Indians of the Ohio

Soon after the first Delawares and Shawnees of Eastern Pennsylvania went to the valleys of the Allegheny and Ohio, Pennsylvania traders followed them to their new forest homes. The first mention of both these traders and the region of the Ohio and Allegheny, in the Pennsylvania Colonial Records, is in the minutes of a conference held at Philadelphia, July 3rd to 5th, 1727, reported in the Pennsylvania Colonial Records, Vol. 3, pages 271 to 276, between the Provincial Council and a number of chiefs of the Six Nations, in which the chiefs requested that "none of the traders be allowed to carry any rum to the remoter parts where James Le Torte trades, that is Allegheny on the Branches of Ohio." Even at this early day, French agents and traders also were among the Delawares and Shawnees of the Allegheny and Ohio; for, in the minutes of this same conference, we find a reference to a "fort" (no doubt a trading house), which the French had erected in the Allegheny Valley. Throughout the passing years, the Pennsylvania trader and the Frenchman sought to gain first place in the hearts of the Indians of these valleys. After the Lancaster Treaty of 1744, the Indian trade of Pennsylvania increased in these valleys and spread as far as the shores of the Great Lakes and the banks of the Wabash, and, at the same time, the French became more active among the Indians in this trackless wilderness.

Two Pennsylvanians realized the importance of keeping the Indians of the western region on friendly terms with the Colony. One was George Croghan, the "king of traders," who wrote to Richard Peters of the Provincial Council, on May 26th, 1747, that "some small presents" should be sent the Indians dwelling in the region of Lake Erie. The other was Conrad Weiser, who wrote Richard Peters, on July 20th, 1747, that "a small present ought to be made to the Indians on Lake Erie to acknowledge the receipt of theirs. It may be sent by some Honest Trader. I think George Croghan is fit to perform it. I always took him for an honest man, and have as yet no Reason to think otherwise of him." The present to which Weiser refers was a French scalp and some wampum which the Lake Erie Indians had just sent by the hand of Croghan for the Governor of Pennsylvania. Croghan had just returned from a trading journey among them, and had found them unfriendly to the French. (See Penna. Archives, Vol. 1, pages 742, 761 and 762.)

Later, in the summer of 1747, it was decided by the Colonial Authorities to send a handsome present to the Indians of the Ohio and Lake Erie. George Croghan was selected as the person to carry the Pennsylvania present to the shores of the Ohio and while arrangements were being made for the mission, ten chiefs from Kuskuskies, among whom was Canachquasy, came to Philadelphia in November, and gave the Provincial Council authentic information of the operations of the French in the western region. They were told by President Palmer that Croghan would bring the Pennsylvania present the following spring. This information soon reached the shores of the Ohio.

Accordingly Croghan took the present to the Indians of the Ohio, in the spring of 1748. At Logstown, on April 28th, he held council with the chiefs of several tribes, and gave them the present of powder, lead, vermillion and flints. When he began to distribute the articles, he found they were not enough to satisfy the fifteen hundred Indians, and so he added much from his own trading stores. He told the Indians that, in answer to their complaints against the whiskey traders, the Governor had issued a proclamation forbidding the carrying of this liquor into the Indian country. Finally he told them that Conrad Weiser would come with a much larger present, on behalf of Pennsylvania, about the first of August.

Conrad Weiser arrived at Logstown on the evening of August 27th as the head of what is generally called the first embassy ever sent by the Colony of Pennsylvania to the Indians of the Ohio and Allegheny, although it would be more nearly correct to say that Croghan's mission of the preceeding April was the first. The Indians had been anxiously awaiting his coming. He notes in his journal that when they saw him, "great joy appeared in their countenances." Weiser distributed the goods making up the Pennsylvania present, and held many conferences with the Indians during his two weeks stay among them. He visited the Delaware town of Sawcunk at the mouth of the Beaver and sent Andrew Montour, who accompanied him, to Kuskuskies to summon the chiefs of that place to councils at Logstown. Kuskuskies was a group of villages on the upper Beaver, its centre being at or near the site of the city of New Castle.

On September 8th, Weiser requested the chiefs with whom he held the conferences at Logstown to give him "a list of their fighting men." The chiefs complied with this request, and under this date he noted in his journal:

"The following is the number of every Nation given to me by their several Deputies in Council in so many sticks tied up in a bundle: The Senecas, 163; Shawonese, 162; Owendaets (Wyandots), 100; Tisagechroanu, 40; Mohawks, 74; Onondagers (Onondagas), 35; Mohickons, 15; Cajukas (Cayugas), 20; Oneidas, 15; Delawares, 165; in all, 789."

While at Logstown, Weiser made George Croghan's trading house his headquarters. He raised the British flag over this famous Indian town. On September 11th, he and Croghan smashed an eight gallon keg of rum which the trader, Henry Norland, had brought to the town. Among the noted sachems with whom he held important conferences were the Oneida chief, Tanacharison, also called the Half King, and the Oneida chief, Scarouady, who, upon the death of Tanacharison in the autumn of 1754, became his successor as "Half King." Tanacharison promised Weiser that he would keep Pennsylvania posted as to the movements of the French in the valleys of the Ohio and "Let us," said he, "keep up true correspondence, and always hear of one another." His protestation of friendship for the English was sincere. He remained faithful to the English interest to the end of his eventful life. Before leaving Logstown, Weiser paid a visit to the aged and infirm Shawnee chief, Kakowatcheky, and presented him with a blanket, a coat, stockings and tobacco. Kakowatcheky had removed from Wyoming to Logstown in 1743 taking many of his tribe with him.

This embassy to the Delawares, Shawnees, Senecas and other Indians on the Ohio was eminently successful. It left Pennsylvania in possession of the Indian trade from Logstown to the Mississippi and from the Ohio to the Great Lakes. Moreover, its success was most gratifying to all the frontier settlers. Not only Pennsylvania, but Maryland and Virginia were active in following up the advantage thus gained. A number of Maryland and Virginia traders pushed into the Ohio region, and presently the Ohio Company, formed by leading men of Virginia and Maryland, among whom were George Washington's half-brothers, Lawrence and Augustine, sought to secure the Forks of the Ohio.

For Weiser's journal of this important mission, the reader is referred to the Pennsylvania Colonial Records, Vol. 5, pages 348 to 358.

Death of Shikellamy

On the 17th day of December in the eventful year of 1748, occurred the death of Shikellamy, "Our Enlightener," the most picturesque and historic Indian character that ever lived in Pennsylvania. As we have seen, his residence was at Sunbury. Conrad Weiser, in the later years of the old chief's life, had built him a substantial house which rested upon pillars for safety, and in which he always shut himself up when any drunken frolic was going on in the village. He had been taken ill in Philadelphia, but so far recovered that he had visited his old friend, Weiser, at his home near Womelsdorf, in April, 1748, and was able to complete his journey to Shamokin. Upon his return to Shamokin, he was again taken ill, and in June the Provincial Council was advised that he was so ill that he might lose his eyesight; but he recovered sufficiently to make a trip to Bethlehem early in December. On his return from that place, he became so ill that he reached home only by the assistance of the Moravian missionary, David Zeisberger. His daughter and Zeisberger were with him during his last illness and last hours. David Zeisberger and Henry Frye made the old chief a coffin, and the Indians painted the body in their gayest colors, bedecked it with his choicest ornaments, and placed with it the old chief's weapons according to the Indian custom. Then, after Christian burial services, conducted by David Zeisberger, Shikellamy was buried in the Indian burying ground of his people in the present town of Sunbury.

Shikellamy left to mourn him his three sons and a daughter. Another son, Unhappy Jake, was killed in the war with the Catawbas. The three sons who survived were: (1) Taghneghdoarus, also known as John Shikellamy, who succeeded his honored and distinguished father in authority, but never gained the confidence with which the father was held by both the Indians and the whites; (2) Taghahjute, or Sayughdowa, better known in history as Logan, Chief of the Mingoes, having been given the name of James Logan by Shikellamy, in honor of the distinguished secretary of the Provincial Council; (3) John Petty. His daughter was the widow of Cajadies, known as the "best hunter among all the Indians," who died in November, 1747. After the death of Shikellamy, Shamokin (Sunbury) rapidly declined as a center of Indian affairs, as his son who succeeded him was not able to restrain the Indians under his authority.

Among the tributes which have been paid to this great chieftain are the following: "He was a truly good man, and a great lover of the English," said Governor Hamilton, of the Colony of Pennsylvania. Said Count Zinzindorf, Moravian missionary, who, like all the prominent leaders of the Moravian Church, had been kindly received by Shikellamy: "He was truly an excellent

SHIKELLAMY'S MARKER, NEAR HIS GRAVE, AT SUNBURY, PA.

A number of years ago, the great Vice-Gerent's grave was opened, and his pipe, a British medal and a number of other articles belonging to him were found therein. His grave is near the bridge leading to Northumberland.

and good man, possessed of many noble qualities of mind, that would do honor to many white men, laying claims to refinement and intelligence. He was possessed of great dignity, sobriety and prudence, and was particularly noted for his extreme kindness to the inhabitants with whom he came in contact." Also, the Moravian historian, Loskiel, says of him: "Being the first magistrate, and the head chief of all the Iroquois Indians living on the banks of the Susquehanna, as far as Onondaga, he thought it incumbent upon himself to be very circumspect in his dealings with the white people. He assisted the Missionaries in building, and defended them against the insults of the drunken Indians; being himself never addicted to drinking, because, as he expressed it, he never wished to become a fool."

The dust of this astute Iroquois statesman reposes at Sunbury on the banks of his long loved Susquehanna; and, as one stands near his grave and looks at the high and rocky river hill on the opposite side of the river, he beholds a strange arrangement of the rocks on the mountainside, resembling the countenance of an Indian warrior, and known locally as "Shikellamy's Profile." Thus, his face carved by nature's hand in the imperishable rock, gazes on the region where "Our Enlightener" had his home for so many years.

The Purchase of 1749

On July 1, 1749, a number of Seneca, Onondaga, Tutelo, Nanticoke, and Conoy chiefs came to Philadelphia to interview Governor Hamilton, with reference to the settlements which the white people were making "on the other side of the Blue Mountains." This delegation had gone first to Wyoming, the place appointed for the gathering of the deputies of the various tribes, had waited there a month for the other deputies, and then decided to go on to Philadelphia. Governor Hamilton advised the chiefs that the Province had been doing everything in its power to prevent persons from settling on lands not purchased from the Indians. Immediately after the conference the Governor issued a proclamation, which was distributed throughout the Province, and posted upon trees in the Juniata and Path valleys, and other places where settlers had built their homes beyond the Blue Mountains, ordering all such settlers to remove from these lands by the first of November. As has already been related in this chapter, these settlers were removed by Conrad Weiser, George

Croghan, Benjamin Chambers, James Galbraith and others, in May, 1750, acting under orders of Lieutenant-Governor Morris.

The delegation of chiefs had left Philadelphia but a short time when Governor Hamilton received word from Conrad Weiser that the other Indian deputies, who had failed to join the previous delegation at Wyoming, were at Shamokin (Sunbury) on their way to Philadelphia. The Governor then sent word to Weiser, urging him to divert this new delegation from coming to the city. Weiser did all in his power to carry out the Governor's orders, but the Indians soon let him see that they were determined to go on to Philladelphia, at which place they arrived on the 16th of August, numbering two hundred and eighty, and led by Canassatego, the speaker at the former treaties at Lancaster and Philadelphia.

Canassatego was the speaker of the Indian delegation at the conferences which were then held with the Governor and Provincial Council. When advised of the efforts that Pennsylvania had made to prevent her people from settling on unpurchased land, Canassatego excused the Government for this, saying: "White people are no more obedient to you than our young Indians are to us." He thus also excused the war parties of young Iroquois who went against the Catawbas. Canassatego further offered to remedy the situation by saying that the Iroquois were "willing to give up the Land on the East side of Susquehannah from the Blue Hills, or Chambers' Mill to where Thomas McGee [McKee], the Indian trader, lives, and leave it to you to assign the worth of them." This great Iroquois statesman complained especially of the settlements on the branches of the Juniata, saying that these were the hunting grounds of the Nanticokes and other Indians under the jurisdiction of the Iroquois. He told the Governor that, when the Nanticokes had trouble with Maryland, where they formerly lived, they had been removed by the Six Nations and placed at the mouth of the Juniata, and that there were three settlements of the tribe still remaining in Maryland. These latter, he explained, wished to join their relatives in Pennsylvania, but that Maryland would not permit them to do so, "where they make slaves of them and sell their Children for Money." He then asked the Governor to intercede with the Governor of Maryland to the end that the Nanticokes in Maryland might be permitted to join their brethren on the Juniata. Explaining why the proposed treaty with the Catawbas had not taken place, Canassatego said that King George's War breaking out had prevented them from getting together, "and now we say we neither offer nor reject Peace." He also let it be known that he did not believe that the Catawbas were sincere in their offers of peace.

Governor Hamilton then took up with Canassatego the proposed sale of lands, and, after much discussion, the Six Nations' deputies sold to the Colony of Pennsylvania a vast tract of land between the Susquehanna and the Delaware, including all or parts of the present counties of Dauphin, Northumberland, Lebanon, Schuylkill, Columbia, Carbon, Luzerne, Monroe, Pike and Wayne. This is known in Pennsylvania history as the "Purchase of 1749," the deed having been signed on the 22nd of August of that year. Nutimus joined in the deed as chief of the Delawares at Nutimus' Town, at the mouth of Nescopeck Creek, Luzerne County. Also, Paxinosa, then residing at Wyoming, and the leading chief of the Shawnees of Eastern Pennsylvania, joined in this deed.

Celoron's Expedition

In the summer of 1749, the year following the treaty of Aix-la-Chapelle, which ended King George's War, Marquis de la Galissoniere, then Governor-General of New France, sent Captain Celoron de Bienville with a detachment composed of one captain, eight subaltern officers, six cadets, one chaplain, twenty soldiers, one hundred and eighty Canadians and about thirty Indians, approximately half of whom were Iroquois, down the valleys of the Allegheny and Ohio to take formal possession of the region drained by these rivers for Louis XV of France. Coming down Conewango Creek to the Allegheny, Celoron, on July 29th, buried a leaden plate on the bank of the river, opposite the mouth of the Conewango, with an inscription thereon proclaiming that all the region drained by the "Beautiful River" and tributaries belonged to the Crown of France forever. This plate was afterwards stolen by some Indians, and several Cayuga chiefs carried it to Sir William Johnson at his residence on the Mohawk, on December 4th, 1750. Then, on January 29th, 1751, Governor George Clinton of New York sent a copy of the inscription on the plate to Governor Hamilton of Pennsylvania.

As Celoron floated down the beautiful and majestic rivers, whose forest-lined banks were clothed with the verdure of midsummer, he buried other leaden plates, mostly at the mouths of tributary streams. One of these was buried near the "Indian God Rock," on the east side of the Allegheny, seven or eight miles below Franklin; one at the mouth of the Monongahela; one at the mouth of the Muskingum, and one at the mouth of the Great Kanawha. The one at the mouth of the Muskingum was found in 1798, and the one at the mouth of the Great Kanawha was found in 1846. The former has been preserved by the American Antiquarian Society, and the latter by the Virginia Historical Society. Several others were buried at places which cannot be definitely ascertained. The last was buried at the mouth of the Great Miami, where Celoron left the Ohio returning to Canada by way of Detroit.

On his way down the Allegheny and Ohio, Celoron stopped at the principal Indian towns and held conferences with the natives,—at the village of Cut Straw, also called Buccaloons, at the mouth of Brokenstraw Creek in Warren County; at Venango (Franklin); at Attique or Attigue (Kittanning); at Chartier's Town, on or near the site of Tarentum; at Logstown and at other places. At Venango he found the English trader, John Frazer, who was driven from that place by the French in the summer of 1753, and removed to the mouth of Turtle Creek on the Monongahela. At Kittanning, he found that the inhabitants had fled to the woods, although he had sent Joncaire ahead to that place to request its chiefs to await his arrival without fear. At Chartier's Town, or probably at Logstown, he found six English traders with fifty horses and one hundred and fifty bales of fur. Ordering these traders to remove, he sent a letter to Governor Hamilton of Pennsylvania, telling him to warn his traders "not to return into these territories" of the French King. This letter was dated August 6th. At or near the site of Pittsburgh, he met Queen Allaquippa of the Senecas, whom he describes in his journal as "entirely devoted to the English." At Logstown, which he reached on August 8th, he ordered the British flag which Conrad Weiser had placed there the preceeding September, to be torn down and the French flag to be raised in its place. At his village on the Miami, Celoron held a conference with Old Britian, or La Demoiselle (the Young Lady), the great chief of the Miamis, and endeavored to draw him into a French alliance, but without success. The Joncaire brothers, Philip and Chabert, who for many years had been active agents of the French among the Indians of the Ohio and Allegheny, accompanied this historic expedition, as did Contrecoeur, who afterwards built Fort Duquesne, and M. de Villiers, who compelled Washington to surrender at Fort Necessity, July 4th, 1754.

On June 30th, 1749, Governor Hamilton, of Pennsylvania, received a letter from Governor Clinton, of New York, advising that he had received information that an army of French was about to make its way into the valley of the "Belle Riviere." This was, of course, Celoron's expedition, just described. Governor Hamilton sent word to George Croghan to go to the Allegheny to ascertain "whether any French were coming into those parts, & if any, in what numbers & what appearance they made, that the Indians might be apprised & put upon their guard." (See Penna. Col. Rec., Vol. V., page 387.) Croghan arrived at Logstown immediately after Celoron had left, and, in councils with Tanacharison and Scarouady, counteracted the influence of the Frenchman.

Attention is called to the fact that, before Croghan left Logstown Tanacharison and Scarouady gave him three deeds for large tracts of land, about 200,000 acres in all. A large part of the city of Pittsburgh and all the towns on the south side of the Ohio River as far as the mouth of Raccoon Creek, in Beaver County, are located on two of these tracts. The third tract, 60,000 acres, was located on the Youghiogheny in the region of the mouth of Big Sewickley Creek, Westmoreland County. These were the first grants of land by the Indian to the white man in the valley of the Ohio. Croghan must have dated the deeds back about a week, as they bear date of August 2nd. Two of these deeds are recited in the records of the office of the Recorder of Deeds of Westmoreland County, one in deed book, No. A. page 395, and the other in deed book, No. A, page 511.

The Virginia Treaty at Logstown

Shortly after the forming of the Ohio Company, in 1748, the King of England granted the company two hundred thousand acres of land to be taken on the south side of the Allegheny and Ohio between the Kiskiminetas River and Buffalo Creek and on the north side of the Ohio between Yellow Creek and Cross Creek, or in such other part of the region west of the Allegheny Mountains as the company should think proper. The grant contained the condition that the company should settle one hundred families thereon within seven years and erect a fort*. On the company's compliance with this condition, it was to receive three hundred thousand acres more, south of the first grant. The company built a storehouse at Will's Creek (Cumberland, Mary-

*The Ohio Company requested Pennsylvania Germans to settle on these lands. They declined, as they desired clergymen of their own language and faith (Lutheran and Reformed) instead of clergymen of the established church of Virginia (Episcopal). Later hundreds of German families received Pennsylvania titles to lands in this region. (Writings of Washington, by Sparks, Vol. 2, page 481).

land), and, in 1751, opened a road towards the Ohio as far as Turkey Foot, Pennsylvania. Pennsylvania claimed that a large part of the company's grant was within the bounds of Charles II's charter to William Penn; and a dispute between Pennsylvania and Virginia, with reference to these lands, continued with varying degrees of intensity until its happy consummation in the Act of the Assembly of Pennsylvania, passed April 1, 1784.

As we have seen, Pennsylvania was following up the advantages gained by Croghan's and Weiser's embassy to Logstown in 1748. In the meantime the Colony of Virginia had not relinquished its claim to the Ohio Valley. In June, 1752, the commissioners of Virginia, Joshua Fry, L. Lomax, and James Patton, held a treaty with the Delawares, Shawnees, and Mingoes of the Ohio Valley, at Logstown. Christopher Gist, the agent of the Ohio Company, George Groghan, and Andrew Montour were present, the latter acting as interpreter. The Great Council of the Six Nations declined to send deputies to attend the treaty. Said they: "It is not our custom to meet to treat of affairs in the woods and weeds. If the Governor of Virginia wants to speak with us, and deliver us a present from our father [the king], we will meet him at Albany, where we expect the Governor of New York will be present."

The object of the treaty was to obtain from the Indians a confirmation of the Lancaster Treaty of 1744, by the terms of which Virginia claimed that the Iroquois had ceded to her their right to all lands in the valley of the Ohio. The task of the Virginia commissioners was not an easy one for the reason that the Pennsylvania traders had prejudiced the Indians against Virginia. However, the commissioners secured permission to erect two forts and to make some settlements. Tanacharison, who was present and took a prominent part in the negotiations, advised that his brothers of Virginia should build "a strong house" at the mouth of the Monongahela to resist the designs of the French. A similar request had been made to the Governor of Pennsylvania by the chiefs at Logstown when George Crogan was at that place in May, 1751.

The Virginians, we repeat, laid claim to all the lands of the Ohio Valley by virtue of the purchase made at the treaty of Lancaster, in 1744, in which the western limit of the Iroquois sale was set forth as the "setting sun." Conrad Weiser had advised the Governor of Pennsylvania that the Six Nations never contemplated such sale, explaining that by the "setting sun" was meant the crest of the Allegheny Mountains, the divide between streams flowing to the Atlantic Ocean on the East and the Mississippi River on the West. At this Logstown treaty one of the Iroquois chiefs told the Virginia commissioners that they were mistaken in their claims. The chiefs agreed with the commissioners not to molest any settlements that might be made on the southeast side of the Ohio. At the treaty, two old chiefs, through an interpreter, said to Mr. Gist: "The French claim all on one side of the river [the Ohio], and the English all on the other side. Where does the Indian's land lie." This question Gist found hard to answer.

During the proceedings of the Virginia treaty, Tanacharison, as the representative of the Six Nations, bestowed, on June 11th, the sachemship of the Delawares on Chief Shingas, later called King Shingas, believed by many authorities to have been a nephew of the great Sassoonan, since whose death, in the autumn of 1747, the kingship of the Delawares had been vacant. Also, Tanacharison's friendship for George Croghan was shown at this treaty. He spoke of him as "our brother, the Buck, who is approved by our Council at Onondaga."

As to the kingship of Shingas, we call attention to the fact that he was not really king of the three Delaware Clans. He belonged to the Turkey Clan. As pointed out, in Chapter II, the head chief of the Turtle Clan was regarded as king of the three Clans of Delawares.

Tanacharison Forbids French to Advance

In the early part of the summer of 1753, the French, coming from Canada, erected Fort Presqu' Isle, where the city of Erie now stands, and later in the same year erected Fort Le Boeuf, where Waterford, Erie County, now stands. But before the erection of these forts, or on May 7, 1753, a message was sent down from Venango to George Croghan at his trading house, near the mouth of Pine Creek, about six miles up the Allegheny from the mouth of the Monongahela, by the trader, John Frazer, to the effect that the French were coming with three brass cannon, amunition and stores. Croghan and his associates were thrown into consternation. On the following day, two Iroquois runners from the Great Council House at Onondaga brought similar news; and on May 12th, a message was received from Governor Hamilton, of Pennsylvania, stating that he had received word from Sir

William Johnson, of New York, that a large French expedition was marching towards the Ohio for the purpose of expelling the English and erecting forts.

The entire party at Croghan's Pine Creek trading house looked to him as leader. A conference was at once held there with Tanacharison and Scarouady. After much deliberation, the sachems decided "that they would receive the French as friends, or as enemies, depending upon their attitude, but the English would be safe as long as they themselves were safe." Croghan's partners, Teafee and Calendar, taking with them the two messengers who had brought Governor Hamilton's warning, returned to Philadelphia, on May 30th, and reported in person. The following day, Governor Hamilton laid the report of Teafee and Calendar before the Pennsylvania Assembly, which, on the same day, made an appropriation of eight hundred pounds for guns and amunition for the friendly Indians on the Ohio. A large part of the Assembly's appropriation was to be a present of condolence to the Twightwees on account of the murder of their king, "Old Britain," at his village on the Miami, on June 21, 1752, by a band of Ottawas and Chippewas, led by Charles Langlade, a Frenchman, of Detroit.

For more than three months, Governor Hamilton held this money. In the meantime, Tanacharison and Scarouady, on June 23d, wrote Governor Dinwiddie, of Virginia, appealing for help in resisting the French invasion. In September, these chiefs sent a delegation of one hundred deputies to Winchester, Virginia, to arrange for aid and supplies at a treaty then and there held between Virginia, in the interest of the Ohio Company, and the Six Nations and their tributary tribes in the valley of the Ohio,—the Delawares, the Shawnees, the Miamis or Twightwees, and the Wyandots. Scarouady headed the delegation of Indian deputies.

While attending the Winchester treaty, the Indians heard of the appropriation which had been voted by the Pennsylvania Assembly; and thereupon, although no invitation had been received by them, they sent a portion of their deputies, under the leadership of Scarouady, to Carlisle, Pennsylvania, to ascertain whether the report were true. This delegation consisted of a number of the important chiefs of the Six Nations, Delawares, Shawnees, Twightwees, or Miamis, and the Owendats, or Wyandots. Governor Hamilton sent Conrad Weiser, Richard Peters, Isaac Norris, and Benjamin Franklin to Carlisle to meet these deputies, October 1st to 4th, 1753. George Croghan was present to give advice. These commissioners had gone to Carlisle without presents, and they had Conrad Weiser interview one of the chiefs to ascertain if it were not possible to go through the forms of condolence on the promise to pay when the goods should arrive later. The chief replied that his people could and would not do any public business while the blood of their tribe remained upon their garments, and that "nothing would wash it unless the presents intended to cover the graves of the departed were actually spread upon the ground before them."

Presently the presents arrived and were distributed.

While the commissioners and Indians were awaiting for the goods to arrive, Conrad Weiser learned from Scarouady that, when the Ohio Indians received the messages in May, 1753, advising them of the threatened French invasion, they at once sent a warning to the French, who were then at Niagara, forbidding them to proceed further toward the Ohio Valley. This notice not deterring the French, the Indians then held a conference at Logstown, and sent a second notice to the French when they were approaching the headwaters of French Creek, as follows:

"Your children on Ohio are alarmed to hear of your coming so far this way. We at first heard that you came to destroy us. Our women left off planting, and our warriors prepared for war. We have since heard that you came to visit us as friends without design to hurt us, but then we wondered you came with so strong a body. If you have had any cause of complaint, you might have spoken to Onas or Corlear [meaning the Governors of Pennsylvania and New York], and not come to disturb us here. We have a Fire at Logstown, where are the Delawares and Shawnees and Brother Onas; you might have sent deputies there and said openly what you came about, if you had thought amiss of the English being there, and we invite you to do it now before you proceed any further."

The French replied to this notice, stating that they would not come to the council fire at Logstown; that they meant no harm to the Indians; that they were sent by command of the king of France, and that they were under orders to build four forts,—one at Venango, one at the Forks of the Ohio, one at Logstown, and another on Beaver Creek. The Ohio Indians then held another conference, and sent a third notice to the French, as follows: "We forbid you to come any farther. Turn back to the place from whence you came."

Tanacharison was the bearer of this third notice to the French, the equivalent of a declaration of war, and very likely, of the other two. Before the conference at Carlisle ended, it was learned that Tanacharison had just returned to Logstown from delivering the third notice; that he had been received in a very contemptuous manner by the French; and that, upon his return, had shed tears, and actually warned the English traders not to pass the Ohio.

For account of the Carlisle Conference of October, 1753, the reader is referred to the Pennsylvania Colonial Records, Vol. 5, pages 665 to 686.

Washington's Mission to the French

The necessity for prompt and energetic action for the vindication of the rights of the English in respect to the valleys of the Ohio and Allegheny became apparent to Governor Dinwiddie of Virginia shortly after Celoron's expedition in the summer of 1749. The French energetically seeking to ingratiate themselves with the Indians of this region, Governor Dinwiddie, in the summer of 1753, sent Captain William Trent to expostulate with the French commander on the Ohio for his invasion of this territory. Captain Trent did not have the qualities necessary for a fit performance of his duties. He came to the Forks of the Ohio (Pittsburgh), and then proceeded to the Indian town of Piqua, in Ohio, where Christopher Gist and George Croghan had been well received some time before. Discovering that the French flag waved there and that the aspect of things on the frontier was more threatening than he had anticipated, Trent abandoned his purpose and returned to Virginia.

Governor Dinwiddie then resolved upon the appointment of Captain Trent's successor; but it was a difficult task to find a person of the requisite moral and physical capacity for so responsible and dangerous an enterprise. The position was offered to several Virginians, by all of whom it was declined, when Dinwiddie received an intimation that it would be accepted by George Washington, then a youth of twenty-one years. Washington had recently come into possession of the fine estate of Mount Vernon, upon the death of his half-brother, Lawrence, and had, therefore, unusual temptations to avoid such a hazardous untertaking. But Washington's whole constitution was heroic. A constant patriot, he did not shrink from any honorable service, however dangerous, which he could render his country. He therefore accepted the appointment and, on the very day he received his commission, October 31st, 1753, he started on his dangerous journey of more than five hundred miles through the wilderness to deliver to St. Pierre, commander of the French forces on the headwaters of the Allegheny, the protest of Governor Dinwiddie against the encroachments of the French on territory claimed by the English.

On November 1st, Washington arrived at Fredericksburg, where he arranged with Jacob Van Braam, a Dutchman, who had been his old fencing master and who claimed to have a knowledge of the French language, to be his interpreter. Washington and Van Braam then proceeded to Alexandria, where they procured a supply of provisions. Proceeding from that place to Winchester, they procured baggage and horses, and from there proceeded to Wills Creek (Cumberland, Maryland), at which place they arrived on November 14th.

At Wills Creek, Washington engaged Christopher Gist, as he says in his journal, "to pilot us out." Gist was a surveyor, and during the years, 1750 and 1751, had made a journey through the Ohio Valley, exploring the region as the agent of the Ohio Company. With only one companion on this journey, Gist proceeded through the wilderness to the Allegheny River, arriving at the same at Shannopin's Town, named for the Delaware chief, Shannopin, a few miles above the mouth of the Monongahela. Swimming the Allegheny at this place, he and his companion then proceeded to what is now the central part of Ohio, thence back to Virginia through the heart of Kentucky, many years before Daniel Boone penetrated its wilderness. It is thus seen that Christopher Gist was well fitted by experience in the wilderness "to pilot" Washington through the forests to the French forts.

At Wills Creek, Washington hired four servants, Barnaby Currin and John McGuire, who were Indian traders, and Henry Stewart and William Jenkins. He and his companions left Wills Creek on November 15th, and on November 22nd, arrived at the cabin of John Frazer, an Indian trader, at the mouth of Turtle Creek. Frazer, as has been seen, had been driven away from Venango by the French in the summer of 1753. From Frazer's, Washington and Gist went overland to Shannopin's Town. From Shannopin's Town, they proceeded to the mouth of the Monongahela, where they met their baggage which had been brought down the Monongahela from Frazer's by the others of Washington's party.

While at the mouth of the Monongahela, Washington was impressed by the desirability of the place for the erection of a fort. From this place, he and his companions proceeded to the site of the present town of McKees Rocks, where he met the Delaware chief, Shingas, and invited him to accompany them to Logstown, at which latter place they arrived on November 24th. At Logstown, Washington held many conferences with Tanacharison and Scarouady, concerning the encroachments of the French. At this famous Indian town, the party was detained until November 30th, on which day they set out for Venango by way of the Venango Indian Trail, accompanied by Tanacharison, Jeskakake, White Thunder, the Hunter, or Guyasuta and John Davidson, Indian interpreter. On December 4th, the entire party arrived at Venango, which Washington describes in his journal as "an old Indian town, situated at the mouth of French Creek, and Ohio, and lies north about sixty miles from Logstown, but more than seventy miles by the way we were obliged to go."

At Venango, they found the French colors hoisted on the trading house from which the French had driven the trader, John Frazer. Washington immediately went to this house and inquired where the commander resided. There were three French officers present, one of whom was Captain Joncaire, who informed him that it would be necessary for him to deliver Governor Dinwiddie's protest to the commander of Fort Le Boeuf, situated on the site of the present town of Waterford, Erie County. The French officers at Venango treated Washington very courteously and invited him to dine with them which invitation he accepted, and during the course of the meal, the officers let it be plainly known that the French were determined to use every means in their power to retain possession of the disputed territory.

At this point we anticipate events somewhat by stating that, in April, 1754, the French erected Fort Machault at Venango (Franklin). The English referred to it as "the French fort at Venango." In 1760, after the close of the French and Indian War, the English erected Fort Venango near where Fort Machault had stood.

Washington remained at Venango until December 7th. During this time, the French officers used every art in their power to alienate Tanacharison from the English interest. Leaving Venango, Washington and his companions proceeded up French Creek to Custaloga's Town, located about twelve miles above the mouth of French Creek and near the mouth of Deer Creek in French Creek Township, Mercer County, and named for the Delaware chief, Custaloga. From Custaloga's Town, they went up French Creek to the Indian town of Cussewago, located on the site of Meadville, Crawford County, and thence to Fort Le-Boeuf (Waterford), at which place they arrived on December 11th. The journey up French Creek was very difficult, by reason of rains, mires and swamps. It was impossible to cross the creek, "either by fording or rafting, the water was so high and rapid."

On December 12th, Washington delivered to St. Pierre, the commander of Fort Le Boeuf, the protest of Governor Dinwiddie. This protest demanded that the French depart from the disputed region. St Pierre's reply was that he would transmit Governor Dinwiddie's protest to Marquis Duquesne, Governor of Canada, "to whom," he observed, "it better belongs than to me to set forth the evidence and reality of the rights of the King, my master, upon the lands situated along the river Ohio, and to contest the pretensions of the King of Great Britain thereto." St. Pierre, like the French officers at Venango, treated Washington with courtesy, but did all in his power to alienate Tanacharison and the other Indians from the English interest. He gave them liquor and presents. Commenting on the efforts of the commander and his officers, Washington says in his journal: "I can not say that ever in my life I suffered so much anxiety as I did in this affair." Under this terrible strain, Washington remained alert and carefully observed that the fort was garrisoned by more than one hundred men and officers and that there were two hundred and twenty canoes in readiness, and many more in process of being built, for the purpose of conveying the French forces down the river in the spring.

Having received St. Pierre's reply, Washington and his companions left Fort Le Boeuf on December 16th, and arrived at Venango on December 22nd, after "a tedious and very fatiguing passage down the creek." The next day, all of Washington's party except Tanacharison and White Thunder started from Venango by the same route which they had followed in the journey from Logstown to that place. White Thunder was sick and unable to walk, and so Tanacharison took him down the Allegheny in a canoe. After Washington and his companions had journied three days on the way south, the horses became weak, feeble and almost unable to travel. Accordingly, on December 26th, Washington and Gist proceeded ahead on foot, leaving the rest of the party to follow by easy stages with Van Bream in charge of the horses and baggage.

Indian Attempts to Kill Washington

On the evening of December 27th, an incident occurred in Washington's journey back to Virginia that has world wide publicity. We refer to the attempt of a hostile Indian to kill him. The exact location of this attempt to kill the future Father of his Country will remain forever unknown, but the approximate location is a few miles from Evans City, Butler County. We shall let Washington relate the incident in his own words as he wrote them in his journal:

"The day following [December 27th], just after we had passed a place called Murdering Town (where we intended to quit the path and steer across the country for Shanapin's Town), we fell in with a party of French Indians, who had laid in wait for us. One of them fired at Mr. Gist or me, not fifteen steps off, but fortunately missed. We took this fellow into custody, and kept him until about nine o'clock at night, then let him go, and walked all the remaining part of the night, without making any stop, that we might get the start so far as to be out of reach of their pursuit the next day, since we were assured they would follow our track as soon as it was light. The next day we continued travelling until quite dark, and got to the river [Allegheny] about two miles above Shahapins."

Christopher Gist, in his journal, describes the attack on Washington in more detail. He says that he and Washington met this Indian at Murdering Town, and believed that they had seen him at Venango. The Indian called Gist by the latter's Indian name and pretended to be very friendly. After some conversation with the Indian, Washington and Gist asked him to accompany them and show them the nearest way to Shannopin's Town. The Indian seemed very glad to accompany them. He led the way from Murdering Town, but seemed to take a course too much to the north-east, which caused both Washington and Gist to mistrust him. Finally, when they came to a snow-covered meadow, the Indian suddenly turned and fired at Washington. He was immediately seized and disarmed before he could re-load his rifle. Gist wanted to kill him on the spot, but Washington would

STATUE TO GEORGE WASHINGTON, ON SITE OF
FORT LE BOEUF, WATERFORD, PA.

The statue represents him in the act of delivering the protest of Governor Dinwiddie to St. Pierre.

not permit him to do so. After he was kept in custody until late in the evening, they let him go. Says Gist: "He was glad to get away. I followed him and listened until he was fairly out of the way, and then we set out about half a mile, when we made a fire, set our compass, and fixed our course, and travelled all night."

For many years, the author felt that a suitable monument should be erected to mark the approximate spot where the hostile Indian attempted to take the life of Washington. During the year 1924, he wrote several articles for the "*Butler Eagle,*" Butler, Pennsylvania, in an effort to arouse interest in the work he had in mind. These appeals through the newspaper brought results. A committee, consisting of Hon. A. E. Reiber, Captain James A. McKee, and the author, erected such monument in the autumn of 1924, and on July 3rd, 1925, it was unveiled with appropriate exercises. The author had the honor of delivering the historical address on this occasion.

At this point, the author asks that the reader indulge him in making the statement that he traces his love for the history of Pennsylvania to the story of the attack on Washington by the hostile Indian on that December evening of 1753, told him under the following circumstances: On the farm on which he was reared in Armstrong County, the ancestral home of his paternal ancestors since 1795, is a high hill, commanding a majestic sweep of the horizon in all directions. To the eastward, the blue outline of the Chestnut Ridge can be seen, on a clear day, almost fifty miles away, while to the westward are the undulating hills of Butler County. One of his earliest recollections is that of his accompanying his revered mother to this hilltop on summer evenings and, with her, watching the sun set in floods of gorgeous and golden beauty behind the western hills. On those occasions she told him that the western region, where the sun was setting, was Butler County, and that it was in this county where George Washington was shot at by a hostile Indian in the dead of winter and in the depth of the forest. The author shall always cherish the recollection of those summer evenings, when, as a child in company with his mother in the grace and beauty of her young womanhood, he watched those golden sunsets bathe the Butler County hills in glory, and in his fancy, pictured the region of the sunset as an enchanted land, inhabited by the ghosts and shadows of the past and hallowed by the footsteps of Washington.

Students of the life of Washington are familiar with the fact that, in crossing the Allegheny on his journey back to Virginia,

Washington was almost drowned in its icy waters. He and Gist were crossing the stream on a raft which they had made. Washington thrust out his pole to propel the raft, but it was caught between blocks of ice with such force as to throw him into the water. Swimming to an island near the Washington Crossing Bridge in the city of Pittsburgh, Washington almost froze to death during the terrible night. This incident took place on December 29th.

On December 30th, Washington and Gist arrived at John Frazer's cabin, at Turtle Creek. The next day, they paid a visit to Queen Allaquippa, who was then residing where McKeesport now stands. Washington presented her with a coat and a bottle of rum, "which latter," he said, "was thought much the best present of the two."

On January 2nd, 1754, Washington and Gist arrived at the latter's plantation near Mount Braddock, Fayette County, where some Virginia families had settled at least as early as the spring of 1753. On January 6th, they arrived at Wills Creek. On the same day, they "met seventeen horses loaded with materials and stores for a fort at the Forks of the Ohio, and the day after, some families going out to settle." Washington arrived at Williamsburg, then the capital of Virginia, on January 16th, and delivered St. Pierre's reply.

The war between the Iroquois and the Cherokees and Catawbas was being carried on during the winter of 1753 and 1754, according to the following statement in Washington's journal, under date of December 30th or 31st, 1753:

"We met here [at Frazer's, at the mouth of Turtle Creek, on the Monongahela] with twenty warriors, who were going to the southward to war; but coming to a place on the head of the Great Kanawha, where they found seven people killed and scalped, (all but one woman with very light hair) they turned about and ran back for fear the inhabitants should rise and take them as the authors of the murder. They report that the bodies were lying about the house, and some of them much torn and eaten by the hogs. By the marks which were left, they say they were French Indians of the Ottoway nation, and who did it."

The author has narrated Washington's mission rather fully on account of its historical importance and for the reason that Pennsylvanians should know the details of the perils which the youthful Washington encountered on Pennsylvania soil in his hazardous journey through the wilderness. As a closing statement, attention is called to the fact that Washington's journal, which was widely published in both England and America, reciting his experiences and giving information of vital import as to the plans for the French for occupying the valleys of the Ohio and Allegheny, made him an outstanding figure in the Colonies.

Clash of Arms About to Begin

This chapter has been devoted to a narration of the leading events in the Indian history of Pennsylvania from the departure of William Penn, in 1701, to the opening of the French and Indian War, the author's purpose being to prepare the reader for a study of the events about to be related. In the next chapter, we shall see the breaking of the storm which had long been gathering over the waters of the Ohio.

CHAPTER V

Opening of the French and Indian War

The French Occupy the Forks of the Ohio

IN January, 1754, George Croghan and Andrew Montour were sent to Logstown by Governor Hamilton of Pennsylvania, to ascertain from Tanacharison and Scarouady a full account of the activities of the French in the valleys of the Allegheny and Ohio, the attitude of the Western Indians, and what assistance in the way of arms and ammunition Virginia had given these Indians. Croghan and Montour found some French soldiers at Logstown, and most of the Indians drunk. John Patten, a trader, who accompanied Croghan and Montour, was captured by the French, but Tanacharison caused his release. The Pennsylvania emissaries remained at Logstown until February 2nd. They found the Indians determined to resist the French. A few days before they left, Tanacharison, Scarouady, and Shingas addressed a speech to Governor Hamilton in which they said: "We now request that our brother, the Governor of Virginia, may build a strong house at the Forks of the Mohongialo [Monongahela], and send some of our young brethren, the warriors, to live in it. And we expect our brother of Pennsylvania will build another house somewhere on the river, where he shall think proper, where whatever assistance he will think proper to send us may be kept for us, as our enemies are just at hand, and we do not know what day they may come upon us."

On February 20th, Andrew Montour was closely examined by Governor Hamilton and the Pennsylvania Assembly as to the location of Shannopin's Town, Logstown and Venango. Montour proved that these towns were all within the limits of the Province of Pennsylvania; but the Assembly decided that the encroachments of the French on the Ohio and Allegheny did not concern Pennsylvania any more than they did Virginia. In the meantime, Governor Dinwiddie, of Virginia, commissioned Captain William Trent to raise a force of one hundred men and proceed to the Forks of the Ohio to erect a fort at that place. Trent raised a force of seventy men and at once proceeded to Cumberland, Maryland; thence along the Nemacolin Indian Trail to Gist's Plantation (Mount Braddock, Fayette County, Pa.); thence by the Redstone trail to the mouth of that creek, where he built a storehouse; thence to the Forks of the Ohio. He arrived at the Forks of the Ohio on February 17th, and immediately began the erection of a fort, called Fort Trent. As Washington was returning to Virginia from his mission to St. Pierre, he met part of the Virginia force, the company consisting of Captain Trent, Lieutenant John Frazer (the former trader at Venango and the mouth of Turtle Creek) and Edward Ward, ensign.*

After the work of erecting Fort Trent was well started, Captain Trent returned to Will's Creek (Cumberland, Maryland), leaving Ensign Edward Ward, a half-brother of George Croghan, in command. The French on the upper Allegheny were promptly warned of the arrival of Trent's forces, and with the opening of spring, marshalled their forces, to the number of about one thousand, including French-Canadians and Indians of various tribes, with eighteen cannon, in all a flotilla of about sixty battaux and three hundred canoes, and descended the Allegheny from Le Boeuff and Venango. The French forces arrived at the Forks of the Ohio on the evening of the 16th of April, under command of Captain Contrecoeur. Planting his artillery, Contrecoeur sent Chevalier Le Mercier, Captain of the artillery of Canada, with a summons to Ensign Ward, demanding immediate surrender. This was the first overt act of war on the part of the French, in the conflict known as the French and Indian War.

Ward thus found himself surrounded by a force of one thousand French and Indians with the fort still uncompleted. Lieutenant Frazer was at his house at Turtle Creek at the time.

The Half King, Tanacharison, was present, and advised Ensign Ward to reply to the demand of Contrecoeur that he was not an officer of rank to answer the demand, and to request a delay until he could send for his superior in command. Contrecoeur, however, refused to parley; whereupon, Ward, having less than forty men, and, therefore, being utterly unable to resist the opposing force, prudently surrendered the half-finished stockade without further hesitation.

Contrecoeur, upon the surrender of Ward, treated him with

*The Ohio Company had intended to erect a fort at the mouth of Chartiers Creek, where McKees Rocks, Allegheny County, now stands.

the utmost politeness, invited him to sup with him, and wished him a pleasant journey back to Virginia. The French commander permitted him to withdraw his men, and take his tools with him; and on the next morning, he started on his return to Virginia going up the Monongahela to the mouth of Redstone Creek (Brownsville, Fayette County), where the Ohio Company had a stockade, erected by Trent on his way to the Ohio Valley. George Croghan, about the time Trent began erecting the fort at the Forks of the Ohio, had contracted with the Ohio Company to furnish provisions for Trent's forces, valued at five hundred pounds, from the back parts of Pennsylvania; and half of these were on their way to the Ohio when Contrecoeur captured the fort.

The French then took possession of the half-finished fort, completed it early in June, and named it Fort Dusquesne, in honor of Marquis DuQuesne, then the Governor-General of Canada. In the meantime, the French destroyed Croghan's trading house at Logstown, taking 20,000 pounds of skins and furs.

Washington's Campaign of 1754

While Captain William Trent was engaged in the work of erecting a fort at the Forks of the Ohio, in the early part of 1754, Colonel Joshua Fry, with George Washington second in command, was raising troops in Virginia to garrison the fort Trent was building. On April 2nd, Washington, with the rank of Lieutenant-Colonel, marched from Alexandria, Virginia, with a detachment of two companies of infantry, commanded by Captain Peter Hogg and Lieutenant Jacob Van Braam, the latter being Washington's interpreter on his mission to the French in the latter part of 1753. About fifteen days later, he was joined by Captain Stephen with a company of men. On April 20th, Washington's forces reached Old Town, Maryland and received information of the surrender of Ensign Ward at the Forks of the Ohio. On April 22nd, Washington reached Will's Creek, where he met Ward and learned the details of his surrender. On April 23d, a council of war was held at Will's Creek, at which it was agreed that it would be impossible to march to the Forks of the Ohio without reinforcements, but that it would be proper to advance as far as Redstone Creek, on the Monongahela, about thirty-seven miles this side of the fort [Fort Duquesne], and there to raise a fortification, "clearing a road wide enough to pass with all our artillery and baggage, and there to await for fresh orders." At Redstone [Brownsville, Fayette County, Pa.], a storehouse had been erected, as we have already seen, by Captain William Trent when on his way to the Forks of the Ohio. Here Washington's cannon and ammunition could be stored until reinforcements should arrive. From Will's Creek, Washington sent Ensign Ward to report to Governor Dinwiddie and a runner to notify Tanacharison, the Half King, of his intention to advance to Redstone with his force of one hundred and fifty men.

Let us now follow Washington as he advances into Pennsylvania over the Nemacolin Indian Trail, in the first military campaign of his illustrious career. On April 25th, he sent a detachment of sixty men to open the road towards Redstone, which detachment was joined by the main body on May 1st. On May 9th, Washington's forces reached the Little Crossings (Grantsville, Md.), having crossed over Will's Mountain, Dan's Mountain, Big Savage Mountain, Little Savage Mountain and Meadow Mountain. On May 11th, Washington sent out a scouting party from the Little Crossings, in command of Captain Stephen and Ensign Peyronie, with instructions to advance along the line of march as far as Gist's Plantation (Mount Braddock, Fayette County) in an effort to discover scouting parties of the French. On May 12th, Washington's forces left the Little Crossings, fording the Castleman River, and, on the same day, the commander received word that Colonel Fry was at Winchester, Virginia, with about one hundred and fifty men, and would join him in a few days; also that Colonel Innis would soon join him with three hundred and fifty men. On May 16th, two traders, fleeing from the French, who had been seen near Gist's Plantation, joined Washington's forces, while, on May 17th, Ensign Ward returned from Williamsburg, Virginia, with the word that Captain Mackay, with an Independent Company of one hundred and fifty men, was on his way to join the forces of the future Father of his Country.

On May 18th, Washington and his troops reached the Great Crossings of the Youghiogheny, at Somerfield, Somerset County, Pennsylvania. Here they were obliged to remain several days on account of the swollen condition of the river. Washington had been told by the two traders, above mentioned, that it was not practicable to open a road to Redstone. Therefore, while at the Great Crossings, he determined to examine the Youghiogheny to ascertain whether or not guns and baggage could be transported down this stream; and, on May 20th, with four white men and an Indian, he went down the river in a canoe as far as Ohiopyle Falls, in Fayette County, and found the stream too rocky and rapid for navigation. On May 21st, he returned to Turkey Foot (Confluence, Somerset County), where he seems to have had an intention of building a fort. From Turkey Foot, Washington returned to his camp at the Great Crossings, from which place he led his forces to the Great Meadows, situated along the National Pike, a few miles east of the Summit, in Fayette County, arriving there on the afternoon of May 24th. "I hurried to this place," says Washington, "as a convenient spot. We have, with nature's assistance, made a good entrenchment, and by clearing the bushes out of the meadows, prepared a charming field for an encounter." Also, on May 24th, two Indian runners came to Washington from the Ohio, with a message from Tanacharison, informing him that the French had marched from Fort Duquesne to meet the Virginians and that Tanacharison would soon join him with other Indian chiefs from the Ohio region.

Also, on the afternoon of May 24th, a trader came to the Great Meadows with the information that he had been at Gist's Plantation the evening before, had seen two Frenchmen there, and had heard that French troops were near Stewart's Crossing, now Connellsville, Fayette County. The next day, Washington sent out several scouting parties from the Great Meadows to examine the woods, the road leading to Gist's Plantation and the surrounding region, in an effort to locate the French force. The scouts returned the same evening without having located the French.

Christopher Gist visited Washington's camp at the Great Meadows early in the morning of May 27th, coming from his plantation at Mount Braddock, thirteen miles distant, and reporting that on May 26th, M. La Force, with fifty French soldiers had been at his plantation the day before, and that on his way to Washington's camp, he had seen the tracks of the same party only five miles from the encampment at the Great Meadows. Tanacharison, with a number of his warriors was but six miles from the Great Meadows, and a little after eight o'clock on the night of the same day, May 27th, he sent Washington intelligence that he had seen the tracks of Frenchmen, and had traced them to an obscure retreat. Washington feared that this might be a stratagem of the French for attacking his camp, and so, placing his ammunition in a place of safety and leaving a strong guard to protect it, he set out before ten o'clock with a band of soldiers, and reached Tanacharison's camp a little before sunrise, marching through a heavy rain, a night of intense darkness and the obstacles offered by an almost impenetrable forest. In a letter to Governor Dinwiddie, he says: "We were frequently tumbled over one another, and often so lost that fifteen or twenty minutes' search would not find the path again."

Just a word, at this point, as to the number of soldiers Washington had with him on this night march through the forest. Most historians have placed the number as forty, but Washington's notes indicate that he left forty soldiers to guard the camp at the Great Meadows and took the rest of his force with him. It will be recalled that his whole force, at that time, consisted of one hundred and fifty men.

Tanacharison Helps Washington Fight First Battle of His Career

At early dawn (May 28th), Washington held a council with Tanacharison at the latter's camp, which was near a spring, now known as Washington's Spring, about two miles north of the Summit on the old National Pike, near Uniontown; and it was agreed at this council to unite in an attack upon the French, Washington's forces to be on the right and Tanacharison's warriors on the left. The French were soon traced to an almost inaccessible rocky glen in the Allegheny Mountains, about three miles north of the Summit. The forces of Washington and Tanacharison advanced until they came so near as to be discovered by the French, who instantly ran to their arms. The firing continued on both sides for about fifteen minutes, when the French were defeated with the loss of their whole party, ten of whom (some authorities say twelve), including their commander, M. de Jumonville, were killed, one wounded, and twenty-one taken prisoners. Of the prisoners, the two most important were an officer named Drouillon, and the redoubtable LaForce. The prisoners were marched to the Great Meadows, and from there sent over the mountains to Virginia. Of Washington's party, only one was killed, and two or three were wounded. Tanacharison's warriors sustained no loss, as the fire of the French was aimed exclusively at Washington and his soldiers.

It is said that Washington fired the first shot in this skirmish, the opening conflict of the French and Indian War. Jumonville was buried where he fell, and a tablet marks the spot where his remains lie. The warriors of Tanacharison and Scarouady scalped the dead Frenchmen, and sent their scalps and a string of black wampum to the tribes on the Ohio, with the request that they take up arms against the French. The scene of this encounter, the first battle of Washington's illustrious career and an event that changed the course of modern history, is almost as wild and primitive as it was on that fateful morning of the 28th day of May, 1754.

At a council held at Philadelphia on December 19th, 1754, between Governor Morris of Pennsylvania, and Scarouady, Jagrea, a Mowhawk, and Aroas, a Seneca, the said Scarouady gave the following account of events leading up to the fight with Jumonville and the part that the Indian allies took in the same:

"This belt [holding up a belt of wampum] was sent by the Governor of Virginia and delivered by Captain Trent. You see in it the representation of an hatchet. It was an invitation to us to join with and assist our brethren to repel the French from the Ohio. At the time it was given, there were but four or five of us, and we were all that knew any thing about the matter; when we got it, we put it into a private pocket on the inside of our garment. It lay next to our breasts.

"As we were on the road going to Council with our brethren, a company of French, in number thirty-one, overtook us and desired us to go and council with them; and when we refused, they pulled us by the arm and almost stripped the chain of covenant from off it, but still I would suffer none to go with them. We thought to have got before them, but they passed us; and when we saw they endeavored to break the chain of friendship, I pulled this belt out of my pocket and looked at it and saw there this hatchet, and then went and told Colonel Washington of these thirty-one French Men, and we and a few of our brothers fought with them. Ten were killed, and twenty-one were taken alive whom we delivered to Colonel Washington, telling him that we had blooded the edge of his hatchet a little."

John Davidson, the Indian trader, acted as interpreter, at the above council. He was in the action, and gave Governor Morris the following account of the same:

"There were but eight Indians, who did most of the execution that was done. Colonel Washington and the Half King [Tanacharison] differed much in judgment, and on the Colonel's refusing to take his advice, the English and Indians separated.

After which the Indians discovered the French in an hollow and hid themselves, lying on their bellies behind a hill; afterwards they discovered Colonel Washington on the opposite side of the hollow in the gray of the morning, and when the English fired, which they did in great confusion, the Indians came out of their cover and closed with the French and killed them with their tomahawks, on which the French surrendered."

In writing to his brother, John Augustine, Washington, referring to the engagement with Jumonville said:

"I have heard the bullets whistle, and believe me, there is something charming in the sound."

This remark was reported later to George the Second, King of England, who commented: "He would not say so if he had been used to hearing many.

Washington Gives Tanacharison an English Name

Two days after the death of Jumonville, Colonel Fry died at the camp at Will's Creek on his way to join the army, and the chief command now devolved upon Colonel Washington. Washington immediately commenced enlarging the intrenchment at the Great Meadows, and erecting palisades, anticipating an attack from the French. The palisaded fort at the Great Meadows having been completed, Washington's forces were augmented to three hundred by the arrival from Will's Creek of the forces which had been under Colonel Fry. With these was the surgeon of the regiment, Dr. James Craik, a Scotchman by birth, who was destined to be a faithful friend of Washington throughout the remainder of his life, and was present at his bedside, when he closed his eyes in death within the hallowed walls of his beloved Mount Vernon.

On the 9th of June, Washington's early instructor, Adjutant Muse, George Croghan and Andrew Montour, then Provincial Captain, arrived at the Great Meadows with reinforcements, powder and ball. Adjutant Muse brought with him a belt of wampum, and a speech from Governor Dinwiddie to Tanacharison, with medals and presents for the Indians under his command. Says Washington Irving in his classic "Life of Washington": "They were distributed with that grand ceremonial so dear to the Red Man. The chiefs assembled, painted and decorated in all their savage finery. Washington wore a medal sent to him by the Governor for such occasions. The wampum and speech having been delivered, he advanced, and, with all due solemnity, decorated the chiefs and the warriors with the medals, which they were to wear in remembrance of their father, the King of England." Among the warriors thus decorated, was Canachquasy, the son of old Queen Allaquippa, who, with her son, had arrived at the Great Meadows on June 1st. Upon his decoration Canachquasy was given the English name of Lord Fairfax. Tanacharison was given the English name of Dinwiddie on this occasion, and returned the compliment by giving Washington the Indian name of Connotaucarius.

On the 10th day of June, Washington wrote Governor Dinwiddie from the camp at the Great Meadows, concerning the decoration of Canachquasy, as follows:

"Queen Allaquippa desired that her son, who was really a great warrior, might be taken into Council, as she was declining and unfit for business; and that he should have an English name given him. I therefore called the Indians together by the advice of the Half-King, presented one of the medals, and desired him to wear it in remembrance of his great father, the King of England; and called him by the name of Colonel Fairfax, which he was told signified 'the First in Council.' This gave him great pleasure."

At the end of the ceremonies of giving English names to Tanacharison and Canachquasy, Washington read the morning service of the Episcopal Church. Dr. James Craik, who was present, said, in a letter home, that the Indians "believed he was making magic."

Washington Advances to Gist's Plantation

On the 10th of June, there was great agitation in the camp at the Great Meadows over the report that a party of ninety Frenchmen were approaching, which report was later found to be incorrect. On the same day, Captain Mackay of the Royal Army, in command of an independent company of one hundred riflemen from South Carolina, arrived at the Great Meadows, increasing Washington's forces to about four hundred men. The arrival of these forces encouraged Washington. He now hoped to capture Fort Duquesne, and selected Mount Braddock as his battle ground. Leaving one company under Captain Mackay to guard the fort, Washington pushed on over the Laurel Hill as far as Christopher Gist's Plantation at Mount Braddock, near Connellsville, Fayette County. So difficult was the passage over Laurel Hill that it took approximately two weeks for Washington's forces to reach Gist's plantation from Great Meadows, a distance of thirteen miles. Washington's Indian allies Tanacharison, Scarouady and others, refused to accompany him as far as Gist's, and returned to the Great Meadows. The trouble was that Washington and Tanacharison could not agree as to the method of conducting the campaign. On the 27th of June, Washington had sent a party of seventy men under Captain Lewis to clear a road from Gist's to the mouth of the Redstone (Brownsville), and another party under Captain Polson was, on the same day, sent ahead to reconnoiter.

While these movements of Washington's forces were taking place, a force of five hundred French and some Indians, afterwards augmented to about four hundred, left Fort Duquesne on the 28th of June to attack Washington, the French being commanded by M. DeVilliers, a half-brother of Jumonville, who it is said, sought the command from Contrecoeur as a special favor that he might avenge his half-brother's "assassination." This force went up the Monongahela in large canoes, and on the 30th of June, reached the mouth of Redstone, and encamped on the rising ground about half a mile from the stockade, which, it will be recalled, Captain Trent had erected during the preceding winter as a storehouse for the Ohio Company. M. DeVilliers described it as "a sort of fort built of logs, one upon another, well notched in, about thirty feet long and twenty feet wide."

While at the mouth of the Redstone, M. DeVilliers learned that Washington's forces were entrenching themselves at Gist's plantation. He thereupon disencumbered himself of all his heavy stores, and leaving a sergeant and a few men to guard the boats, pushed on in the night, cheered by the hope that he was about to capture the forces of Washington. Arriving at Gist's Plantation in the early morning of July 2nd, he saw the intrenchments which Washington had there begun to erect, at once invested them, and fired a general volley. No response came from the intrenchments; for the prey had escaped. However, at Mr. Gist's house, some Indians with the French captured Elizabeth Williams and three of James Lowrey's traders, named Andrew McBriar, John Kennedy and Nehemiah Stevens. (Pa. Col. Rec. Vol. 6, pages 142-143.) M. DeVilliers was then about to retrace his steps, when a deserter named Barnabas Devan, coming from the Great Meadows, disclosed to him the whereabouts and the half-famished condition of Washington's forces. Having made a prisoner of the deserter with a promise to reward or hang him after proving his story true or untrue, M. DeVilliers continued the pursuit. While he is pursuing Washington, we will relate how the latter's forces escaped capture.

At Gist's Plantation, on June 28th, Washington held a council of war, upon receipt of intelligence that the French in large numbers, accompanied by many Indians, were marching against him. At this council, it was resolved to send a message to Captain Mackay, who was then at the Great Meadows, desiring him to join Washington at once, and also to call in Captain Lewis and Captain Polson, who, as we have seen, had been sent forward to cut the road from Gist's to Redstone, and to reconnoiter. Captain Mackay and his company arrived on the evening of the 28th, and the foraging parties on the morning of the 29th, when a second council of war was held, and it was decided to retreat as speedily as possible. In order to expedite the retreat to the Great Meadows, Washington impressed the pack-horses of George Croghan, who had been furnishing flour and ammunition for the Virginians.

Washington Surrenders at Fort Necessity

The troops, with great difficulty, succeeded in retreating to the Great Meadows. Here they halted on July 1st. The suffering among Washington's forces was great. For eight days they had no bread, and had taken little of any other food. It was not the intention of Washington at first to halt at this place, but his men had become so fatigued from great labor and hunger that they could draw the swivels no further. Here, then, it was resolved to make a stand. Trees were felled, and a log breastwork was raised at the fort, in order to strengthen it in the best manner that the circumstances would permit. Washington now named the stockade "Fort Necessity" from the circumstances attending its erection. At this critical juncture, many of Washington's Indian allies, under Tanacharison, deserted him, being disheartened at the scant preparations of defense against the superior force, and offended at being subject to military command. On July 2nd, Washington received information that the French were at Gist's Plantation.

Early on the morning of July 3rd an alarm was received from a sentinel, who had been wounded by the enemy, and, at nine o'clock, word was received that the whole body of the French and Indian allies amounting, as some authorities say, to nine hundred men, was only four miles off. Before noon, distant firing was heard, and the enemy reached a woods about a third of a mile from the fort. Washington had drawn his men up on the open and level ground outside the trenches, and waited for the attack, which he thought would be as soon as the enemy emerged from the woods; and he ordered his troops to reserve their fire until they should be near enough to do execution. The French did not incline to leave the woods and to attack the fort by assault. Washington then drew his men back within the trenches, and gave them orders to fire at their discretion, as suitable opportunities might present themselves. The enemy remained on the side of the rising ground next to the fort, and were sheltered by the trees. They kept up a brisk fire of musketry, but never appeared in open view. In the meantime, rain was falling in torrents, the trenches were filled with water, and many of the arms of Washington's men were out of order. Until eight o'clock at night—the rain falling without intermission—both parties kept up a desultory fire, the action having started at about eleven o'clock in the morning. By that time, the French had killed all the horses and cattle at the fort.

At eight o'clock at night, the French requested a parley, but Washington, suspecting this to be a feint to procure the admission of an officer into the fort to discover his condition, declined. They repeated their request with the additional request than an officer might be sent to them, they guaranteeing his safety. Washington then sent Captain Jacob Van Braam, the only person under his command who understood the French language, with the exception of Chevalier de Peyrouny, an Ensign in the Virginia regiment, who was dangerously wounded. Van Braam returned and brought with him from M. DeVilliers, the French commander, the proposed articles of capitulation. Villiers was a half-brother of the ill-fated Jumonville. Owing to the overpowering number of the enemy, Washington decided to come to terms. After a notification of the proposed articles, he consented to leave the fort the next morning, July 4, 1754, but was to leave it with the honors of war, and with the understanding that he should surrender nothing but the artillery.

French Accuse Washington of Having Assassinated Jumonville

Considerable dissatisfaction was expressed with regard to several of the articles of capitulation when they were made public.

One of these was an article, by consenting to which Washington virtually admitted that Jumonville had been "assassinated" in the action of May 28th. Another was an article, by consenting to which, Washington virtually admitted the validity of the French claim to the Ohio Valley. M. De Villiers, the commandant of the French forces, in his account of the march from Fort Duquesne and the affair at the Great Meadows said, "We made the English consent to sign that they had assassinated my brother in his camp." A copy of the capitulation was subsequently laid before the House of Burgesses of Virginia, with explanations. The conduct of Washington and his officers was properly appreciated, and they received a vote of thanks for their gallant defense of their country. However, from this vote of thanks, two officers were excepted—Major Muse, who was charged with cowardice, and Captain Jacob VanBraam, who was accused of treachery in purposely misinterpreting the articles of capitulation. The truth is that Washington had been greatly deceived by VanBraam, through either ignorance or design. An officer of his regiment, who was present at the reading and signing of the articles of capitulation, wrote a letter to a friend, in which he discusses the true intent and meaning of the articles and of their bungling translation by VanBraam, as follows:

"When Mr. VanBraam returned with the French proposals, we were obliged to take the sense of them from his mouth; it rained so hard that he could not give us a written translation of them; we could scarcely keep the candle lighted to read them by; and every officer there is ready to declare that there was no such word as 'assassination' mentioned. The terms expressed were 'the death of Jumonville.' If it had been mentioned, we would by all means have had it altered, as the French, during the course of the interview, seemed very condescending and desirous to bring things to a conclusion; and, upon our insisting, altered the articles relating to the stores and ammunition, which they wanted to detain; and that of the cannon, which they agreed to have 'destroyed,' instead of 'reserved for their use.'

"Another article, which appears to our disadvantage, is that whereby we oblige ourselves not to attempt an establishment beyond the mountains. This was translated to us, not 'to attempt' buildings or 'improvements on the lands of his most Christian Majesty.' This we never intended, as we denied he had any there, and therefore thought it needless to dispute this point.

"The last article, which relates to the hostages, is quite different from the translation of it given to us. It is mentioned 'for the security of the performance of this treaty,' as well as for the return of the prisoners. There was never such an intention on our side, or mention of it made on theirs, by our interpreter. Thus, by the evil intention or negligence of VanBraam, our conduct is scrutinized by a busy world, fond of criticizing the proceedings of others, without considering circumstances, or giving just attention to reasons which might be offered to obviate their censures.

"VanBraam was a Dutchman, and had but an imperfect knowledge of either the French or English language. How far his ignorance should be taken as an apology for his blunders, is uncertain. Although he had proved himself a good officer, yet there were other circumstances, which brought his fidelity in question. Governor Dinwiddie, in giving an account of this affair to Lord Albermarle says: 'In the capitulation they made use of the word 'assassination,' but Washington, not understanding French, was deceived by the interpreter, who was a paltroon, and though an officer with us, they say he has joined the French."

Also, Washington expressed himself on Van Braam's translation, as follows:

"That we were willfully or ignorantly deceived by out interpreter in regard to the word 'assassination,' I do aver and will to my dying moment; so will every officer who was present. The interpreter was a Dutchman little acquainted with the English tongue, and therefore might not advert to the tone and meaning of the word in English; but whatever his motives were for so doing, certain it is he called it the 'death' or the 'loss' of the Sieur Jumonville. So we received and so we understood it until, to our great surprise and mortification, we found it otherwise in a literal translation."

Washington Marches Out With Honors of War

On the morning of July 4th, Washington and his forces marched out of the Fort with the honors of war, taking with them their regimental colors, but leaving behind a large flag, too cumberous to be transported. His forces set out for Will's Creek, but had scarcely left the Great Meadows when they encountered one hundred Indian allies of the French, who, in defiance of the terms of capitulation, began plundering the baggage, and committing other irregularities. Seeing that the French did not or could not prevent their Indian allies, Washington's men destroyed their powder and other stores, including even their private baggage, to prevent its falling into the hands of the Indians. M. DeVilliers sent a detachment to take possession of the fort as soon as Washington's forces defiled therefrom. Washington's regiment left twelve dead on the ground, and the number left by Captain Mackay's company is not known. DeVillier said that the number of dead excited his pity. He reported that the "English have had 70 or 80 men killed or mortally wounded, and many others slightly;" that two French-Canadians were killed and seventy wounded, and that two Indian allies of the French were wounded. (Pa. Archives, Sec. Series, Vol. 6, pages 168-170.)

Thus ended the affair at the Great Meadows, Washington's first and last surrender. On reaching Will's Creek, where his half-famished troops found ample provisions in the military magazine, he hastened with Captain Mackay, to Governor Dinwiddie, at Williamsburg, whom they particularly informed of the events of their expedition. Washington soon thereafter resigned his commission, and retired to private life at Mount Vernon. His first act, after relinquishing his command, was to visit his mother, inquire into the state of her affairs, and look after the welfare of his younger brother and his sister, Betty. He continued his residence at Mount Vernon until the following year, when he again entered the service of Virginia in the army of General Braddock.

DeVilliers' Indian allies were Nipissings and Algonquins from Canada, and when he advanced from Gist's Plantation towards Fort Necessity, they were reluctant to accompany him. At this point, attention is called to the fact that DeVilliers had two reasons, both unknown to Washington, for requesting the cessation of hostilities, which led to Washington's surrender. One was the fact that the Indian allies of the French commander intended to leave him the next day, which would have reduced his force to five hundred Frenchmen, and the other was that the French were almost out of ammunition.

Fearing that Washington would be reinforced, the French commander, after destroying Fort Necessity, the cannon and a quantity of rum, which he did not wish to fall into the hands of his Indian allies, hastened away from the Great Meadows. On the morning of the 5th of July, he arrived at Gist's Plantation, where his forces demolished the stockade which Washington had erected. All the houses in the settlement were burned, including one which had been built in 1753 by William Stewart, where Connellsville now stands. On July 6th, DeVilliers' forces arrived at Redstone (Brownsville), where they burned the storehouse or Hangard which Captain Trent had erected near that place early in 1754. On July 7th, they arrived at Fort Duquesne. A little later they rebuilt Logstown which had been burned by Scarouady about June 24th.

Washington's surrender might well have filled the English with gloom, says Dr. George P. Donehoo, in his "Pennsylvania—A History:"

"When Washington's force marched out of Fort Necessity, carrying the British flag with them, the flag of France flew over the continent from the waters of the Potomac and Susquehanna to the Mississippi. The British dominated the narrow strip along the Atlantic, and that was all. There was not left a single trading house or dwelling place of the English west of the blue ridges of mountains. France had its chain of forts connecting the possessions in Canada with the Ohio Valley, and it was only a question of time when this chain would be completed to the possessions on the Mississippi. The prospect for the Anglo-Saxon conquest of the continent was not a bright one."

Washington's Love for the Great Meadows

To the day of his death, Washington loved the Great Meadows. While the spot on which Jumonville was slain is the site of the first skirmish in which the Revolutionary General was engaged, the Great Meadows is the the site of his first real battle. Here he erected Fort Necessity. Here he valiantly defended the fort against overpowering numbers and amid the drenching rain. Here he occupied a position against which the heaviest fire of the French and Indians was directed. Here he saw his companions sink in death. Here he was compelled to surrender, but with honor. It was the memory of these things that caused the Great Meadows to have a lasting place in his affections. In 1769, he acquired a pre-emption right to two hundred and thirty-four acres of these meadows, including the site of the fort. Later his title was confirmed by Pennsylvania. He referred to these meadows in his will; he owned them at the time of his death, and they were sold by his executors. Throughout our country's history to the last, may the traveler on the National Pike pause amid the mountains of Fayette County to pay homage to the memory of Washington on the spot where he, a Virginia youth, received his baptism of fire and blood.

Captains Van Braam and Stobo

According to the terms of Washington's capitulation, Jacob Van Braam and Robert Stobo, the engineer of Fort Necessity, were given up as hostages to the French until the British should return to Fort Duquesne the French prisoners taken when Jumonville was slain. The Governor of Virginia refused to return the French prisoners, and Van Braam and Stobo were then taken to Canada. While a prisoner at Fort Duquesne, Stobo wrote two letters to the Governor of Virginia, which were entrusted to two Indians friendly to the British, and safely delivered. The first letter, written on July 28th, 1754, and sent by the Indian, Moses, advised the Governor that the French had circulated a rumor among the Indians at and in the vicinity of Fort Duquesne, that Scarouady and other Indians friendly to the British had been killed and their wives and children delivered to the Cherokees and Catawbas for torture. The second letter, written the following day, and sent by Delaware George, contained a sketch of Fort Duquesne. These letters were carefully kept, and delivered to General Braddock, when he took command of the expedition against Fort Duquesne the following year. They were found among his effects on the field of battle, and were sent to Canada. Stobo, who was then a prisoner at Quebec, was tried, and sentenced to be executed, but made his escape. After the close of the French and Indian War, Van Braam lived in Wales and England until the outbreak of the Revolution, when, much against his will, it seems, he entered the service of the British against the Colonies. After the close of the Revolution, Washington received a long letter from his former fencing master and interpreter, giving an account of his experiences after the surrender at Fort Necessity and stating that he was spending his declining days in France. Here this interesting character disappears from history. (See Stobo's letters in Vol. 6 of Colonial Records of Pennsylvania, pages 141 and 161.)

Croghan, Montour and Gist

At this point, it will be well to devote a few paragraphs to three noted characters whom we have met a number of times thus far in this history and who assisted Washington in his campaign of 1754,—George Croghan, Andrew Montour and Christopher Gist.

Croghan was born in Ireland and educated in Dublin. He came to America somewhere between the years 1740 and 1744. He engaged in the Indian trade and appears to have been first licensed as an Indian trader in Pennsylvania, in 1744. In 1746, he was located in Silver Spring Township, in the present county of Cumberland, a few miles west of Harris'Ferry, now Harrisburg. During the same year, he was made a counsellor of the Six Nations at Onondaga, according to his sworn statement; and in March, 1749, he was appointed by the Governor and Council of Pennsylvania one of the justices of the peace in Common Pleas for Lancaster County.

As early as the years 1746 and 1747, he had gone as far as the southwestern border of Lake Erie in his trading expeditions. In 1748, he had a trading house at Logstown, which was made the headquarters of Weiser upon his visit to the Indians of that place, in the month of September, 1748. He had also branch trading establishments at the principal Indian towns in the valleys of the Ohio and Allegheny, one being on the northwestern side of the Allegheny River, at the mouth of Pine Creek, five or six miles above the forks of the Ohio. From this base of operations and from Logstown, trading routes "spread out like the sticks of a fan." One of these routes went up the Allegheny past Venango, (Franklin), where Croghan had a trading house and competed with John Frazer, a Pennsylvania trader from Paxtang, who for some years, had traded at Venango, maintaining both a trading house and gunsmith shop until he was driven off by the French, as has already been seen. Croghan's abilities and influence among the Indians soon attracted the attention of Conrad Weiser, who, in 1747, recommended him to the Pennsylvania Authorities, and, in this way, he entered the service of the Province.

His part in Washington's campaign consisted in furnishing the Virginia forces with flour and ammunition. On May 30th, 1754, he contracted with Governor Dinwiddie, at Winchester, Virginia, to transport to Redstone ten thousand pounds of flour by means of packhorses. Much of the powder and lead used by Washington at Fort Necessity was furnished by Croghan and Captain William Trent, who was his partner and brother-in-law. However, Croghan was so much delayed in furnishing flour that, as we have seen, Washington's forces suffered greatly from hunger in the latter days of the campaign.

The outbreak of the French and Indian War ruined Croghan's prosperous trading business. He was brought to the verge of bankruptcy and threatened with imprisonment for debt. Then the Pennsylvania Assembly passed an act giving him immunity from arrest for ten years, in order that the Province might have the benefit of his services and influence among the Indians. To add to his financial troubles, the Irish traders, because most of them were Roman Catholics, fell under suspicion of acting as spies for the French, and Croghan was unjustly suspicioned by many in authority. He was granted a captain's commission to command the Indian allies during Braddock's campaign, and was at Braddock's defeat.

Early in 1756, Croghan resigned from the Pennsylvania service and went to New York, where his distant relative, Sir William Johnson, chose him deputy Indian agent, and appointed him to manage the Allegheny and Susquehanna tribes. From this time, he was engaged for several years in important dealings with the Western Indians, and had much to do in swaying them to the British interest and making possible the success of General Forbes, in 1758. In 1763, he went to England on private business, and was shipwrecked upon the coast of France. Upon his return to America in 1765, he was dispatched to Illinois, going by way of the Ohio River, and was taken prisoner near the mouth of the Wabash, and carried to the Indian towns upon that river. Here he not only secured his own release, but conducted negotiations putting an end to Pontiac's War. He also took part in the Great Treaty of Fort Stanwix (Rome, New York), in 1768, and, as a reward, was given a grant of land in Cherry Valley, New York. Shortly prior to this, however, he had purchased a tract on the Allegheny, about four miles above the mouth of the Monongahela, where he entertained George Washington in 1770. When the Revolutionary War came on, it seems he embarked in the patriotic cause, and later was an object of suspicion; and then Pennsylvania proclaimed him a public enemy, and his place as Indian agent was conferred upon Colonel George Morgan. He continued, however, to reside in Pennsylvania—the scene of his early activities and the Colony which he rendered such signal service—and died at Passayunk on August 31, 1782. His funeral was conducted at the Episcopal Church of St. Peter's in Philadelphia, but the place of his burial remains unknown.

Croghan's Mohawk daughter became the third wife of the celebrated Mohawk Chief, Joseph Brant.

Andrew Montour, the "Half Indian," whose Indian name was Sattelihu, was the eldest and most noted of the children of Madam Montour. He is one of the most picturesque Indian characters in the early history of Pennsylvania, and accompanied George

Croghan on many of his missions to the Indians of the Ohio and Allegheny valleys. Governor Dinwiddie gave him a captain's commission "to head a select company of friendly Indians, as scouts for our small army," when Virginia was raising forces for the occupation of the Forks of the Ohio, early in 1754. Montour, however, did not organize a company of Indians, as he had been instructed, but raised a company of traders and woodsmen, who had been driven from the valley of the Ohio on the approach of the French. His company consisted of eighteen men, and with these, he and Croghan joined Washington at the Great Meadows on the 9th of June. Montour and his forces assisted Washington in the battle of Fort Necessity, on July 3rd and 4th, where two of his men, Daniel Lafferty and Henry O'Brien, were taken prisoners

In the spring of 1755, Montour and Croghan, with about fifty Indian braves, joined Braddock's army at Cumberland; but after the army began to advance on Fort Duquesne, many of these Indian allies deserted or were dismissed by Braddock. However, Montour continued with the army and took part in its overwhelming defeat. Throughout the French and Indian War, he took part as interpreter in many Indian councils with the Pennsylvania and New York authorities, and was sent on a number of important missions. In Pontiac's War, he was also faithful to the English. He was one of the interpreters at the treaty with the Six Nations at Fort Stanwix (Rome, N. Y.), in October, 1768, at which the Penns made their last purchase of lands from the Indians. During the year 1769, Montour was granted a tract of three hundred acres, situated on the south side of the Ohio River opposite Montour's Island, about nine miles below the mouth of the Monongahela. Soon thereafter this picturesque character disappears from history. A town, a creek, an island, a county, a mountain range—all in Pennsylvania—are named for him and his mother.

We have met Christopher Gist a number of times in this history—as the explorer and surveyor of the Ohio Company, as Washington's guide on his mission to St. Pierre, and in Washington's campaign of 1754. At least as early as the spring of 1753, this noted pathfinder had made a settlement of some Virginia families in the vicinity of what is now Mount Braddock, Fayette County. He served faithfully in Braddock's campaign of 1755 and with his sons, Nathaniel and Thomas, was in the terrible defeat of the haughty British general on the banks of the Monongahela. After Braddock's defeat, he raised a company of scouts in Virginia and Maryland and rendered service on the harried frontier, being then called Captain Gist. In 1756, he was sent to the Carolinas to enlist the Cherokee Indians in the British service in the French and Indian War. In 1757, he became deputy Indian agent in the South, a position "for which," said Washington, "I know of no person so well qualified. He has had extensive dealings with the Indians, is in great esteem among them, well acquainted with their manners and customs, indefatigable and patient." According to most authorities, he died of smallpox in the summer of 1759, in either South Carolina or Georgia.

This trusted friend of Washington deserves to be remembered for all time. He was one of the earliest Anglo-Saxon explorers of the vast region comprising the states of Ohio and Kentucky. Concerning this region he reported to the Ohio Company: "Nothing is wanted but cultivation to make this a most delightful country."

(For account of Christopher Gist's explorations for the Ohio Company, the reader is referred to William M. Darlington's "Christopher Gist's Journals.")

The Albany Treaty and Purchase of 1754

In order to combine the efforts of the Colonies in resisting the encroachments of the French, a conference was ordered by the British Ministry, to be held at Albany, New York, in June and July, 1754, to which the Six Nations were invited. Governor Hamilton, of Pennsylvania, unable to be present, commissioned John Penn and Richard Peters of the Provincial Council, and Isaac Norris and Benjamin Franklin, of the Assembly, to attend the conference in his stead. Conrad Weiser also attended the conference as interpreter in the negotiations with the Six Nations. At this conference, a plan was proposed for a political union, and adopted on the very day that Washington surrendered at Fort Necessity. It was subsequently submitted to the Home Government and the Provincial Assemblies. The Home Government condemned it, according to Franklin, on account of its being too democratic; and the various Provincial Assemblies objected to it as containing too much power of the King. Pennsylvania negatived it without discussion.

At this Albany Conference, the title of the Iroquois to the Ohio Valley was recognized, and the Pennsylvania commissioners secured from the Iroquois a great addition to the Province, to which the Indian title was not extinct. The deed, which was signed by the chiefs of the Six Nations on July 6, 1754, conveyed to Pennsylvania all the land extending on the west side of the Susquehanna River from the Blue Mountains to a mile above the mouth of Kayarondinhagh (Penn's) Creek; thence northwest by west to the western boundary of the Province; thence along the western boundary to the southern boundary; thence along the southern boundary to the Blue Mountains; and thence along the Blue Mountains to the place of beginning.

Although the Great Council of the Iroquois declared at the Albany Treaty that they would not sell their lands in the Wyoming Valley to either Pennsylvania or Connecticut, but would reserve them as a hunting ground and for the residence of such Indians as cared to remove from the French and settle there, and also declared that the Onondaga Council had appointed Shikellamy's son, John, in charge of this territory; yet, before the Treaty was closed, the Mohawks very irregularly sold the Wyoming lands to Connecticut.

This Albany Treaty, which secured the neutrality of the Six Nations during the French and Indian War, was the first official acknowledgment of the independence of the Iroquois Confederation by delegates from all the Colonies. It was a truly historic assembly. Even until the present day, the Iroquois Confederation has been considered an independent Nation by the United States Government. (For account of the Albany Conference and Treaty, see Penna. Col. Rec. Vol. 6, pages 57 to 128.)

Tanacharison Complains of Washington and Protests Albany Purchase

After the defeat of Washington at the Great Meadows, Tanacharison and Scarouady, with some of their followers, "came down to the back parts of Virginia," and then with Seneca George and about three hundred Mingos (Iroquois), retreated to George Croghan's trading post at Aughwick, now Shirleysburg, Huntingdon County. At about the same time, some Shawnees, Delawares, and an inconsiderable number of renegades of the Seneca tribe of the Six Nations, joined the French. Tanacharison and Scarouady after retreating to Aughwick, sent out messages to assemble the friendly Delawares and Shawnees at that place, and asked the Colony of Pennsylvania to support their women and children while the warriors fought on the side of the English, whom they expected speedily to take decisive steps against the French. In response to these messages, great swarms of excited Indians came to Aughwick, clamoring for food, and were fed at the expense of the Colony throughout the fall and winter. Here most of them remained until General Braddock's army arrived at Cumberland Maryland, in the spring of 1755, when they went to join his army. Here, also Queen Allaquippa died in December, 1754.

George Croghan was in charge of distributing provisions and supplies to the friendly Indians, who had assembled at Aughwick after Washington's surrender at Fort Necessity. The bills which he was sending the Colonial Authorities for feeding these Indians having grown rather large, Croghan was suspicioned as not being reliable, and finally there were hints that he was in league with the French. The Pennsylvania Assembly then cut down his bills, and he decided to leave Aughwick. Conrad Weiser was then directed by the Colonial Authorities to go to Aughwick, and make a report on Croghan. He reached this place on August 31st, 1754, being accompanied by Tanacharison from Harris' Ferry, now Harrisburg.

"On the way," says Weiser, "Tanacharison complained very much of the behavior of Colonel Washington, (though in a very moderate way, saying the Colonel was a good-natured man, but had no experience); that he took upon him to command the Indians as his slaves, and would have them every day upon the Out Scout, and attack the Enemy by themselves, and that he would by no means take advice from the Indians; that he lay at one place from one full moon to another, and made no fortifications at all but that little thing upon the meadow, [Fort Necessity] where he thought the French would come up to him in open field; that had he taken the Half King's advice and made such fortifications as the Half King advised him to make, he would certainly have beat the French off; that the French had acted as great cowards and the English as fools in that engagement; that he [the Half King] had carried off his wife and children; so did other Indians before the battle begun, because Colonel Washington would never listen to them, but was always driving them on to fight by his directions."

Weiser found that Croghan was entirely worthy of being trusted. He also found that the inhabitants of Cumberland County caused much trouble in selling so much strong liquor to the Indians assembled at Aughwick. In the conferences which he held with Tanacharison, Scarouady, King Beaver, and various other chiefs, he completely won old Tanacharison and his people back to the English cause after their anger at Washington and the Virginians. Moreover, at these conferences, Weiser learned that the Shawnees and Delawares had formed an alliance; that the French had offered them presents, either to join them or to remain neutral, and that to these proposals, the Delawares made no reply, but at once sent their deputies to Aughwick for the purpose, as Weiser thought, of learning the attitude of the English.

Near the close of the conference, Tanacharison and Scarouady pressed Weiser to tell them what transpired at the Albany Treaty; and he then told them all about the purchase of the vast tract west of the Susquehanna. "They seemed not to be very well pleased," says Weiser, "because the Six Nations had sold such a large tract." Weiser then explained that the purchase was made in order to frustrate land schemes of the Connecticut interests, and of the French on the Ohio. This appeared to satisfy them, though they resented not receiving a part of the consideration. For a time they were content, not knowing that the purchase included most of the lands on the West Branch of the Susquehanna. The Shawnee and Delaware deputies then went back to the Ohio into danger and temptations, and to learn from the French that their vast hunting grounds on the West Branch of the Susquehanna had been sold to the Province of Pennsylvania at the Albany Treaty.

No wonder that Tanacharison and Scarouady complained to Weiser. The Albany purchase was a very powerful factor in alienating, not only the Delawares, but the other Indians, from Pennsylvania. The Shawnees and Delawares of the Munsee Clan (Monseys) in the valleys of the Susquehanna, Juniata, Allegheny, and Ohio, thus found their lands "sold from under their feet" which the Six Nations had guaranteed to them, so they claimed, on their migration to these valleys. It was provided in the contract of sale of these lands that half of the purchase price should be paid upon delivery of the deed, and the remainder was not to be paid until the settlers had actually crossed the Allegheny Mountains, and taken up their abode in the purchased territory. The Indians declared in July, 1755, that they would not receive the second installment, but the Mohawk chief, Hendricks, persuaded them to stand by the deed. After Braddock was defeated on July 9, 1755, the entire body of dissatisfied Indians on the Albany Purchase took bitter vengeance on Pennsylvania. After three years of bloodshed, outrage and murder, Conrad Weiser persuaded the Proprietaries of Pennsylvania to deed back to the Indians that part of the Albany purchase which lay west of the Allegheny Mountains. This was done at the treaty at Easton, in October, 1758, which treaty will be discussed in a later chapter.

Death of Tanacharison

After the series of conferences with Conrad Weiser at Aughwick, in September, 1754, Tanacharison returned to the trading house of John Harris, at Harris' Ferry, where he became dangerously ill; and a conjuror, or "medicineman," was summoned to make inquiry into the cause and nature of his malady. The "medicineman" gave it as his opinion that the French had bewitched Tanacharison in revenge for the great blow he had struck them in the affair of Jumonville; for the Indians gave him the whole credit of that success, Tanacharison having made it clear that it was he who killed Jumonville, in revenge of the French, who, as he declared, had killed, boiled, and eaten his father. Furthermore, Tanacharison had sent around the French scalps taken at that action, as trophies. All the friends of the old chieftain concurred in the opinion of the "medicineman," and when Tanacharison died at the house of John Harris, on October 4, 1754, there was great lamentation among the Indians, mingled with threats of immediate vengeance. Thus was this noted sachem gathered to his fathers in the "Happy Hunting Ground," at a time when his services and influence among the Western Indians were greatly needed by the English.

CHAPTER VI

General Braddock's Campaign

THE news of Washington's surrender at the Great Meadows produced a feeling of alarm throughout the Colonies and also among the members of the King's cabinet. The Treaty of Aix-la-Chapelle, which closed King George's War, was still in force. Officially, at least, Great Britain and France were at peace. Yet the British Government realized that France meant to take and retain possession of the valleys of the Ohio and Allegheny by force of arms. Great Britain, therefore, began to make arrangements for sending troops to America to resist the aggressions of the French. General Edward Braddock was selected as commander-in-chief of these forces.

Braddock sailed for Virginia on December 21st, 1754, with his staff and a small part of his troops, leaving the main body to follow on January 14th, 1755. On February 20th, he arrived in Virginia. At a council of Governor Shirley of Massachusetts, Governor Dinwiddie of Virginia, Governor Delancy of New York, Governor Morris of Pennsylvania, Governor Sharpe of Maryland and Governor Dobbs of North Carolina, held at Alexandria, Virginia, on April 14th, 1755, the plans of military operations were definitely formed. Three expeditions were decided upon: one against Niagara and Frontenac, under General Shirley; one against Crown Point, under General William Johnson; and one against Fort Duquesne, under General Braddock. The expedition against Fort Duquesne was considered the most important, and is the only one we shall discuss in this history. It was made up of the Forty-fourth and Forty-eighth Royal Regiments of Foot, commanded by Sir Peter Halket and Colonel Thomas Dunbar, of New York Independent Companies of Foot, and of South Carolina, Maryland and Virginia troops.

The Army Assembles at Cumberland

Without setting forth the details of the forming of Braddock's expedition, we state that his army assembled at Will's Creek, or

Fort Cumberland, where the city of Cumberland, Maryland now stands. Braddock joined his forces here early in May. Here came Colonel George Washington, who was chosen as one of Braddock's aides-de-camp. Here, also, Braddock received two hundred wagons and two hundred and fifty horses from York and Lancaster Counties, Pennsylvania, principally through the efforts of Benjamin Franklin, who, in the latter part of April, sent handbills throughout the counties of York, Lancaster and Cumberland, containing the threat of Quartermaster-General Sir John St. Clair to send an armed force into these counties to seize wagons and horses for the expedition.

In this connection we state that Braddock told Franklin he was sure his army would not be detained long at Fort Duquesne and that, after capturing that place, he would press on to Niagara and Frontenac without any obstruction being offered. Franklin then warned him of the danger of being ambushed by Indian allies of the French. "He smiled at my ignorance," says Franklin in his Autobiography, "and replied: 'These savages may indeed be a formidable enemy to your raw American militia, but upon the King's regular and disciplined troops, sir, it is impossible that they should make any impression.' "

Braddock planned to advance on Fort Duquesne over the route followed by Washington's expedition of the preceeding summer, which, it will be recalled, was originally the Nemacolin Indian Trail. In order that his army might procure food and other supplies from the fertile counties of Eastern Pennsylvania, the Province of Pennsylvania directed Colonel James Burd to cut a road from McDowell's Mill, in the western part of Franklin County, to join the Braddock road at or near Turkey Foot, now Confluence. Braddock was very anxious that the Burd road be completed before his army would arrive at the Great Crossings of the Youghiogheny (Somerfield, Somerset County). He issued orders later that the work of cutting a road from Raystown (Bedford, Pa.) to Fort Cumberland be left unfinished until Colonel Burd would finish cutting the road to Turkey Foot, and he sent one hundred troops from Fort Cumberland under Captain Hogg to act as a guard for Burd's road-cutters. However, Colonel Burd had cut his road only to the crest of the Allegheny Mountains by the time of Braddock's defeat.

Most students of Braddock's expedition are of the opinion that the starting place for Fort Duquesne should have been Philadelphia or Carlisle. Probably the starting place would have been in Pennsylvania, if the Pennsylvania Assembly had realized the impending danger of a successful French invasion and occupation of the valleys of the Ohio and Allegheny, and had not spent its time disputing with Governor Morris. After the Governor had called the attention of the Assembly to the fact that the French had invaded a large part of the Province, this body replied, on January 3d, 1755, that "the French Forts and their other Acquisitions on the Ohio are constantly considered and called in Great Britain an Invasion upon His Majesty's Territory of Virginia." Pennsylvania had been requested to enlist men to fill the gaps in the Forty-fourth and Forty-eighth Regiments. This was not done. Furthermore, early in January, the Assembly adjourned until May, without doing anything to put the Province in a state of defense. Governor Morris then told the Assembly that "all the fatal Consequences that may attend your leaving the Province in this defenseless State must lie at your Doors." (Pa. Col. Rec., Vol. 6, pages 227 to 247, especially pages 233, 234, 240 and 247.)

Without going further into the dispute between the Pennsylvania Assembly and Governor Morris, we state that, on account of this dispute and consequent inaction on the part of Pennsylvania, the British Government realized that any movement of troops against Fort Duquesne would have to be made from Virginia and by Virginia's assistance.

Braddock's Indian Allies

Braddock expected to receive many Indian allies, especially Catawbas and Cherokees of the South, which Governor Dinwiddie had promised. None of these southern warriors came. He urged George Croghan, Cristopher Gist and Governor Morris, of Pennsylvania, to persuade Indians of the Ohio and Allegheny to join his forces. But the Delawares and Shawnees of these valleys, alienated from the English interest by the fraudulent Walking Purchase of 1737, the land sales at the Treaty of 1736, and especially by the Albany Purchase of 1754, were in no frame of mind to take up arms against the sympathizing French. At best, they were waiting to see which side would win in the impending contest. Finally, in the latter part of May, George Croghan and Andrew Montour brought from Aughwick (Shirleysburg, Pa.) to Braddock's camp at Cumberland about fifty warriors, mostly of the Six Nations. Many of these Indians had been in Washington's campaign of the preceeding summer, had deserted him before the battle at Fort Necessity, and then had been fed at the expense of Pennsylvania, by Croghan, at Aughwick, throughout the autumn and winter.

Scarouady, successor to Tanacharison, was the leader of the Indians brought by Croghan and Montour. Other chiefs were White Thunder (The Belt), Silver Heels (Aroas), so called, probably, on account of being fleet of foot, Canachquasy (Captain New Castle) and Carondowanen (Great Tree). Scarouady addressed the assembled Indians, and urged them to take up the English cause with vigor.

Washington Irving's "Life of Washington" contains the following interesting paragraphs concerning the assembling of Scarouady and his warriors at Cumberland.

"Notwithstanding his secret contempt for the Indians, Braddock, agreeably to his instructions, treated them with great ceremony. A grand council was held in his tent, at Fort Cumberland, where all his officers attended. The chiefs, and all the warriors, came painted and decorated for war. They were received with military honors, the guards resting on their firearms. The general made tham a speech through his interpreter, expressing the grief of their father, the great King of England, at the death of the Half King, Tanacharison, and made them presents to console them. They in return promised their aid as guides and scouts, and declared eternal enmity to the French, following the declaration with the war song, 'making a terrible noise.'

"The general, to regale and astonish them, ordered all the artillery to be fired, 'the drums and fifes playing and beating the point of war;' the fete ended by their feasting in their own camp on a bullock which the general had given them, following up their repast by dancing the war dance round a fire, to the sound of their uncouth drums and rattles, 'making night hideous,' by howls and yellings.

"For a time all went well. The Indians had their separate camp, where they passed half the night singing, dancing, and howling. The British were amused by their strange ceremonies, their savage antics, and savage decorations. The Indians, on the other hand, loitered by day about the English camp, fiercely painted and arrayed, gazing with silent admiration at the parade of the troops, their marchings and evolutions; and delighted with the horse-races, with which the young officers recreated themselves.

"Unluckily the warriors had brought their families with them to Will's Creek, and the women were even fonder than the men of loitering about the British camp. They were not destitute of attractions; for the young squaws resemble the gypsies, having seductive forms, small hands and feet, and soft voices. Among those who visited the camp was one who no doubt passed for an Indian princess. She was the daughter of the sachem, White Thunder, and bore the dazzling name of Bright Lightning. The charms of these wild-wood beauties were soon acknowledged. 'The squaws,' writes Secretary Peters, 'bring in money plenty; the officers are scandalously fond of them.'

"The jealousy of the warriors was aroused; some of them became furious. To prevent discord, the squaws were forbidden to come into the British camp. This did not prevent their being sought elsewhere. It was ultimately found necessary, for the sake of quiet, to send Bright Lightning, with all the other women and children, back to Aughwick. White Thunder, and several of the warriors, accompanied them for their protection.

"As to the Delaware chiefs, they returned to the Ohio, promising the general they would collect their warriors together, and meet him on his march. They never kept their word. 'These people are villians, and always side with the strongest,' says a shrewd journalist of the expedition.

"Either from disgust thus caused, or from being actually dismissed, the warriors began to disappear from the camp. It is said that Colonel Innes, who was to remain in command at Fort Cumberland, advised the dismissal of all but a few to serve as guides; certain it is, before Braddock recommended his march, none remained to accompany him but Scarouady and eight of his warriors."

Neither White Thunder nor any of the other Indians who conducted the Indian women back to Aughwick returned to Braddock's army. The faithful eight Iroquois chiefs who remained with the army and fought in the battle on the banks of the Monongahela, were thanked by Governor Morris, of Pennsylvania, at a meeting of the Provincial Council, held on August 15th, 1755, in whose minutes their names are given. They were at the meeting. (See Pa. Col. Rec., Vol. 6, page 524).

"Captain Jack"

At this point attention is called to the fact that many historians have made the statement that, when Braddock arrived at the

Little Meadows, soon to be mentioned again, "Captain Jack, the Wild Hunter of the Juniata," offered him the services of himself and his band of backwoodsmen, which offer was distainfully refused. But "Captain Jack, the Wild Hunter," was a mythical character. He never existed, except as the beau ideal of the period. Many legends concerning this mythical frontiersman, "with the eye of an eagle and an aim that was unerring, are given in McKnights "Captain Jack, the Scout."

Many have confused the mythical "Captain Jack" with the real Captain Patrick Jack, of the Cumberland Valley, who, it is claimed, at the suggestion of Benjamin Franklin, offered Braddock the services of his band of foresters as guides, which offer the General declined to accept, giving as a reason that he already had secured guides for his expedition. At least this is the tradition that has been handed down to the descendants of Captain Patrick Jack. Many, too, have confused the mythical character with Andrew Montour, the Half Indian; others with the White Mingo; and others with Captain William Patterson, of the Juniata Valley. (See Frontier Forts of Penna., Sec. Edition, Vol. 2, page 643; also Hanna's "Wilderness Trail," Vol. 2, page 57).

The March from Cumberland to the Fatal Field

On June 7th, Sir Peter Halket's division took up the march from Cumberland, followed, on June 8th, by Lieutenant-Colonel Burton's division, and, on June 10th, by Colonel Thomas Dunbar's division, accompanied by Braddock and his aides. Colonel Innes was left in command of Fort Cumberland, with a detachment of Colonial troops.

On June 16th, the army reached the Little Meadows, about three miles east of Grantsville, Maryland. Here Braddock decided to divide his army. On the 18th of June, four hundred men were sent forward to cut the road to the Little Crossing, (Grantsville) and, on the following day, Braddock followed with a detachment of five hundred men, the officers, and the "two eldest Grenadier Companies," making, in all, somewhat more than twelve hundred officers and men. The rest of the army about eight hundred and fifty men and officers, under command, of Colonel Dunbar, was to follow by slower stages, with the heavy baggage, heavy artillery and stores and with most of the women accompanying the army. It was Washington who advised hastening forward with the best troops and as little baggage as possible.

For several days he had been very ill of fever. On account of this illness, he was left, on June 19th, at the camp at the Little Crossing, under the care of Dr. Craik, by the positive orders of Braddock. He traveled with Dunbar's division, until July 3d, then hastened forward from a point near the Great Meadows, weak as he was, and joined the main army under Braddock the day before the battle.

Leaving Colonel Dunbar, we shall follow General Braddock's army on its march through the wilderness and over the mountains to the fatal field. On June 19th, his army reached Bear Camp, which was almost on the Maryland and Pennsylvania line, about three miles southeast of Addison, Somerset County. During this day's march, Scarouady and his son, who were marching with the other Indian allies as an advanced party and were some distance from the line of march, were surrounded and captured by some French and Indians. The son escaped and brought the intelligence to the warriors, who hastened to rescue or avenge the aged chief, but found him tied to a tree. The French had been disposed to kill him; but the Indians with them declared that they would abandon the French should they do so, thus showing some tie of friendship or kindred with Scarouady, who then rejoined Braddock's forces unharmed.

By the 23rd of June, the army reached Squaw Fort, situated a short distance southeast of Somerfield, Somerset County. On June 24th, it passed over the Great Crossing of the Youghiogheny and encamped three or four miles east of the Great Meadows, the site of Fort Necessity, where Washington surrendered the year before. On June 25th, it marched over the very spot where Braddock was buried a fortnight later, and encamped at the Orchard Camp, where he died on the night of July 13th. Both the Orchard Camp and the place of Braddock's burial are not far from the Summit on the National Pike, in Fayette County. On the morning of this day (June 25th), three men, venturing beyond the sentinels, were shot and scalped by Indians. On June 26th, the army encamped at Rock Fort Camp, not far from Washington's Spring, where, it will be remembered, Tanacharison was encamped with his warriors when he and Washington set out to make the attack on Jumonville. On June 27th, the army reached Gist's Plantation, the present Mount Braddock, in Fayette County. On June 28th, the army reached Stewart's Crossing on the Youghiogheny, at Connellsville, Fayette County, where it encamped on the western side of this stream. The army remained in camp all day during the 29th, and crossed to the eastern side of the Youghiogheny, on the 30th, encamping about a mile from the river.

At this point, attention is called to the fact that, from Gist's Plantation to Stewart's Crossing, Braddock's army followed the course of the Catawba Indian Trail, leading from the domain of the Senecas and other members of the Iroquois Confederation to the territory of the Catawbas and Cherokees; also to the fact that, at his camp on the eastern side of the Youghiogheny, on June 30th, General Braddock wrote what was very likely the last letter, official or otherwise, penned by his hand. This was a letter to Governor Morris, urging that Colonel Burd's road be speedily completed and advising of attacks upon some settlers near Fort Cumberland by hostile Indians. (Pa. Col. Rec., Vol. 6, pages 475–476).

On July 1st, the army encamped at what is known as the Camp at the Great Swamp, the location of which was near the old Iron Bridge, southeast of Mount Pleasant, Westmoreland County, and near the headwaters of Jacob's and Mount's creeks. On July 2nd, the army encamped at Jacob's Cabin, making a march of about six miles. This "cabin" belonged to the famous Delaware chief, Captain Jacobs. On July 3rd, the army passed near Mount Pleasant, and encamped at the headwaters of Sewickley Creek, about five miles southeast of Madison, Westmoreland County. The camp at this place was called Salt Lick Camp. On July 4th, the army encamped at Thicketty-Run (Sewickley Creek), about a mile west of Madison. From this camp two Indians were sent forward as scouts, as was also Christopher Gist. All three returned on the 6th, the Indians bringing the scalp of a French officer they had killed near Fort Duquesne. Mr. Gist had intended to spy around the fort at night, but was discovered and pursued by two Indians. He narrowly escaped with his life. On July 6th, the army reached Camp Monacatoocha, so named in honor of Scarouady, or Monacatoocha, on account of the following sad event:

On the 6th of July, three or four soldiers, loitering in the rear of Braddock's forces, were killed and scalped by the Indian allies of the French, and several of the grenadiers set off to take revenge. These came upon a party of the Indians who held up boughs and grounded their arms as the sign of amity. Either Braddock's grenadiers did not perceive this sign, or else misunderstood it. At any rate, they fired upon the Indians and one of them fell, who proved to be the son of Scarouady. The grenadiers brought the body of the young warrior to camp. Braddock then sent for Scarouady and the other Indians, and condoled with them on the lamentable occurrence, making them the customary presents to wipe away their tears. He also caused the young man to be buried with the honors of war, and at his request the officers attended the funeral and fired a volley over the grave. The camp that night, located about two miles southeast of Irwin, Westmoreland County was given the name of Camp Monacatoocha, in honor of Scarouady. Says Irving:

"These soldier-like tributes of respect to the deceased and sympathy with the survivors, soothed the feelings and gratified the pride of the father, and attached him more firmly to the service. We are glad to record an anecdote so contrary to the general contempt for the Indians with which Braddock stands charged. It speaks well for the real kindness of his heart."

On July 7th, Braddock on advice of Gist and Montour, abandoned the Indian trail, in order to avoid the dangerous Narrows of Turtle Creek; and turning sharply westward, the army followed the valley of Long Run at or near Stewartsville, and encamped on the night of July 8th, about two miles from the Monongahela and an equal distance from the mouth of the Youghiogheny, near McKeesport, Allegheny County. This was the last camp of the army before the fatal encounter. Here George Washington, who had been left at the Little Crossing near Grantsville, Maryland, on June 19th, on account of illness, rejoined the army on the evening of July 8th, bringing with him from Dunbar's division a detachment, sent to guard a pack-horse train carrying provisions for Braddock's army. It is seen, therefore, that Washington had not been with Braddock's army during the long march from the Little Crossing, near Grantsville, Maryland.

After the arrival of Washington's detachment, Braddock's forces numbered 1,460 officers and men besides women and camp followers. July 9th dawned bright and clear. Braddock would reach Fort Duquesne before evening. He felt certain of victory. Although French and Indians had lurked in the woods, near his line of march, from the time his army left Cumberland, yet there had been no ambush of his forces, owing to the vigilance of Christopher Gist, Andrew Montour, Scarouady and other scouts. As has been seen, his Indian scouts had approached near the fort. They and Gist reported, on July 6th, that there were no signs of ambush and no signs of preparations for resistance. Nor, in fact, was Braddock ambushed on the fatal ninth day of July, when his army went down to overwhelming and inglorious defeat at the hands of the French and their Indian allies. It is true that the French officer, Beaujeu, had planned an ambush, and picked a place for it on the evening of July 8th. In the meantime, Braddock had crossed the Monongahela and started up the slopes of the field of encounter before the French and Indians arrived at the place which they had selected for ambushing him. We think it well to point out this fact before we describe the battle (See the French account of the battle, in Pa. Archives, Sec. Series, Vol. 6, page 256).

But to return to the early morning of the fatal day. To reach Fort Duquesne, it was necessary for Braddock's army to cross to the south side of the Monongahela, march some distance along the south bank, then return to the north bank by again fording the stream.

At three o'clock on the morning of July 9th, Colonel Gage was sent with about four hundred men to secure both fords of the river and to hold the northern bank of the second ford. At four o'clock, Sir John St. Clair, with a detachment of two hundred and fifty men, was sent to make a road for transporting the artillery and baggage. At eight o'clock, Braddock crossed the first ford to the south bank of the Monongahela. Here his forces took up the line of march along the south shore, and, when they had gone about a mile, Braddock received word from Colonel Gage that he had carried out the General's orders and posted himself on the north bank to secure the second ford. Presently the entire army crossed the second ford, and formed along the north shore, just below the mouth of Turtle Creek, where the town of Braddock now stands.

The march along the south shore of the Monongahela was an imposing spectacle—with arms cleaned the night before, gleaming in the summer sunshine, with officers and men, clad in their best uniforms, stepping buoyantly to the inspiring music of the "Grenadiers' March," which the drums and fifes were beating and playing, with the flag of England flying in the breeze. Washington looked upon the scene with deep emotion, and, in after years, spoke of it as the most beautiful sight he ever beheld. The fording to the north shore was made with bayonets fixed, drums beating, fifes playing and colors flying, as before.

The Battle of the Monongahela

The army is now on the north shore of the Monongahela. Fort Duquesne is only ten miles away. It is almost two o'clock. After a halt, General Braddock has arranged the order of march. First moves the advance, under Colonel Gage, preceeded by the engineers and six light horsemen. These are followed by Sir John St. Clair and the working party, with wagons and two cannon, four flanking parties being thrown out on each side. General Braddock is soon to follow with the main body, the artillery and baggage, preceeded and flanked by light horse and infantry; while the Virginia and other Colonial troops are to form the rear guard.

The advanced party, under Gage, has proceeded beyond the first high ground and is just going up the second when one of the engineers, marking the course of the road, sees French and Indians directly in front of him. He gives the alarm, "French and Indians"! Beaujeu, their leader, is wearing a gay hunting shirt and silver gorget on his breast, as he leads them on. They are on the run, indicating that they have just come from Fort Duquesne. Both sides are equally surprised. Both sides fire upon each other. Beaujeu is killed at the first fire. Upon his fall, the Indians begin to waver, terrified at the roar of St. Clair's cannon. The command of the French and Indians now devolves upon M. Dumas. With great presence of mind, he rallies the Indians and orders his officers to lead them to the wings and attack the British on the flank, while he, with the French soldiers, will maintain a position in front. His orders are promptly obeyed.

General Braddock hears the quick and heavy firing in front and the terrible yelling of the Indians. He orders Colonel Burton to hasten to the assistance of the advanced party, with the van guard, eight hundred strong. The rest of the army, four hundred strong, are halted and posted to protect the artillery and baggage. The General sends an aid-de-camp forward to bring him an account of the attack. He does not wait for the aid-de-camp's return, but, finding the turmoil and uproar increasing, he and Washington move forward, leaving Sir Peter Halket in charge of the baggage.

In the meantime Gage has ordered his men to fix bayonets and form in order of battle. They do so in terror, and he now orders them to scale the hill on the right from which there is the heaviest firing, but they will not quit the line of march, dismayed by the terrible yells of the Indians, who have now extended themselves along the hill and in the ravines which traverse the field.

The whereabouts of the Indians are known only by their blood-curdling cries and the puffs of smoke from their rifles. The soldiers fire when they see the smoke. The officers' orders are not heeded. The men shoot at random, killing some of their own flanking parties and of the van guard. In a few minutes most of the officers and men of the advance are killed or wounded. Gage himself is wounded. His detachment falls back upon the detachment which followed.

Braddock has now arrived, and is trying to rally the men, but they heed neither his entreaties nor his threats. They will not fight when they can not see the enemy. The Virginia troops, however, accustomed to the Indian mode of fighting, spring into the forest, take post behind trees and rocks, and, in this manner, pick off some of the lurking foe. Washington urges Braddock to adopt the same plan with the regulars, but he persists in forming them into platoons. Consequently they are cut down without mercy. Some, indeed, attempt to take to trees, but the General storms at them and calls them cowards. He even strikes them with the flat of his sword. In the meantime, the regulars kill many of the Virginians, firing as they see the puffs of smoke from their rifles in the forest.

The slaughter of the officers is terrible. The Indians fire from their coverts at every one on horseback, or who appears to have command. Colonel Burton, and Sir John St. Clair are wounded. Sir Peter Halket is shot down at the head of his regiment. Secretary Shirley is shot through the head, falling by the side of Braddock, who still remains in the center of the field in the hope of retrieving the fortunes of the day. He has seen his trusted officers shot down all around him. Two of his aides, Captain Robert Orme and Captain Roger Morris, are wounded. Four horses have now been shot and killed under Braddock; still he keeps his ground. At length, as he mounts a fifth horse, a bullet passes through his right arm and lodges itself in his lungs. He falls from his horse into the arms of Captain Robert Stewart, of the Virginia Light Horse. The mortally wounded General asks to be left amid the dead and dying on the scene of slaughter, but Captain Stewart and another Virginian officer assisted by Braddock's servant, Bishop, later carry him from the field in his military scarf.

Amid the carnage, with the war-whoop of the Indians ringing in his ears, with the groans of the dying bringing unutterable sadness to his soul, Washington distinguishes himself by his courage and presence of mind. His brother aides, Orme and Morris, having been wounded early in the action, the whole duty of carrying the orders of the General has devolved on him. He dashes to every part of the field, and is a conspicuous mark for the rifles of the Indians. A chief and his warriors single him out, and, after firing at him many times, the chief orders the warriors to desist, believing the life of the brave young Virginian is protected by the Great Spirit. (When Washington, in 1770, in company with Dr. Craik and William Crawford, made a journey down the Ohio River to explore lands given the Virginia soldiers, the Indian chief who fired at him so often in this battle, made a long journey to meet him.) The men who should have served Sir Peter Halket's cannon are paralyzed with terror. Washington springs from his horse, wheels and points a brass field-piece with his own hands, and directs an effective discharge into the woods. Two horses are shot under him. Four bullets pass through his coat. Dr. James Craik, as he attends the wounded, watches him with great anxiety, as he dashes from place to place in the most exposed manner. Yet Washington miraculously escapes without a wound.

The battle lasted until five o'clock. Just before Braddock was shot, the drums beat a retreat, but, by this time, most of the survivors, abandoning their arms, had crossed the Monongahela in headlong flight, at the same ford across which they had come, in proud array, to the field of death a few hours before. Neither the French nor the Indians pursued the fugitives. The Indians remained on the field to scalp and plunder the dead. This saved the life of many a fugitive. Had the French and Indians followed the broken fragments of the army, it is likely that none would have escaped. Later many of the Indians returned home, being dissatisfied with their share of the spoils.

This was the most crushing defeat ever administered to a British army on American soil. Throughout that dreadful afternoon, death, like a hungry Moloch, eager for a royal feast, stalked by the side of Mars and drank his fill of blood amid the gloom of the forest. The slaughter of trained soldiers by Indians, in this battle, has no comparison except the slaughter of General George A. Custer's troops at the battle of the Little Big Horn, on June 25th, 1876.

Of the 1460, besides women and other camp followers, who on that July day crossed the sparkling Monongahela, 456 were killed and 421 wounded, many of them mortally. Out of 89 commissioned officers, 63 were killed or wounded. In no other battle in history were so many officers slain in proportion to the number engaged. The Virginians suffered the most. One company was almost annihilated, and another, besides those killed and wounded in its ranks, lost all its officers, even to the corporal. Of the three Virginia companies, Washington said that they "behaved like men and died like soldiers" and that "scarce thirty men were left alive."

The French Account of the Battle

The French account of the battle, among other things, bears out the contention that Braddock was not ambushed. In this account, we read:

"That officer (Contrecoeur, commander of Fort Duquesne) employed the next day (July 8th) in making his arrangements; and on the ninth detached M. de Beaujeu, seconded by Messers. Dumas and de Lignery, all three Captains, together with four Lieutenants, 6 Ensigns, 20 cadets, 100 soldiers, 100 Canadians and 600 Indians, with orders to lie in ambush at a favorable spot, which had been reconnoitered the previous evening. The detachment, before it could reach its place of destination, found itself in the presence of the enemy within three leagues of that fort. M. de Beaujeu, finding his ambush had failed, decided upon an attack. This he made with so much vigor as to astonish the enemy, who were waiting for us in the best possible order; but their artillery, loaded with grape (a cartouche) having opened fire, our men gave way in turn. The Indians, also frightened by the report of the cannon rather than by any damage it could inflict, began to yield, when M. de Beaujeu was killed. M. Dumas began to encourage his detachment."

(See Pa. Archives, Sec. Series, Vol. 6, page 256.)

The French account, just quoted, goes on to state that "the enemy left more than 1,000 men on the field of battle;" while, in the "Memoirs des Pouchot," Vol. 1, page 37, the following is stated:

"There were counted dead on the battle field six hundred men, on the retreat about four hundred; along a little stream three hundred. Their total loss was reckoned at twelve hundred and

THE SITE OF THE BATTLE OF THE MONONGAHELA, AS IT APPEARED IN 1803

seventy . . . The wounded were abandoned, and almost all perished in the woods."

The official reports of the French show that Contrecoeur, frightened by the exaggerated statements given him as to the number of Braddock's forces, had prepared to surrender Fort Duquesne when the British army should arrive at that place. Reluctantly did he give assent to any resistance; and when his officers selected a place of ambush on the evening of June 8th, it was merely to dispute the passes of the Monongahela and to annoy and retard the march of Braddock's army.

In this connection we state that there were few, if any, Delawares and Shawnees among the Indian allies of the French at Braddock's defeat. These tribes did not go over to the French to the extent of taking up arms against the English until after Braddock's defeat. They were simply waiting to see which side would win. The Indians with the French at this battle were the Tisagechroann, Chippewas, Ottawas and other tribes from the region of the Great Lakes. Contrary to the statements of many historians, it may well be doubted that Pontiac commanded the Ottawas at this battle. (See W. N. Loudermilk's "History of Cumberland," page 177.) It has also been stated that the Seneca chief, Cornplanter, fought on the side of the French in this battle. This, too, may well be doubted.

The Retreat—Death of Braddock

At the time of the battle, Colonel Dunbar, who followed, as has been seen, with the heavy artillery and heavy stores, was in camp at a place since known as "Dunbar's Camp," and located not far from the spot where Jumonville was killed in Washington's campaign of 1754. This place is almost fifty miles from the place of Braddock's defeat. Dunbar has been greatly criticised on account of the slowness with which he followed Braddock; but it should be remembered that he had the poorest troops, many of whom sickened and died on the way; that he had the heaviest stores, and an insufficient number of horses to transport them; and that he was almost constantly harrassed by French and Indians, as his poor, jaded horses dragged the heavily laden wagons up the mountain sides in the summer heat. Moreover, the Indians got in his rear and cut off much of his supplies.

When General Braddock was carried from the field, he was taken to the other side of the Monongahela, where about one hundred men had gathered, among them being Washington, the aides, Orme and Morris, and Dr. Craik, who here dressed the General's wound. This place was about a quarter of a mile from the ford. From here Braddock ordered Washington to go to Dunbar's camp with orders to send wagons for the wounded, hospital stores, provisions and other supplies, escorted by two Grenadier companies. Colonel Burton posted sentries here and intended to hold the place until he could be reinforced. But most of the men took to flight within an hour, and then Burton retreated up and across the stream to the camp ground from which the army had marched on the morning of that fatal day. Here Burton and his companions were joined by Colonel Gage and eighty men whom he had rallied. From this place, Burton and Gage, uniting their detachments and carrying the wounded General with them, marched all that night and the next day, and arrived at Gist's Plantation at ten o'clock at night. Around the Indian spring at Gist's, on that warm, summer night, the dying General and the other wounded lay sleepless and hungry, waiting for surgical aid and food from the camp of Dunbar.

Now, to return to Washington. After receiving the General's orders to hasten to Dunbar's camp, he with two companions, rode all through the melancholy, dark and rainy night, and arrived at the camp in the evening of July 10th. But the tidings of Braddock's defeat had preceded Washington. These were borne by wagoners, who had mounted their horses when the day was lost, and fled from the field of battle. Haggard and terrified, the Indian yell ringing in their ears, these wagoners had ridden into Dunbar's camp at noon, on July 10th, exclaiming, "All is lost! Braddock is killed! The troops are cut to pieces!" A panic then fell upon the camp, which Washington found still prevailing upon his arrival. The orders which he brought with him were executed during the night. Early the next morning (July 11th), he accompanied the convoy of supplies to Gist's Plantation, eleven miles away. Here he found General Braddock suffering intense agony of body and mind. In this agony the dying General's thoughts were on the poor soldiers, who were wandering in the woods to die from their wounds, from exhaustion, from starvation, or at the hands of the Indians.

The wounded were attended to at Gist's on the 11th. Then the survivors retreated to Dunbar's camp. Here confusion still reigned. Orme says in his journal that Dunbar's forces "seemed to have forgot all discipline." Dunbar's wagoners were nearly all Pennsylvanians, and, like those who were with Braddock, had fled, taking the best horses with them.

All the wagons being needed to carry the wounded, most of Dunbar's ammunition and other military stores were destroyed and buried to prevent their falling into the hands of the French.

General Braddock died at the Orchard Camp, west of the Great Meadows, during the night of July 13th, and was buried in the middle of the road, the troops, horses and wagons passing over the grave to obliterate its traces and thus prevent its desecration by the Indians. Some historians say that the time of the burial was before daylight and that Washington read the burial service amid the flickering light of torches, after the manner of the burial of Sir John Moore. However, Veech, in his "Monongahela of Old," says the burial took place after daylight, on the morning of the 14th.

After the burial of Braddock, the wreck of his former proud array continued its retreat without molestation. Had the French known the fear and panic that seized Dunbar's soldiers and that no reinforcements were coming, they would no doubt have annihilated the remnants of the British forces.

Hon. William Findley, of Westmoreland County, wrote that Washington advised him that he intended to erect a monument at the place where Braddock was buried, but had no opportunity to do so until after the Revolutionary War; that in 1784, he made diligent search for the grave, but could not find it. (See Niles' Register, XIV, page 179.)

Colonel James Burd located the grave in 1759 when on his way to Redstone, and said that it was "about two miles from Fort Necessity, and about twenty yards from a little hollow, in which there was a small stream of water, and over it a bridge." In 1812, some workmen, under the direction of Abraham Stewart, repairing the road at a point near the place mentioned by Colonel Burd, unearthed the skeleton and trappings of a British officer. These were, very probably, General Braddock's bones. Some of the bones were taken away by relic hunters, but all were later collected by Mr. Stewart. In 1820, the skeleton was reinterred a few rods from the original grave. A monument now marks the spot where these bones repose in the soil of the historic county of Fayette. Thousands of travelers on the National Pike pause at "Braddock's Grave" to pay tribute to the memory of the haughty and unfortunate British General. Peace to his ashes!

Thomas Fossit

Thomas Fossit (Fausset), a soldier in Braddock's army, said by some to have been enlisted at Shippensburg, maintained to the end of his long life that he fired the bullet that gave General Braddock his mortal wound. Fossit claimed that his brother, Joseph, was killed by Braddock for attempting to seek shelter, during the battle; whereupon he, in revenge, shot the General. For a number of years, Fossit conducted a small tavern not far from Braddock's burial place, where he related his story to the passing traveler. Some historians, among them Bancroft and Egle, accept Fossit's story as true; others give it little or no credence. Perhaps the fairest comment to make is to say that the truth of the old soldier's statement can be neither proved nor disproved.

Torture of the Prisoners

James (later Colonel) Smith, a young man eighteen years of age, was one of the force of three hundred men, under Colonel James Burd, engaged in cutting the Pennsylvania road from McDowell's Mill to Turkey Foot as Braddock was marching on Fort Duquesne. At a point four or five miles above Bedford, he was captured, about July 5th, by Indian allies of the French and carried to Fort Duquesne, where he was a prisoner on the day of Braddock's defeat. He gives the following description of the happenings at the fort on that dreadful day:

"Shortly after this, on the 9th day of July, 1755, in the morning, I heard a great stir in the fort. As I could then walk with a staff in my hand, I went out of the door, which was just by the wall of the fort, and stood upon the wall and viewed the Indians in a huddle before the gate, where were barrels of powder, bullets, flints, &c., and every one taking what suited; I saw the Indians also march off in rank entire—likewise the French Canadians, and some regulars. After viewing the Indians and French in different positions, I computed them to be about four hundred, and wondered that they attempted to go out against Braddock with so small a party. I was then in high hopes that I would soon see them fly before the British troops, and that General Braddock would take the fort and rescue me.

"I remained anxious to know the advent of this day; and, in the afternoon, I again observed a great noise and commotion in the fort, and though at that time I could not understand French, yet I found that it was the voice of joy and triumph, and feared that they had received what I called bad news.

"I had observed some of the old country soldiers speak Dutch [German]; as I spoke Dutch, I went to one of them, and asked him, what was the news? He told me that a runner had just arrived, who said that Braddock would certainly be defeated; that the Indians and French had surrounded him, and were concealed behind trees and in gullies, and kept a constant fire upon the English, and that they saw the English falling in heaps, and if they did not take the river, which was the only gap, and make their escape, there would not be one man left alive before sundown. Some time after this, I heard a number of scalp halloos, and saw a company of Indians and French coming in. I observed they had a great many bloody scalps, grenadiers' caps, British canteens, bayonets, &c., with them. They brought the news that Braddock was defeated. After that, another company came in which appeared to be about one hundred, and chiefly Indians, and it seemed to me that almost every one of this company was carrying scalps; after this, came another company with a number of wagon horses, and also a great many scalps. Those that were coming in, and those that had arrived, kept a constant firing of small arms, and also the great guns in the fort, which were accompanied with the most hideous shouts and yells from all quarters; so that it appeared to me as if the infernal regions had broke loose.

"About sundown I beheld a small party coming in with about a dozen prisoners, stripped naked, with their hands tied behind their backs, and part of their bodies blackened,—these prisoners they burned to death on the bank of the Allegheny River opposite the fort. I stood on the fort wall until I beheld them begin to burn one of these men; they had him tied to a stake, and kept touching him with fire-brands, red-hot irons, &c., and he screaming in the most doleful manner,—the Indians in the meantime yelling like infernal spirits. As this scene appeared too shocking for me to behold, I retired to my lodgings both sore and sorry."

This is the first torture of white prisoners by Indians that we have seen thus far in this volume. We shall see many others before the end of the book. In this connection we state that Hon. Warren K. Moorehead, of the United States Board of Indian Commissioners, who has made the American Indians a life study, believes that they learned their cruel treatment of prisoners from the early Spanish explorers. However this may be, certainly the

Indians never exceeded the Spanish explorers in cruelty. And the eternal pages of history will say that the American Indians never inflicted more horrible tortures on prisoners, white or red, than civilized white men—Christians, both Catholic and Protestant—inflicted on one another, in religious persecutions only a few centuries ago. It is well to keep this great fact of history in mind as we read the accounts of Indian tortures.

But to quote a little more from James Smith's account:

"When I came into my lodgings, I saw Russel's Seven Sermons, which they had brought from the field of battle, which a Frenchman made a present of to me. From the best information I could receive, there were only seven Indians and four French killed in this battle, and five hundred British lay dead on the field, besides what were killed in the river on their retreat. The morning after the battle, I saw Braddock's artillery brought into the fort; the same day I also saw several Indians in British officers' dress, with sash, half moons, laced hats, &c., which the British then wore."

Smith was a native of Franklin County, Pennsylvania. He remained in captivity among the Indians at Fort Duquesne, Mahoning, and Muskingum. He was adopted by his captors. During his captivity among the Indians, he was carried from place to place, spending most of his time at Mahoning and Muskingum. In about 1759, he accompanied his Indian relatives to Montreal, where he managed to secrete himself on board a French ship. He was again taken prisoner and confined for four months, but was finally exchanged and reached his home in 1760, to find the sweetheart of his boyhood married, and all his friends and relatives supposing him dead. He became a very prominent man on the Pennsylvania frontier, and during the Revolution, was a captain on the Pennsylvania line, being promoted, in 1778, to the rank of colonel. In 1788, he removed to Kentucky, where he at once took a prominent part in public affairs, serving in the early Kentucky conventions and in the legislature. He died in Washington County, Kentucky, in 1812, leaving behind him as a legacy to historians a very valuable account of his Indian captivity.

A Final View of the Field

Let us take a final view of the field of blood and death by the limpid waters of the Monongahela. Hundreds of scalped and mutilated bodies lie amid the ferns, the laurel, the clinging vines, and by the mossy logs of these sylvan shades. They lie on the bank of the river; they lie on the sides of the ravines; they lie by the rivulets. The ferns, the laurel, the vines, the moss are stained with blood. The rivulets run red with blood. Far from the scene of battle, bodies lie—bodies of the wounded who dragged themselves deeper into the forest to die, or perished on the flight from the scene of slaughter. Soon these bodies will be torn asunder by wild beasts. Soon wolves and bears will devour their flesh and crunch their bones. Later the voice of lamentation will be heard in hundreds of homes, far away from the banks of the Monongahela—agonizing cries of fathers, of mothers, of sisters, of brothers, of wives, of sweethearts of the fallen. For long, sad years, the mystic cords of memory and affection, stretching from hundreds of homes in Virginia, in Maryland, and across the sea, will bind these homes to this Monongahela battle ground—bind them until these relatives, wives and sweethearts meet the loved and lost in the land where there are no wars, no partings and no death.

General Forbes captured Fort Duquesne, on November 25th, 1758. Three days later he sent a detachment to bury the bones of the soldiers slain at Braddock's defeat. Among those who went to the scene of the battle was the then Sir Peter Halket, son of the Sir Peter Halket who was killed at the battle, as was also one of his sons. Young Sir Peter Halket had accompanied the Highlanders to America in the hope of finding the bones of his father and brother. By interrogating some Indians who had fought against Braddock young Sir Peter Halket found one who stated that at the massacre he had seen an officer fall near a tree, that a young subaltern ran to his assistance, was shot when he reached the spot, and fell across the other's body. On hearing the Indian's story, Halket had a mournful conviction that the two officers were his father and brother.

Captain West, a brother of the famous painter, Benjamin West, piloted by Indians who had been in the battle, led the detachment which buried the bones of Braddock's soldiers. In Galt's "Life of Benjamin West," we learn that the Indian who told young Sir Peter Halket the incident just related, accompanied the latter and companions to the scene of the battle. They found the ground covered with skeletons. Some were lying across trunks of fallen trees. Skulls and bones were scattered on the ground—a certain indication that the bodies had been torn asunder and devoured by wild beasts. In a short time, the Indian informant uttered a cry, announcing that he had found the tree near which he had seen the officers fall on the day of battle. Then the Indian removed the leaves which thickly covered the ground. Presently two skeletons were found, as the Indian had expected, lying one across the other. Young Peter Halket then remembering that his father had an artificial tooth, examined the jaw bones of the skeletons for this mark of identification. In a short time he exclaimed, "It is my father!" and fell into the arms of his companions. The two skeletons, covered with a Highland plaid, were then buried together.

Sargent, one hundred years after Braddock's defeat, published his "History of Braddock's Expedition." He describes the appearance of the place of battle as then being a tranquil, rural landscape of rare charm and beauty, where

"*Peaceful smiles the harvest,*
And stainless flows the tide."

Today, one hundred and seventy-four years after the battle, the town of Braddock has replaced the forest of 1755 and the rural landscape of 1855. Today the greater part of the battlefield is covered by the Edgar Thompson Steel Works, where men face the hot furnaces, instead of the rifle of the Indian—where men labor amid the clang and roar of machinery, instead of being shot down with the blood-curdling yells of the Indians ringing in their ears.

Some of the Survivors

Among the survivors of the Braddock campaign, were men who lived to take a prominent part in the Revolutionary War. Colonel Gage who led the advance on the day of battle, was the General Gage who led the British forces at Bunker Hill. Captain Horatio Gates, who commanded one of the New York independent companies in the Braddock campaign, was the General Gates to whom Burgoyne surrendered at Saratoga. Captain Hugh Mercer who was in the battle on the banks of the Monongahela, was the General Mercer who laid down his life for the American cause at the battle of Princeton. General Daniel Morgan, whose famous riflemen from Pennsylvania and Virginia rendered the American cause such great service during the Revolutionary War, was a teamster in Braddock's army. For some real or supposed affront, a haughty British officer caused him to be whipped on the bare back.

Daniel Boone, the famous Kentucky pioneer, was in Braddock's fatal expedition. (Hanna's Wilderness Trail, Vol. 2, pages 213 and 214.)

Effects of Braddock's Defeat

The news of Braddock's defeat quickly spread throughout the settlements of Pennsylvania, Maryland and Virginia and later to the other Colonies, filling the hearts of all, especially the inhabitants of the frontiers, with dismay. Fear traveled on the wings of the wind, bringing terror to those who had believed Braddock's proud army to be invincible but now learned that it was overwhelmingly defeated.

The terrified Colonel Dunbar, with 1,800 troops, 300 of whom were sick and wounded, continued his retreat to Fort Cumberland, at which place he arrived on July 22nd. About the only reason he gave for retreating was that that many of his soldiers had lost their clothes in the battle. It was midsummer. Why he should attach so much importance to lack of clothes at this time of year, as a reason for retreating, especially when he had so great a supply of ammunition and other supplies that he had to destroy most of the same, is hard to see. Then, on August 2nd, he marched away to "winter quarters" at Philadelphia, shamefully leaving Fort Cumberland, the only fort on the frontier, with a small garrison and four hundred sick and wounded soldiers. On October 1st, his army, fifteen hundred strong, took up the march from Philadelphia to New York and Albany. When the news of Dunbar's cowardly and traitorous action spread throughout the settlements, the terror in the log cabins on the frontier was greatly increased.

If, instead of destroying the larger part of his stores and ammunition and then retreating, Dunbar had rested his troops and gotten reinforcements from Fort Cumberland, he could no doubt have captured Fort Duquesne. This is unquestionably what he should have done. With reinforcements from Fort Cumberland, he would have had about three times as many troops as had the French at Fort Duquesne. The French were nearly as badly frightened as was he. They expected the British army to be reinforced and then return. Moreover, nearly all of their Indian allies had returned to their forest homes along the Great Lakes. Gist, Scarouady, Montour and the other scouts with Dunbar, could easily have ascertained the situation and number of the French. Had poor Braddock lived, he would undoubtedly have done just what we say Dunbar should have done.

The news of Dunbar's action soon spread among the Delawares and Shawnees. Hesitating no longer, they went over to the French and prepared to strike the frontier settlements. The Delawares threw off the yoke of subserviency to the Six Nations. In doing this, they declared they were no longer "women" but MEN with the right to determine their own actions. Soon the mountains of Pennsylvania were filled with war parties of Delawares and Shawnees, coming from the valleys of the Ohio and Allegheny. They rushed down the Braddock road into Maryland, and killed and scalped settlers almost up to the gates of Fort Cumberland. A little later, they entered the Pennsylvania settlements by way of the various Indian trails, traders' routes and the road Colonel Burd had cut to the crest of the Allegheny Mountains.

The bitter fruits of the fraudulent Walking Purchase of 1737 and the Albany Purchase of 1754 are about to be gathered. The Delawares and Shawnees are about to wreak terrible and bloody vengeance on defenseless Pennsylvania. In our next chapter, we shall see the beginning of their work of blood and death.

A Final Word as to General Braddock

General Edward Braddock was born in Perthshire, Scotland, in 1695. He became Lieutenant-Colonel, in 1745, Brigadier-General, in 1746, and Major-General, in 1754. He fought valiantly at Fontenoy and Culloden.

General Braddock's principal shortcomings were that he paid too little attention to those who warned him of the dangers of Indian warfare and that he underestimated the worth of the Colonial troops. We have already called attention to the fact that he told Benjamin Franklin that it was impossible for the Indians to make any impression whatever on the British regulars. But it must be remembered that it was natural for him to have an exalted opinion of the efficiency of the mode of warfare in which he had been schooled since his fifteenth year, at which early age he entered the British army as an Ensign in the Coldstream Guards, a very aristocratic division of the army, the bodyguard of British Royalty. He could hardly be expected suddenly to adopt a radically different mode of warfare in his sixtieth year.

His Secretary, William Shirley, son of Governor Shirley, of Massachusetts, wrote Governor Morris, of Pennsylvania, from Fort Cumberland, almost a month before the army left that place for Fort Duquesne: "We have a general most judiciously chosen for being disqualified for the service he is employed in, in almost every respect." (Pa. Col. Rec., Vol. 6, page 405.) Washington, too, criticised him "for want of that temper and moderation which should be used by a man of sense" and for being incapable of arguing military questions without inordinate warmth of feeling. (Washington's letter of June 7th, 1755, to William Fairfax.) Also, the Indian chief, Scarouady, at a meeting of the Provincial Council of Pennsylvania, on August 22nd, 1755, complained to Governor Morris concerning Braddock: "It is now well known to you how unhappily we have been defeated by the French near Monongahela. We must let you know that it was the pride and ignorance of that great general that came from England. He is now dead; but he was a bad man when he was alive; he looked upon us [the Indians who were with Braddock] as dogs; would never hear anything that was said to him. We often endeavored to advise him, and to tell him of the danger he was in with his soldiers; but he never appeared pleased with us, and that was the reason a great many of our warriors left him, and would not be under his command." (Pa. Col. Rec., Vol. 6, page 589.)

Bitterly criticised in life, reproach did not spare the unfortunate Braddock in his grave. In both England and America, the failure of the expedition was attributed to his obstinacy, pedantry and conceit. But the mistakes of a man who fails are always magnified. Furthermore, his bitterest critics and defamers were compelled to admit his bravery. He was as brave as the bravest of the brave. Nor was he without kindness of heart. Before he closed his eyes in death, in that Allegheny Mountain camp, he acknowledged his mistake in not heeding the advice of Washington to order the British regulars to fight the Indians in the manner of the Virginia troops. "We shall know better how to deal with them another time," he said. It is also said that, in the shadows of the receding world, he bequeathed Washington his favorite charger and his body servant, Bishop, an evidence of his affection for the Virginia youth. And we call attention to the fact that Washington, in mature years, after his military judgement had been strengthened and broadened amid the mighty throes of the American Revolution, said the following of his former General:

"True, he was unfortunate, but his character was much too severely treated. He was one of the honestest and best men of the British officers. Even in the manner of fighting he was not more to blame than others, for of all that were consulted, only one person [probably, Washington, himself] objected to it. He was both my General and my physician."

General Braddock and the soldiers who went down to death in his campaign against Fort Duquesne, did not die in vain. From the time of his bloody defeat, the frontiersmen of Virginia, Maryland and the other American Colonies, had no doubt that they were the equal of the British regulars. Therefore, they did not fear to take up arms against them later on, in resisting British tyranny. It is not too much to say, then, that Braddock's defeat was the first step in the direction of American independence—that, in the Providence of God, his defeat was one of the links in the chain of events that led to American independence—that, out of that travail of blood and death on the banks of the Monongahela, was born the greatest Nation that ever stepped forth upon the stage of time.

But—

> "*No farther seek his merits to disclose,*
> *Or draw his frailties from their dread abode.*"

Let us hope that, after the warfare of life, General Braddock and those who criticised him so severely, have reached a common consummation. Let us hope that his soul and theirs found the golden key that unlocked the palace of a peaceful eternity.

CHAPTER VII

The First Delaware Invasion

IT is the autumn of 1755. By this time, nearly all the Delawares and Shawnees have gone over to the French. They are about to invade the Pennsylvania settlements with rifle, tomahawk and scalping knife. The storm which has been gathering in the valleys of the Ohio and Allegheny, is about to pass over the Allegheny Mountains and deluge the frontiers with indescribable horror.

But, before taking up the recital of the massacres of the autumn of 1755, let us again call attention to the defenseless condition of the Pennsylvania frontier. When Governor Morris of Pennsylvania, learned that Colonel Dunbar was bringing his army to Philadelphia to go into "winter quarters" in midsummer, leaving the Pennsylvania frontier exposed and unprotected, he was astounded, and wrote Governor Shirley of Massachusetts to this effect. (Pa. Col. Rec., Vol. 6, page 513.) Shirley was now commander-in-chiefs, after the death of Braddock. Furthermore, Governor Morris wrote Dunbar, urging him to keep his army on the frontiers for the protection of the settlers. Colonel James Burd urged the same in an interview with Dunbar at Cumberland. When Governor Shirley received the information that Dunbar intended to march to Philadelphia, he wrote that there never was any thing equal to Braddock's defeat "unless the retreat of the 1,500 men and the scheme of going into Winter Quarters when his Majesty's Service stands so much in need of the troops." (Pa. Col. Rec., Vol. 6, page 548.) Then, on August 6th, Governor Shirley ordered Dunbar to proceed to Albany, New York, with his troops. Six days later, he ordered him, with the assistance of troops to be raised in Pennsylvania, to attack Fort Duquesne and Fort Presu' Isle, and, in case of failure in both these attempts, then to make such a disposition of his troops as to protect the frontiers of Pennsylvania, especially in the neighborhood of Shippensburg, Carlisle and McDowell's Mill. In these orders of August 12th, Shirley told him that, should he, "through any unforeseen Accident," find it "absolutely impracticable" to put them into execution, then he was to carry out the orders of August 6th, and come to Albany. The orders of August 6th were the orders Dunbar found "practicable." He led his army from Philadelphia to New York, as was seen in the preceding chapter. Furthermore, Governor Morris was not able to raise troops in Pennsylvania, and wrote Governor Shirley, on August 19th, telling him that "uncommon pains have been taken by the Quakers to dissuade the people from taking up arms upon the present occasion," and explaining that a great majority of the Pennsylvania Assembly were Quakers. Such was the state of affairs in Pennsylvania when the Delawares and Shawnees, in the autumn of 1755, began their bloody invasion of the frontier settlements. (See Pa. Col. Rec., Vol. 6, pages 558 to 563.)

On October 9th, George Croghan wrote from Aughwick to Charles Swaine at Shippensburg that a friendly Indian, coming from the Ohio, warned him that one hundred and sixty Indians were ready to set out for the Pennsylvania settlements. (Pa. Col. Rec., Vol. 6, page 642.) This Indian gave it as his opinion that these Indians would attack the Province as soon as they could persuade the Indians on the Susquehanna to join them. Said Croghan: "He desires me, as soon as I see the Indians remove from Susquehanna back to Ohio, to shift my quarters, for he says that the French will, if possible, lay all the back frontiers in ruins this Winter." In a postscript to this letter, Croghan asks for guns and powder, and says that he is building a stockade, which he expects to complete by the middle of the next week.

Penn's Creek Massacre

On October 16th, 1755, just one week after George Croghan wrote the foregoing letter, began the terrible massacre of the German settlers along Penn's Creek, which empties into the Susquehanna near Selinsgrove, Snyder County—the first Indian outrage in Pennsylvania, after Braddock's defeat, and the first actual violation, by the Delawares, of the treaty of peace which William Penn entered into with the great Tamanend shortly after his arrival in the Province. The massacre extended from a point near New Berlin, Union County to a point near Selinsgrove, and lasted for two days, according to the statements of Barbara Leininger and Marie le Roy (Mary King), two girls captured on this occasion. The Indians, fourteen in number, and all Delawares, came from the Allegheny Valley, principally from Kittanning, over the trail used by the Delawares in their first great exodus from the region of Shamokin to the valleys of the Ohio and Allegheny. One of the leaders of the Indian band was the chief, Keckenepaulin, who lived for some time near Jenners' Cross Roads, in Somerset County, and whose name has been applied to the Shawnee town at the mouth of the Loyalhanna, possibly due to the fact that he resided there for a time. Other members of the band were Joseph Compass, young James Compass, young Thomas Hickman, Kalasquay, Souchy, Machynego and Katoochquay.

The first account of this massacre was given by John Harris (later founder of Harrisburg), writing from his trading house at Paxtang (Harrisburg), to Governor Morris, on October 20th:

"I was informed last night by a person that came down our river that there was a Dutch [German] woman who had made her escape to George Gabriel's, [near Selinsgrove], and informs that last Friday Evening on her way home from this Settlement to Mahanoy [Penn's Creek] where her family lived, she called at a Neighbor's House and saw two persons laying by the door of said house murdered and scalped, that there were some Dutch [German] familys that lived near left their places immediately, not thinking it safe to stay any longer. It's the opinion of the people up the river that the familys on Penn's Creek, being but scattered, that few in number are killed or carried off, except the above said woman, the certainty of which will soon be known, as there are some men gone out to bury the dead." (Pa. Col. Rec. Vol. 6, page 645.)

In a postscript to the above letter, Harris says that a man has just arrived with additional information as to the number of settlers killed and captured along Penn's Creek. He adds that the Indians at Paxtang, mostly of the Six Nations, urge the Governor to put the Province in a state of defense. Their chief, Belt of Wampum, strongly insisted on this. Then Conrad Weiser, on October 22nd, wrote from Reading to the Governor, stating that information has been received that six families have been murdered on Penn's Creek, about four miles from its mouth; that altogether twenty-eight are missing; that the people of those parts are leaving their plantations in consternation, and that two of his sons have gone to Penn's Creek to help one of their cousins and his family escape with their lives.

On the same day (October 20th), the following petition of the inhabitants "living near the mouth of Penn's Creek on the West side of the Susquehanna," signed by seventeen, giving some of the details of the massacre, was sent the Governor:

"That on or about the sixteen of this instant, October, the Enemy came down upon the said Creek and killed, scalped and carried away all the men, women and children, amounting to 25 persons in number, and wounded one man who fortunately made his escape and brought us the news; whereupon we, the Subscribers, went out and buried the dead, whom we found most barbarously murdered and scalped. We found but 13, which were men and elderly women, and one child of two weeks old, the rest being young women and children we suppose to be carried away prisoners; the House (where we suppose they finished their Murder), we found burnt up, and the man of it, named Jacob King, a Swissar, lying just by it; he lay on his back barbarously burnt and two Tomahawks sticking in his forehead; one of the tomahawks, marked newly with W. D., we have sent to your Honour. The terror of which has drove away almost all these back inhabitants except us, the Subscribers, with a few more who are willing to stay and endeavor to defend the land; but as we are not able of ourselves to defend it for want of Guns and Ammunition, and but few in number, so that, without assistance we must fly and leave the Country at the mercy of the Enemy." (Pa. Col. Rec., Vol. 6, pages 647-648.)

The persons captured during this horrible massacre were: Barbara Leininger, Rachel (Regina) Leininger, Marie le Roy, Jacob le Roy, Marian Wheeler, Hanna, wife of Jacob Breylinger, and two of their children, one of whom died at Kittanning of starvation, Peter Lick and his two sons, John and William. (Pa. Archives, Vol. 3, page 633.)

Barbara Leininger and Marie le Roy were neighbor girls, aged about twelve years, living about one half mile apart and near the present town of New Berlin. Marie le Roy was a daughter of Jean Jaques le Roy, alias Jacob King, one of the victims of the massacre. The Indians took these girls and others with them. When they arrived at Chinklacamoose (Clearfield), Marie's brother Jacob was left with the Delawares of that place. The Indians then took the two girls to Punxsutawney, thence to Kittanning, at which place they arrived in December and remained until after Colonel John Armstrong destroyed this noted Delaware town, September 8th, 1756. Here they were compelled to witness the torture of some English prisoners. In their "Narrative," found in Pa. Ar., Sec. Series Vol. 7, pages 401 to 412, they describe one of these tortures, that of a woman who had attempted to escape. It is a shocking recital. After the woman was dead, "an English soldier, named John ——, who escaped from prison at Lancaster, and joined the French, had a piece of flesh cut from her body, and ate it."

Barbara and Marie were taken to Fort Duquesne soon after Colonel Armstrong's expedition, where they remained for two months. They say that the French at the fort tried to persuade them to leave the Indians captors and stay with them, but that they "could not abide the French," and felt that they were better off among the Indians. From Fort Duquesne, they were taken to Sauconk, at the mouth of the Beaver, where they remained until the spring of 1757, when they were taken up the Beaver to Kuskuskies. They were among the Delawares at Kuskuskies when Christian Frederick Post visited that place, in the autumn of 1758, on his peace mission to the Western Delawares. They met him, but the Indians did not permit them to speak with him. Shortly after General Forbes captured Fort Duquesne, on November 25th, 1758, they were taken to the Muskingum, to which place the Delawares then fled from Sauconk, Logstown, Kuskuskies, Shenango (located on the Shenango River, just below the town of Sharon, Mercer County) and other Indian towns in Western Pennsylvania. From Muskingum, the girls made their escape, on March 16th, 1759, coming to the newly erected Fort Pitt, thence by way of Ligonier, Bedford and Carlisle to Philadelphia, at which place they arrived on May 6th, being conducted part of the way from Fort Pitt by soldiers commanded by Captain Samuel Weiser, son of the famous Indian interpreter of Pennsylvania, Conrad Weiser. After arriving at Philadelphia, they appeared before the Provincial Council, and gave an account of their terrible experiences. (See Pa. Archives, Vol. 3, page 633.) Later they published their "Narrative," from which we quote the following about the Penn's Creek massacre:

"Early in the morning of the 16th of October, 1755, while le Roy's [the father of Marie] hired man went out to fetch the cows, he heard the Indians shooting six times. Soon after, eight of them came to the house, and killed Barbara (Marie) le Roy's father with tomahawks. Her brother defended himself desperately for a time, but was at last overpowered. The Indians did not kill him, but took him prisoner, together with Marie le Roy and a little girl who was staying with the family. Thereupon they plundered the homestead, and set it on fire. Into this fire they laid the body of the murdered father, feet foremost, until it was half consumed. The upper half was left lying on the ground, with the two tomahawks with which they had killed him, sticking in his head. Then they kindled another fire, not far from the house. While sitting around it, a neighbor of le Roy, named Bastian, happened to pass by on horseback. He was immediately shot down and scalped.

"Two of the Indians now went to the house of Barbara Leininger, where they found her father, her brother, and her sister, Regina. Her mother had gone to the mill. They demanded rum, but there was none in the house. They then called for tobacco, which was given them. Having filled and smoked a pipe, they said: 'We are Allegheny Indians, and your enemies. You must all die!' Thereupon, they shot her father, tomahawked her brother, who was twenty years of age, took Barbara and her sister Regina prisoners, and conveyed them into the forest for about a mile. They were soon joined by the other Indians, with Marie le Roy and the little girl.

"Not long after, several of the Indians led the prisoners to the top of a high hill, near the two plantations. Toward evening the rest of the savages returned with six fresh and bloody scalps, which they threw at the feet of the poor captives, saying that they had a good hunt that day.

"The next morning we were taken about two miles further into the forest, while the most of the Indians again went out to kill and plunder. Toward evening they returned with nine scalps and five prisoners.

"On the third day the whole band came together and divided the spoils. In addition to large quantities of provisions, they had taken fourteen horses and ten prisoners, namely: One man, one woman, five girls and three boys. We two girls, as also two of the horses, fell to the share of an Indian named Galasko. We traveled with our new master for two days. He was tolerably kind, and allowed us to ride all the way, while he and the rest of the Indians walked."

It is significant that the Penn's Creek Massacre took place almost on the line of the Albany Purchase of July, 1754, which so offended the Delawares and Shawnees. It is said that the line would have passed through the land of Jacob King, alias le Roy. The Penn's Creek settlers had come to this place in 1754.

Also, it is a strange anomaly in the record of Pennsylvania's relations with the Indians that the first blow struck by the Indians against the Province fell upon the German settlers, who had always treated the Indian kindly. While others went to the Indian "with a musket in one hand and a bottle of rum in the other," the German settlers on the border land did not cheat him or take advantage of him in any way. There is no sublimer chapter in American history than the account, for instance, of the efforts of the Moravian Missionaries, Germans, to win the Indians of Pennsylvania to the Christian faith.

Attack on John Harris

On October 23d, John Harris, Thomas Forster, Captain McKee and Adam Terence went from Harris' trading house at Paxtang to Penn's Creek, with a force of between forty and fifty men, to bury the dead of the massacre of October 16th and 17th. When they arrived, they found that this had already been done. They then decided to return immediately to the settlement at Paxtang, but were urged by John Shikellamy, son of the vice-gerent of the Six Nations, and the Belt of Wampum, (or the Belt, also called White Thunder), a Seneca chief, to go to Shamokin (Sunbury), about five miles farther up the Susquehanna, in order to ascertain the feelings of the Indians at that place, which they did.

Harris and his companions found many strange Delawares at Shamokin, all painted black, Andrew Montour being with them and also painted black. These Delawares had come from the valleys of the Ohio and Allegheny to advise the Delawares at Shamokin and other places on the Susquehanna that the Delawares of the Ohio and Allegheny had taken up arms against the English, and to warn all those of this tribe on the Susquehanna who would not join them to move away.

Harris and his men spent the night (October 24th) at Shamokin. In the night time, Adam Terrence overheard Delawares talking as follows: "What are the English [Harris and his men] come here for? To kill us, I suppose. Can't we then send off some of our nimble young men to give our friends notice that will soon be here." Then, after they had sung a war song, four of them went off, well armed, in two canoes, one across the Susquehanna and the other down the river.

At this point, we call attention to the fact that, after the councils held at Shamokin that night and later, the hostile Delawares gathered at Nescopeck, at the mouth of the creek of the same name, in Luzerne County, where later many a bloody expedition was planned by Shingas, Captain Jacobs, Teedyuscung and other of their chiefs. Also, at the time of these councils at Shamokin, the Moravian missionary, Keifer, was residing at that place, exposed to imminent danger, whereupon the friendly Shawnee chief, Paxinosa, of Wyoming, sent two of his sons who rescued the missionary and conducted him safely to the Moravian mission at Gnadenhuetten.

But to return to Harris and his band. They left Shamokin on the morning of October 25th. Before leaving they were advised by Scarouady and Andrew Montour, who were present, not to follow the western side of the river on their return. However, disregarding this advice, they marched down the west side of the river. When they reached the mouth of Penn's Creek, they were fired upon by Delawares hidden in the bushes. Harris describes the attack as follows:

"We were attacked by about twenty or thirty Indians, received their fire, and about fifteen of our men and myself took to the trees and attacked the villians, killed four of them on the spot, and lost but three men, retreating about half a mile through the woods and crossing the Susquehanna, one of which was shot from off an horse, riding behind myself through the river. My horse before was wounded, and falling in the river, I was obliged to quit and swim part of the way. Four or five of our men were drowned crossing the river." (Pa. Col. Rec., Vol. 6, pages 654, 655.)

John Harris gave the above account in a letter written to Governor Morris, on October 28th. He adds:

"The old Belt of Wampum promised me at Shamokin to send out spies to view the enemy, and upon his hearing of our Skirmish was in a rage, gathered up 30 Indians immediately and went in pursuit of the enemy, I am this day informed . . . The Indians are all assembling themselves at Shamokin to counsel; a large body of them were there four days ago. I cannot learn their intentions, but it seems Andrew Montour and Scarouady are to bring down the news from them. There is not a sufficient number of them to oppose the enemy; and perhaps they will all join the enemy against us. There is no dependence on Indians, and we are in imminent danger.

"I got information from Andrew Montour and others that there is a body of French with fifteen hundred Indians coming upon us, —Picks, Ottawas, Orandox, Delawares, Shawnees, and a number of the Six Nations,—and are not many days march from this Province and Virginia, which are appointed to be attacked. At the same time, some of the Shawnee Indians seem friendly, and others appear like enemies. Montour knew many days ago of the Indians being on their march against us before he informed; for which I said as much to him as I thought prudent, considering the place I was in."

"I just now received information that there was a French Officer, supposed to be a Captain, with a party of Shawonese, Delawares, etc., within six miles of the Shamokin two days ago, and no doubt intends to take possession of it, which will be of dreadful consequence to us if suffered. The inhabitants are abandoning their plantations, and we are in a dreadful situation."

Then in a postscript, he says: "The night ensuing our attack the Indians burnt all George Gabriel's Houses, danced around them, etc."

The report to the effect that there was a "body of French with fifteen hundred Indians" on the march from the Ohio to the Pennsylvania settlements was but one of the rumors that, at that dreadful time, filled the unprotected frontier with terror.

Massacre on East Side of the Susquehanna

On the same day that the Delawares made the attack on John Harris, or probably the next day, they crossed the Susquehanna and killed many settlers from Thomas McKee's to Hunter's Mill. Conrad Weiser, in a letter, written from his home near Womelsdorf to James Reed at Reading late in the night of October 26th, describes this incursion as follows:

"This evening, about an hour ago, I received the news of the Enemy having crossed the Susquehanna and killed a great many people from Thomas McKee's down to Hunter's Mill. Mr. Elders [the Rev. John Elder, pastor of the Presbyterian Church at Paxtang, later Colonel], the minister of Paxton, wrote this to another Presbyterian Minister in the neighborhood of Adam Reed Esq." (Squire Adam Read who lived on Swatara Creek.) (Pa. Col. Rec., Vol. 6, page 650.)

Learning of this incursion so closely following the Penn's Creek massacre and the attack on his party, John Harris nevertheless determined not to flee. On October 29th, (Pa. Col. Rec., Vol. 6, page 656), he wrote Edward Shippen, of Lancaster, that he had that day cut holes in his trading house and "determined to hold out to the last extremity." "We expect the Enemy upon us every day, and the Inhabitants are abandoning their Plantations," further wrote Harris, in his letter.

Attention is called to the fact that in this same letter John Harris urged the erection of a fort at some "convenient place up the Susquehannah," as a gathering place for friendly Delawares on this river as well a place for the defense of the Province by its white inhabitants. In doing this he was in line with the urgent request of the Belt, the friendly Seneca. There is no doubt that the lack of such a fort had much to do with the going over to the French of many Delawares and Shawnees on the Susquehanna, who otherwise would have remained at peace with Pennsylvania. The English trade was blotted out by the French, who, after having gotten complete possession of the Ohio and Allegheny and the allegiance of the Delawares and Shawnees of their valleys, were now planning to take possession of the Susquehanna and erect a fort at Shamokin. The French and their Indian allies had the supplies the Delawares and Shawnees on the Susquehanna so sorely need, and being unable to get ammunition and other supplies from the English, many of the Indians on the Susquehanna now turned to the French.

Weiser Plans Defense of the Province

The news of the massacres at Penn's Creek and its vicinity spread fast, and from a letter written from Reading by Conrad Weiser to Governor Morris on October 30th, (Pa. Col. Rec., Vol. 6, pages 656-659), we find that he immediately alarmed the settlers of Berks County. The farmers, to the number of more than two hundred, armed with guns, swords, axes, pitchforks and whatever they chanced to possess, gathered at Benjamin Spicker's near Stouchsburg, about six miles from Weiser's home. Weiser sent privately for Rev. J. N. Kurtz, a Lutheran clergyman, who resided about a mile from Spicker's, and after an exhortation and prayer by this clergyman, the farmers were divided into companies of thirty, each under a captain selected by themselves. Weiser then took up his march towards the Susquehanna in the early morning of October 28th, having sent fifty men "to Tolheo in order to possess themselves of the Capes or Narrows of Swahatawro, where we expected the enemy would come through." These carried a letter from Weiser to William Parsons, who happened to be at his plantation. Weiser's force increased rapidly in number on the way, and at ten o'clock (October 28th), reached Adam Read's on Swatara Creek, in East Hanover Township, Lebanon County. Here intelligence was received of the attack on John Harris and his party who had gone to bury the dead of the Penn's Creek Massacre. This news dampened the ardor of Weiser's men, and they concluded that they could afford more protection to their families by remaining at home. They accordingly wended their way back to their homes, hearing a rumor as they were returning, that the Indians had already made their way through Tolheo Gap and killed a number of people.

William Parsons received the letter sent him by Weiser. In a letter, found in Pa. Archives, Vol. 2, page 443, he tells that he met the advance guard of Weiser's forces, and advised them to make a breastwork of trees at Swatara Gap. They went as far as the top of the mountain, fired their guns in the air, and then came back, firing the whole way to the terror of the inhabitants. Presently came the news of the murder of a certain Henry Hartman, who lived over the mountain just beyond Swatara Gap. As Mr. Parsons and a party were on their way to bury Hartman's body, they were told of two more men who had recently been killed and scalped, and of several others who were missing. It was a terrible time. The roads were filled with settlers fleeing from their homes. Confusion reigned supreme. Though the settlers lacked military experience, they were, at heart, brave and true men. Governor Morris, on October 31st, answered Weiser's letter of October 30th, commending his conduct and zeal, and enclosing him a commission as Colonel that he might have greater authority in those trying times. A few days later, Weiser accompanied Scarouady, Andrew Montour and "drunken Zigrea" to Philadelphia, where Scarouady held the important conferences with Governor Morris, on November 8th to 14th, described later in this history.

Benjamin Spicker or Spycker, above mentioned, lived in what is now Jackson Township, Lebanon County, not far from the Berks County line. Several miles west of Spicker's and a short distance east of Myerstown, Lebanon County, was the fortified house of Philip Breitenbach. On several occasions, when there were Indian alarms, Mr. Breitenbach took a drum and beat it on a little hill near his house, to collect his neighbors from their labors into the blockhouse. On one occasion, the Indians pursued them so close to the blockhouse that one of the inmates shot one of the red men dead on the spot.

Regina, the German Captive

We close this chapter with the interesting narrative of "Regina, the German Captive," first quoting it as it appears in "The Frontier Forts of Pennsylvania," and then adding some comments which show that its inclusion in the present chapter is not inappropriate. The story is as follows:

"The Rev. Henry Melchior Muhlenberg [a son-in-law of Conrad Weiser] relates in the 'Hallische Nachrichten,' page 1029, a touching incident, which has been frequently told, but is so 'apropos' to this record that it should not be omitted. It was of the widow of John Hartman who called at his house in February, 1765, who had been a member of one of Rev. Kurtz's [a Lutheran pastor in Berks County] congregations. She and her husband had emigrated to this country from Reutlingen, Wurtemberg, and settled on the frontiers of Lebanon County. The Indians fell upon them in October, 1755, killed her husband, one of the sons, and carried off two small daughters into captivity, whilst she and the other son were absent. On her return she found the home in ashes, and her family either dead or lost to her, whereupon she fled to the interior settlements at Tulpehocken and remained there.

"The sequel to this occurrence is exceedingly interesting The two girls were taken away. It was never known what became of Barbara, the elder, but Regina, with another little girl two years old, were given to an old Indian women, who treated them very harshly. In the absence of her son, who supplied them with food, she drove the children into the woods to gather herbs and roots to eat, and, when they failed to get enough, beat them cruelly. So they lived until Regina was about nineteen years old and the other girl eleven. Her mother was a good Christian woman, and had taught her daughters their prayers, together with many texts from the Scriptures, and their beautiful German hymns, much of which clung to her memory during all these years of captivity.

"At last, in the providence of God, Colonel Bouquet brought the Indians under subjection in 1764, [at the end of Pontiac's War] and obliged them to give up their captives. More than two hundred of these unfortunate beings were gathered together at Carlisle, amongst them the two girls, and notices were sent all over the country for those who had lost friends and relatives, of that fact. Parents and husbands came, in some instances, hundreds of miles, in the hope of recovering those they had lost, the widow being one of the number. There were many joyful scenes, but more sad ones. So many changes had taken place, that in many instances, recognition seemed impossible. This was the case with the widow. She went up and down the long line, but, in the young women who stood before her, dressed in Indian costume, she failed to recognize the little girls she had lost. As she tood, gazing and weeping, Colonel Bouquet compassionately suggested that she do something which might recall the past to her children. She could think of nothing but a hymn which was formerly a favorite with the little ones:

'Allein, und doch nicht ganz allein,
Bin ich in meiner Einsamkeit.'

[The English translation of the first stanza of this hymn is as follows:

'Alone, yet not alone am I,
Though in this solitude so drear;
I feel my Saviour always nigh,
He comes the very hour to cheer;
I am with Him, and He with me,
E'en here alone I cannot be.']

"She commenced singing, in German, but had barely completed two lines, when poor Regina rushed from the crowd, began to sing also and threw her arms around her mother. They both wept for joy and the Colonel gave the daughter up to her mother. But the other girl had no parents, they having probably been murdered. She clung to Regina and begged to be taken home with her. Poor as was the widow she could not resist the appeal and the three departed together."

The foregoing account is all based on the original account written by the Rev. Henry Melchior, Muhlenberg, D.D., in his "Hallische Nachrichten," with the exception of the family name of the mother and daughter. Muhlenberg does not give the name of the family and does not definitely give the location of the tragedy. In time the belief became quite general among Pennsylvania historians that Regina was a daughter of John Hartman, born June 20th, 1710, and that the scene of the tragedy is at or near the site of the town of Orwigsburg, Schuylkill County.

Captain H. M. M. Richards, a descendant of Muhlenberg, contends in his "The Pennsylvania-German in the French and Indian War" (Vol. XV of the Publications of the Pennsylvania German Society), that Regina was none other than Regina Leininger, who, as we have seen, was captured at the Penn's Creek massacre of October 16th, 1755, the very date Muhlenberg gives as the date of the tragedy described in his account. In addition to the date of the alleged Hartman tragedy being the same as the date of the Leininger tragedy, the following points of similarity in the narrative of Rev. Muhlenberg and the narrative of Marie Le Roy and Barbara Leininger will be noted: In each tragedy, the mother was absent, the father was killed, a son was killed and two daughters, one named Regina and the other Barbara, were captured.

Furthermore, Muhlenberg says that the father "was already advanced in years, and too feeble to endure hard labor;" but John Hartman would have been only forty-five years old at the time of the tragedy. Also, there is no record of Indian outrages east of the Susquehanna until after the attack on John Harris (October, 25th), and none in the neighborhood of Orwigsburg until at least the middle of November.

We believe that any one who will closely compare the narrative of Barbara Leininger and Marie le Roy with Muhlenberg's account will agree with Captain Richards that each narrative describes the same tragedy—that Regina "Hartman" was Regina Leininger, and that she became permanently separated from her sister Barbara at the time of the flight of the Indians and their captives from Kuskuskies to the Muskingum, after General Forbes captured Fort Duquesne.

"Regina, the German Captive," and her mother are said to be buried in Christ Lutheran Cemetery, near Stouchsburg, Berks County. Whether or not the dust of this daughter of the Pennsylvania frontier reposes in this cemetery, and whether her name was Regina Leininger or Regina Hartman, God knows where she sleeps and has written her name in his book of everlasting remembrance.

CHAPTER VIII

Invasion of Great and Little Coves and the Conolloways

ON October 31st, 1755, one hundred Delawares and Shawnees from the Ohio and Allegheny began an invasion of the Scotch Irish settlements in the Great or Big Cove and along the Big and Little Conolloway Creeks in Fulton County and the Little Cove in Franklin County. This incursion lasted for several days and virtually blotted out these settlements. Of the ninety-three settlers in the Great Cove, forty-seven were killed and captured. No pen can describe the horrors of this bloody incursion. Infuriated Indians dashed out the brains of little children against the door-posts of cabins of the settlers in the presence of shrieking mothers, and, it is said, in some cases, cut off the heads of children and drank their warm blood. Wives and mothers were tied to trees, and compelled to witness the torture of their husbands and children. One woman, over ninety years of age, was found with her breasts cut off and a stake driven through her body. Scores of houses and barns were burned. Horses and cattle were killed or driven off. The captured settlers were taken to Kittanning and other Delaware and Shawnee towns in the valleys of the Allegheny and Ohio, and later to the Tuscarawas and Muskingum, few of whom ever returned.

The leader of the Indians was Shingas, the "Delaware King," a brother of King Beaver or Tamaque, and Pisquetomen and said by some authorities to have been a nephew of the great Sassoonan, or Allumapees. This was the first of those incursions which made the name of Shingas "a terror to the frontier settlements of Pennsylvania." Heckewelder says of him: "Were his war exploits all on record, they would form an interesting document, though a shocking one. Conococheague, Big Cove, Sherman's Valley and other settlements along the frontier felt his strong arm sufficiently that he was a bloody warrior, cruel his treatment, relentless his fury. His person was small, but in point of courage and activity, savage prowess, he was said to have never been exceeded by any one." Yet Heckewelder further says that, though Shingas was terrible and vindictive in battle, he was nevertheless kind to prisoners whose lives he intended to spare. "One day," he says, "in the summer of 1762, while passing with him [Shingas] near by where two prisoners of his, boys about twelve years of age, were amusing themselves with his own boys, as the chief observed that my attention was arrested by them, he asked me at what I was looking. Telling him in reply that I was looking at his prisoners, he said: 'When I first took them, they were such; but now they and my children eat their food from the same bowl, or dish.' Which was equivalent to saying that they were, in all respects, on an equal footing with his own children, or alike dear to him." Shingas was at that time living on the Muskingum.

But let us return to the scenes of blood and death in the Coves and along the Conolloways. The following letters vividly tell the story of this incursion:

Benjamin Chambers (later Colonel), writing from his home at Falling Springs, now Chambersburg, Franklin County, on November 2nd, "to the inhabitants of the lower part of the County of Cumberland," tells of this bloody incursion as follows:

"If you intend to go to the assistance of your neighbours, you need wait any longer for the certainty of the news. The Great Cove is destroyed; James Campbell left this company last night and went to the fort at Mr. Steel's meeting house, and there saw some of the inhabitants of the Great Cove, who gave this account that, as they came over the hill, they saw their houses in flames. The messenger says that there is but 100, and that they divided into two parts. The one part to go against the Cove and the other against the Conolloways, and that there are no French among them. They are Delawares and Shawnees. The part that came against the Cove are under the command of Shingas, the Delaware King; the people of the Cove that came off saw several men lying dead; they heard the murder shout and the firing of guns, and saw the Indians going into the houses that they had come out of before they left sight of the Cove. I have sent express to Marsh Creek at the same time that I send this, so I expect there will be a good company from there this day, and as there is but 100 of the enemy, I think it is in our power (if God permit) to put them to flight, if you turn out well from your parts. I understand that the west settlement is designed to go if they can get any assistance to repel them." (Pa. Col. Rec., Vol. 6, pages 675-676.)

Likewise, John Armstrong (later Colonel) wrote Governor Morris from Carlisle, on November 2nd:

"At four o'clock this afternoon by expresses from Conegochego, we are informed that yesterday about 100 Indians were seen in the Great Cove. Among whom was Shingas, the Delaware King; that immediately after the discovery, as many as had notice fled, and looking back from an high hill, they beheld their houses on fire, heard several guns fired and the last shrieks of their dying neighbours; 'tis said the enemy divided and one part moved towards Canallowais. Mr. Hamilton was here with 60 men from York County when the express came, and is to march early tomorrow to the upper part of the county. We have sent out expresses everywhere, and intend to collect the forces of this lower part, expecting the enemy every moment at Sherman's Valley, if not nearer hand. I'm of opinion that no other means than a chain of block houses along or near the south side of the Kittatinny Mountain, from Susquehannah to the temporary line, can secure the lives and properties even of the old inhabitants of this county, the new settlement being all fled except Sherman's Valley, whom (if God do not preserve) we fear will suffer very soon." (Pa. Col. Rec., Vol. 6, page 676.)

The following day (November 3d), Adam Hoops wrote Governor Morris, from Conococheague, concerning the same incursion, as follows:

"I am sorry I have to trouble you with this melancholy and disagreeable news, for on Saturday I received an express from Peters Township that the inhabitants of the Great Cove were all murdered or taken captive and their houses and barns all in flames. Some few fled, upon notice brought them by a certain Patrick Burns, a captive, that made his escape that very morning before this sad tragedy was done.

"Upon this information, John Potter, Esq., and self, sent express through our neighborhood, which induced many of them to meet with us at John McDowell's Mill, where I with many others had the unhappy prospect to see the smoke of two houses that were set on fire by the Indians, viz, Matthew Patton's and Mescheck James', where their cattle were shot down, the horses standing bleeding with Indian arrows in them, but the Indians fled.

"The Rev. Mr. Steel, John Potter, Esq., and several others

with us, to the number of about an hundred, went in quest of the Indians, with all the expedition imaginable, but to no success. These Indians have likewise taken two women captives, belonging to said township. I very much fear the Path Valley has undergone the same fate. George Croghan was at Aughwick, where he had a small fort and about 35 men, but whether he has been molested or not we cannot say.

"We, to be sure, are in as bad circumstances as ever any poor Christians were in, for the cries of the widowers, widows, fatherless and motherless children, with many others, for their relations, are enough to pierce the hardest of hearts; likewise it's a very sorrowful spectacle to see those that escaped with their lives with not a mouthful to eat, or bed to lie on, or clothes to cover their nakedness, or keep them warm, but all they had consumed into ashes.

"These deplorable circumstances cry aloud for your Honour's most wise consideration, that you would take cognizance of and grant what shall seem most meet, for it is really very shocking, it must be, for the husband to see the wife of his bosom, her head cut off, and the children's blood drank like water by these bloody and cruel savages as we are informed has been the fate of many.

"Whilst I am writing, I had intelligence by some that fled out of the Coves that chiefly the upper part of it was killed and taken. One, Galloway's son, escaped after he saw his grand-mother shot down and other relations taken prisoners. Likewise, from some news I have likewise heard, I am apprehensive that George Croghan is in distress, though just now Mr. Burd, with about 40 men, left my house and we intend to join him tomorrow at McDowell's Mill, with all the force we can raise, in order to see what damages are done, and for his relief. As we have no magazines at present to supply the guards or scouts, the whole weight of their maintenence lies chiefly upon a few persons." (Pa. Archives, Vol. 2, pages 462 and 463.)

Also, on November 3d, John Potter, Sheriff of Cumberland County, wrote Secretary Richard Peters, from Conococheague, as follows:

"Sir: This comes ye melancholy account of the ruin of the Great Cove, which is reduced to ashes, and numbers of the inhabitants murdered and taken captives on Saturday last about three of the clock in the afternoon. I received intelligence in conjunction with Mr. Adam Hoopes, and sent immediately and appointed our neighbors to meet at McDowell's. On Sunday morning, I was not there six minutes till we observed, about a mile and half distant, one Mathew Patton's house and barn in flames, on which we sat off with about forty men, tho' there was as least one hundred and sixty there. Our old officers hid themselves for (ought as I know) to save their scalps until afternoon when danger was over; we went to Patton's with a seeming resolution and courage but found no Indians there, on which we advanced to a rising ground, where we immediately discovered another house and barn on fire belonging to Mesach James, about one mile up the creek from Thomas Bar's; we set off directly for that place, but they had gone up the creek to another plantation left by one widow Jordan the day before, but had unhappily gone back that morning with a young woman, daughter to one William Clark, for some milk for childer, were both taken captives but neither house nor barn hurt. I have heard of no more burnt in that valley yet, which makes me believe they have gone off for some time, but I much fear they will return before we are prepared for them, for it was three of the clock in the afternoon before a recruit came of about sixty men. Then we held council whether to pursue up the valley all night or return to McDowell's, the former of which I and Mr. Hoop and some others plead for, but could not obtain without putting it to votes, which done, we were out voted by a considerable number, upon which I and my company was left by them that night and came home, for I will not guard a man that will not fight when called in so eminent manner, for there was not six of these men that would consent to go in pursuit of the Indians.

"I am much afraid that Juniata, Tuscaroro, and Sherman's Valley hath suffered. There is two-thirds of the inhabitants of this valley who hath already fled, leaving their plantations, and, without speedy succor be granted, I am of opinion this county will be lead dissolute without inhabitant. Last night I had a family of upwards of an hundred of women and children who fled for succor. You cannot form no just idea of the distressed and distracted condition of our inhabitants unless your eyes seen and your ears heard their crys. I am of opinion it is not in the power of our representatives to meet in assembly at this time. If our Assembly will give us any additional supply of arms and ammunition, the latter of which is most wanted, I could wish it were put into the hands of such persons as would go out upon scouts after the Indians rather than for the supply of forts." (Pa. Col. Rec., Vol. 6, pages 673, 674.)

Then, on November 6th, Adam Hoops again wrote Governor Morris, from Conococheague:

"I have Sent in Closed, Is 2 qualifications of which is Patrick Burns, who is the bearer, and a tameyhak which was found Sticking in the brest of one, David McClellan. The people of the path valley is all Gethered Unto a small fort, and the last account, was Safe. The Great Cove and Kennalaways is all Burned to Ashes, and about 50 persons killed or taken. There is numbers of the inhabitants of this County have moved their families, Sum to York County, and Sum to Maryland; Hans Hamilton, Esq. is now at John McDowell's mill with upwards of 200 men and about 200 from this County, in all about four hundred men, and tomorrow we entends To go into the Cove and to the Path Valley, in order To Bring what Cattle and horses that the Indians hath Left alive; we are informed by a Dolloway Indian, which lives munghts us, on the same day The Murder was Committed, he Seen four hundred Indians in the Cove, and we have Sum Reason to Believe they are about there yet; the people of Sheer Man's Crick and Juneate is all Cum away and left there houses, and there is now about 30 miles Of this County laid waste, and I am afraid there will Be Soon more.

"P. S. I just now have received ye Account of one, George McSwane, who was taken captive about 14 Days ago, and has made his Escape, and has brought two Scalps and a Tomahawk with Him." (Pa. Archives, Vol. 2, pages 474, 475.)

The Pennsylvania *Gazette*, November 13th, 1755, gives a partial list of those killed and captured in the Great Cove, Little Cove and the Conolloways, as follows: Elizabeth Galloway, William Fleming's son and one, Hicks, Henry Gilson, Robert Peer and David McClellan were all killed; while John Martin's wife and five children, William Galloway's wife and two children, a certain young woman, Charles Stewart's wife and two children, David McClellan's wife and two children and William Fleming and wife were captured.

Other captives, taken in this incursion and later delivered up by the Delaware chief, King Beaver, at the Lancaster Council of August, 1762, were Elizabeth McAdam and John Lloyd, from the Little Cove, and Dorothy Shobrian, from the Big Cove. (Pa. Col. Rec., Vol. 8, page 728.) Many of the captives, taken in this incursion, were delivered up to Colonel Bouquet at the time of his expedition to the Muskingum, in the autumn of 1764.

In the Penna. Col. Records, Vol. 6, page 767, is found another reference to this incursion, as follows:

"October 31st. An Indian Trader and two other men in the Tuscarora Valley were killed by Indians, and their Houses burnt, on which most of the Settlers fled and abandoned their Plantations.

(One of these men was the Indian trader, Peter Shaver, for whom Shaver's Creek, in Huntingdon County, is named. Another was John Savage.)

"November 3d. Two women are carried away from Conegochege (Conococheague) by the Indians, and the same day the Canalaways and Little Cove, two other considerable settlements, were attacked by them, their Houses burnt, and the whole Settlement deserted."

The Pennsylvania *Gazette*, February 12th, 1756, gives the number of people murdered and captured along the Conolloways. James Seaton, Catherine Stillwell and one of her children were killed and scalped, while two others of her children, one aged eight years and the other three, were captured. Richard Stillwell, her husband, was at a neighbors when the tragedy at his home occurred, and made his escape to a block house in the neighborhood. The houses of Elias Stillwell, John McKinney and Richard Malone were burned.

Rev. John Steel

The "fort at Mr. Steel's meeting house," mentioned in Benjamin Chambers' letter of November 2nd, where the survivors of the Great Cove massacre found refuge, was named in honor of the Presbyterian minister, Rev. John Steel, and was one of the first forts erected after Braddock's defeat, being a stockade around the church, and located about three miles east of Mercersburg, Franklin County. It was known as the "Old White Church," and was subsequently burned by the Indians in one of their forays. In 1756, Rev. Steel was appointed Captain in a company in the pay of the Province, and for a time, made his headquarters at McDowell's Mill, or Fort McDowell, located in the western part of Franklin County. From this place he detached parties from time to time to scour the woods in search of hostile Indians. About 1758, he took charge of the Presbyterian church at Carlisle, where he ended his days. In March and April, 1768, he and John Allison, Cristopher Lemes and James

Potter were sent by Governor John Penn to warn the settlers in the vicinity of Redstone (Brownsville) to remove from lands not purchased from the Indians. Rev. Steel and his men are frequently mentioned in the records of the troublesome times of which we are writing. On page 553 of Vol. 1 of "The Frontier Forts of Pennsylvania," we read the following concerning this preacher and soldier of the Pennsylvania frontier:

"At one time, it is stated, Rev. Steel was in charge of Fort Allison, located just west of the town, near what afterward became the site of McCaulay's Mill. At this time the congregation had assembled in a barn . . . During this period, when Mr. Steel entered the church and took his place back of the rude pulpit, he hung his hat and rifle behind him, and this was done also by many of his parishoners. On one occasion, while in the midst of his discourse, some one stepped into the church quietly, and called a number of the congregation out, and related the facts of a murder of a family by the name of Walker by the Indians at Rankin's Mill. The tragic story was soon whispered from one to another. As soon as Mr. Steel discovered what had taken place, he brought the services to a close, took his hat and rifle, and at the head of the members of his congregation, went in pursuit of the murderers."

The murder above mentioned, was probably that of William Walker, in Silver Spring Township, Cumberland County, on May 13th, 1757.

Capture of the Martin and Knox Families

Among the outrages committed by Shingas during the above incursion into Fulton County, was as has been seen, the capture of the family of John Martin, a settler in the Big Cove. On Saturday morning, November 1, 1755, Mrs. Martin learned that Indians were in the neighborhood, and, thereupon, sent her son, Hugh, aged seventeen, to their neighbor, Captain Stewart, requesting him to come and take her family with his to the blockhouse, as her husband, John Martin, had gone to Philadelphia for supplies for the family, and had not returned. When Hugh came in sight of his home on his way back from Captain Stewart's, whose house was burned, he saw the Indians capture his mother; his sister, Mary, aged nineteen; his sister, Martha, aged twelve; his sister, Janet, aged two; his brother, James aged ten; and his brother, William, aged eight. Hugh hid where a fallen tree lay on the bank of Cove Creek not far from the Martin house, which the Indians now burned to the ground.

It has been said that there were some Tuscaroras among the band that captured Mrs. Martin and her children. At least such is the tradition among her descendants. It may be that some of this tribe were among the hostile Delawares and Shawnees in this incursion, as there is evidence that there were a few Tuscaroras lingering in the Tuscarora or Path Valley as late as 1755, stragglers of the Tuscarora migration to New York. These may have been influenced by the hostile Delawares and Shawnees.

After the Indians left, Hugh started toward Philadelphia to meet his father. All that day he found nothing but desolation, and in the evening, he came to a stable with some hay in it. Here he lay until morning. During the night something jumped on him, which proved to be a dog. In the morning he found some fresh eggs in the stable, which he ate. When he was ready to leave, a large colt came to the stable. Making a halter of rope, he mounted the colt and rode on his way. In the afternoon, he met some men who had gathered to pursue the Indians, among them being the owner of the colt, who was much surprised to find it so easily managed, as it was considered unruly. It is not known when Hugh met his father, but, at any rate, they returned and rebuilt the house.

Mrs. Martin and her children were taken to the Indian town of Kittanning. A warrior wished to marry Mary, which made the squaws jealous and they beat her dreadfully, so much so that her health rapidly declined, and one morning she was found on her knees dead in the wigwam. An Indian squaw claimed little Janet, and tied her to a rope fastened to a post. While she was thus confined, a French trader named Baubee came to the child, and she reached out her arms and called him father. He then took her in his arms, and the Indian woman who claimed her sold her to the trader for a blanket, who carried her to Quebec intending to adopt her. Later, Mrs. Martin was bought by the French, and also taken to Quebec, not knowing her child was there. Still later, Mrs. Martin bought her own freedom, and one day she found little Janet on the streets of Quebec. Janet was well dressed and had all appearances of being well cared for, but did not recognize the mother. Mrs. Martin followed Janet to the home of the French family who had her, identified her by some mark, and the family reluctantly gave up the child to the mother, who paid them what they had paid the Indians for her.

Mrs. Martin then sailed with Janet to Liverpool, England, from which place she took ship to Philadelphia, and joined her husband.

The boys, James and William, and the daughter, Martha, were taken to the Tuscarawas and Muskingum, in the state of Ohio. After Mrs. Martin and Janet returned to their home in the Big Cove, Mr. Martin, upon the close of the French and Indian War, endeavored to recover his child from the Indians. Traveling on horseback to the Ligonier Valley, he found an encampment of Indians, and tried to make arrangements with them for the return of his children, when they claimed to have raised his family and wanted pay. Being unable to pay them, he said something about not having employed them to raise his family; thereupon, they became angry, and he made his escape as fast as he could, being chased by two Indians on horseback to a point on the Allegheny Mountain, where the sound of the bells of the Indian horses ceased.

In the Penna. Archives (Vol. 4, page 100), is a petition of John Martin, dated August 13th, 1762, presented to Governor James Hamilton at the Lancaster Council of that month and year, in which he says:

"I, one of the bereaved of my wife and five children, by savage war, at the captivity at the Great Cove, after many and long journeys, lately went to an Indian town, *viz.*, Tuskoraways [Tuscarawas, a Delaware and Wyandot village on the Tuscarawas River just above the mouth of Big Sandy Creek, in Tuscarawas County, Ohio] 150 miles beyond Fort Pitt, and entreated in Colonel Bouquet's and Colonel Croghan's favour, so as to bear their letters to King Beaver and Captain Shingas, desiring them to give up one of my daughters to me, while I have yet two sons and one other daughter, if alive, among them—and after seeing my daughter with Shingas, he refused to give her up, and after some expostulating with him, but all in vain, he promised to deliver her up with the other captives, to your Excellency."

Many captives were delivered by King Beaver at the Lancaster Council of August, 1762, but the Martin children were not among them. These Martin children, James, William and Martha, were finally liberated by Colonel Henry Bouquet when he made his expedition to the Muskingum and Tuscarawas, in the late autumn of 1764. He brought them to Pittsburgh. Here Mr. Martin received them on November 28th, 1764, and then returned with them to his home, taking with him another liberated captive, John McCullough, who was captured in Franklin County, on July 26th, 1756. (*See John McCullough's "Narrative.") Martha could read when captured, but during her captivity, she had forgotten this art. William and James, during their captivity, assisted the squaws in raising vegetables, caring for the children and old people, and grew up as Indians, in contrast to their brother, Hugh, who had escaped capture and became a man of considerable influence on the Pennsylvania frontier. Before being taken to the Muskingum, Martha, James, and William spent some time with their Indian captors on Big Sewickley Creek, in Westmoreland County. The boys became attached to the locality, and after their return, they patented two tracts of land in that vicinity, and lived there most of their lives.

Janet Martin, in 1774, married John Jamison. She has many descendants in Western Pennsylvania, especially in Westmoreland County, among them being the well-known Robert S. Jamison family, of Greensburg.

During the same incursion, occurred the capture of the Knox family, who lived some distance from the Big Cove. On Sunday morning, November 2nd, 1755, while the family were engaged in morning worship, they were alarmed by the barking of their dogs. Then, two men of their acquaintance, who had come to the Knox home on Saturday evening for the purpose of attending religious services the next day, went to the door. They were immediately shot down by the Indians, and the rest of the family taken prisoners. After the Indians returned to the town from where they had come, no doubt Kittanning, each warrior who had lost a brother in the incursion was given a prisoner to kill. As there were not enough men to go around, little Jane Knox was given to one of the warriors as his victim. Placing her at the root of a tree, this savage commenced throwing his tomahawk close to her head, exclaiming that his brother, who was killed, was a warrior, and that the other Indians had given him only a squaw to kill. Jane expected that every moment would be her last. Presently, an Indian squaw came running and claimed Jane as her child, thus saving her life. She later returned to the settlements, and became the wife of Hugh Martin, mentioned above.

---

* While this is McCullough's statement, data in the possession of the descendants of Janet Martin indicates that the Martin children were delivered by the Shawnees to George Croghan, at Fort Pitt, early in May, 1765.

Conclusion

In concluding this chapter on the bloody incursion of the Delawares and Shawnees into the Scotch-Irish settlements in Fulton and Franklin Counties, in the late autumn days of 1755, we call attention to the fact that some historians have erroneously stated that the massacres mentioned in Penna. Archives, Vol. 2, page 375, and Pa. Col. Rec., Vol. 6, pages 641 and 642, took place on Pennsylvania soil, the former in the Great Cove and on the Conolloways, in Fulton County, and the latter in the vicinity of Patterson's Fort, in Juniata County. The former took place in the vicinity of Cumberland, Maryland, shortly after General Braddock's army left that place on its March against Fort Duquesne. The latter took place, October 2nd, 1755, on Patterson's Creek, Maryland, a few miles from its mouth. The error on page 600 of Vol. 1 of "The Frontier Forts of Pennsylvania" in stating that this massacre of October 2nd took place near Patterson's Fort, in Juniata County, no doubt is due to confusing Patterson's Creek, in Maryland, with Patterson's Fort, in Juniata County, Pennsylvania. As stated in Chapter VII, the Penn's Creek massacre of October 16th, 1755, was the first massacre committed by the Indians on Pennsylvania soil following Braddock's defeat.

We also, at this point, call attention to the fact that Scotch-Irish settlers entered Franklin County prior to 1730. In this year, Benjamin and Joseph Chambers located at Falling Springs, now Chambersburg, coming from the east side of the Susquehanna above Harrisburg, and erecting a log house, a saw mill and grist mill at Falling Springs. After Braddock's defeat, Benjamin (Colonel) Chambers erected a large stone house at Falling Springs for the security of his family and neighbors. It was surrounded by water from the spring, the roof was of lead to prevent its being set on fire by the Indians, and it was also stockaded. The stockade also included the mill near the house. This fort was known as Chambers' Fort.

About 1740, many Scotch Irish settlers, mostly from Maryland entered the Great Cove and the valleys of the Conolloways.

As was pointed out in Chapter IV, in connection with the account of the Treaty of 1742, the Iroquois complained at this treaty, through their spokesman, Canassatego, that Pennsylvania was permitting squatters to remain on lands not purchased from the Six Nations—in the Juniata Valley, in the Great and Little Coves, in the valleys of Big and Little Conolloways, in the valley of Aughwick Creek, in Path Valley and Sherman's Valley.

But Pennsylvania made no really energetic effort to remove these settlers until May, 1750, when, as was also pointed out in Chapter IV, they were removed by Richard Peters, George Croghan, Conrad Weiser, James Galbraith and others by authority of Lieutenant-Governor Morris. Many of their cabins were burned on this occasion. But the restless spirit of these settlers impelled them to return to their desolated homes, and with them came others willing to risk the wrath of the Indians. Then came the Albany Purchase of July 6th, 1754, by which the Iroquois conveyed these lands to Pennsylvania—a purchase which mortally offended the Delawares and Shawnees, who claimed that the Six Nations, their conquerors, had guaranteed these lands to them upon their migration from the Susquehanna. "Our lands are sold from under our feet," said they. Later came Braddock's defeat, which gave the Delawares and Shawnees an opportunity to wreak awful vengenance upon the Scotch-Irish settlers within the bounds of the Albany Purchase.

CHAPTER IX

Massacres of November and December, 1755

THIS chapter will be devoted principally to massacres east of the Susquehanna in November and December, 1755, but, before narrating their details, we shall devote a few paragraphs to events that preceded them.

On November 3d, 1755, Governor Morris received John Armstrong's letter, quoted in Chapter VIII, advising him of the murder of the settlers in the Great Cove. He immediately called the attention of the Assembly to the acts of the hostile Indians and the terror throughout the frontier, and asked that something be done to put the Province in a state of defense. The Assembly replied, on November 5th, that it "requires great Care and Judgement in conducting our Indian Affairs at this critical Juncture," and requested the Governor to inform the House "if he knew of any injury which the Delawares and Shawnees had received to alienate their affections, and whether he knew the part taken by the Six Nations in relation to this incursion."

Robert Strettell, Joseph Turner, and Thomas Cadwalader, were appointed a committee to inspect all "minutes of Council and other books and papers" relating to Pennsylvania's transactions with the Delawares and Shawnees from the beginning of the Colony. The committee made an elaborate report, which was approved and sent to the House on November 22nd, setting forth the findings of the committee that "the conduct of the Proprietaries and this Government has been always uniformly just, fair, and generous towards these Indians."

In the meantime, the Governor had informed the inhabitants of the frontier counties from whom he received petitions for arms and ammunition that, if they would organize themselves into companies, he would give commissions to fit persons as officers. As a result of his offer, companies were raised and officers commissioned. Then, on November 8th, the Governor sent a message to the Assembly in which he said: "You have now been sitting six days, and instead of strengthening my Hands and providing for the safety and defense of the people and Province in this Time of imminent danger, You have sent me a message wherein you talk of retaining the Affections of the Indians now employed in laying waste the Country and butchering the Inhabitants, and of inquiring what injustice they have received, and into the Causes of their falling from their alliance with us and taking part with the French." In the same message, he informed the Assembly that the Provincial Council had advised him to visit the frontiers in order to superintend the work of organizing the settlers for defense; that he had waited to see what the Assembly would do before his setting out, but now realizing that the Assembly would do nothing, he proposed to start on his journey at once. However, Conrad Weiser, Scarouady, Andrew Montour and "drunken Zigrea," a Mohawk, arrived at Philadelphia that very day (November 8th) for the councils presently to be mentioned, which caused the Governor to postpone his trip until early in 1756. The cause of the lack of action to put the Province in a state of defense at this terrible time was the endless discussion, to be mentioned later in this chapter, between the Governor and the Assembly as to whether the proprietary estates should be taxed in raising money for defense. (Pa. Col. Rec., Vol. 6, pages 676 to 681.)

Scarouady Threatens to Go to the French

While the terrible things related in Chapter VIII were happening, Scarouady was exerting his utmost influence on behalf of the English. On November 1st, he and Andrew Montour came from Shamokin to Harris' Ferry, where he delivered a message to John Harris, who forwarded it to the Governor, advising, among other things, that "about twelve days ago the Delawares sent for Andrew Montour to go to Big Island [Lock Haven], on which he [Scarouady] and Montour with three more Indians went up immediately, and found there about six of the Delawares and four Shawnees, who informed them that they had received a hatchet from the French, on purpose to kill what game they could meet with, and to be used against the English if they proved saucy."

At this time (November 1st), Scarouady and Montour both told John Harris that a fort should immediately be erected at

Shamokin. "They said that our own Neglect had brought all this upon us; That the Delawares being asked why they took up the Hatchet, said the English had for some time called them Frenchmen, and yet fell upon no measures to defend themselves, whereupon they thought it not safe to stick by Us, and would now publicly declare themselves Frenchmen. That Scarouady Enquiring from George Croghan was answered by Mr. Buchannan he was fortified at Aughwick, whereupon the Indian desired Mr. Buchannan to give him speedy notice to remove, or he would certainly be killed. They say Carlisle is Severly threatened, and Adviseth that the Women and Children be removed." (Pa. Archives, Vol. 2, page 452.)

On November 8th, Scarouady and Montour, accompanied by Conrad Weiser, appeared before the Provincial Council, and, gave additional details of their trip to Big Island. Scarouady said that two Delawares from the Ohio appeared at the meeting at Big Island and spoke as follows: "We the Delawares of Ohio, do proclaim war against the English. We have been their friends many years, but now have taken up the hatchet against them, and will never make it up with them whilst there is an English man alive.

"When Washington was defeated, we, the Delawares, were blamed as the cause of it. We will now kill. We will not be blamed without a cause. We make up three parties of Delawares. One party will go against Carlisle; one down the Susquehanna; and . . . another party will go against Tulpehocken to Conrad Weiser. And we shall be followed by a thousand French and Indians, Ottawas, Twightwees, Shawnees, and Delawares."

It will be noted that the Delawares gave their being blamed for Washington's defeat at the Great Meadows, in the summer of 1754, as the cause of their having taken up arms against Pennsylvania. Later they told the Shawnee chief, Paxinosa, of Wyoming, that the cause of their hostility was the Walking Purchase of 1737 and the Albany Purchase of 1754; and the great Delaware chief, Teedyuscung, stoutly insisted that it was these wrongs upon the Delawares that caused these friends of William Penn to take up arms against the Colony he founded.

On the afternoon of the same day, November 8th, Scarouady again appeared before the Governor, his Council, and the Provincial Assembly, and told them of the journey which he had recently made in the interest of the English, up the North Branch of the Susquehanna "as far as the Nanticokes live." He stated that he had told the Nanticokes and other Indians on the Susquehanna that the defeat of General Braddock had brought about a great turn of affairs; that it was a great blow, but that the English had strength enough to recover from it. He further said that there were three hundred friendly Indians on the Susquehanna. (Delawares and Nanticokes) "who were all hearty in the English interest." For these he desired the Colony's assistance with arms and ammunition. He insisted that they should be given the hatchet and that a fort should be built for the protection of their old men, women, and children. They had told him, he said, that whichever party, the French or English, would seek their assistance first, would be first assisted; and that he "should go to Philadelphia and apply immediately to the Government and obtain explicit answer from them whether they would fight or no." These Indians "waited with impatience to know the success of his application."

Then the old chief threw down his belts of wampum upon the table before the members of the Assembly and said: "I must deal plainly with you, and tell you if you will not fight with us, we will go somewhere else. We never can nor ever will put up the affront. If we cannot be safe where we are, we will go somewhere else for protection and take care of ourselves. We have no more to say, but will first receive your answer to this, and as the times are too dangerous to admit of our staying long here, we therefore entreat you will use all the dispatch possible that we may not be detained." It is possible that Scarouady meant that he and his followers would go to one of the other colonies, but he was understood as meaning that, unless the Pennsylvania Authorities acted promptly, he and his followers would go over to the French.

Governor Morris then said to the Provincial Assembly: "You have heard what the Indians have said. Without your aid, I can not make a proper answer to what they now propose and expect of us." The Assembly replied that, as Captain General, the Governor had full authority to raise men, and that "the Bill now in his hands granting Sixty Thousand Pounds will enable him to pay the expenses." This was a bill just passed by the Assembly, granting this sum for the defense of the Colony, to be raised by a tax on estates. The Governor opposed the bill on the ground that the Proprietary estates should not be taxed. He then explained to Scarouady how his controversy with the Assembly stood, and that he did not know what to do. Scarouady was amazed and said that Pennsylvania's failure to comply with his (Scarouady's) request in behalf of his three hundred friendly Indians would mean their going over to the French. However, he still offered his own services and counseled the Governor not to be cast down, but to keep cool.

After long consultations between Scarouady and Conrad Weiser, it was determined that Scarouady could render an important service to the Colony by visiting the Six Nations and Sir William Johnson, and, after gaining what intelligence he could on his way to New York, as to the actions of the Indians on the Susquehanna, by laying before the Great Confederation such intelligence as well as the recent conduct of the Delawares.

Scarouady's decided stand had a good effect on the Governor and Council. On November 14th, the old chief and Andrew Montour were sent by the Governor on a mission to the Six Nations. They were instructed to convey the condolence of Pennsylvania to the Six Nations on the death of several of their warriors who had joined General Shirley and General Johnson and had fallen in battle with the French, and to advise the Six Nations how the Delawares had, in a most cruel manner, fallen upon and murdered so many of the inhabitants of Pennsylvania. In a word, Scarouady was to give the Six Nations a complete account of the terrible invasion of the Delawares and Shawnees and to ascertain whether or not this invasion was made with the knowledge, consent, or order of the Six Nations, and whether the Six Nations would chastise the Delawares. (For account of above conferences between Scarouady and the Governor, see Pa. Col. Rec., Vol. 6, pages 682 to 689.)

Swatara and Tulpehocken Massacres

While Conrad Weiser, Scarouady and Andrew Montour were holding their final councils with Governor Morris, on November 14th, the hostile Delawares, possibly accompanied by some Shawnees, entered Berks County, the home of Weiser, and committed terrible atrocities upon the German settlers. On this day, as six settlers were on their way to Dietrick Six's plantation, near what is now the village of Millersburg, they were fired upon by a party of Indians. Hurrying toward a watch-house, about half a mile distant, they were ambushed before reaching the same, and three of them killed and scalped. A settler named Ury, however, succeeded in shooting one of the Indians through the heart, and his body was dragged off by the other savages. The Indians then divided into two parties. The one party, lying in ambush near the watch-house, waylaid some settlers who were fleeing toward that place, and killed three of them.

The next night some savages crept up to the home of Thomas Bower, on Swatara Creek, and pushing their guns through a window of the house, killed a cobbler who was repairing a shoe. They set fire to the house before being driven off. The Bower family, having sought refuge through the night at the home of a neighbor, named Daniel Snyder, and returning to their home in the morning, saw four savages running away and having with them the scalps of three children, two of whom were still alive. They also found the dead body of a woman with a two week's old child under her body, but unharmed.

Such, in brief, is the account of the atrocities committed in Berks County during the absence of Weiser at Philadelphia. It is interesting to read his report of the same, written to Governor Morris on November 19th, after arriving at his home in Heidelberg Township, as follows:

"On my return from Philadelphia, I met in the township of Amity, in Berks County, the first news of our cruel enemy having invaded the Country this Side of the Blue Mountains, to witt, Bethel and Tulpenhacon [Tulpehocken]. I left the papers as they were in the messengers Hands, and hastened to Reading, where the alarm and confusion was very great. I was obliged to stay that Night and part of the next Day, to witt, the 17th of this Instant, and sat out for Heidelberg, where I arrived that Evening. Soon after, my sons Philip and Frederick arrived from the Persuit of the Indians, and gave me the following Relation, to witt, that on Saturday last about 4 of the Clock, in the Afternoon, as some men from Tulpenhacon were going to Dietrich Six's Place under the Hill on Shamokin Road to be on the watch appointed there, they were fired upon by the Indians but none hurt nor killed, (Our people were but Six in number, the rest being behind.) Upon which our people ran towards the Watch-house which was about one-half mile off, and the Indians persued them, and killed and scalped several of them. A bold, Stout Indian came up with one Christopher Ury, who turned about and shot the Indian right through his Breast. The Indian dropped down dead, but was dragged out of the way by his own Companions. (He was found next day and scalped by our People.)

"The Indians devided themselves into two Parties. Some came this way to meet the Rest that was going to the Watch, and killed some of them, so that six of our men were killed that Day, and a few wounded.

"The Night following the Enemy attacked the House of Thos. Bower, on Swatara Creek. They came to the House in the Dark night, and one of them put his Fire-arm through the window and shot a Shoemaker (that was at work) dead upon the spot. The People being extremely Surprised at this Sudden attack, defended themselves by firing out of the windows at the Indians. The Fire alarmed a neighbor who came with two or three more men; they fired by the way and made a great noise, scared the Indians away from Bower's House, after they had set fire to it, but by Thomas Bower's Deligence and Conduct was timely put out again, So Thos. Bower, with his Family, went off that night to his neighbour, Daniel Schneider, who came to his assistance.

"By 8 of ye Clock, Parties came up from Tulpenhacon and Heidelberg. The first Party saw four Indians running off. They had some Prisoners whom they scalped immediately, three children lay scalped yet alive, one died since, the other two are likely to do well. Another Party found a woman just expired, with a male Child on her side, both killed and scalped. The woman lay upon her Face, my son Frederick turned her about to see who she might have been and to his Companion's Surprize they found a Babe of about 14 Days old under her, rapped up in a little Cushion, his nose quite flat, which was set right by Frederick, and life was yet in it, and recovered again. Our people came up with two parties of Indians that Day, but they hardly got sight of them, the Indians Ran off Immediately. Either our party did not care to fight them if they could avoid it, or (which is most likely) the Indians were too alarmed first by the loud noise of our People coming, because no order was observed. Upon the whole, there is about 15 killed of our People, Including men, women and children, and the Enemy not beat but scared off. Several Houses and Barns are Burned; I have not true account how many. We are in a Dismal Situation, Some of this murder has been committed in Tulpenhacon Township. The People left their Plantation to within 6 or 7 miles from my house [located near the present town of Wolmesdorf] against another attack.

"Guns and Ammunition is very much wanted here, my Sons have been obliged to part with most of that, that was sent up for the use of the Indians. I pray your Honour will be pleased, if it lies in your Power, to send us up a quantity upon any Condition. I must stand my Ground or my neighbours will all go away, and leave their Habitations to be destroyed by the Enemy or our own People.

"P. S. I am creditably informed just now that one Wolf, a Single man, killed an Indian the same Time when Ury killed the other but the Body is not found yet. The Poor Young Man since died of his wound through his Belly." (Pa. Archives Vol. 2, pages 503, 504.)

The following is a partial list of the slain:

A man named Beslinger, Sebastian Brosius, the wife and eight-year-old child of a settler named Cola, Rudolph Candel, John Leinberger, Casper Spring, a child of Jacob Wolf and a young man also named Wolf.

Following the murders, the Rev. J. N. Kurtz conducted funeral services for seven of the victims of the Indians' wrath who were buried from his church, Christ Lutheran, near Stouchsburg, at one time. The opening hymn at these solemn services was Martin Luther's famous "Ein' feste Burg ist unser Gott" (A Mighty Fortress is Our God). Rev. Kurtz was pastor of the Lutheran congregation at Tulpehocken to which Conrad Weiser and many of his neighbors belonged.

At various other times during the French and Indian War, the soil of Berks County was stained with the blood of the German settlers. It is claimed that, during this conflict, almost one hundred and fifty inhabitants of Bethel and Tulpehocken Townships were slain, and more than thirty carried into captivity, most of whom never returned.

Weiser and Scarouady in Danger from Settlers

Conrad Weiser, as has been seen, returned home from Philadelphia on November 17th, accompanied by Scarouady and Andrew Montour on their way to the Six Nations. He found the Berks County settlers in a state of great excitement, on account of the Indian outrages. The settlers of Berks County knew that he had frequently accompanied delegations of friendly Indians to Philadelphia. To many of the settlers whose homes and barns were destroyed and whose dear ones were murdered or carried into captivity, all Indians looked alike. Consequently, many of the settlers were now suspicious of Weiser, and believed that he was protecting Indians who did not deserve it. Consequently, also, he had now great difficulty in conducting Scarouady and Montour towards the Susquehanna. Said he, in another letter to Governor

Morris on November 19th: "I made all the haste with the Indians [Scarouady and Montour] I could, and gave them a letter to Thomas McKee, to furnish them with necessaries for their journey. Scarouady had no creature to ride on. I gave him one. Before I could get done with the Indians, three or four men came from Benjamin Spikers to warn the Indians not to go that way for the people were so enraged against all the Indians and would kill them without distinction. I went with them. So did the gentlemen before named. When we came near Benjamin Spikers, I saw about 400 or 500 men, and there was loud noise. I rode before, and in riding along the road and armed men on both sides of the road, I heard some say: 'Why must we be killed by the Indians, and not kill them. Why are our hands so tied.' I got the Indians into the house with much ado, where I treated them with a small dram, and so parted in love and friendship. Captain Diefenback undertook to conduct them, with five of our men, to the Susquehanna." (Pa. Archives, Vol. 2, pages 504 to 506.)

Continuing the above letter, Weiser says:

"After this, a sort of a counsel of war was held by the officers present, the before named, and other Freeholders.

"It was agreed that 150 men should be raised immediately to serve as out scouts, and as Guards at Certain Places under the Kittitany Hills for 40 days. That those so raised to have 2 Shillings a Day and 2 Pounds of Bread, 2 Pounds of Beaff and a jill of rum, and Powder and lead. Arms they must find themselves.

"This Scheme was signed by a good many Freeholders, and read to the people. They cried out that so much for an Indian scalp would they have, be they friends or enemies, from the Governor. I told them I had no such power from the Governor nor Assembly. They began some to curse the Governor; some the Assembly; called me a traitor of the country, who held with the Indians, and must have known this murder beforehand. I sat in the house by a lowe window; some of my friends came to pull me away from it, telling me some of the people threatened to shoot me.

"I offered to go out to the people and either pasefy them or make the King's Proclamation. But those in the house with me would not let me go out. The cry was, The Land was betrayed and sold. The common people from Lancaster [now Lebanon County] were the worst. The wages they said was a Trifle and some Body pocketed the Rest, and they would resent it. Some Body had put it in their head that I had it in my power to give them as much as I pleased. I was in danger of being shot to death.

"In the meantime, a great smoke arose under Tulpenhacon Mountain, with the news following that the Indians had committed a murder on Mill Creek (a false alarm) and set fire to a barn; most of the people ran, and those that had horses rode off without any order or regulation. I then took my horse and went home, where I intend to stay and defend my own house as long as I can. The people of Tulpenhacon all fled; till about 6 or 7 miles from me some few remains. Another such attack will lay all the country waste on the west side of Schuylkill."

In a subsequent chapter will be found Scarouady's report of his mission to the Six Nations. In the meantime, the Indians, entering the passes of the Blue Mountains, committed many murders and devastations in Berks, Lebanon, Northampton and Carbon Counties. Independent companies were hastily organized which later were incorporated into the Provincial Regiment. Captain Thomas McKee ranged the territory along the Susquehanna; Colonel Conrad Weiser, Captain Adam Read, of Swatara Creek and Captain Peter Heydrick, of Swatara Gap, ranged the territory between the Susquehanna and Schuylkill Rivers; the two Captains Wetterholt ranged the district along the Lehigh; and Captains Wayne, Hays, Jenning, McLaughlin and Van Etten ranged the territory between the Lehigh and Delaware. Nevertheless, the Indians crept stealthily upon the settlers, murdered them in cold blood, often in the dead hours of the night, and then disappeared before the alarm could be spread to the citizen soldiers.

The Kobel Atrocity

On November 24th, 1755, Governor Morris received a letter from Conrad Weiser in which he describes the attack on the Kobel family, one of the atrocities committed by the Indians in the invasion of Berks County, described in this chapter. The letter, found in Pa. Archives, Vol. 2, pages 511 and 512, is as follows:

"I cannot forbear to acquaint your Honor of a certain Circumstance of the late unhappy Affair: One............Kobel, with his wife and eight children, the eldest about fourteen Years and the youngest fourteen Days, was flying before the Enemy, he carrying one, and his wife and a Boy another of the Children, when they were fired upon by two Indians very nigh, but hit only the Man upon his Breast, though not Dangerously. They, the Indians, then came with their Tomahawks, knocked the woman down, but not dead. They intended to kill the Man, but his Gun (though out of order so that he could not fire) kept them off. The Woman recovered so farr, and seated herself upon a Stump, with her Babe in her Arms, and gave it Suck, and the Indians driving the children together, and spoke to them in High Dutch, 'Be still; we won't hurt you.' Then they struck a Hatchet into the woman's Head, and she fell upon her Face with her Babe under her, and the Indian trod on her neck and tore off the scalp. The children then run; four of them were scalped, among which was a Girl of Eleven Years of Age, who related the whole Story; of the Scalped, two are alive and like to do well. The Rest of the Children ran into the Bushes and the Indians after them, but our People coming near to them, and hallowed and made noise; the Indians Ran, and the Rest of the Children were saved. They ran within a Yard by a Woman that lay behind an Old Log, with two Children; there was about Seven or Eight of the Enemy."

Other Atrocities of 1755

Other atrocities, committed in the autumn of 1755, were the following:

Two brothers, named Ney, were ambushed by Indians, in the Tulpehocken region, while gathering a load of fire wood for winter. The one brother, Michael, was killed and scalped. The other brother was tomahawked and left for dead, but afterwards regained consciousness and made his way back home. Some neighbors then went in pursuit of the Indians. They found the body of Michael, but the Indians had fled.

As the Indian depredations spread eastward from Swatara Gap, they reached the vicinity of the present town of Pine Grove, Schuylkill County. Here George Everhart and his entire family except his little daughter, Margaret, were killed. The little girl was taken captive. She was released by Colonel Bouquet, when he made his expedition to the Muskingum, in the autumn of 1764, and returned to her friends. (H. M. M. Richards' "Pennsylvania Germans in the French and Indian War," pages 79 to 81.)

Moravians Massacred

Scarouady was hardly started on his journey to the Six Nations when the tomahawk and scalping knife of the Delawares became stained anew with the blood of the settlers of Eastern Pennsylvania. On November 24th, the Moravian missionaries at Gnadenhuetten, Carbon County, were cruelly murdered by a band of twelve warriors of the Munsee Clan of Delawares, led by Jachebus, chief of the Assinnissink, a Munsee town in Steuben County, New York. The bodies of the dead were placed in a grave. A monument marks the spot where the dust of these victims of savage cruelty reposes, a short distance from Lehighton, and bears the following inscription:

"To the memory of Gottlieb and Joanna Anders, with their child, Christiana; Martin and Susanna Nitschman; Anna Catherine Senseman; John Gattermeyer; George Fabricius, clerk; George Schweigert; John Frederick Lesly; and Martin Presser; who lived here at Gnadenhuetten unto the Lord, and lost their lives in a surprise from Indian warriors, November 24, 1755. Precious in the sight of the Lord is the death of his saints."

Bishop Loskiel's "History of the Moravian Mission" thus describes the massacre of the Moravians at Gnadenhuetten:

"The family were at supper; and on the report of a gun, several ran together to open the house-door; the Indians instantly fired and killed Martin Nitschman. His wife and some others were wounded, but fled with the rest to the garret, and barricaded the door. Two escaped by leaping out of a back window. The savages pursued those who had taken refuge in the garret, but finding the door too well secured, they set fire to the house, which was soon in flames. A boy and a woman leaped from the burning roof, and escaped almost miraculously. Br. Fabricius then leaped off the roof, but he was perceived by the Indians, and wounded with two balls; they dispatched him with their hatchets, and took his scalp. The rest were all burnt alive, except Br. Senseman, who got out at the back door. The house being consumed, the murderers set fire to the barns and stables, by which all the corn, hay and cattle were destroyed."

The light of the burning buildings was seen at Bethlehem, although nearly thirty miles distant and with the ridge of the Blue Mountains between.

On the day of the massacre, the Moravian missionary, David

Zeisberger, had been sent from Bethlehem to Gnadenhuetten, bearing a letter relative to the convoy of some friendly Indians at Wyoming who wished to visit the Governor. He had reached the Lehigh River and was just ready to cross to the other side, before it became quite dark, when he heard gun-shots, which he supposed to be those of militia patroling the woods. Suddenly a piteous cry floated on the evening air, but Zeisberger did not hear it, as his horse was now wading the river and the splashing water and the crack of the stones under his horse's hoofs prevented his hearing anything else. Nor did he see the flames, as the thick underbrush of the river bank and the bluff beyond concealed their light from him. Having reached the west shore, he paused a moment and took in the awful situation, just as young Joseph Sturgis, who had escaped with a slight wound on his face, rushed down to the river. Turning his horse, he crossed back to the east side of the stream, where he found some Moravian Indians in great terror. Gathering what particulars he could, he rode through the night to Bethlehem, arriving there at three o'clock in the morning and telling Bishop Spangenberg of the Moravian Church the terrible story. (See Pa. Col. Rec., Vol. 6, pages 736, 737.)

For some time prior to the massacre of the Moravian missionaries, these good people had been suspected of being in sympathy with the French and their Indian allies—an altogether unjust suspicion. Just prior to the outbreak of the war, unfriendly Indians made frequent visits to the Delawares who had been converted to the Christian religion by the Moravians, and made efforts to win them to their cause. Some of the Christianized Delawares yielded to the persuasion of the unfriendly Indians, and, in time, were recognized among the marauders. Then the cry went up that the Moravian missionaries were training the Indians for the French service. Furthermore, the fact that the missionaries spoke German, a language foreign to that of their English and Scotch-Irish neighbors, tended to put them under suspicion. But now that these missionaries fell victims to the wrath of the Indians in league with the French, the eyes of their traducers were opened. Even before the corpses of the murdered Moravians were buried, it is said, many people came to the scene of the massacre and shed tears of penitence.

In closing the account of this terrible atrocity, we call attention to the fact that Susanna Nitschman, long believed to have been killed at the time of the massacre of the other missionaries, was, according to De Schweinitz's "Life of David Zeisberger," carried to Tioga, where she was compelled to share the wigwam with a brutal Indian and where, having lapsed into profound melancholy, death came to her relief after a half year of captivity.

Attack on the Hoeth and Brodhead Families

On December 10th and 11th, 1755, occurred the attack on the Hoeth and Brodhead families. The Frederick Hoeth family lived on Poco-Poco Creek, afterwards known as Hoeth's Creek, and now generally known as Big Creek, a tributary to the Lehigh above Weissport. The Indians attacked the house on the evening of the 10th, killing and capturing all the family except a son and a smith, who made their escape. This son, John Michael Hoeth, or Hute as he is called in the Pennsylvania Colonial Records, made a deposition before William Parsons at Easton, on December 12th, as follows:

"The 12th Day of December, 1755, Personally appeared before me, William Parsons, one of his Majesty's Justices of the Peace for the County of Northampton, Michael Hute, aged about 21 Years, who being duly sworn on the Holy Evangelists of Almighty God did depose and declare that last Wednesday, about 6 of the Clock, Afternoon, a Company of Indians, about 5 in number, attacked the House of Frederick Hoeth, about 12 miles Eastward from Gnadenhutten, on Pocho-Pocho Creek. That the family being at Supper, the Indians shot into the House and wounded a woman; at the next shot they killed Frederick Hoeth himself, and shot several times more, whereupon all ran out of the house that could. The Indians immediately set fire to the House, Mill and Stables. Hoeth's wife ran into the Bakehouse, which was also set on fire. The poor woman ran out thro' the Flames, and being very much burnt she ran into the water and there dyed. The Indians cut her belly open, and used her otherwise inhumanely. They killed and Scalped a Daughter, and he [Hute] thinks that three other Children who were of the Family were burnt. Three of Hoeth's Daughters are missing with another Woman, who are supposed to be carried off. In the action one Indian was killed and another wounded." (Pa. Col. Rec., Vol. 6, pages 758, 759.)

Attention is called to the fact that Barbara Leininger and Marie le Roy, in their Narrative, recorded in Pa. Archives, Sec. Series, Vol. 7, pages 401 to 412, state that, at the time of their escape from the Indians, March 16th, 1759, three sisters "from the Blue Mountains, Mary, Caroline and Catherine Hoeth," were still in captivity among the Indians, but do not state whether at Sauconk, Kuskuskies or Muskingum.

The Hoeth tragedy occurred in the vicinity of where Fort Norris, about a mile southeast of Kresgeville, Monroe County, was afterwards built. Other families in the vicinity of the Hoeths —the Hartmans, the Culvers and the McMichaels—were attacked by daylight the next morning. Many of their members were killed and captured, and their buildings were burned. Terror spread throughout the region upon the report that there were two hundred Indians ravaging that part of the frontier. Families fled to the Moravian stockades at Nazareth, Northampton County, and the infants of that place were taken to Bethlehem for greater security. Among the fugitives who took refuge among the Moravians at Nazareth were a poor German, his wife and child, the latter only several days old. It was late at night when he received word of the tragedy at Hoeth's. Taking his wife and child on his back, he fled for his life.

On the morning of December 11th, the Indians who committed the atrocities at Hoeth's and in the vicinity, made an assault on Brodhead's house, near the mouth of Brodhead Creek, not far from where Stroudsburg, Monroe County, now stands. The barracks and barn at Brodhead's were set on fire. Refugees hastening to Easton heard firing and crying at Brodhead's throughout the day. However, the Indians met such a determined resistance by the Brodhead family that they were finally obliged to retire. All the members of this family were noted for their bravery. Among the sons was the famous Colonel (later General) Brodhead of the Revolutionary War, who no doubt aided in the defense of his father's home. For account of the outrages at Hoeth's and Brodhead's, the reader is referred to Pa. Col. Rec., Vol. 6, pages 756 to 760.

Massacres Continue

The Indians continued their murders and depredations in Monroe, Carbon and Northampton Counties throughout the month of December and into the following January, as we shall see in the next chapter. The following quotation from Pa. Col. Rec., Vol. 6, page 767, briefly describes, under date of December 29th, their atrocities and devastation in this region in December:

"During all this month [December, 1755] the Indians have been burning and destroying all before them in the County of Northampton, and have already burned fifty houses here, murdered above one hundred persons, and are still continuing their Ravages, Murders and Devastations, and have actually overrun and laid waste a great part of that County, even as far as within twenty miles of Easton, its chief Town. And a large Body of Indians, under the Direction of French Officers, have fixed their head Quarters within the Borders of that County for the better security of their Prisoners and Plunder . . . All the settlements between Shamokin and Hunter's Mill for a space of 50 Miles along the River Susquehanna were deserted."

Continuing, the same account describes the horrors on the Pennsylvania frontier at the time of which we are writing, as follows:

"Such schocking descriptions are given by those who have escaped of the horrid Cruelties and Indecencies committed by these merciless Savages on the Bodies of the unhappy wretches who fell into their Barbarous hands, especially the Women, without regard to Sex or Age, as far exceeds those related of the most abandoned Pirates; which has occasioned a general Consternation and has struck so great a Pannick and Damp upon the Spirits of the people that hitherto they have not been able to make any considerable resistance or stand against the Indians."

One of the atrocities, committed in the Minisink region, in December, 1755, was that described in the affidavit of Daniel McMullen, found in Pa. Col. Rec., Vol. 7, pages 282 and 283. A party of five Delawares captured McMullen and a woman, and at the same time, killed eight men in the neighborhood. McMullen and the woman were taken to Tioga, where McMullen was sold to a Mohawk, who treated him very kindly, and afterwards sold him to the daughter of French Margaret, who was the daughter of Madam Montour. Later French Margaret's daughter went to see Colonel Johnson in order to ransom the woman who was taken when McMullen was captured. While French Margaret's daughter was absent on this journey, McMullen made his escape, and he and Thomas Moffit, another captive belonging to French Margaret's daughter, made their way down the Susquehanna to Fort Augusta, in September, 1756.

In December, 1755, Nicholas Weiss was killed, near Fennersville, Monroe County, and his family captured and taken to Canada (Egle's "History of Pennsylvania," page 948.)

During November and December, 1755, as stated in a former chapter, the Shawnee and Delaware town of Nescopeck at the site of the present town of Nescopeck, in Luzerne County, was the rallying point for the Indians who were devastating the settlements and murdering the inhabitants. Many bloody expeditions were sent out from this place until the building of Fort Augusta, at Shamokin (Sunbury), in the summer and autumn of 1756, drove the hostile Indians away from Nescopeck. They then went up the North Branch of the Susquehanna to the Delaware town of Assarughney, located about two miles north of the mouth of the Lackawanna, near the present town of Ransom, in Luzerne County. At the time of the assembling of the hostile Indians at Nescopeck, John Shikellamy, son of the great vicegerent of the Six Nations, moved away from that place to Wyoming, near Plymouth, Luzerne County, where the friendly Shawnee chief, Paxinosa, lived.

About the middle of December, some settlers at Paxtang "took an enemy Indian on the other side of the Narrows above Samuel Hunter's and brought him down to Carson's, where they examining him, the Indian begged for his Life and promised to tell all what he knew tomorrow morning, but (shocking to me) they shot him in the midst of them, scalped him and threw his Body into the River. The Old Belt told me that, as a child of Onontio [the French], he deserved to be killed, but that he would have been glad if they had delivered him up to the Governor in order to be examined stricter and better." Thus wrote Conrad Weiser to Governor Morris, on December 22nd.

Capture of Peter Williamson

Loudon's "Indian Narratives" contains an account of the capture and subsequent experiences of Peter Williamson, who, according to Loudon, was living near the "Forks of the Delaware" in the terrible autumn of 1755. He was alone at midnight, when the Indians came upon him, his wife being away visiting relatives at the time. They made him prisoner, burned his house, barn, cattle and 200 bushels of grain. Taking him with them, they fell upon the Jacob Snyder family "at the Blue Hills near the Susquehanna," killing the parents and their five children, burning the house, and capturing the hired man, whom they tortured to death after going some distance. The band then lay hid near the Susquehanna for several days. They then attacked the home of an old man, named John Adams, burning the home and killing Mrs. Adams and her four small children before the eyes of the horrified father. Taking Mr. Adams with them, they went to the "Great Swamp," where they remained eight or nine days, inflicting many cruelties on Mr. Adams in the meantime. While at the "Great Swamp," twenty-five Indians arrived one night from the Conococheague, with twenty scalps and three prisoners. This second band had murdered John Lewis, his wife and three small children, also Jacob Miller, his wife and six children. The prisoners from the Conococheague were tortured to death at the "Great Swamp." Peter Williamson was then taken to the Indian town of Alamingo, where he remained two or three months until the snow was gone. In the spring, one hundred and fifty Indians left Alamingo, taking Williamson with them, to attack the settlements along the base of the Blue Mountains and along the Conococheague. Arriving near the settlements, the Indians separated into small bands. Williamson and ten Indians were left behind at a certain place to await the return of the rest who went to kill and scalp the settlers. Before the marauders returned, Williamson made his escape from his ten Indian companions. For some time he hid in a hollow log, and then made his way through the forest and over the mountains to the home of his father-in-law, in Chester County to receive the sad news that his wife had died two months before his return.

Murder of William McMullin and James Watson

In Loudon's "Indian Narratives" is found the account of the murder of William McMullin and his brother-in-law, James Watson. This murder most likely occurred in November, 1755. These men went from a block house between the Conodoguinet Creek, in Cumberland County, and the Blue Mountains to their home to look after things there. While in the barn, they were attacked by Indians. They then started to flee to the block house, and, as they were running through a buckwheat field, other Indians hidden there, attacked them, and fatally wounded McMullin, who crawled into a thicket, where he died and his body was afterwards found. During this attack, Watson shot four or five Indians in a running fight. Finally, while going up a hill, he was shot, then tomahawked and scalped. When found, his hands were full of an Indian's hair.

Samuel Bell

In Loudon's "Indian Narratives" is also found the account of the experiences of Samuel Bell, who, in the late autumn of 1755, with his brother, James, left their home on Stony Ridge, five miles below Carlisle, Cumberland County, to go into Sherman's Valley, Perry County, to hunt deer. The brothers agreed to meet at Croghan's (now Sterret's) Gap, in the Blue Mountains, but for some reason they failed to meet. Samuel spent the night in a deserted cabin on Sherman's Creek, belonging to a Mr. Patton. In the morning he had not gone far before he saw three Indians, who saw him at same time and each party fired at the other. Samuel wounded one of the Indians and several bullets passed through his own clothes. Each side took to trees. Samuel took his tomahawk and stuck it into the tree, so that he might be prepared if the Indians advanced. The tree was hit with several bullets. After some time, the two Indians carried the wounded one over the fence, and one ran one direction and the other another, trying to get on both sides of the tree where Bell was. Bell shot one of them dead and the other took the dead Indian on his back with a leg over each shoulder. Bell ran after him and fired a bullet through the dead Indian's body into the body of the one who was carrying him. The Indian dropped the dead companion and ran off. Bell then ran away, and found the first Indian dead, and later the bodies of the three were found.

Hugh McSwane

Loudon also relates the account of the experiences of Hugh McSwine (McSwane), who was captured by a band of Delawares, led by the noted Delaware chief, Captain Jacobs, during one of the incursions into the counties of Fulton, Franklin and Cumberland, in the autumn of 1755. McSwine was away from home at the time when the Indians came into his neighborhood. He followed them, and the place of his capture was at Tussey's Narrows. There was with the Indians a man named Jackson, who had joined them. Captain Jacobs left McSwine and another prisoner under care of Jackson and another Indian, while the rest went against other settlers. The Indian and Jackson, with two prisoners, travelled all night, and then they entered a deserted cabin and sent McSwine to cut rails to make a fire. McSwine took his ax and killed the Indian and then tried to kill Jackson. They had a desperate struggle. Both were very strong. McSwine's strength began to fail and he kept calling on the other white man to assist, but he stood trembling. Finally McSwine got hold of one of the guns and killed Jackson and scalped both him and the Indian. The next evening McSwine arrived at Fort Cumberland with Captain Jacobs' gun and horse, which had been left with him. George Washington sent McSwine to Winchester where he got paid for horse, gun, and scalps, and was made a lieutenant.

About this time the Cherokees came to help Pennsylvania. They pursued a band of Indians to the west side of Sidling Hill where they started back. Among the Cherokees was Hugh McSwine. On their way back they fell in with another party of Indians and had a battle with them. McSwine was parted from the rest. He was pursued by three Indians. He turned and shot one, and ran some distance and turned and shot another. Then the third Indian turned back. The Cherokees soon after brought 14 scalps and two prisoners, one of whom was a squaw who had been twelve times at war.

About the same time some Cherokees and white men scouted in neighborhood of Fort Duquesne. Coming back the white men were not able to keep up with the Indians and arrived home in very distressing condition. Hugh McSwine later was killed by the Indians, near Ligonier.

Such is Loudon's account. It may be that Hugh McSwane was the same person mentioned by Adam Hoops in a letter written from Conococheague to Governor Morris, on November 6th: "I just now have received ye account of one George McSwane, who was taken Captive about 14 Days ago, and has made his escape, and has brought two Scalps and a Tomahawk with Him."

Assistance of Cherokees and Catawbas

Loudon, as has been seen, mentions the fact that the Cherokees of the South helped the English to resist the bloody incursions of the Delawares and Shawnees. In the latter part of 1755, Governor Dinwiddie, of Virginia, succeeded in persuading the Cherokees to declare war against the Shawnees. They then sent one hundred and thirty of their warriors to protect the frontiers of Virginia, and later sent many to assist Pennsylvania, especially into the Cumberland Valley. The Cherokees occupied a very dangerous position on the Pennsylvania frontier, especially among the Scotch-Irish settlers of the Cumberland Valley, who, on account of the terrible atrocities committed upon them, were ready to shoot and scalp any Indian on sight. Colonel John Armstrong, in a letter written to Governor Denny, from Carlisle, on May 5th, 1757, and recorded in Pa. Col. Rec., Vol. 7, pages 503-505, mentions a case in point. The Catawbas also sent many of their warriors to assist Pennsylvania, as will be seen later in this history. While these Southern tribes were assisting the English, the French were busy in efforts to persuade them to join the Delawares and Shawnees in their incursions into the English settlements.

Tom Quick

Frederick A. Godcharles, in his "Daily Stories of Pennsylvania," gives an interesting account of the experiences of Tom Quick, "the Indian killer," who is said to have declared on his death bed, in 1795, that he had killed ninety-nine Indians, and begged that an old Indian, who lived near, might be brought to him in order that he might kill this old red man and thus bring his record to an even hundred. Early in the French and Indian War, no doubt in the autumn of 1755, Tom Quick's father, also named Tom, was killed by the Delawares, in Pike County, in the presence of the son and his brother-in-law. Young Tom was wounded at the same time, and almost frantic with rage and grief, he swore that he would never make peace with the Indians as long as one remained on the banks of the Delaware. Some years later, he met an Indian, named Muskwink, at Decker's Tavern, on the Neversink. Muskwink, on this occasion, claimed that it was he who scalped the elder Quick. Tom followed him from the tavern about a mile, and then shot him dead. Some time later, he espied an Indian family in a canoe on Butler's Rift. Concealing himself in the tall grass, he shot the Indian warrior, and then tomahawked his squaw and three children. He sank the bodies, and destroyed the canoe. Upon being asked later why he killed the children, he replied: "Nits make lice." On another occasion, several Indians came to him while he was splitting rails, and told him to go along with them. Quick asked them to help him to split open the last log, and as they put their fingers in the crack to help pull the log apart, Tom knocked out the wedge, and thus caught them all. He then killed them. On another occasion, he killed an Indian, while hunting with him, by shooting him in the back. At another time he killed an Indian, while hunting with him, by pushing him off the high rocks into the ravine below.

Egle, in his "History of Pennsylvania," says that Tom Quick made a vow early in life to kill one hundred Indians; that he took seriously ill before he had slain the hundred, and prayed earnestly for life and health to carry out his "project;" that he eventually recovered, and succeeded in bringing the number to one hundred; whereupon he laid aside his rifle, and died soon thereafter. He is buried on the banks of the Delaware, between the towns of Milford and Shohola, Pike County.

Governor and Assembly Dispute as Settlers Die

Indeed, from the Penn's Creek massacre until well into the year of 1756, terror reigned throughout the Pennsylvania settlements. It is a sad fact, already referred to in this chapter, that, while the Delawares and Shawnees were thus burning and scalping on the frontier, the Assembly and Governor, instead of putting the Province in a state of defense, spent their time in disputes as to whether or not the Proprietary estates should be taxed to raise money to defend the settlers against the hostile Indians. Noted men on the frontier, such as Rev. John Elder, pastor of the Presbyterian church at Paxtang, raised their voice in protest against such action on the part of the Colonial Authorities. William Plumstead, Mayor of Philadelphia, and the Aldermen and Common Council of that city remonstrated in the most forceful language. The smoke of burning farm houses darkened the heavens; the soil of the forest farms of the German and Scotch-Irish settlers was drenched with their blood; the tomahawk of the savage dashed out the brains of the aged and the infant; hundreds were carried into captivity, many of whom were tortured to death by fire at Kittanning and other Indian towns in the valleys of the Allegheny and the Ohio to which they were taken—all of these dreadful things were taking place as the disputes between the Governor and the Assembly continued.

Says Egle, in his "History of Pennsylvania:" "The cold indifference of the Assembly at such a crisis awoke the deepest indignation throughout the Province. Public meetings were held in various parts of Lancaster and in the frontier counties, at which it was resolved that they would repair to Philadelphia and compel the Provincial authorities to pass proper laws to defend the country and oppose the enemy. In addition, the dead bodies of some of the murdered and mangled were sent to that city and hauled about the streets, with placards announcing that these were the victims of the Quaker policy of non-resistance. A large and threatening mob surrounded the house of Assembly, placed the dead bodies in the doorway, and demanded immediate relief for the people of the frontiers. Such indeed were the desperate measures resorted to for self defense."

Some of these dead bodies were those of the victims of the raids of Shingas in October and November, described in Chapter VIII.

Finally, on November 26th, the very day that the news reached Philadelphia of the slaughter of the Moravian missionaries at Gnadenhuetten, "An Act For Granting 60,000 pounds to the King's Use" was passed, after the Proprietaries had made a grant of 5,000 pounds in lieu of the tax on the Proprietary estates.

Pennsylvania Begins Erection of Chain of Forts

Pennsylvania then began erecting a chain of forts and block-houses to guard the frontier. These forts extended along the Kittatinny or Blue Mountains from the Delaware River to the Maryland line, and the cost of erection was eighty-five thousand pounds. They guarded the important mountain passes, were garrisoned by from twenty-five to seventy-five men in pay of the Province, and stood almost equi-distant, so as to be a haven of refuge for the settlers when they fled from their farms to escape the tomahawk and scalping knife. The Moravians at Bethlehem cheerfully fortified their town and took up arms in self-defense. Benjamin Franklin and James Hamilton were directed to go to the Forks of the Delaware and raise troops in order to carry the plan into execution. On December 29th, 1755, they arrived at Easton, and appointed William Parsons major of the troops to be raised in the county of Northampton. In the meantime, Captain Hays had been ordered to New Gnadenhuetten, the scene of the massacre of the Moravian missionaries on November 24th, with his militia from the Irish settlement in the county. The attack on these militia on New Year's Day, 1756, will be described in Chapter X. Finally, the Assembly requested Franklin's appearance, and, responding to this call, he turned his command over to Colonel William Clapham.

This chain of forts began with Fort Dupui, erected on the property of the Hugenot settler, Samuel Dupui, in the present town of Shawnee, on the Delaware River, in Monroe County.

Next came Fort Hamilton, on the site of the present town of Stroudsburg, in Monroe County. Fort Penn was also erected in the eastern part of this town. These three forts were in the heart of the territory of the Munsee Clan of Delawares. Next was Fort Norris, about a mile southeast of Kresgeville, Monroe County; and fifteen miles west was Fort Allen where Weissport, Carbon County now stands. Then came Fort Franklin near Snydersville Schuylkill County; and nineteen miles west was, Fort Lebanon, also known as Fort William, not far from the present town of Auburn, in Schuylkill County. Then came Fort Henry at Dietrick Six's, near Millersburg, Berks County. This post is sometimes called "Busse's Fort" from its commanding officer, also the "Fort at Dietrick Six's." Fort Lebanon and Fort Henry were twenty-two miles apart, and midway between them was the small post, Fort Northkill, near Strausstown, Berks County. Next came Fort Swatara, located in the vicinity of Swatara Gap, or Tolihaio Gap, Lebanon County; then Fort Manada at Manada Gap, Dauphin County; then Fort Hunter, on the east bank of the Susquehanna River at the mouth of Fishing Creek, six miles north of Harrisburg; then Fort Halifax at the mouth of Armstrong Creek, half a mile above the present town of Halifax, on the east bank of the Susquehanna, in Dauphin County; then Fort Augusta at Sunbury, Northumberland County. While there were numerous block-houses, these posts were the principal forts east of the Susquehanna.

Crossing the Susquehanna, we find Fort Patterson in the Tuscarora Valley at Mexico, Juniata County; Fort Granville, near Lewistown, Mifflin County; Fort Shirley, at Shirleysburg, Huntingdon County; Fort Lyttleton at Sugar Cabins, in the northeastern part of Fulton County; Fort McDowell, where McDowell's Mill, Franklin County, now stands; Fort Loudon, about a mile distant from the town of Loudon, Franklin County; Fort Morris at Shippensburg, Cumberland County; and Fort Lowther, at Carlisle, Cumberland County. Like the forts east of the Susquehanna, these forts were supplemented with blockhouses in the vicinity. The erection of the entire chain of forts was completed in 1756.

To garrison these forts and intervening posts and for patroling the neighborhood of each, a body of troops, called the "Pennsylvania Regiment," was organized, of which the Governor was, ex-officio, commander-in-chief. It was divided into three battalions. The First Battalion, commanded by Lieutenant-Colonel Conrad

Weiser, consisting of ten companies and five hundred men, guarded the territory along the Blue or Kittatinny Mountains from the Susquehanna to the Delaware. The Second Battalion, commanded by Lieutenant-Colonel John Armstrong, consisting of eight companies and four hundred men, guarded the district west of the Susquehanna. The Third Battalion, commanded by Colonel William Clapham, consisting of eight companies and four hundred men, guarded the region at and around Fort Augusta. Because of its location, it was called the "Augusta Regiment." Major James Burd was also in command of this regiment for a time. The troops not only garrisoned the regular forts, but were also located at stockaded mills and farm houses, from three to twenty at a place, at the disposition of the captains of the companies.

A final word as to the distinction between the various places of defense and refuge. Reference is made in all chronicles dealing with the border wars in Pennsylvania to "forts," "block-houses" and "stations." Frequently the term "fort" is applied as well to "block-houses" and "stations." A "fort," especially the forts erected by the Colony of Pennsylvania, was a strong place of defense and refuge, stockaded and embracing cabins for the accommodation of the garrison and of families who sought refuge there. A "station" was a parallelogram of cabins, so united by palisades as to present a continued wall on the outer side. A "block-house" was a strong, square, two-storied structure, having the upper story projecting over the lower about two feet, so that the inmates could shoot from above upon the Indians attempting to fire the building, to burst open the door or to climb its walls. Many stations and block-houses were erected by the harrassed settlers at their own expense and by their own labors.

CHAPTER X

Massacres Early In 1756

GOVERNOR MORRIS spent the greater part of January, 1756, in visiting the frontiers for the purpose of seeing to the erection of forts and block houses. He was at Reading on January 5, and attended the Carlisle council of January 13th to 17th, to be described in Chapter XI. Taking leave, very largely, of the Governor, the Provincial Council and the Assembly for a time, we shall devote the present chapter to the narration of Indian atrocities in the early part of 1756.

Massacre of Soldiers at Gnadenhuetten

After the massacre of the Moravian missionaries at Gnadenhuetten, now Weissport, Carbon County, on the evening of November 24th, 1755, the surviving missionaries and the Christianized Delawares of that place hastened to Bethlehem, leaving their effects and harvest behind. As stated in Chapter IX, the hostile Indians spread devastation and death throughout that region in the closing weeks of 1755, and a thorough and systematic plan of defense was formulated. Benjamin Franklin and James Hamilton, being selected to execute this plan, went to Easton, and, on December 29th, after their arrival, appointed William Parsons Major of the troops to be raised in Northampton County. In the meantime, Captain Hayes had been ordered to lead his company of troops from the Irish Settlement in Northampton County to Gnadenhuetten to guard the mills of the Moravians, which were filled with grain and had escaped the torch of the Indians, to keep the property of the Christian Delawares from being destroyed, and to protect the few settlers who still remained in the neighborhood. Hayes stationed his troops in the forsaken village and erected a temporary stockade.

Then, on January 1st, 1756, a number of the soldiers, due to their lack of experience, fell victims to an Indian stratagem. While amusing themselves by skating on the Lehigh River, not far from the stockade, they saw two Indians farther up the stream, and, thinking to kill or capture them, gave chase while the Indians ran further up the river. These two Indians were decoys, who skillfully drew the soldiers into an ambush. After the soldiers had pursued them for some distance, a large party of Indians rushed out behind the troops, cut off their retreat, fell upon them with great fury, and quickly dispatched them. Some of the soldiers, remaining in the stockade, terrorized and horrified by the murder of their companions, deserted, while the others, despairing of defending the place, fled, leaving the mills, the stockade and the houses of the Christian Indians to be burned to ashes by the hostile Indians.

Massacres in Monroe County

Also, on January 1st, 1756, the Delaware chief, Teedyuscung led a band of about thirty Indians into lower Smithfield Township, Monroe County, destroying the plantation of Henry Hess, killing Nicholas Colman and a laborer named Gotlieb, and capturing Peter Hess and young Henry Hess, son of Peter Hess and nephew of Henry Hess, the owner of the plantation. This attack took place about nine o'clock in the morning. Teedyuscung's band then went over the Blue Mountains and overtook five Indians with two prisoners, Leonard and William Weeser, and a little later killed Peter Hess in the presence of his son.

In a few days the Indians over-ran the country from Fort Allen as far as Nazareth, burning plantations, and killing and scalping settlers. During this same month, the Delawares entered Moore Township, Northampton County, burning the buildings of Christian Miller, Henry Shopp, Henry Diehl, Peter Doll, Nicholas Scholl, and Nicholas Heil, and killing one of Heil's children and John Bauman. The body of Bauman was found two weeks later, and buried in the Moravian cemetery at Nazareth.

Young Henry Hess, one of the captives in this incursion, was delivered up by the Indians at the Easton Conference of November, 1756, at which conference he made an affidavit, recorded in Pa. Archives, Vol. 3, page 56, from which the following statements are taken:

That, on January 1st, 1756, he was at the plantation of his uncle, Henry Hess, in Lower Smithfield Township, and that his father, Peter Hess, Nicholas Coleman and one, Gotlieb, a laborer, were also there; that, about nine o'clock in the morning, they were surprised by a party of twenty-five Indians, let by Teedyuscung, some of whom were then attending the Easton Conference, namely, Peter Harrison, Samuel Evans, Christian, and Tom Evans; that the Indian band killed Nicholas Coleman and Gotlieb, took him and his father prisoners, set fire to the stable, and then hunted up the horses and took three of them; that the Indians then went over the second range of the Blue Mountains, and overtook five other Indians with two prisoners, Leonard and William Weeser; that a little later, they killed and scalped his father, Peter Hess, in his presence; that the two bands, now being united, stopped in the evening, kindled a fire, tied him and the two Weesers to a tree with ropes, in which manner they remained all night, although the night was extremely cold, the coldest night of the year; that the next day he and the other prisoners were taken to Wyoming, which they found deserted, its Indian population having fled to the Delaware village of Tunkhannock, the site of the present town of the same name, in Wyoming County; that their captors then took them to Tunkhannock, where they found about one hundred and fifty Indians; that after the severe weather abated, all the Indians left Tunkhannock, taking the prisoners with them, and went to Tioga, near the present town of Athens, Bradford County; that, during his stay with the Indians, small parties of five or six warriors, occasionally went to war, and returned with scalps and captives, which they said they had taken at Allemangle, in the northern part of Berks County, and in the Minisink region; and that he frequently heard his captors say that "all the country of Pennsylvania did belong to them, and the Governors were always buying their lands from them but did not pay them for it."

Leonard Weeser, one of the captives taken in this incursion, was also delivered up at the Easton Conference of November, 1756, at which conference he made the following affidavit, giving the date of the beginning of the incursion as December 31st, 1755:

"This examinant says that on the 31st of Dec'r last, he was at his father's House beyond the Mountains, in Smithfield Township, Northampton County, w'th his Father, his Bro'r William and Hans Adam Hess; that Thirty Indians from Wyomink surrounded them as they were at Work, killed his Father and Hans Adam Hess and took this Examinant and his Brother William, aged 17, Prisoners. The next day the same Indians went to Peter Hess's, Father of the s'd Hans Adam Hess; they killed two young men, one Nicholas Burman, ye others name he knew not, and took Peter Hess and his elder son, Henry Hess, and went off ye next morning at the great Swamp, distant about 30 miles from Weeser's Plantation; they killed Peter Hess, sticking him with their knives, as this Examinant was told by ye Indians, for he was not present. Before they went off, they burned the Houses and a Barrack of Wheat, killed all ye Cattle and Horses and Sheep and destroyed all they could. Thro' ye Swamp they went directly to Wyomink, where they stayed only two days and then went up the river to Diahogo [Tioga], where they stayed till the Planting Time, and from thence they went to little Passeeca, an Indian Town up the Cayuge Branch, and there they stayed till they brought him [Leonard Weeser] down. Among the Indians who made this attack and took him Prisoner, were Teedyuscung, alias Gideon, alias Honest John, and three of his Sons, Amos and Jacob, ye other's name he knew not. Jacobus and his Son, Samuel Evans and Thomas Evans were present; Daniel was present, one Yacomb, a Delaware who used to live in his Father's Neighborhood. They said that all the country was theirs and they were never paid for it, and this they frequently gave as a reason for their conduct. The King's [Teedyuscung] Son, Amos, took him, this Examinant, and immediately gave him over to his Father . . . This Examinant saw at Diahogo a Boy of Henry Christmans, who lived near Fort Norris, and one Daniel William's Wife and five children. Ben Feed's wife and three children; a woman, ye wife of a Smith, who lived with Frederick Head, and three children; a woman taken at Cushictunk, a boy of Hunt's who lived in Jersey, near Canlin's Kiln and a Negro man; a boy taken about four miles from Head's, called Nicholas Kainsein, all of which were prisoners with the Indians at Diahogo and Passeeca, and were taken by the Delaware Indians; that Teedyuscung did not go against the English after this Examinant was taken, Tho' his Sons did." (Pa. Archives, Vol. 3, page 45.)

It will be noted that, in the above affidavit, Leonard Weeser says that the Indians said "that all the country was theirs and they were never paid for it, and this they frequently gave as a reason for their conduct." The murders that these Delawares committed were within the bounds of the "Walking Purchase." In a subsequent chapter, we shall find the able Delaware chief, Teedyuscung, of the Turtle Clan, boldly telling Governor Denny at the Easton Conference of November, 1756, that the injustice done the Delawares in this fraudulent land purchase was the principal reason why they took up arms against the Province.

Not only the atrocities we are now describing, but those at Hoeth's and Brodheads, described in Chapter IX, were committed within the bounds of the "Walking Purchase." It was natural that the Delawares of the Munsee Clan headed for their own locality in striking their blows against the Province.

The massacres of the first week in January filled the Province with alarm and confusion. Governor Morris was discouraged, as is shown in his letter written from Reading, on January 5th, to the Provincial Council, recorded in Pa. Col. Rec., Vol. 6, pages 771 and 772:

"The Commissioners [Benjamin Franklin and James Hamilton] have done everything that was proper in the County of Northampton, but the People are not satisfied, nor, by what I can learn from the Commissioner, would they be unless every Man's House was protected by a Fort and a Company of Soldiers, and themselves paid for staying at home and doing nothing. There are in that County at this time three hundred Men in Pay of the Government, and yet from Disposition of the Inhabitants, the want of Conduct in the Officers and of Courage and Discipline in the Men, I am fearful that the whole Country will fall into the Enemy's Hands.

"Yesterday and the day before I received the melancholy News of the Destruction of the Town of Gnadenhuetten, and of the greatest part of the Guard of forty Men placed there in order to erect a Fort. The particulars you will see by the inclosed Papers, so far as they are yet come to hand, but I am in hourly Expectation of further Intelligence by two Men that I dispatched for that Purpose upon the first News of the Affair, whose long stay makes me apprehend some mischief has befallen them.

"Last night an Express brought me an acco't that seven Farm Houses between Gnadenhuetten and Nazareth were on the First Instant burnt, about the time that Gnadenhuetten was, and some of the People destroyed, and the accounts are this date confirmed.

"Upon this fresh alarm it is proposed that one of the Commissioners return to Bethlehem and Easton, and there give fresh Directions to the Troops and post them in the best Manner for the Protection of the remaining Inhabitants."

The commissioner, selected to "return to Bethlehem and Easton, and there give fresh direction to the troops," was Benjamin Franklin. This energetic and capable man at once went to Bethlehem from which place he wrote Governor Morris, on January 14th, telling him of the progress already made in raising additional troops and bringing order out of chaos. He then went to Gnadenhuetten, and superintended the erection of Fort Allen at that place, the site of which is now occupied by the "Fort Allen Hotel," at Weissport. He tells in his "Autobiography" some of the details of erecting Fort Allen, as follows:

"Our first work was to bury more effectually the dead we found there, who had been half interred by the country people; the next morning our fort was planned and marked out, the circumference measuring four hundred fifty-five feet, which would require as many palisades to be made, one with another of a foot diameter each. Each pine made three palisades of eighteen feet long, pointed at one end. When they were set up, our carpenters made a platform of boards all round within, about six feet high, for the men to stand on when to fire through the loop holes. We had one swivel gun, which we mounted on one of the angles, and fired it as soon as fixed, to let the Indians know, if any were within hearing, that we had such pieces; and thus our fort (if that name may be given to so miserable a stockade) was finished in a week, though it rained so hard every other day that the men could not well work."

Franklin's letter to Governor Morris of January 25th, and his official report of January 26th, give the details of the erecting of Fort Allen. These are found in Pa. Col. Rec., Vol. 7, pages 15 and 16. He named the fort in honor of Judge William Allen, father of James Allen, who laid out Allentown in 1762, and was Chief Justice of the Province of Pennsylvania. Franklin, early in 1756, also superintended the erection of Fort Franklin, in the southeastern part of Schuylkill County, Fort Hamilton, where the town of Stroudsburg, Monroe County, now stands, Fort Hyndshaw, in Monroe County, about one mile from the Delaware River and near the Pike County line, and Fort Norris, near Kresgeville, Monroe County. Forts Hamilton and Hyndshaw stood in the very heart of the Minisink region, occupied by the Munsee or Wolf Clan of Delawares until their expulsion following the fraudulent "Walking Purchase" of 1737.

In his official report, above mentioned, Franklin said that he had 522 men under his command, divided into companies whose heads were officers Trump, Aston, Wayne, Foulk, Trexler, Wetterholt, Orndt, Craig, Martin, Van Etten, Hays, McLaughlin and Parsons.

This bloody incursion caused the settlers to flee in terror from their forest farms, and seek safety within the more thickly settled parts of the Province. As pointed out in Chapter IX, hundreds fled to the Moravian settlement at Nazareth, where, in Decemebr, 1755, sentry boxes had been erected near the principal buildings, and stockades near by, at Gnadenthal (Vale of Grace), Friedensthal (Vale of Peace), Christian's Spring and the Rose Inn. On January 29th, 1756, according to the annals of the Moravians, there were 253 fugitives at Nazareth, 52 at Gnadenthal, 48 at Christian's Spring, 21 at the Rose Inn and 75 at Friedensthal. Of these fugitives, 226 were children.

Other forts, stockades and block houses, not already mentioned, erected at about the time the stockades at Nazareth were erected, and a little later, were: Breitenbach's Block House, near Myerstown, Lebanon County; Brown's Fort, in East Hanover Township, Dauphin County; Davis' Block House, in the south-western part of Franklin County; Doll's Block House, in Moore Township, Northampton County; Fort Everett, near where the town of Lynnport, Lehigh County, now stands; Harper's Block House, in East Hanover Township, Lebanon County; Hess' Block House, in Union Township, Lebanon County; the Fort or Block House at Lehigh Gap, on the north side of the Blue Mountains, in Carbon County, and, a little later, the stockade at Trucker's (Kern's) mill, three or four miles south of Lehigh Gap and in Lehigh County; Fort McCord, in Hamilton Township, Franklin County; Bingham's Fort, in Tuscarora Township, Juniata County; McKee's Fort, on the east shore of the Susquehanna, in the southern part of Northumberland County; Ralston's Fort, in the Irish Settlement in Northampton County, about five miles northwest of Bethlehem; Read's Block House, the stockaded residence of Adam Read, on Swatara Creek, in East Hanover Township, Lebanon County; Robinson's or Robeson's Fort, a stockaded mill, in East Hanover Township, Dauphin County; Robinson's Fort, or Block House, in Sherman's Valley, Perry County; Dietrich Snyder's Stockade, erected around his residence, in Berks County, on the road leading from the vicinity of Fort Northkill, near Strausstown, over the Blue Mountains to Pottsville, Schuylkill County; Benjamin Spycker's (Spiker) Stockade, around his residence in Jackson Township, Lebanon County, not far from the Berks County line and not far from Stouchsburg, Berks County, at which fortified house the German farmers, under Conrad Weiser, rendezvoused, in the latter part of October, 1755, as described in Chapter VII; Ulrich's Fort, near Annville, Lebanon County, being a mural dungeon or vault built into the hillside, with an air hole walled out and closed by a large stone on which was the inscription, "So oft die Dier den Ankel went, An deinen Tod, O Mensch, gedenk" (As oft as this door on its hinge doth swing, To thee, O Man, thought of death may it bring); Wind Gap Fort, near Wind Gap, Northampton County; and Zeller's Block House, near Newmanstown, in the south-eastern part of Lebanon County.

Teedyuscung

We shall meet Teedyuscung again in the course of this history, not as a bloody warrior, but as an advocate of peace between the Eastern Delawares and the Province; but, inasmuch as he was the leader of the incursion of January 1st, just described, we deem it appropriate to give a short sketch, at this point, of his life up to the time of which we are writing. He was the son of the Delaware chief, John Harris, of the Turtle Clan, and was born at Trenton, New Jersey, about 1705. The early part of his life is clouded in obscurity; but, when he was about fifty years of age, he was chosen chief of the Delawares on the Susquehanna, and from that time until his tragic death on April 16th, 1763, he was one of the chief figures in the Indian history of Pennsylvania.

He came under the influence of the Moravian missionaries, and was baptized by them as Brother Gideon. Honest John was also a name applied to him by the Moravians and others. Later he became an apostate, and endeavored to induce the Christian Delawares of Gnadenhuetten to remove to Wyoming, actually succeeding in gaining a party of seventy of the converts, who left Gnadenhuetten, April 24th, 1754, and took up their abode at Wyoming.

In April, 1755, he attended a conference with the Provincial Authorities at Philadelphia, assuring them of his friendship for the English. At that time, he was living at Wyoming. His friendship for the English and Pennsylvania did not continue long after the conference of April, 1755. When the Delawares and Shawnees took up arms against Pennsylvania following Braddock's defeat, Teedyuscung, at Nescopeck with Shingas and other leaders of the hostile Indians, planned many a bloody expedition against the frontiers of Eastern Pennsylvania.

In March, 1756, he and the Delawares under him left the town of Wyoming and removed to Tioga (now Athens, Bradford County), followed at about the same time by the Shawnees from their town where Plymouth, Luzerne County, now stands, under the leadership of Paxinosa. After the death of Shikellamy, in 1748, some of the Shamokin Delawares had settled at Tioga, and upon Teedyuscung's removal to that place, they and the Delawares of the Munsee Clan chose him "King of the Delawares." He was at that time busily engaged in forming an alliance between the three clans of Delawares and the Shawnees, Nanticokes, and Mohicans of northeastern Pennsylvania.

Massacre Near Schupp's Mill

On January 15th, some refugees at Bethlehem went out into the country to look after their farms and cattle, among them being Christian Boemper. The party and some friendly Indians who escorted them, were ambushed by hostile Delawares near Schupps Mill, and all were killed except one named Adam Hold, who was so severely wounded that it was necessary later to amputate his arm. Those killed were Christian Boemper, Felty Hold, Michael Hold, Laurence Knuckel, and four privates of Captain Trump's Company then stationed at Fort Hamilton (Stroudsburg).

At about the same time, a German, named Muhlhisen while breaking flax on the farm of Philip Bossert, in Lower Smithfield Township, Monroe County, was fatally wounded by an unseen Indian. One of Bossert's sons, hearing the report of the Indian's rifle, ran out of the house and was killed. Then old Philip Bossert, the owner of the farm, appeared on the scene, wounded one of the Indians, and was himself wounded badly. Neighbors then arrived upon the scene, and the Indians retreated. ("Frontier Forts of Penna.," Vol. 1, pages 200-201.)

Massacres in Juniata and Perry Counties

On January 27th, a band of Delawares from the Susquehanna, attacked the home of Hugh Mitchelltree, near Thompsontown, Juniata County, killing Mrs. Mitchelltree and a young man, named Edward Nicholas, Mr. Mitchelltree being then absent at Carlisle. The same band then went up the Juniata River. William Wilcox at that time lived on the opposite side of the river, whose wife and eldest son had come over the river on some business. The Indians came while they were there and killed old Edward Nicholas and his wife and took Joseph Nicholas, Thomas Nicholas, Catherine Nicholas, John Wilcox and Mrs. James Armstrong and two children prisoners. An Indian named James Cotties and an Indian boy went to Sherman's Creek, Perry County, and killed William Sheridan and his family, 13 in number. They then went down the creek to where three old persons lived, two men and a woman by the name of French whom they killed. Cotties afterward boasted that the boy took more scalps than the whole party.

The above is the account of this massacre, found in Loudon's "Indian Narratives." In Pa. Archives, Vol. 2, page 566, is found the following letter of Governor Morris, dated February 3d, relative to this massacre:

"I have just received the melancholy intelligence from Cumberland County that a fresh party of Indians are again fallen upon ye settlements, on Juniata, and have carry'd off several of ye people there to ye number of 15 or upwards."

Also, on page 568 of the same volume of the Pennsylvania Archives, is found the letter of Rev. Thomas Barton, dated February 6th, referring to this massacre, as follows:

"Within three miles of Patterson's Fort was found Adam Nicholson and his wife, dead and scalped; his two sons and a Daughter are carried off, Hugh Mitchelltree and a son of said Nicholson, dead and scalped, with many children, in all about 17. The same Day, one Sherridan, a Quaker, his wife, three children and a Servant were kill'd and scalped, together with one, Wm. Hamilton and his Wife, his Daughter and one, French, within ten miles of Carlisle, a little beyond Stephen's Gap.

"It is dismal, Sir, to see the Distress of the People; women and Children screaming and lamenting, men's hearts failing them for Fear under all the Anguish of Despair. The Inhabitants over the Hills are entirely fleeing, so that in two or three Days the North Mountain will be the Frontier. Industry droops, and all Sorts of Work seem at an End. In short, Sir, it appears as if this Part of the Country breath'd its last. I remember you dreaded this blow would be struck in February; and now we know that our Danger hastens with the Encrease of the Moon, and we expect nothing but Death and Ruin every night."

Mrs. James Armstrong later escaped, and waded across the Susquehanna to Fort Augusta, June 26th, 1757, where her husband was then a soldier. On April 12th, 1759, the Iroquois delivered up one of the children, Elizabeth Armstrong, at Canajoharie, New York. She had been given to them by the Delawares, and was then only four years old.

Loudon relates of the Indian, James Cotties, that in the autumn of 1757, he went to Fort Hunter, and killed a young man, named William Martin, while gathering chestnuts; also, that after the French and Indian War, he came to Fort Hunter and boasted what a good friend he had been to the white people during the war, whereupon a friendly Delaware, named Hambus, accused him of having killed young Martin, and the two Indians began to fight. A little later in the day, Cotties got drunk and fell asleep near the fort, whereupon Hambus slipped up and killed him with his tomahawk.

During the incursion of January 27th, occurred the murder of the Woolcomber family, Quakers, on Sherman's Creek, Perry County, thus described in Loudon's "Indian Narratives," as if it took place in the latter part of 1755:

"The next I remember of was in 1755, the Woolcombers family on Shearman's Creek; the whole of the inhabitants of the valley was gathered at Robinson's, but Woolcomber would not leave home, he said it was the Irish [Scotch-Irish] who were killing one another; these peaceable people, the Indians would not hurt any person. Being at home and at dinner, the Indians came in, and the Quaker asked them to come and eat dinner; an Indian announced that he did not come to eat, but for scalps; the son, a boy of fourteen or fifteen years of age when he heard the Indian say so, repaired to a back door, and as he went out he looked back, and saw the Indian strike the tomahawk into his father's head. The boy then ran over the creek, which was near the house, and heard the screams of his mother, sisters and brother. The boy came to our Fort [Robinson] and gave us the alarm; about forty went to where the murder was done and buried the dead."

A few days after the massacre of January 27th, some Indians, probably members of this same band, had a skirmish with thirteen soldiers from Croghan's Fort, at Aughwick, within a short distance of the fort. One of the soldiers was wounded, and two of the Indians were killed, on this occasion. (Pa. Archives, Vol. 2, page 571.)

Two months later, or on March 29th, 1756, the Indians again came to the neighborhood where the murders of January 27th were committed. They attacked Patterson's Fort, and, according to a letter written by Captain Patterson to his wife,they carried off Hugh Mitchelltree, about five o'clock in the evening, while foddering his cattle within sight of the fort. Evidently, then, Rev. Thomas Barton was mistaken in his letter, quoted above, in saying that Hugh Mitchelltree was killed in the massacre of January 27th. (Pa. Archives, Vol. 2, page 613.)

On March 24th, Captain William Patterson with a scouting party had an encounter with a party of Delawares on Middle Creek, in what is now Snyder County, killing and scalping one and routing the rest. On his return to his fort, he reported that the country from the forks of the Susquehanna (Sunbury) to the Juniata was "swarming with Indians, looking for scalps and plunder, and burning all the houses and destroying all the grain which the fugitive settlers had left in the region." ("Frontier Forts of Penna.," Vol. 1, pages 594–595.)

Patterson's Fort near which some of the murders of January 27th, were committed, was the fortified residence of Captain James Patterson, situated where the town of Mexico, Juniata County, now stands. The residence was fortified before the close of 1755. Captain James Patterson was the father of Captain William Patterson. The son lived opposite Mexico, and had a fortified residence, also called Fort Patterson, but it seems that the son's fort was not erected until the time of Pontiac's War.

There has been much confusion as to these two forts. By instructions given by Benjamin Franklin to George Croghan, on December 17th, 1755, the latter was to "fix on proper places for erecting three stockades, one back of Patterson's." This stockade "back of Patterson's" was to be called Pomfret Castle, and was to be erected on Mahantango Creek, near Richfield, Juniata County, but within the limits of Snyder County. Many historians doubt whether Pomfret Castle was ever erected. Governor Morris wrote on January 29th, 1756, saying it was erected. Then, hearing of the massacre of January 27th, he wrote to Captain Burd, on February 3d, reprimanding him and Captain Patterson for being remiss in *not* having erected the fort that was "order'd to be built at Matchitongo." (Pa. Archives, Vol. 2, pages 556 and 566.)

Capture of John and Richard Coxe and John Craig

On February 11th, 1756, occurred the capture of John Coxe, his brother Richard, and John Craig, thus described in the "Frontier Forts of Pennsylvania":

"At a council, held at Philadelphia, Tuesday, September 6th, 1756, the statement of John Coxe, a son of the widow Coxe, was made, the substance of which is: He, his brother Richard, and

John Craig were taken in the beginning of February of that year by nine Delaware Indians from a plantation two miles from McDowell's mill, [Franklin County], which was between the east and west branches of the Conococheague Creek, about 20 miles west of the present site of Shippensburg, in what is now Cumberland County, and brought to Kittanning on the Ohio. On his way hither he met Shingas with a party of 30 men, and afterward Capt. Jacobs and 15 men, whose design was to destroy the settlements on Conococheague. When he arrived at Kittanning, he saw here about 100 fighting men of the Delaware tribe, with their families, and about 50 English prisoners, consisting of men, women and children. During his stay here, Shingas' and Jacobs' parties returned, the one with nine scalps and ten prisoners, the other with several scalps and five prisoners. Another company of 18 came from Diahogo with 17 scalps on a pole, which they took to Fort Duquesne to obtain their reward. The warriors held a council, which, with their war dances, continued a week, when Capt. Jacobs left with 48 men, intending as Coxe was told, to fall upon the inhabitants at Paxtang. He heard the Indians frequently say that they intended to kill all the white folks, except a few, with whom they would afterwards make peace. They made an example of Paul Broadley, who, with their usual cruelty, they beat for half an hour with clubs and tomahawks, and then, having fastened him to a post, cropped his ears close to his head, and chopped off his fingers, calling all the prisoners to witness the horrible scene."

Additional details of the incursion which the Coxe boys and John Craig were captured are given in Egle's "History of Pennsylvania," as follows:

"In February, 1756, a party of Indians made marauding incursions into Peters Township. They were discovered on Sunday evening, by one Alexander, near the house of Thomas Barr. He was pursued by the savages, but escaped and alarmed the fort at McDowell's mill. Early on Monday morning a party of fourteen men of Captain Croghan's company, who were at the mill, and about twelve other young men, set off to watch the motion of the Indians. Near Barr's house they fell in with fifty, and sent back for a reinforcement from the fort. The young lads proceeded by a circuit to take the enemy in the rear, whilst the soldiers did attack them in front. But the impetuosity of the soldiers defeated their plan. Scarce had they got within gunshot, they fired upon the Indians, who were standing around the fire, and killed several of them at the first discharge. The Indians returned fire, killed one of the soldiers, and compelled the rest to retreat. The party of young men, hearing the report of firearms, hastened up, finding the Indians on the ground which the soldiers had occupied, fired upon the Indians with effect; but concluding the soldiers had fled, or were slain, they also retreated. One of their number, Barr's son, was wounded, would have fallen by the tomahawk of an Indian, had not the savage been killed by a shot from Armstrong, who saw him running upon the lad. Soon after soldiers and young men being joined by a reinforcement from the mill, again sought the enemy, who, eluding the pursuit, crossed the creek near William Clark's, and attempted to surprise the fort; but their design was discovered by two Dutch lads, coming from foddering their master's cattle. One of the lads was killed, but the other reached the fort, which was immediately surrounded by the Indians, who, from a thicket, fired many shots at the men in the garrison, who appeared above the wall, and returned the fire as often as they obtained sight of the enemy. At this time, two men crossing to the mill, fell into the middle of the assailants, but made their escape to the fort, though fired at three times. The party at Barr's house now came up, and drove the Indians through the thicket. In their retreat they met five men from Mr. Hoop's, riding to the mill; they killed one of these and wounded another severely. The sergeant at the fort having lost two of his men, declined to follow the enemy until his commander, Mr. Crawford, who was at Hoop's, should return, and the snow falling thick, the Indians had time to burn Mr. Barr's house, and in it consumed their dead. On the morning of the 2nd of March, Mr. Crawford, with fifty men, went in quest of the enemy, but was unsuccessful in his search."

John Coxe further said in his statement, which is found in Pa. Col. Rec. Vol. 7, pages 242 and 243, that in March following his capture, he was taken by three Indians to Tioga, where he found about fifty warriors of the Delawares and Mohicans, and about twenty German captives; that, while he was there, the Indians frequently went out in parties of twelve to murder the settlers and as often returned with scalps but no prisoners; that, on the 9th of August, he left Tioga with his Indian master, Makomsey, and came down the Susquehanna to the Indian town of Gnahay, whose location is unknown, to get some corn; and that he here made his escape, on August 14th, and arrived at Fort Augusta (Sunbury) that evening.

The following letter, written by Captain William Trent, at Carlisle, on Sunday evening, February 15th, 1756, and sent to Richard Peters, fixes the date of the capture of the Coxe boys and John Craig, and shows how Shingas and Captain Jacobs were keeping the settlers in a state of terror:

"Wednesday evening two lads were taken or killed at the Widow Cox's, just under Parnell's Knob, and a lad who went from McDowell's Mill to see what fire it was never returned, the horse coming back with the Reins over his Neck; they burnt the House and shot down the Cattle. Just now came News that a Party of Indian Warriors were come out against the Inhabitants from some of the Susquehanna Towns, and yesterday some people who were over in Sherman's Valley, discovered fresh Tracks; all the People have left their Houses betwixt this and the Mountain, some coming to town [Carlisle] and others gathering into little Forts; they are moving their Effects from Shippensburg, every one thinks of flying; unless the Government fall upon some Method, and that immediately, of securing the Frontiers, there will not be one Inhabitant in this Valley one Month longer." (Pa. Archives, Vol. 2, page 575.)

Murder of Frederick Reichelsdorfer's Daughters

"The Frontier Forts of Pennsylvania" contains the following account of one of the saddest tragedies of the terrible winter of which we are writing, the date of the atrocity being February 14th, 1756:

"The Rev. Henry Melchior Muhlenberg, D. D., in the Hallische Nachrichten, tells the soul-stirring story of Frederick Reichelsdorfer, whose two grown daughters had attended a course of instruction, under him, in the Catechism, and been solemnly admitted by confirmation to the communion of the Ev. Lutheran Church, in New Hanover, Montgomery County.

"This man afterwards went with his family some distance into the interior, to a tract of land which he had purchased in Albany Township, Berks County. When the war with the Indians broke out, he removed his family to his former residence, and occasionally returned to his farm, to attend to his grain and cattle. On one occasion he went, accompanied by his two daughters, to spend a few days there, and bring away some wheat. On Friday evening, after the wagon had been loaded, and everything was ready for their return on the morrow, his daughters complained that they felt anxious and dejected, and were impressed with the idea that they were soon to die. They requested their father to unite with them in singing the familiar German funeral hymn,

'Wer weiss wie nahe meine Ende.'

[Who knows how near my end may be.]

after which they commended themselves to God in prayer, and retired to rest.

"The light of the succeeding morn beamed upon them, and all was yet well. Whilst the daughters were attending to the dairy, cheered with the joyful hope of soon greeting their friends, and being out of danger, the father went to the field for the horses, to prepare for their departure home. As he was passing through the field, he suddenly saw two Indians, armed with rifles, tomahawks and scalping knives, making towards him at full speed. The sight so terrified him that he lost all self command, and stood motionless and silent. When they were about twenty yards from him, he suddenly and with all his strength, exclaimed 'Lord Jesus, living and dying, I am thine!' Scarcely had the Indians heard the words 'Lord Jesus' (which they probably knew as the white man's name of the Great Spirit), when they stopped short, and uttered a hideous yell.

"The man ran with almost supernatural strength into the dense forest, and by taking a serpentine course, the Indians lost sight of him, and relinquished the pursuit. He hastened to an adjoining farm, where two German families resided, for assistance, but on approaching near it, he heard the dying groans of the families, who were falling beneath the murderous tomahawks of some other Indians.

[One of these families was the family of Jacob Gerhart. One man, two women and six children were murdered. Two children hid under the bed, one of which was burned to death, and the other escaped and ran a mile for help. ("Frontier Forts of Pennsylvania," Vol. 1, pages 152 and 153.)]

"Having providentially not been observed by them, he hastened back to learn the fate of his daughters. But, alas! on arriving within sight, he found his home and barn enveloped with flames. Finding that the Indians had possession here too, he hastened to another adjoining farm for help. Returning, armed with several men, he found the house reduced to ashes and the Indians gone. His eldest daughter had been almost entirely burnt up, a few remains only of her body being found. And, awful to relate, the younger daughter though the scalp had been cut from her head, and her body horribly mangled from head to foot with the tomahawk, was yet living. 'The poor worm,' says Muhlenberg, 'was able to state all the circumstances of the dreadful scene.' After having done so she requested her father to stoop down to her that she might give him a parting kiss, and then go to her dear Saviour; and after she had impressed her dying lips upon his cheek, she yielded her spirit into the hands of that Redeemer, who, though His judgments are often unsearchable, and His ways past finding out, has nevertheless said, ' I am the resurrection and the life; if any man believe in me, though he die yet shall he live.' "

Attack on Andrew Lycans and John Rewalt

On March 7th, Andrew Lycans and John Rewalt, settlers in the Wiconisco, or Lykens Valley in Dauphin County, went out early in the morning to feed their cattle when they were fired upon by Indians. Hastening into the house, they prepared to defend themselves. The Indians concealed themselves behind a pig-pen some distance from the dwelling. Lycans' son, John, John Rewalt, and Ludwig Shutt, a neighbor, upon creeping out of the house, in an effort to discover the whereabouts of the Indians, were fired upon and each one wounded, Shutt very dangerously. At this point Andrew Lycans discovered an Indian named Joshua James and two white men running away from their hiding place near the pig-pen. The elder Lycans then fired, killing the Indian; and he and his party then sought safety in flight, but were closely pursued by at least twenty of the Indians. John Lycans and John Rewalt, although badly wounded, made their escape with the aid of a negro servant, leaving Andrew Lycans, Ludwig Shutt, and a boy to engage the Indians. The Indians then rushed upon these and, as one of their number, named Bill Davis, was in the act of striking the boy with his tomahawk, he was shot dead by Shutt, while Andrew Lycans killed another and wounded a third. Andrew Lycans also recognized two others of the band, namely, Tom Hickman and Tom Hays, members of the Delaware tribe. The Indians then momentarily ceased their pursuit, and Lycans, Shutt, and the boy, weak from the loss of blood, sat down on a log to rest, believing that they were no longer in imminent danger. Later, Lycans managed to lead his party to a place of concealment and then over the mountain into Hanover Township, where they were given assistance by settlers. Andrew Lycans, however, died from his wounds and terrible exposure. His name has been given to the charming valley of the Wiconisco. (Penna. Gazette, March 18th, 1756.)

Attack on Zeislof and Kluck Families

On March 24th, some settlers with ten wagons went to Albany, Berks County, for the purpose of bringing a family with their effects to a point near Reading. As they were returning, they were fired upon by a number of Indians on both sides of the road. The wagoners, leaving the wagons, ran into the woods, and the horses, frightened at the terrible yelling of the Indians, ran off. The Indians on this occasion, killed George Zeislof and his wife, a boy aged twenty, another aged twelve, and a girl aged fourteen. Another girl of the party was shot through the neck and mouth, and scalped, but made her escape.

On the same day the Indians burned the home of Peter Kluck, about fourteen miles from Reading, and killed the entire family. While the Kluck home was burning, the Indians assaulted the house of a settler named Lindenman nearby, in which there were two men and a woman, all of whom ran upstairs, where the woman was killed by a bullet which penetrated the roof. The men then ran out of the house. Lindenman was shot through the neck. In spite of his wound, Lindenman succeeded in shooting one of the Indians.

At about the same time a boy named John Schoep, who lived in this neighborhood, was captured and taken seven miles beyond the Blue Mountains where, according to the statement of Schoep, the Indians kindled a fire, tied him to a tree, took off his shoes, and put moccasins on his feet. They then prepared themselves some mush, but gave him none. After supper they took young Schoep and another boy between them, and proceeded over the second mountain. During the second night of his captivity, when the Indians were asleep, young Schoep made his escape, and returned home.

During the raid in which the above outrages occurred, the Indians killed the wife of Baltser Neytong, and captured his son aged eight. And in November, the Indians entered this region, and carried off the wife and three children of Adam Burns, the youngest child being only four weeks old. They also killed a man named Stonebrook, and captured a girl in this raid. ("Frontier Forts of Penna.," Vol. 1, pages 153 to 155.)

Shingas Burns McCord's Fort

On April 1st, 1756, Shingas attacked and burned Fort McCord, a private fort, erected in the autumn of 1755, and located several miles north-east of Fort Loudon, Franklin County, and not far from the Yankee Gap in the Kittatinny Mountains, west of Chambersburg. All the inmates of the fort, twenty-seven in number, were either killed or captured. After the destruction of the fort, Shingas' band was pursued by three bodies of settlers and soldiers. One body, commanded by Captain Alexander Culbertson, overtook the Indians on Sideling Hill. Here a fierce battle was fought for two hours, but Shingas being reinforced, the white men were defeated with great loss, twenty-one killed and seventeen wounded.

Among the killed were: Captain Alexander Culbertson, John Reynolds, William Kerr, James Blair, John Leason, William Denny, Francis Scott, William Boyd, Jacob Painter, Jacob Jones, Robert Kerr and William Chambers. Among the wounded were Francis Campbell, Abraham Jones, William Reynolds, John Barnet, Benjamin Blyth, John McDonald and Isaac Miller. The Indians, according to the statement of one of their number who was captured, lost seventeen killed and twenty-one wounded in this engagement.

Another body, commanded by Ensign Jamison, from Fort Granville, went in pursuit of the same band of Indians, and was also defeated. Among the killed were: Daniel McCoy, James Robinson, James Pierce, John Blair, Henry Jones, John McCarty and John Kelly. Among the wounded were: Ensign Jamison, James Robinson (There were two James Robinsons in Ensign Jamison's party), William Hunter, Matthias Ganshorn, William Swails and James Louder, the last of whom later died of his wounds.

Captain Hance Hamilton, in a letter written to Captain Potter, dated Fort Lyttleton, April 4th, and recorded in Pa. Col. Rec., Vol. 7, page 77, says the following concerning the terrible events of which we are writing:

"These come to inform you of the melancholy news of what occurred between the Indians, that have taken many captives from McCord's Fort and a party of men under the command of Captain Alexander Culbertson and nineteen of our men, the whole amounting to about fifty, with the captives, and had a sore engagement, many of both parties killed and many wounded, the number unknown. Those wounded want a surgeon, and those killed require your assistance as soon as possible, to bury them. We have sent an express to Fort Shirley for Doctor Mercer, supposing Doctor Jamison is killed or mortally wounded in the expedition. He being not returned, therefore, desire you will send an express, immediately, for Doctor Prentice to Carlisle; we imagining Doctor Mercer cannot leave the fort under the circumstances the fort is under. Our Indian, Isaac, has brought in Captain Jacobs' scalp."

The scalp brought in by the friendly Indian, Isaac, was not that of Captain Jacobs. This chief was not killed until the destruction of Kittanning, by Colonel John Armstrong and his Scotch-Irish troops from the Cumberland Valley, September 8th, 1756.

Likewise, Robert Robinson thus describes the attack on McCord's Fort and the pursuit of the savages:

"In the year 1756 a party of Indians came out of the Conococheague to a garrison named McCord's Fort, where they killed some and took a number prisoners. They then took their course near to Fort Lyttleton. Captain Hamilton being stationed there with a company, hearing of their route at McCord's Fort, marched with his company of men, having an Indian with him who was under pay. The Indians had McCord's wife with them; they cut off Mr. James Blair's head and threw it into Mrs. McCord's lap, saying that it was her husband's head; but she knew it to be Blair's."

Mrs. McCord was taken to Kittanning, where she was rescued when Colonel John Armstrong's forces destroyed this noted stronghold of the Delawares.

The terrible disaster of Fort McCord and vicinity caused the greatest consternation among the harried settlers of the Cumberland Valley. Block houses and farms were abandoned, and refugees came streaming into Carlisle.

A monument now marks the site of Fort McCord, having thereon a list of the killed and wounded—members of the leading pioneer families of the present counties of Cumberland, Franklin and Fulton.

Conclusion

This chapter brings us up to the time of Pennsylvania's declaration of war against the Delawares and Shawnees. It is a story of outrage, devastation and murder. But many of the horrors on the Pennsylvania frontier during the early part of 1756 will remain forever unrecorded. The statement of the French that, from Braddock's defeat until the middle of March, 1756, more than seven hundred people in Pennsylvania, Virginia and North Carolina were killed and captured by the Delawares and Shawnees, gives one an idea of the appalling tragedies in the cabin homes of the pioneers.

CHAPTER XI

Carlisle Council—War Declared

ON January 13th to January 17th, 1756, an important Indian council was held at Carlisle between Governor Morris, James Hamilton, Richard Peters, William Logan, Joseph Fox, Conrad Weiser and George Croghan, on the one hand, and the following Indians, on the other hand: The Belt of Wampum, Aroas (Silver Heels), Jagrea (Zigera, Sata Karoyis), Canachquasy (Kos Showweyha, Captain New Castle), Seneca George, Isaac, and several chiefs of the Conestogas. The council had particular reference to affairs on the Ohio.

George Croghan reported, at this council, that, in the latter part of 1755, at the request of Governor Morris, he had sent Delaware Jo, a friendly Indian, to the Ohio to gain what information he could about the attitude and actions of the Delawares and Shawnees of that place. Delaware Jo returned to Croghan's fortified trading house, often called Croghan's Fort, at Aughwick, now Shirleysburg, Huntingdon County, on January 8th, 1756. On his journey to the Ohio, he visited Kittanning and Logstown. He reported that, at Kittanning, then the residence of Shingas and Captain Jacobs, he found one hundred and forty warriors, mostly Delawares and Shawnees, and about one hundred English prisoners, captured on the frontiers of Virginia and Pennsylvania; that, at Kittanning, he met the Delaware chief, King Beaver, or Tamaque, a brother of Shingas and Pisquetomen, and that King Beaver told him that the French had often offered the Delawares and Shawnees the "French Hatchet," but they had refused it until April or May, 1755, when some Iroquois, Adirondack and Caughnawage warriors, stopping at Fort Duquesne, on their way to attack the Catawbas and Cherokees, were prevailed upon by the French to offer the "French Hatchet" to the Delawares and Shawnees, who then and there accepted the hatchet, and went with the other Indians into Virginia. King Beaver further told Delaware Jo that neither he nor the other chiefs of the Delawares and Shawnees approved the action of the members of their tribes who had accepted the "French Hatchet," that they were sorry for this action, and wished to "make Matters up with the English."

At Logstown, Delaware Jo found about one hundred Indians and thirty English prisoners. These prisoners had been captured on the frontiers of Virginia. The French had tried to buy the prisoners, but the Indians refused to sell them until they should hear from the Six Nations. Delaware Jo further reported that there were some warriors of the Six Nations living with the Delawares and Shawnees on the Allegheny and Ohio, and that they often went with them in their incursions into the settlements. When at Logstown, this friendly Delaware intended to go to Fort Duquesne to see what the French were doing, but found he could not cross the river for the driving of the ice. He was informed, however, that the number of the French did not exceed four hundred. From Logstown, he returned to Kittanning, and there learned that ten Delawares had recently left for the Susquehanna, "as he supposed to persuade those Indians to strike the English, who might perhaps be concerned in the Mischief lately done in the County of Northampton"—atrocities described in Chapter X. (Pa. Col. Rec., Vol. 6, pages 781, 782.)

James Hamilton reported, at this council, that, in November, 1755, he had sent Aroas, or Silver Heels, to the Indian towns on the Susquehanna to gain information, whereupon Aroas was called in and gave the following account of his journey:

"That he found no Indians at Shamokin, and therefore proceeded higher up Sasquehanna, as far as to Nescopecka, where he saw one hundred and forty Indians, all Warriors; that they were dancing the war dance; expressed great bitterness against the English, and were preparing for an expedition against them, and he thought would go to the Eastward. He did not stay with them, finding them in this disposition, but went to the House of an uncle of his, at a little distance from Nescopecka, between that and Wyoming, who told him the Delawares and Shawnees on the Ohio were persuaded by the French to strike the English, and had put the Hatchet into the Hands of the Susquehannah Indians, a great many of whom had taken it greedily, and there was no persuading them to the Contrary, and that they would do abundance of mischief to the People of Pennsylvania, against whom they were preparing to go to War." (Pa. Col. Rec., Vol. 6, page 783.)

The Belt of Wampum, at this council, made a long speech in

which he reviewed the events that had taken place on the Ohio and Allegheny from the time the French had first occupied this region until the Delawares and Shawnees took up arms against Pennsylvania. Being the official keeper of the wampum belts, this chief was well qualified to review these events. Among other things, he said that, after Tanacharison had delivered his third notice to the French to withdraw from the valleys of the Allegheny and Ohio, it was learned that "the French had prevailed upon the Shawonese, who were a Nation in alliance with the Six Nations, and living by their Sufferance upon a part of their Country, and upon the Delawares, who were a tribe conquered by and entirely dependent upon them, to enter into a separate and private Treaty with them, by which they, the Shawonese and Delawares, had agreed not only to permit the French to take Possession of the Country upon the Ohio, as far as they would, but to assist them against the English, if their Aid should be found necessary in the Contest, which the taking Possession of that Country should occasion. That, in consequence of this secret Treaty, and upon the Persuasions of the French, who have acquired a considerable Influence over these Two Tribes, they had fallen upon the English and done the mischief already complained of without any just Reason or Cause." (Pa. Col. Rec., Vol. 6, pages 3 and 4.)

There are several significant things in the above statement of the Belt of Wampum. One is that the Delawares and Shawnees were endeavoring to break away from the overlordship of the Six Nations, their conquerors, and to make treaties for themselves. Another is, as Dr. George P. Donehoo points out in his "Pennsylvania—A History," that "the attempts of the Quaker element in the Assembly to justify the action of these hostile tribes, from the standpoint of the Six Nations, was without any real foundation." This is evident from the great historical fact that those Iroquois on the Ohio and Allegheny who went with the Shawnees and Delawares on their incursions into the settlements were not genuine members of the great Iroquois or Six Nation Confederation, but a mixture of Iroquoian stock on the outskirts of the habitat of the Senecas. In other words, these Indians who joined the Delawares and Shawnees, were a mongrel population of the Ohio and Allegheny valleys, known as the Mingoes; they were not true representatives of the Confederation of the Six Nations, and were beyond the jurisdiction of the historic Confederation.

George Croghan said, at this Carlisle council, that he believed the Delawares and Shawnees were acting in their hostile manner with the approval of the Six Nations; but he should have considered that the Mingoes were a rabble element beyond the jurisdiction of the Six Nations, and that the true representatives of the great Iroquois Confederation on the Ohio, such as Tanacharison, Scarouady, The Belt of Wampum, Captain New Castle and Seneca George, never wavered in their friendship for the English and always disapproved of the hostile actions of the Mingoes. They even succeeded in keeping many of the Delawares and Shawnees friendly to the English.

Scarouady Returns From His Mission to the Six Nations

We shall now learn from Scarouady the real attitude of the Six Nations. As stated in Chapter IX, Governor Morris, in the middle of November, 1755, sent Scarouady and Andrew Montour on a mission to the Six Nations—a mission in which they were instructed to give the real authorities of the Six Nations a complete account of the bloody invasion of the Delawares and Shawnees and to ascertain whether or not this invasion was made with the knowledge, consent or order of the Six Nations, also to ascertain whether the Six Nations would chastise the Delawares and Shawnees for their hostile action.

Scarouady and Montour returned to Philadelphia from this mission on March 21, 1756, and on the 27th of that month, they appeared before the Provincial Council, and made a report of their journey. They had gone by way of Tulpehocken and Thomas McKee's trading post to Shamokin; and from there through Laugpaughpitton's Town and Nescopeck to Wyoming (Plymouth, Luzerne County). At Wyoming they found a large number of Delawares, some Shawnees, Mohicans, and members of the Six Nations. They next came to Asserughney, a Delaware Town, twelve miles above Wyoming, near the junction of the Susquehanna and Lackawanna. Their next stop was at Chinkannig (Tunkhannock), twenty miles farther up the Susquehanna, where they found the great Delaware chief, Teeduscung, with some Delawares and Nanticokes. Their next stop was at Diahogo (Tioga), a town composed of Mohicans and Delawares of the Munsee Clan, located where Athens, Bradford County, now stands, at which place they found ninety warriors. About twenty-five miles beyond, they came to the deserted town of Owegy.

Leaving this place they arrived at Chugnut, about twenty miles distant. About five miles above Chugnut, was the town of Otseningo, where they found thirty cabins and about sixty warriors of the Nanticokes, Conoys, and Onondagas. Fourteen miles beyond this place they came to Oneoquagque, where they sent a message to the Governor of Pennsylvania, written by Rev. Gideon Hawley. From there they proceeded to Teyonnoderre and Teyoneandakt, and next to Caniyeke, the Lower Mohawk Town, located about two miles from Fort Johnson, and about forty miles from Albany, New York. At Fort Johnson, they held a conference in February, 1756, with Sir William Johnson and the chiefs of the Six Nations, who expressed great resentment over the action of the hostile Delawares.

This was a very dangerous journey for Scarouady and Montour. While they were at Wyoming, their lives were threatened by a party of eighty Delaware warriors, who came soon after their arrival. While Scarouady was consulting with the oldest chief in the evening, the rest cried out of doors: "Let us kill the rogue; we will hear of no mediator, much less of a master; hold your tongue, and be gone, or you shall live no longer. We will do what we please." Said Scarouady: "All the way from Wyoming to Diahogo, a day never passed without meeting some warriors, six, eight, or ten in a party; and twenty under command at Cut Finger Pete, going after the eighty warriors which we saw at Wyoming. . . . All the way we met parties of Delawares going to join the eighty warriors there."

Scarouady reported that, at Wyoming he and Montour found John Shikellamy, son of the great vice-gerent of the Six Nations, with the hostile Delawares. They took him aside, and upbraided him severely for his ingratitude to Pennsylvania, "which had ever been extremely kind to his father when alive." Then John Shikellamy explained that he was with the enemies of the Colony, because he could not help it, as they had threatened to kill him if he did not join them.

Scarouady again appeared before the Provincial Council on April 3d and gave additional details of his journey. Said he: "You desired us in your instructions to inquire the particular reasons assigned by the Delawares and Shawnees for their acting in the manner they do against this Province. I have done it and all I could get from the Indians is that they heard them say their brethren, the English, had accused them very falsely of joining with the French after Colonel Washington's defeat, and if they would charge them when they were innocent, they could do no more if they were guilty; this turned them against their brethren and now indeed the English have good reason for any charge they may make against them, for they are heartily their enemies."

As to the attitude of the Six Nations, Scarouady reported: "The Six Nations in their reply expressed great resentment of the Delawares; they threatened to shake them by the head, saying they were drunk and out of their senses and would not consider the consequences of their ill behavior and assured them that, if they did not perform what they had promised they should be severely chastized." At this meeting of the Provincial Council and at others held early in April, Scarouady expressed himself as favoring a declaration of war by Pennsylvania against the Delawares, and ventured the opinion that the Six Nations would approve of such action. (Pa. Col. Rec., Vol. 7, pages 64 to 72.)

Pennsylvania Declares War Against Delawares and Shawnees, and Offers Rewards for Scalps

Not only Scarouady, but many other prominent men, including James Hamilton, strongly urged that Pennsylvania should declare war against the Delawares and Shawnees, and offer bounties for their scalps. As a result of the foregoing conferences with Scarouady, Governor Morris, on April 8th, 1756, delivered an address to this great sachem and Andrew Montour, which had been approved by the Provincial Council, in which he said:

"I therefore, by this Belt, declare War against the Delawares and all such as act in conjunction with them. I offer you the Hatchet, and expect your hearty Concurrence with us in this just and Necessary War. I not only invite you, but desire you will send this Belt to all your Friends everywhere, as well on the Susquehannah, as to the Six Nations and to their Allies, and engage them to join us heartily against these false and perfidous Enemies. I promise you and them Protection and Assistance, when you shall stand in need of it against your Enemies.

"For the Encouragement of you, and all who will join you in the Destruction of our Enemies, I propose to give the following Bounties or Rewards, Vist: for every Male Indian Prisoner above Twelve Years Old that shall be delivered at any of the Government's Forts, or Towns, One Hundred and Fifty Dollars.

"For every Female Prisoner, or Male Prisoner of Twelve years old, one hundred and thirty Dollars.

"For the Scalp of every male Indian of above Twelve Years old, one hundred and thirty dollars.

"For the scalp of every Indian Woman, Fifty Dollars.

"To our own People, I shall observe our own forms; to you I give the Hatchet according to yours.

"Agreeable to your repeated Request, I am now going to Build a Fort at Shamokin. Forces are raising for that Purpose, and everything will soon be in Readiness." (Pa. Col. Rec., Vol. 7, pages 75 and 76.)

Having used the Indian forms in declaring war, the Governor now made good his promise to Scarouady to "observe our own forms to our own people." The formal declaration of war and the bounty offered for prisoners and scalps was signed by the Commissioners, James Hamilton, Joseph Fox, Evan Morgan, John Mifflin and John Hughes. Then, against the protests of Samuel Powell and others, on behalf of the Quakers, the proclamation of war against the Delawares and Shawnees, was "published at the Court House, on April 14th, in the presence of the Provincial Council, Supreme Judges, Magistrates, Officers and a large Concourse of People." The language of that part of the formal declaration, relating to the bounties offered for Indian scalps, is as follows:

"For every male Indian enemy above twelve years old, who shall be taken prisoner and delivered at any fort, garrisoned by the troops in pay of this Province, or at any of the county towns to the keepers of the common jail there, the sum of 150 Spanish dollars or pieces of eight; for the scalp of every male enemy above the age of twelve years, produced to evidence of their being killed the sum of 130 pieces of eight; for every female Indian taken prisoner and brought in as aforesaid, and for every male Indian prisoner under the age of twelve years, taken and brought in as aforesaid, 130 pieces of eight; for the scalp of every Indian woman, produced as evidence of their being killed, the sum of fifty pieces of eight, and for every English subject that has been killed and carried from this Province into captivity that shall be recovered and brought in and delivered at the City of Philadelphia, to the Governor of this Province, the sum of 130 pieces of eight, but nothing for their scalps; and that there shall be paid to every officer or soldier as are or shall be in the pay of the Province who shall redeem and deliver any English subject carried into captivity as aforesaid, or shall take, bring in and produce any enemy prisoner, or scalp as aforesaid, one-half of the said several and respective premiums and bounties." (Pa. Col. Rec., Vol. 7, pages 88 and 89.)

The Scalp Act had the effect of causing hundreds of brave warriors of the Delawares and Shawnees who were up to that time undecided, to take up arms against the Colony. "A mighty shout arose which shook the very mountains, and all the Delawares and Shawnees, except a few old sachems, danced the war dance."

James Logan, a prominent Quaker member of the Provincial Council, and former Secretary of the same, opposed the declaration of war, though he was a strict advocate of defensive warfare. Conrad Weiser was in favor of the declaration of war, but strongly opposed to offering rewards for scalps. He said that the Colony might offer rewards for Indian prisoners, but that a bounty for scalps would certainly tend to aggravate existing affairs. He argued that anyone could bring in these scalps, and there was no means of distinguishing the scalps of friendly Indians. "Indeed," says Walton, "this was the core of the whole difficulty. Scalps of friendly Indians were taken, and the peace negotiations with the Eastern Indians frustrated."

Sir William Johnson was displeased with Pennsylvania's declaration of war and offering of bounties for scalps, at a time when a great council was about to be held at Onondaga. The opposition of the Quakers to these measures was due largely to the fact that they believed the Delawares had been unjustly treated by the Province, after the Six Nations came into such prominence in Pennsylvania's relations with the Indians. The Quakers called attention to the fraudulent "Walking Purchase," by which the Delawares had been compelled by the Iroquois to surrender possession of their ancestral possessions, and to the Purchase of July, 1754, by which the Iroquois sold the land of the Delawares and Shawnees "from under their feet." The land sales drove the Delawares from one place to another. Wherever they went, the land on which they erected their wigwams was sold by their Iroquois conquerors without their being consulted or having any say whatever in the matter. Therefore, it is no wonder that the Quakers sympathized with the Delawares, the affectionate friends of the greatest of the Quakers, William Penn, the Founder of the Province.

Great Britain did not declare war against France until May 17th, 1756, an act which was not known in Pennsylvania until about two months later. The declaration was published at Easton, July 30th, and a little later in Philadelphia.

CHAPTER XII

Atrocities in the Summer and Autumn of 1756

THE erection of frontier forts, the organization of military companies, and the scalp bounties did not prevent the Delawares and Shawnees from making bloody raids into the settlements. Crossing the mountains through the various gaps, the Indians fell upon the settlements along the Conococheague, in Franklin County, along Tuscarora Creek, in Juniata County, also upon various settlements in the counties of Perry, Dauphin, Cumberland, Lebanon, Schuylkill, Carbon, Berks, Lehigh, Northampton and Monroe.

The failure of the "Scalp Act" to bring the desired results is seen in a letter sent to Governor Morris, on June 14th, 1756, by the Commissioners, Benjamin Franklin, John Mifflin, Joseph Fox, Evan Morgan and John Hughes, in which they say that they are disappointed in the number of persons volunteering to "go out on the Scalping." They then add:

"We think, however, that the Indians ought to be persued and Hunted; and as the back Inhabitants begin now to request Guards to protect them in getting in their Harvest, we submit it to the Governor's Consideration whether the best means of affording them the Protection will not be to order out parties from the Forts to range on the West side of Susquehannah, quite to the Ohio and the Neighbourhood of Fort Duquesne, to Annoy the Enemy, take Prisoners, and obtain Intelligence, which may be of great use," etc. (Pa. Col. Rec., Vol. 7, page 153.)

The harvest of the summer of 1756 was, according to Joseph Armstrong and Adam Hoops, the most bountiful in the "Memory of Man." Yet, on account of the tomahawk, rifle, scalping knife and torch of the Delawares and Shawnees, the settlers fled from their farms, leaving their abundant crops of grain and corn standing in the fields. Every time an attempt was made to harvest the crops, it was necessary to guard the farmers by Provincial troops. Even then, many troops and farmers were killed and captured by the lurking foe.

In June, 1756, a Mr. Dean, who lived about a mile east of Shippensburg, Cumberland County, was found murdered in his cabin, his skull having been cleft with a tomahawk; and it was supposed that the deed was committed by some Indians who had been seen in the neighborhood the day before. On the 6th of this month, a short distance from where Burd's Run crosses the road leading from Shippensburg to Middle Spring Church, a band of Indians killed John McKean and John Agnew, and captured Hugh Black, William Carson, Andrew Brown, James Ellis and Alex McBride. A party of settlers from Shippensburg pursued the Indians through McAllister's Gap into Path Valley. On the morning of the third day of the pursuit, they met all the prisoners except James Ellis, on their way home, after having made their escape. Ellis was never heard from again. The pursuers returned with the men who had escaped. A few days before the murder of Mr. Dean, John Wasson was murdered and his body frightfully mangled, in Peters Township, Franklin County.

On June 8th, a band of Indians crept up on Felix Wuench as he was ploughing on his farm near Swatara Gap, and shot him through the breast. The poor man cried lamentably and started to run, defending himself with a whip; but the Indians overtook him, tomahawked and scalped him. His wife, hearing his cries and the report of the guns, ran out of the house, but was captured with one of her own and two of her sister's children. A servant boy who saw this atrocity ran to a neighbor named George Miess, who, though he had a crippled leg, ran directly after the Indians and made such a noise as to scare them off.

On June 24th, Indians attacked the home of Lawrence Dieppel, in Bethel Township, Berks County, carrying off two of the children, one of whom they later killed and scalped. (Penna. *Gazette*, June 17th, 1756; Pa. Col. Rec., Vol. 7, page 164.)

On June 26, in the same neighborhood in which the above atrocities were committed, a band of Indians surprised and scalped Franz Albert and Jacob Handschue, also two boys, Frederick Weiser and John George Miess, who were plowing in the field of a settler named Fischer. (See "Frontier Forts," Vol. I, page 65.)

Burning of Bingham's Fort

On June 11th or 12th, 1756, Bingham's Fort, the stockaded home of Samuel Bingham, or Bigham, in Tuscarora Township, Juniata County, was attacked and burned by a band of Indians led by the Delaware chief, King Beaver. All the occupants of the fort were either killed or captured. On the day of the attack, John Gray and Francis Innis were returning from Carlisle, where they had gone for salt. As they were descending the Tuscarora Mountain, in a narrow defile, Gray's horse taking fright at a bear which crossed the road, became unmanageable and threw him off. Innis, anxious to see his wife and family, went on, but Gray was detained for nearly two hours in catching his horse and righting his pack. In the meantime, Innis pressed on rapidly toward the fort. What happened to him, we shall presently see. John Gray's detention saved him from death or capture. He arrived at the fort just in time to see the last of its timbers consumed. With a heart full of anguish, he examined the charred remains of the bodies inside the fort, in an effort to ascertain whether any were those of his family. It subsequently was found that his wife, Hannah, and his only daughter, Jane, three years of age, were among the captured.

The Pennsylvania *Gazette*, June 24th, 1756, gave the following list of persons killed and captured on this occasion:

"The following is a list of persons killed and missing at Bingham's Fort, namely: George Woods, Nathaniel Bingham, Robert Taylor, his wife and two children, Francis Innis, his wife and three children, John McDonnell, Hannah Gray and one child, missing. Some of these are supposed to be burnt in the fort, as a number of bones were found there. Susan Giles was found dead and scalped in the neighborhood of the fort. Robert Cochran and Thomas McKinney found dead and scalped. Alexander McAllister and his wife, James Adams, Jane Cochran and two children missed. McAllister's house was burned and a number of cattle and horses driven off. The enemy was supposed to be numerous, as they did eat and carry off a great deal of beef they had killed."

All the prisoners taken at Bingham's Fort were marched to Kittanning and from there to Fort Duquesne, where they were parceled out and adopted by the Indians. George Woods, one of these prisoners, was given to an Indian named John Hutson, who removed him to his own wigwam. Woods later purchased his ransom, and returned to the settlements. He was a surveyor, and followed this vocation in the counties of Juniata, Bedford and Allegheny. When Pittsburgh was laid out, in 1784, he assisted in this work, and one of its principal streets, Wood Street, is named for him.

Hannah Gray and her daughter, Jane, were carried to Canada. Later in the summer of 1756, her husband, John Gray, joined Colonel John Armstrong's expedition against Kittanning, in the hope of either recovering his wife and daughter or gaining some intelligence of their whereabouts. He returned disappointed, and a few years thereafter died. After about four years of captivity, Mrs. Gray, by the assistance of some traders, made her escape, and reached her home in safety, but unhappily, was compelled to leave her daughter with the Indians. The little girl never returned. At the close of Pontiac's War, many children, captured by the Indians during this and the French and Indian War, were delivered up to Colonel Bouquet, and brought to Carlisle and Philadelphia to be recognized and claimed by their relatives and friends. Mrs. Gray, at Philadelphia, searched in vain among these returned captives for her daughter, and then took one of them, a girl of about her daughter's age. The taking of this child in the place of her own daughter brought on a famous law suit over the title of the farm her husband had devised to her and the daughter in case they returned from captivity. This law suit is known as "Frederick et al. *versus* Gray. It finally reached the Supreme Court of Pennsylvania, and is reported in the Reports of this tribunal, in No. 10 Sergeant and Rawle, pages 182 to 188.

Francis Innis and his wife were sold to the French and taken to Canada in December, 1756, after the wife had been severely injured in running the gauntlet. While the Indians were taking the family to Montreal, they put the youngest of the children, who was sickly, under the ice of one of the rivers. While in Montreal, another child, James, was born. Mr. and Mrs. Innis were released by the French, and returned to their home. Their surviving children remained among the Indians until the autumn of 1764, when they were delivered up to Colonel Bouquet, and soon returned to their parents. (Frontier Forts of Penna., Vol. 1, pages 586 to 591; Day's Historical Collections," pages 383 to 385.)

Capture of John McCullough

On July 26th the Indians entered the valley of the Conococheague, in Franklin County, killing Joseph Martin, and taking captive two brothers, John and James McCullough. James McCullough, the father of these boys, had only a few years before removed from Delaware into what is now Montgomery Township, Franklin County. At the time of this Indian incursion, the McCullough family were residing temporarily in a cabin three miles from their home, and the parents and their daughter, Mary, on the day of the capture, went home to pull flax. A neighbor, named John Allen, who had business at Fort Loudon, accompanied them to their home, and promised to return that way in the evening, and accompany them back to their cabin. However, he did not keep his promise, and returned by a circuitous route. When he reached the McCullough cabin on his return, he told John and James to hide, that Indians were near and that he supposed they had killed Mr. and Mrs. McCullough. John was but eight years old, and James but five at the time. They alarmed their neighbors, but none would volunteer to go to the McCullough home to warn Mr. and Mrs. McCullough, being too much interested in making preparations to hurry to the fort a mile distant for safety.

Then the boys determined to warn their parents themselves. Leaving their little sister, Elizabeth, aged two, asleep in bed, they proceeded to a point where they could see the McCullough home, and began to shout. When they had reached a point about sixty yards from the house, five Indians and a Frenchman, who had been secreted in the thicket, rushed upon them and took them captive. The parents were not captured, inasmuch as the father, hearing the boys shout, had left his work and thus the Indians missed him, and they failed to notice the mother and Mary at work in the field.

John and James were taken to Fort Duquesne. From this place James was carried to Canada, and all trace of him became lost. John was taken to Kittanning, Kuskuskies, Shenango, Mahoning and the Muskingum, was adopted by the Delawares, and remained among them for nine years until liberated by Colonel Bouquet in the autumn of 1764. At one time his father came to Venango (Franklin) to recover him, and at another time to Mahoning, for the same purpose, but the boy had been so long among the Indians that he preferred the Indian life to returning with his father, and succeeded in eluding him. After his liberation by Colonel Bouquet, he returned to the community from which he had been taken nine years before, and lived there nearly sixty years. He wrote a most interesting account of his captivity, which sheds much light on the manners and customs of the Delawares at that time.

Other Outrages In Perry, Franklin and and Cumberland Counties

During the same month (July), Hugh Robinson was captured and his mother killed at Robinson's Fort, in Perry County. Hugh, after being carried to the western part of the state, made his escape. Also, during this same month a number of Indians appeared near Fort Robinson, killed the daughter of Robert Miller, the wife of James Wilson, and a Mrs. Gibson, and captured Hugh Gibson and Betty Henry.

Robert Robinson, in his Narrative, says that nearly all the occupants of the fort were out in the harvest fields reaping their grain, when the Indians waylaid the place. The reapers, forty in number, returned to the fort, and the Indians then fled. While one of the Indians was scalping the wife of James Wilson, Robert Robinson shot and wounded him. The captives were taken to Kittanning.

Hugh Gibson was 14 years old at the time of his capture. He was adopted by an Indian, named Busqueetam, who was lame from a knife wound, received when skinning a deer. Gibson had to build a lodge for the Indian. At one time the lodge fell down on the Indian and injured him. He then called for his knife and ordered Gibson and some Indians to carry him into another hut. While they were carrying the Indian, Gibson saw him hunt for the knife and Gibson's Indian mother concealed it. When they put the Indian to bed, the Indian mother ordered Gibson to conceal himself, and he afterwards heard the Indian reprove his wife for hiding the knife. The old Indian soon forgot his anger and treated Gibson well thereafter.

Sometime later all the prisoners were collected to see the torture of a woman prisoner. She had fled to the white men at the time Colonel Armstrong burned Kittanning. They stripped her naked, bound her to a post and applied hot irons to her, while the skin stuck to the irons at every touch. Thus was she tortured to death.

Also, in July, 1756, a band of Indians attacked the plantation of Robert Baskins, who lived near Baskinsville railroad station. They murdered Mr. Baskins, burned his house, and captured his wife and children. Part of the same band captured Hugh Carroll and his family. The Indians, committing these outrages, were Delawares, who had come down the Juniata into Perry County after having appeared near Fort Granville, July 22nd, and challenged the garrison to fight—a challenge which was declined on account of the weakness of the garrison.

About the same time, according to Egle's "History of Pennsylvania," a band of Indians murdered a family of seven persons, on Sherman's Creek, Perry County, and then passed over the Kittatinny or Blue Mountains at Sterrett's Gap, wounding a man and capturing a Mrs. Boyle, her two sons and a daughter, living on Conodoguinet Creek, Cumberland County. These are probably the same atrocities mentioned by Colonel John Armstrong in a letter written from Carlisle to Governor Morris, on July 23d, 1756, and recorded in Pa. Archives, Vol. 2, page 719, in which he says:

"Being just got home, I am unable to furnish your Honor with the Occurrences of these two days past, in which time the Indians have begun to take advantage of the Harvest Season. Seven people on this side of the Kittatinney Hills being Kill'd and missing within this county, and two on the South Side of the Temporary line."

About this time, occurred the Williamson and Nicholson tragedies in Mifflin Township, Cumberland County, though neither the date nor the details of the same can be definitely set forth. It seems that eight or nine members of the Williamson family, all except Mrs. Williamson and her babe, were victims of the tomahawk, rifle and scalping knife of the Indians. Mr. Nicholson was shot at the door of his cabin, but his wife and brother within, succeeded in keeping the Indians at bay until morning, when they left the neighborhood. Tradition says that the mother and brother each mounted a horse, the former carrying two children and the latter his slain brother, and rode to Shippensburg, where they buried the murdered man. (See "History of Cumberland and Adams Counties," Werner, Beers and Co., Chicago, 1886, pages 308, 309.)

Probably during the summer of 1756, though Loudon gives the date as April 2nd, 1757, William McKinney, who had sought shelter with his family at Fort Chambers, where Chambersburg, Franklin County, now stands, ventured out of the fort, accompanied by his son, for the purpose of visiting his dwelling and plantation. They were surprised by the Indians, and both were killed and scalped. Their bodies were brought to the fort and buried. (Frontier Forts of Penna., Vol. 1, page 532.)

Egle, in his "History of Pennsylvania," mentions another tragedy which, he says happened in Franklin County, in the summer of 1756, as follows:

"William Mitchell, an inhabitant of Conococheague, had collected a number of reapers to cut down his grain; having gone out to the field, the reapers all laid down their guns at the fence, and set in to reap. The Indians suffered them to reap on for some time, till they got out in the open field. They secured their guns, killed and captured every one."

James Young's letter, written at Carlisle on July 22nd, 1756, and recorded in Pa. Archives, Vol. 2, pages 716 and 717, describes other atrocities, committed in Franklin and Cumberland counties during the terrible summer of which we are writing:

"On the 20th Inst., in the morning, a party of Indians Surpriz'd two of Captain Steel's [Rev. John Steel] men on this side McDowell's mill; they killed and scalped one; the other they carried off; the Reapers made their escape; also, one of the soldiers from McDowell's Mill that went with two Women to the Spring for some water is missing; the women got off safe to the fort, and almost at the same time, a man and a women were scalped a few miles on the other side of the mill. And yesterday morning, Eight Indians came to the house of Jacob Peeble, near the great Spring and McCluker's Gap, about ten miles from this place, on this side the mountain; they killed an Old Woman and carried off two children, and an old man is missing; they pursued a boy who was on horse back a long way, but he escaped; there were some people Reaping at a small distance from the house, but knew nothing of what was doing at home, for the Indians did not fire a Gun . . . A party went from this town to bury the dead, and are returned again; they inform me that the Country People are all leaving their houses to come down, as there is great reason to fear many more Indians will soon be among them."

On August 28th, according to Loudon, Betty Ramsey, her son and cropper were killed, and her daughter was taken captive, probably in Franklin County. This same authority relates that on one occasion, probably in 1756, a band of Indians came into the valley of the Conococheague, and killed and scalped many persons, whereupon a large party of settlers pursued them, overtaking them on Sideling Hill, and compelling them to flee leaving their guns behind.

At the time of these murders, incursions were being made into that part of Maryland lying south of Franklin County, Pennsylvania. On August 27th, occurred the terrible massacre on Salisbury plain, near the mouth of the Conococheague, in which thirty-nine persons were killed. An attack was made on a funeral party, in which fifteen were killed and many wounded. The same day six men went from Israel Baker's on a scout. Of these, four were killed, one was captured, and another, though wounded, escaped. The same day, also, some soldiers going from Shirley's Fort, were killed and captured. On the following day Captain Emmett and a party of scouts were attacked while crossing the South Mountain. Three of them were killed and two wounded.

Massacre Near McDowell's Mill

Early in November, 1756, the beautiful valley of the Conococheague, in Franklin County, was again devastated and many of its inhabitants were killed by the hostile Indians. Robert Callender, writing from Carlisle, on November 4th, thus informed Governor Denny of these atrocities:

"This Day I received Advice from Fort McDowell that, on Monday or Tuesday last, one Samuel Perry, and his two Sons went from the Fort to their Plantation, and not returning at the Time they proposed, the Commanding Officer there sent a Corporal and fourteen Men to know the Cause of their Stay, who not finding them at the Plantation, they marched back towards the Fort, and on their Return found the said Perry killed and scalped, and covered over with Leaves; immediately after a Party of Indians, in Number about thirty, appeared and attacked the Soldiers, who returned the Fire, and fought for Sometime until four of our People fell; the rest then made off, and six of them got into the fort, but what became of the rest is not yet known; there are also two families cut off, but cannot tell the Number of People. It is likewise reported that the Enemy in their Retreat burnt a Quantity of Grain and sundry Houses in the Coves." (Pa. Archives, Vol. 3, page 29.)

Four days later, Colonel John Armstrong wrote Governor Denny, from Carlisle, giving the list of the killed and missing in this bloody raid, as follows:

"Soldiers Kill'd—James and William McDonald, Bartholomew McCafferty, Anthony McQuoid.

"Of the Inhabitants Kill'd—John Culbertson, Samuel Perry, Hugh Kerrel, John Woods, with his Wife and Mother-in-law, Elizabeth Archer, Wife to Jno. Archer.

"Soldiers Missing—James McCorkem, William Cornwall.

"Of the Inhabitants Missing—Four Children belonging to John Archer, Samuel Neely, a Boy, James McQuoid, a Child." (Pa. Archives, Vol. 3, pages 40 and 41.)

Attack on the Boyer Family

Sometime during the summer of 1756, though authorities differ as to the exact date, occurred the attack on the Boyer family, who lived in the vicinity of Fort Lehigh, at Lehigh Gap. The "Frontier Forts of Pennsylvania" thus describes this event:

"His [Boyer's] place was about 1½ miles east of the Fort, on land now owned by Josiah Arner, James Ziegenfuss and George Kunkle. With the other farmers he had gathered his family into the blockhouse for protection. One day, however, with his son Frederick, then thirteen years old, and the other children, he went home to attend to the crops. Mr. Boyer was ploughing and Fred was hoeing, whilst the rest of the children were in the house or playing near by. Without any warning they were surprised by the appearance of Indians. Mr. Boyer, seeing them, called to Fred to run, and himself endeavored to reach the house. Finding he could not do so, he ran towards the creek, and was shot through the head as he reached the farther side. Fred, who had escaped to the wheat field, was captured and brought back. The Indians, having scalped the father in his presence, took the horses from the plough, his sisters and himself, and started for Stone Hill, in the rear of the house. There they were joined by another party of Indians and marched northward to Canada. On the march the sisters were separated from their brother and never afterwards heard from. Frederick was a prisoner with the French and Indians in Canada for five years, and was then sent to Philadelphia. Of Mrs. Boyer, who remained in the blockhouse, nothing further is known. After reaching Philadelphia, Frederick made his way to Lehigh Gap, and took possession of the farm. Shortly after he married a daughter of Conrad Mehrkem, with whom he had four sons and four daughters. He died October 31, 1832, aged 89 years."

Murder at the Bloody Spring

During July, Samuel Miles and Lieutenant Atlee were ambushed by three Indians near a spring about half a mile from Fort Augusta, at Sunbury. A soldier who had come to the spring for a drink, was killed. Miles and Atlee made their escape. A rescuing party came out from the fort, and found the soldier scalped, with his blood trickling into the spring, giving its waters a crimson hue. The spring was ever afterwards called the Bloody Spring. (Frontier Forts of Penna., Vol. 1, page 362.)

Captain Jacobs Captures Fort Granville

On August 1st, 1756, the Delaware chief, Captain Jacobs, at the head of a band of his tribe from Kittanning, accompanied by some French soldiers, captured and burned Fort Granville, on the Juniata, near Lewistown, Mifflin County. We quote the following account of this event from the "Frontier Forts of Pennsylvania":

"The attack upon Fort Granville was made in harvest time of the year 1756. The Fort at this time was commanded by Lieut. Armstrong, a brother of Colonel Armstrong, who destroyed Kittanning. The Indians, who had been lurking about this fort for some time, and knowing that Armstrong's men were few in number, sixty of them appeared, July 22nd, before the fort, and challenged the garrison to a fight; but this was declined by the commander in consequence of the weakness of his force. The Indians fired at and wounded one man, who had been a short way from it, yet he got in safe; after which they divided themselves into small parties, one of which attacked the plantation of one Baskins, near the Juniata, whom they murdered, burnt his house and carried off his wife and children. Another made Hugh Carroll and his family prisoners.

"On the 30th of July, 1756, Capt. Edward Ward, the commandant of Granville, marched from the fort with a detachment of men from the garrison, destined for Tuscarora Valley, where they were needed as guard to the settlers while they were engaged in harvesting their grain. The party under Capt. Ward embraced the greater part of the defenders of the fort, under command of Lieut. Edward Armstrong. Soon after the departure of Capt. Ward's detachment, the fort was surrounded by the hostile force of French and Indians, who immediately made an attack, which they continued in their skulking, Indian manner through the afternoon and following night, but without being able to inflict much damage on the whites. Finally, after many hours had been spent in their unsuccessful attacks, the Indians availed themselves of the protection afforded by a deep ravine, up which they passed from the river bank to within twelve or fifteen yards of the fort, and from that secure position, succeeded in setting fire to the logs and burning out a large hole, through which they fired on the defenders, killing the commanding officer, Lieut. Armstrong, and one private soldier and wounding three others.

"They then demanded the surrender of the fort and garrison, promising to spare their lives if the demand was acceded to. Upon this, a man named John Turner, previously a resident in the Buffalo valley, opened the gates and the besiegers at once entered and took possession, capturing as prisoners twenty-two men, three women and a number of children. The fort was burned by the chief, Jacobs, by order of the French officer in command, and the savages then departed, driving before them their prisoners, heavily burdened with the plunder taken from the fort and the settlers' houses, which they had robbed and burned. On their arrival at the Indian rendezvous at Kittanning, all the prisoners were cruelly treated, and Turner, the man who had opened the gate at the fort to the savages, suffered the cruel death by burning at the stake, enduring the most horrible torment that could be inflicted upon him for a period of three hours, during which time red hot gun barrels were forced through parts of his body, his scalp torn from his head and burning splinters were stuck in his flesh, until at last an Indian boy was held up for the purpose who sunk a hatchet in the brain of the victim and so released him from this cruel torture."

Colonel John Armstrong, brother of Lieutenant Edward Armstrong who was killed at the destruction of Fort Granville, wrote Governor Morris, from Carlisle, on August 20th, giving additional details of this event. Lieutenant Armstrong behaved with greatest bravery to the last, "despising all the Terrors and Threats of the Enemy, whereby they Often urged him to Surrender. Tho' he had been near two Days without Water, but a little Ammunition left, the Fort on Fire, and the Enemy situate within twelve or fourteen Yards of the Fort, he was as far from Yielding as when at first attacked. A French Man in our Service, fearful of being burned up, asked leave of the Lieutenant to treat with his Country Men in the French Language. The Lieutenant answered,

'The First word of French you speak in this Engagement, I'll blow your brains out,' telling his Men to hold out bravely for the flame was falling and he would soon have it extinguished, but soon after received the fatal Ball. The French Officers refused the Soldiers the Liberty of interring his Corps, though it was to be done in an instant, where they raised the Clay to quench the Fire."

The above information came to Colonel Armstrong from Peter Walker, one of the captives taken at Fort Granville and later escaping. Walker had been informed by an interpreter for the French, named McDowell, that the Indians "designed very soon to attack Fort Shirley with four hundred men," and that "Captain Jacobs said he could take any Fort that would Catch Fire, and would make Peace with the English when they had learned him to make Gunpowder." (Pa. Col. Rec., Vol. 7, pages 231 to 233.)

For many years, the friendly Shawnee chief, Kishacoquillas, lived at the mouth of the creek of this name, a few miles from Fort Granville. He died in the summer of 1754. He was a firm friend of Arthur Buchanan, who lived near Fort Granville. Some of the followers of Kishacoquillas are said to have warned Buchanan and his sons of the expected attack on the fort, enabling them and their families to escape to Carlisle.

The destruction of Fort Granville exposed the whole western frontier to Indian incursions. Settlers fled in terror from the Juniata Valley, Sherman's Valley, the Tuscarora Valley, and the valleys of the Conococheague and Conodoguinet. Rev. Thomas Barton, writing from Carlisle, on August 22nd, described the dismal situation on the frontier, as follows:

"I came here this Morning, where all is Confusion. Such a Panick has seized the Hearts of the People in general, since the Reduction of Fort Granville, that this County is almost relinquished, and Marsh Creek in York [Adams] County is become a Frontier." (Pa. Archives, Vol. 2, page 756.)

Captain Jacobs

Captain Jacobs, the destroyer of Fort Granville, was one of the Delaware chiefs who took up arms against Pennsylvania after Braddock's defeat. He had at one time resided near Lewistown, where he sold lands to Colonel Buchanan, who gave him the name of Captain Jacobs, because of his close resemblance to a burly German in Cumberland County. Later he resided at "Jacob's Cabin," not far from Mount Pleasant, Westmoreland County. His principal residence was the famous Indian town of Kittanning, Armstrong County, which, as we have seen in an earlier chapter, was the first town established by the Delawares on their migration into the Allegheny Valley with the consent of the Iroquois Confederation. From this town, he and that other noted chief, Shingas, led many an expedition against the frontier settlements. In our next chapter, we shall record the fate that befell Captain Jacobs at the hands of Colonel John Armstrong.

Murders Near Brown's Fort and Fort Swatara

On August 6th, 1756, a soldier named Jacob Ellis, of Brown's Fort, located several miles north of Grantville, Dauphin County, desired to cut some wheat on his farm, a few miles from the fort, and, accordingly, took with him a squad of ten soldiers as a guard. At about ten o'clock, a band of Indians crept up on the reapers, shot the corporal dead, and wounded another of the soldiers. After this attack, a soldier named Brown was missing, and the next morning his body was found near the harvest field. (Pa. Archives, Vol. 2, pages 738, 740.)

On October 12th, 1756, a band of Shawnees entered the neighborhood near where the murders of August 6th were committed. Adam Read, writing from his stockaded residence, on Swatara Creek, in East Hanover Township, Lebanon County, thus describes the murder of Noah Frederick, by this hostile band:

"Last Tuesday, the 12th of this Instant, ten Indians came on Noah Frederick plowing in his Field, killed and Scalped him, and carried away three of his Children that was with him, the eldest but Nine Years old, plundered his House, and carried away every thing that suited their purpose, such as Cloaths, Bread, Butter, a Saddle and good Riffle Gun, it being but two short miles from Captain Smith's Fort [Fort Swatara, in Union Township, Lebanon County], at Swatawro Gap, and a little better than two from my House." (Pa. Col. Rec., Vol. 7, page 303.)

Noah Frederick's wife and small daughter were at the barn, where the mother was threshing the seed wheat, when the Indians made their appearance. They saw the murderers in time to make their escape. The captured children, one of whom was named Thomas, after a few days of captivity, were separated. They never met again. Thomas was carried to the Muskingum, where he grew up with the Indians and was given the name, Kee-saw-so-so. He was one of the prisoners delivered up by the Shawnees at the close of Pontiac's War, most likely at Fort Pitt, on May 9th, 1765. He then went to Philadelphia, where he learned the shoemaker trade. Several years later, he went to the neighborhood where he had been captured. Here he was so fortunate as to find his mother, who identified him by a certain scar on his neck. He left numerous descendants, among whom is C. W. Frederick, of Rochester, N. Y., who furnished the author with some of the material used in this paragraph.

The above letter of Adam Read describes other atrocities in the same neighborhood in which Noah Frederick was killed:

"Yesterday Morning, two miles from Smith's Fort, at Swataro, in Bethel Township, as Jacob Fornwall was going from the House of Jacob Meyler to his own, he was fired upon by two Indians and wounded, but escaped with his life, and a little after, in the said Township, as Frederick Henley and Peter Stample was carrying away their Goods in Waggons, was met by a parcel of Indians and all killed, five lying Dead in one place and one man at a little distance, but what more is done is not come to my Hand as yet, but that the Indians was continuing their Murders. The Frontiers is employed in nothing but carrying off their Effects, so that some Miles is now waist."

Loudon, in his "Indian Narratives," mentions the following events, which he says took place in Dauphin County, probably in 1756. He does not give the exact location of the first, but its scene was probably near Fort Manada, a stockade erected in the autumn of 1755, near the east bank of Manada Creek, in East Hanover Township, a few miles north-west of Grantville. Here is Loudon's account:

"At another time they [the Indians] attacked a man in Dauphin County who was endeavoring to move off in a wagon with some others. Those in the wagon fled to a fort. The men in the fort came to see what was happening and met a woman running toward them crying. They then came to where the wagon stood and behind it found the owner, a German, tomahawked and scalped but still breathing. The next day twelve men were sent to inform the soldiers at the next fort about eight miles distance, but were fired upon from ambush and all but two were killed. These two were wounded but made their escape.

"Mrs. Boggs in the same neighborhood while riding to a neighbors house was fired upon and her horse killed and she, with a young child, taken prisoner. The child was badly treated and after three days, they murdered it.

"Four men living in one house, in Paxton, erected a stockade around it. A Captain and his company, being overtaken at night, stopped to pass the night. They went in but had neglected to fasten the gate. A party of Indians entered the gate and closed it, and then called upon those in the house to open the door. The Indians likely did not know that there were soldiers in the house. The Captain opened the door, keeping some of his men in reserve. When the Indians entered, they were fired upon and began to retreat. The soldiers in reserve then pursued them, and, since they had closed the gate of the stockade, they could not get out, and were slain to a man."

Expedition Against Great Island and Other Indian Strongholds

During the summer of 1756, Fort Augusta was built and garrisoned, at Sunbury. At this fort, on October 18th of this year, Colonel William Clapham, the commander, was informed by Ogagradarisha, a Six Nations scout, that, as the result of a treaty recently held by the commander of Fort Duquesne with the Chippewas, Tawas, Twightwees (Miamis), Notowas, Delawares and Shawnees, a large body of French and one thousand Indians "were getting ready for an Expedition against this place, and are determined to take your Fort" (Augusta). (Col. Rec., Vol. 7, pages 299 to 302.) Colonel Clapham immediately got ready for any attack that might be made on Fort Augusta. Scouting parties were sent out in an endeavor to locate the French and Indian forces. It seems that the invaders did march from Fort Duquesne, but, probably because they learned through their scouts that Fort Augusta and other frontier forts had received information as to their advance, their large force was divided into smaller bodies, which made incursions into the frontier settlements.

Colonel Clapham directed Captain John Hambright, of Lancaster, to lead a company of thirty-eight men against the Indian towns of Chincklacamoose (Clearfield, Clearfield County), Great Island (Lock Haven, Clinton County) and other places on the West Branch of the Susquehanna. (Pa. Archives, Vol. 3, pages 41 and 42). There is no doubt that Captain Hambright carried out his instructions, but, unhappily, no records giving the details of his expedition are to be found. In this connection, we state that Colonel Clapham was one of the most conspicuous figures on the frontier. In the early spring of 1763, he removed with his family to Sewickley Creek, where the town of West Newton, Westmoreland County, now stands. Here he and his entire family were cruelly murdered on the afternoon of May 28, 1763, by The Wolf, Kekuscung, and two other Indians, one of whom was called Butler.

Massacres Near Forts Henry, Lebanon, Northkill and Everett

On October 19, 1756, Conrad Weiser wrote Governor Denny that the Indians had again entered Berks County, killing and scalping two married women and a boy fourteen years old, wounding two children about four years of age, and capturing two more, near Fort Henry. One of the wounded children, he said, was scalped and likely to die, while the other had two cuts on her forehead, inflicted by an Indian when making an unsuccessful attempt to scalp her. (Pa. Col. Rec., Vol. 7, page 302.)

Captain Jacob Morgan, writing to Governor Denny from Fort Lebanon, on November 4th, 1756, describes the following murders which were committed by the Indians, near the fort on the preceding day:

"Yesterday morning, at break of day, one of the neighbors discovered a fire at a distance from him. He went to the top of another mountain to take a better observation, and make a full discovery of the fire, and supposed it to be about seven miles off, at the house of John Finsher [Fincher]. He came and informed me of it. I immediately detached a party of ten men (we being but 22 men in the fort) to the place where they saw the fire at the said Finsher's house, it being nigh Schuylkill; and the men, anxious to see the enemy if there, ran through the water and bushes to the fire, where, to their disappointment, they saw none of them, but the house, barn and other out-houses all in flames, together with a considerable quantity of corn. They saw a great many tracks, and followed them, and came to the house of Philip Culmore, thinking to send from thence to alarm the other inhabitants to be on their guard, but instead of that, found the said Culmore's wife and daughter and son-in-law all just killed and scalped. There is likewise missing out of the same house Martin Fell's wife and child about one year old and another boy about seven years of age. The said Martin Fell was killed. It was done just when the scouts came there, and they seeing the scouts, ran off. The scouts divided into two parties. One came to some other houses nigh at hand, and the other to the fort, it being within half a mile of the fort [Fort Lebanon], to inform me. I immediately went out with the scouts again, and left in the fort no more than six men, but could not make any discovery, but brought all the families to the fort, where now, I believe, we are upward of sixty women and children that are fled here for refuge.

"And at twelve o'clock at night, I received an express from Lieutenant Humphreys, commander at Fort Northkill, who informed me that the same day, about eleven o'clock in the forenoon, about half a mile from his fort, as he was returning from his scout, came upon a body of Indians to the number of twenty at the house of Nicholas Long, where they had killed two old men and taken another captive, and doubtless would have killed all the family, there being nine children in the house. The Lieutenant's party, though seven in number, fired upon the Indians, and thought they killed two . . . The Lieutenant had one man shot through the right arm and right side, but hopes not mortal, and he had four shots through his own clothes." (Pa. Archives, Vol. 3, pages 28, 30, 31 and 36.)

James Read, Esq., writing Governor Denny from Reading, on November 7th, gives an account of the murders near Fort Lebanon, stating that the sister and mother of Mrs. Martin Fell were scalped, the young woman not being dead when the scouts arrived, "but insensible, and stuck in the throat as butcher's kill a pig." The poor woman soon died.

Fort Lebanon was not far from the town of Auburn, Schuylkill County; Fort Northkill was in upper Tulpehocken Township, Berks County, eleven miles from Fort Lebanon; and Fort Henry was near Millersburg, Berks County.

Near Adam Harper's fortified residence, at a place now known as "Harper's Tavern" in East Hanover Township, Lebanon County, hostile Indians, in October, 1756, killed five or six settlers. They scalped a woman, a sister of Major Leidig, who nevertheless lived for many years thereafter. One of the families murdered in this raid was that of Andrew Berryhill. On October 22nd, John Craig and his wife were killed, and a boy was captured. The next day a German settler was killed and scalped.

Timothy Horsfield, writing Governor Denny from Bethlehem, on November 30th, 1756, which letter is reported in Pa. Archives,

Vol. 3, page 77, says that, on the evening on November 28th, a band of Indians came to the home of a settler named Schlosser, most likely in Lynn Township, Lehigh County, killing a man named Stonebrook and capturing a child. At first two children were captured, but some of the men at the house fired upon the Indians, wounding one, whereupon one of the children, a girl, made her escape.

At the same time he informed the Governor of the attempt by some settlers to kill one of the Christian (Moravian) Delawares, near Bethlehem. In the terror and excitement on the frontier, the settlers sometimes made no distinction between hostile Indians and friendly Indians.

Some events that took place in Lebanon County, probably in Union Township, during the French and Indian War, and likely in 1756, were the following:

Philip Mauer was shot dead by Indians while reaping oats. A Mr. Noacre or Noecker was shot dead while plowing. Mathias Boeshore fled from Indians to the house of Martin Hess. Just as he got inside the house, he leveled his rifle at one of his pursuers, and was in the act of pulling the trigger, when a bullet from the rifle of one of the Indians struck that part of Boeshore's weapon, to which the flint was attached, and glancing, wounded him in the left side. On one occasion Indians entered the neighborhood in great numbers, when nearly all the settlers were in their houses. Peter Heydrich gave immediate notice to all the people to resort to a blockhouse in the neighborhood, probably that of Martin Hess. In the meantime, taking a fife and drum from the blockhouse, he went into the woods or thicket nearby. Now beating the drum, then blowing the fife, then again giving the word of command in a loud and distinct voice, as if to a large force, he managed to keep the Indians away, and collect his neighbors safely. (Frontier Forts of Penna., Vol. 1, pages 58 and 59.)

The Prowess of Mrs. Zellers

On page 63 of Vol. I, of the "Frontier Forts of Pennsylvania," is the following account of the attack on the fortified home of Heinrich Zellers, near Newmanstown, Lebanon County, some time during the French and Indian War, probably in 1756:

"It is related of the original Mrs. Zellers that she superintended the construction of the house, whilst her husband was out on an expedition against the Indians, and that her laborers were colored slaves. It is said, also, of this same Christine Zellers that one day, whilst alone in the fort, she saw three prowling savages approaching and heading for the small hole in the cellar shown on the picture attached. She quickly descended the cellar steps and stationed herself at this window with an uplifted axe. Presently the head of the first Indian protruded through the hole, when she quickly brought down the weapon with an effective blow. Dragging the body in, she disguised her voice and in Indian language, beckoned his companions to follow, which they did and were all dispatched in like manner."

As stated formerly, in this history, hundreds of the atrocities of the French and Indian War, in Pennsylvania, will remain forever unrecorded. However, the present chapter, like several that have preceded it, gives one an idea of the horrors of the crimson tide that flowed down from the mountains into the Pennsylvania settlements during the first two years of this tragic period.

CHAPTER XIII

Destruction of Kittanning

September 8th, 1756

AS stated, in Chapter XII, the destruction of Fort Granville left the frontiers of the counties of Juniata, Perry, Fulton, Franklin and Cumberland exposed to the bloody incursions of the Delawares and Shawnees of the valleys of the Ohio and Allegheny, especially the Delawares of Kittanning. In Chapter XII, also, as well as in chapters preceding it, we saw the horrors of the incursions which these Indians made into the counties above named—families murdered at midnight and their cabin homes burned to ashes; parents and children captured and, in many cases, separated forever; captives tortured to death at Kittanning and other Indian towns; relief parties burying the mutilated bodies of the dead amid the shades of the forest; the pale and tear-stained faces of women, with babes in their arms, and the anxious faces of men, fleeing in terror to the more thickly settled parts of the Province with the war-whoop of the Indian ringing in their ears.

In the letter written by Colonel John Armstrong, at Carlisle, on August 20th, quoted in part, in Chapter XII, he calls attention to the unprotected state of the Cumberland and Franklin County frontier, as follows:

"Lyttleton, Shippensburg, and Carlisle (the last two not finished), are the only Forts now built that will, in my Opinion, be Serviceable to the public. McDowell's or thereabouts is a necessary Post, but the present Fort not defencible. The Duties of the Harvest has not admitted me to finish Carlisle Fort with the Soldiers; it shou'd be done, and a Barrack erected within the Fort, otherwise the Soldiers cannot be so well governed, and may be absent or without the Gates at a time of the greatest necessity."

On the very day Colonel Armstrong's letter was written, Governor Morris was superseded by Governor William Denny—a change of governors at a most critical time—but, before Governor Denny's arrival, Governor Morris, in response to the cries for help from the frontier, especially from Cumberland County, had arranged with Colonel Armstrong for an expedition against the Indian town of Kittanning. Colonel Armstrong had urged Governor Morris to give him permission to make this expedition, and Benjamin Franklin had earnestly advocated this plan of attacking this Indian stronghold from which Shingas, Captain Jacobs and King Beaver had led so many incursions into the Pennsylvania settlements.

Colonel Armstrong's small army consisted of about three hundred men, Scotch-Irish from the Cumberland Valley, divided into seven companies whose captains were himself, Hance Hamilton, Dr. Hugh Mercer, Edward Ward, Joseph Armstrong, John Potter and Rev. John Steel. Armstrong marched from Fort Shirley (Shirleysburg, Huntingdon County), on August 30th, and arrived at the "Beaver Dams," near Hollidaysburg, on September 3d, where his forces joined the advance party. Leaving this place on September 4th and following the Kittanning Indian Trail, his army arrived at a point within fifty miles of Kittanning two days later. From this point Armstrong sent out scouts to reconnoitre the famous Delaware town and get information as to the number of the Indians there. The day following, the scouts returned and reported that the road was clear of the enemy, but it appeared later that they had not been near enough the town to learn its exact situation or the best way to approach the same.

Armstrong then continued his march. At about ten o'clock on the night of September 7th, one of his guides reported that he had discovered a fire by the road, a short distance ahead and within six miles of Kittanning, with three or four Indians seated around the fire. Deeming it not prudent to attack this party, Lieutenant Hogg and thirteen men were left to watch them, with orders to attack them at break of day. The main body then, making a circuit, stole silently through the night to the Allegheny, reaching it just before the setting of the moon, about three o'clock in the morning, and at a point about one hundred perches below the town. They learned the position of the town by the beating of a drum and the whooping of the warriors at a dance.

Colonel Armstrong's Account of the Battle

We shall now let Colonel Armstrong describe the battle, quoting from his report, written at Fort Littleton, on September 14th, 1756, and sent to Governor Denny:

"It then, after ascertaining the location of the town, became us to make the best use of the remaining Moon Light, but ere we were aware, an Indian whistled in a very singular manner, about thirty perches from our front in the foot of a Corn Field; upon which we immediately sat down, and after passing Silence to the rear, I asked one Baker, a Soldier, who was our best assistant, whether that was not a Signal to the Warriors of our Approach. He answered no, and said it was the manner of a Young Fellow's calling a Squaw after he had done his Dance, who accordingly kindled a Fire, cleaned his Gun and shot it off before he went to Sleep. All this time we were obliged to lie quiet and hush, till the Moon was fairly set. Immediately after, a Number of Fires appeared in different places in the Corn Field, by which Baker said the Indians lay, the night being warm, and that these fires would immediately be out, as they were designed to disperse the Gnats.

"By this time it was break of Day, and the Men, having marched thirty Miles, were most asleep; the line being long, the Companies of the Rear were not yet brought over the last precipice. For these, some proper Hands were immediately dispatched, and the weary Soldiers, being roused to their Feet, a proper Number under sundry Officers were ordered to take the End of the Hill, at which we then lay, and march along the top of the said Hill at least one hundred perches, and so much further, it then being day light, as would carry them opposite the upper part or at least the body of the Town. For the lower part thereof and the Corn Field, presuming the Warriors were there, I kept rather the larger Number of the Men, promising to postpone the Attack in that part for eighteen or twenty Minutes, until the Detachment along the Hill should have time to advance to the place assigned them, in doing of which they were a little unfortunate. The Time being elapsed, the Attack was begun in the Corn Field, and the Men, with all Expedition possible, dispatched thro' the several parts thereof; a party being also dispatched to the Houses, which were then discovered by the light of the Day. Captain Jacobs immediately gave the War-Whoop, and with sundry other Indians, as the English Prisoners afterwards told, cried the White Men were at last come, they would then have Scalps enough, but at the same time ordered their Squaws and Children to flee to the Woods.

"Our Men with great Eagerness passed thro' and fired in the Corn Field, where they had several Returns from the Enemy, as they also had from the opposite side of the River. Presently after, a brisk fire began among the Houses, which, from the House of Captain Jacobs, was returned with a great deal of Resolution; to which place I immediately repaired, and found that from the Advantage of the House and the Port Holes, sundry of our People were wounded, and some killed; and finding that returning the Fire upon the House was ineffectual, ordered the contiguous houses to be set on fire; which was performed by sundry of the Officers and Soldiers with a great deal of Activity, the Indians always firing whenever an object presented itself, and seldom missed of wounding or killing some of our People; From which House, in moving about to give the necessary orders and directions, I received a wound from a large Musket Ball in the Shoulder. Sundry persons during the action were ordered to tell the Indians to surrender themselves prisoners; but one of the Indians, in particular, answered and said he was a Man and would not be a Prisoner, upon which he was told in Indian he would be burnt. To this he answered he did not care for he would kill four or five before he died, and had we not desisted from exposing ourselves, they would have killed a great many more, they having a number of loaded Guns by them.

"As the fire began to approach and the Smoak grew thick, one of the Indian Fellows, to show his manhood, began to sing. A Squaw, in the same House, and at the same time, was heard to cry and make Noise, but for so doing was severely rebuked by the Men; but by and by the Fire being too hot for them, two Indian Fellows and a Squaw sprung out and made for the Corn Field, who were immediately shot down by our People then surrounding the House. It was thought Captain Jacobs tumbled himself out at a Garret or Cock Loft Window, at which he was shot, our Prisoners offering to be qualified to the powder horn and pouch there taken off him, which, they say, he had lately got from a French Officer in exchange for Lieutenant Armstrong's Boots, which he carried from Fort Granville, where the Lieutenant was killed. The same Prisoners say they are perfectly assured of his Scalp, as no other Indians there wore their Hair in the same Manner. They also say they knew his Squaw's Scalp by a particular bob; and also knew the Scalp of a young Indian called the King's Son.

"Before this time, Captain Hugh Mercer, who early in the Action was wounded in the Arm, had been taken to the top of a Hill above the Town, to whom a number of Men and some of the Officers were gathered, from whence they had discovered some Indians cross the River and take the Hill with an intent, as they thought, to surround us and cut off our retreat, from whom I had sundry pressing Messages to leave the Houses and retreat to the Hill or we should all be cut off; but to this could by no means consent until all the Houses were set on fire. Tho' our spreading upon the Hills appeared very necessary, yet did it prevent our Researches of the Corn Field and River side, by which means sundry Scalps were left behind, and doubtless some Squaws Children and English Prisoners that otherwise might have been got. During the burning of the Houses, which were near thirty in number, we were agreeably entertained with a quick succession of charged Guns gradually firing off as reached by the Fire, but much more so with the vast explosion of sundry Bags and large Cags of Gunpowder, wherewith almost every House abounded; the Prisoners afterwards informing that the Indians had frequently said they had a sufficient stock of ammunition for ten Years War with the English.

"With the roof of Captain Jacobs' House, when the powder blew up, was thrown the Leg and Thigh of an Indian with a Child three or four years old, such a height that they appeared as nothing and fell in the adjacent Corn Field. There was also a great Quantity of Goods burnt, which the Indians had received in a present but ten days before, from the French. By this time I had proceeded to the Hill to have my wound tyed up and the Blood stopped, where the Prisoners, which in the Morning had come to our People, informed me that that very day two Battoas of French Men, with a large party of Delaware and French Indians, were to join Captain Jacobs at the Kittanning, and to set out early the next Morning to take Fort Shirley, or as they called it, George Croghan's Fort, and that twenty-four Warriors who had lately come to the Town, were set out before them the Evening before, for what purpose they did not know, whether to prepare Meat, to spy the Fort, or to make an attack on some of our back inhabitants. Soon after, upon a little Reflection, we were convinced these Warriors were all at the Fire we had discovered the Night before, and began to doubt the fate of Lieutenant Hogg and his Party, from the Intelligence of the Prisoners.

"Our Provisions being scaffolded some thirty miles back, except what were in the Men's Haversacks, which we left with the Horses and Blankets with Lieutanant Hogg and his Party, and a number of wounded People then on hand, by the advice of the

Officers it was thought imprudent then to wait for the cutting down the Corn Field (which was before designed), but immediately to collect our Wounded and force our march back in the best manner we could, which we did by collecting a few Indian horses to carry off our wounded. From the apprehension of being waylaid (especially by some of the Woodsmen), it was difficult to keep the men together, our march for sundry miles not exceeding two miles an hour, which apprehensions were heightened by the attempts of a few Indians who for some time after the march fired upon each wing and immediately ran off, from whom we received no other Damage but one of our men's being wounded thro' both Legs. Captain Mercer, being wounded, was induced, as we have reason to believe, by some of his Men, to leave the main Body with his ensign, John Scott, and ten or twelve men, they being heard to tell him they were in great Danger, and that they could take him into the Road a nigh Way, is probably lost, there being yet no Account of him; the most of the Men come in detachment was sent back to bring him in, but could not find him, and upon the return of the detachment, it was generally reported he was seen with the above number of Men taking a different Road.

"Upon our return to the place where the Indian Fire had been discovered the Night before, we met with a Sergeant of Captain Mercer's Company and two or three other of his Men who had deserted us that Morning, immediately after the action at Kittanning. These men, on running away, had met with Lieutenant Hogg, who lay wounded in two different parts of his Body by the Road side. He there told them of the fatal mistake of the Pilot, who had assured us there were but three Indians, at the most, at this Fire place, but when he came to attack them that Morning according to orders, he found a number considerably superior to his, and believes they killed and mortally wounded three of them the first fire, after which a warm engagement began, and continued for above an Hour, when three of his best men were killed and himself twice wounded; the residue fleeing off, he was obliged to squat in a thicket, where he might have laid securely until the main Body had come up, if this cowardly Sergeant and others that fled with him had not taken him away; they had marched but a short Space when four Indians appeared, upon which these deserters began to flee. The Lieutenant then, notwithstanding his wounds, as a brave Soldier, urging and commanding them to stand and fight, which they all refused. The

Indians pursued, killing one Man and wounding the Lieutenant a third time through the Belly, of which he died in a few Hours; but he, having some time before been put on Horse back, rode some miles from the place of action. But this last attack of the Indians upon Lieutanant Hogg and the deserters was, by the before mentioned Sergeant, represented to us in quite a different light, he telling us that there were a far larger number of the Indians there than appeared to them, and that he and the Men with him had fought five Rounds; that he had there seen the Lieutenant and sundry others killed and scalped, and had also discovered a number of Indians throwing themselves before us, and insinuated a great deal of such Stuff, as threw us into much Confusion, so that the Officers had a great deal to do to keep the Men together, but could not prevail with them to collect what Horses and other Baggage that the Indians had left after their Conquest of Lieutenant Hogg and the Party under his command in the Morning, except a few of the Horses, which some of the bravest of the Men were prevailed on to collect; so that, from the mistake of the Pilot, who spied the Indians at the Fire, and the cowardice of the said Sergeant and other Deserters, we have sustained a considerable loss of our Horses and Baggage.

"It is impossible to ascertain the exact number of the Enemy killed in the Action, as some were destroyed by Fire and others in different parts of the Corn Field, but, upon a moderate Computation, it is generally believed there cannot be less than thirty or Forty killed and mortally wounded, as much Blood was found in sundry parts of the Corn Field, and Indians seen in several places crawl into the Weeds on their Hands and Feet, whom the Soldiers, in pursuit of others, then overlooked, expecting to find and scalp them afterwards; and also several killed and wounded in crossing the River. On beginning our March back, we had about a dozen of Scalps and eleven English Prisoners, but now find that four or five of the Scalps are missing, part of which were lost on the Road and part in possession of those Men who, with Captain Mercer, separated from the main Body, with whom also went four of the Prisoners, the other seven being now at this place [Fort Littleton], where we arrived on Sunday Night, not being ever separated or attacked thro' our whole March by the Enemy, tho' we expected it every Day. Upon the whole, had our Pilots understood the true situation of the town and the paths leading to it, so as to have posted us at a convenient place, where the disposition of the Men and the Duty assigned to them could have been performed with greater Advantage, we had, by divine Assistance, destroyed a much greater Number of the Enemy, recovered more Prisoners, and sustained less damage than what we at present have; but tho' the Advantage gained over these, our Common Enemy, is far from being satisfactory to us, must we not despise the smallest degrees of Success that God has pleased to give, especially at a time of such general Calamity, when the attempts of our Enemys have been so prevalent and successful." (Pa. Col. Rec., Vol. 7, pages 257 to 263.)

Such is the account of the destruction of Kittanning, written by the leader of the heroic men who inflicted this telling blow upon the Indians. Hitherto the English had not attacked the Indians in their towns, which led the leaders of the bloody incursions to fancy that the settlers would not venture to follow them into their western strongholds. But now the Western Delawares dreaded that, when absent on incursions into the settlements, their wigwams might be burned to ashes by the outraged frontiersmen. From now on, they feared Colonel Armstrong and his Scotch-Irish troops. Most of the Indians, therefore, left Kittanning, refusing to settle east of Fort Duquesne, and determined to place this fort between them and the English. They went to Logstown, located on the north bank of the Ohio, just below the site of the present town of Ambridge, Beaver County; to Sauconk, located at or near the mouth of the Beaver, and known also as Shingas' Old Town and King Beaver's Town; to Kuskuskies, a group of villages whose centre was at or near the present city of New Castle; to Shenango, located on the river of this name, a short distance below the present town of Sharon, Mercer County, and to other towns in the western region. However, Kittanning was not deserted, though it ceased to be a gathering place for the hostile Delawares during the French and Indian War. As we saw in Chapter XII and as we shall see in subsequent chapters, the destruction of Kittanning did not put an end to the Indian raids. But it did have a great moral effect. It struck fear into the hearts of the Indians, and it caused the forntiersmen to have confidence in their ability to meet the Indians on their own ground and defeat them.

"The corporation of Philadelphia, on occasion of this victory, on the 5th of January following, addressed a complimentary letter to Colonel Armstrong, thanking him and his officers for their gallant conduct, and presented him with a piece of plate. A medal was also struck, having for device an officer followed by two soldiers, the officer pointing to a soldier shooting from behind a tree, and an Indian prostrate before him; in the background Indian houses in flames. Legend: Kittanning, destroyed by Colonel Armstrong, September the 8th, 1756. Reverse device: The Arms of the corporation. Legend: The gift of the corporation of Philadelphia."—Egle's "History of Pennsylvania."

The report of the explosion of the magazine at Kittanning was heard at Fort Duquesne, upon which some French and Indians set off from that place to Captain Jacobs' stronghold, but did not reach the town until the next day. They found among the ruins the blackened bodies of the fallen chieftain, his wife and his son. Robert Robinson says in his Narrative that a boy named Crawford, then a captive among the Delawares, told him that he accompanied the French and Indians on this occasion. He also says that, after Armstrong's forces had returned to the east side of the Allegheny Mountains, one of his soldiers, named Samuel Chambers, disregarding the advice of the Colonel, went back to the "Clear Fields," in Clearfield Township, Cambria County, to get his coat and three horses; that, at the top of the mountain, he was fired upon by Indians, and then fled towards the Great Island; and that the Indians pursued him, and, on the third day, killed him on French Margaret's Island, as they later told Captain Patterson.

Many blankets of Armstrong's soldiers were afterwards found on the ground where Lieutenant Hogg and his party were defeated. Hence this place has ever since been called "Blanket Hill." It is in Kittanning Township, Armstrong County.

List of the Slain—The English Prisoners

Colonel Armstrong's report of the destruction of Kittanning is also found in Pa. Archives, Vol. 2, pages 767 to 775, with a list of the killed, wounded and missing, as well as a list of the English prisoners recovered. This list is as follows:

"Lieutenant-Colonel John Armstrong's Company—killed; Thomas Power and John McCormick. Wounded: Lieutenant-Colonel John Armstrong, James Carruthers, James Strickland and Thomas Foster.

Captain Hance Hamilton's Company—Killed: John Kelley.

Captain Hugh Mercer's Company—Killed: John Baker, John McCartney, Patrick Mullen, Cornelius McGinnis, Theophilus Thompson, Dennis Kilpatrick and Bryan Carrigan. Wounded:

Marker at the Site of the Delaware Indian Town of Kittanning, near the bridge across the Allegheny River, at Kittanning, Pa.

In the foreground Chief Strong Wolf, of the Ojibway Tribe, and Hon. James W. King, President of the Armstrong County Historical Society.

From a photograph taken on the occasion of the dedication of the Marker, September 8th, 1926, the One Hundred and Seventieth Anniversary of the Destruction of Kittanning by Colonel John Armstrong.

Richard Fitzgibbins. Missing: John Taylor, John —, Francis Phillips, Robert Morrow, Thomas Burk and Philip Pendergrass.

Captain Joseph Armstrong's Company—Killed: Lieutenant James Hogg, James Anderson, Holdcraft Stringer, Edward Obrians, James Higgins and John Lasson. Wounded: William Findley, Robert Robinson, John Ferrol, Thos. Camplin and Charles O'Neal. Missing: John Lewis, William Hunter, William Baker, George Appleby, Anthony Grissy and Thos. Swan.

Captain Edward Ward's Company—Killed: William Welch. Wounded: Ephriam Bratten. Missing: Patrick Myers, Lawrence Donnahow and Samuel Chambers.

Captain John Potter's Company—Wounded: Ensign James Potter and Andrew Douglass.

Captain John Steel's Company—Missing: Terrence Cannaberry."

The English prisoners recovered from the Indians at the destruction of Kittanning were:

Ann McCord, wife of John McCord, and Martha Thorn, a child seven years of age, both captured at Fort McCord, on April 1st, 1756; Barbara Hicks, captured at Conolloways; Catherine Smith, a German child captured near Shamokin; Margaret Hood, captured near the mouth of the Conococheague, Maryland; Thomas Girty, captured at Fort Granville; Sarah Kelly, captured near Winchester, Virginia; a woman, a boy, and two little girls, who were with Captain Mercer and Ensign Scott, and had not reached Fort Littleton when Colonel Armstrong made his report.

Barbara Leininger and Marie Le Roy, who, it will be recalled, were captured at the Penn's Creek massacre of October 16th, 1755, were prisoners among the Indians at Kittanning at the time when Colonel Armstrong destroyed the town. However, they were on the other (west) side of the river at the time the attack began, and were then taken ten miles back into the interior, in order that they might not have a chance to escape. After Armstrong's forces had withdrawn, Barbara and Marie were brought back to the ruins of the town. Here they witnessed the torture of a woman who had attempted to escape with Armstrong's troops, but was recaptured. An English renegade ate a piece of the woman's flesh.

After describing the torture of the woman, Barbara and Marie, in their Narrative, relate the following:

"Three days later an Englishman was brought in, who had likewise attempted to escape with Col. Armstrong, and he was burned alive in the same village. His torments, however, continued only about three hours; but his screams were frightful to listen to. It rained that day very hard, so that the Indians could not keep up the fire. Hence they began to discharge gunpowder at his body. At last, amidst his worst pains, when the poor man called for a drink of water, they brought melted lead, and poured it down his throat. This draught at once helped him out of the hands of the barbarians, for he died on the instant."

Relatives of Captain Jacobs, who were also killed at the destruction of Kittanning, are mentioned in a letter written at Carlisle, on December 22nd, 1756, by Adam Stephen: "A son of Captain Jacobs is kill'd and a Cousin of his about seven foot high, call'd young Jacob, at the Destroying of the Kittanning." (Pa. Archives, Vol. 3, page 83.) Probably another relative was the Delaware Chief, called Captain Jacobs, who attended the conference held at Fort Pitt in April and May, 1768. (Pa. Col. Rec. Vol. 9, page 543.)

A Retrospect

The author was born and reared within ten miles of Kittanning. Often he has stood on the river hill above the site of the former Indian town, and contemplated its history. On these occasions, the past rose before him, as a dream. He could see the Delawares, in the course of their westward migration, as early as 1724, floating down the beautiful Allegheny, in their canoes, from the mouth of the Mahoning, and erecting their wigwams on the wide flats, naming the town "Kittanning," that is *Kit*, "great"; *hanna*, "a stream"; *ing*, "at, or at the place of"—"at the great river." He could see Jonas Davenport, James Le Tort and other traders, a few years later, visit the place and barter with the Indians, giving them rum, powder, lead, guns, knives and blankets in exchange for skins and furs. He could see French emisaries holding councils with the Indians here, as early as 1727, and for many years thereafter. He could see Celoron visit the town, in the summer of 1749. He could see the clouds of war gathering over the valley for many years, and finally breaking in a storm of fury, in the autumn of 1755. He could see Shingas, King Beaver and Captain Jacobs holding their councils of war here, far into the night, and inflaming the wild passions of the warriors as the council fire lit up their savage features, and as their shouts echoed from hill to hill. He could see bands of warriors go forth from the town on bloody incursions into the settlements of Pennsylvania,

Maryland and Virginia, and return with sorrowing, sad-faced captives and the bloody scalps of the slain. He could see hundreds of these captives tortured to death—burned to death, tied to the black post in the village. He could see their bodies pierced with red-hot gun barrels and their bloody scalps torn from their heads. He could hear their agonizing cries and see the fiendish looks of their tormentors. He could see Colonel John Armstrong's forces wend their way silently over the forest-covered mountains, and, in the early hours of that September morning, visit retribution and vengeance on Captain Jacobs and his warriors. He could see the village sink in flames, and hear the death chants of the warriors, as they perished in the fire. He could see the Indian women and children fleeing in terror to the forest, as their husbands, fathers and brothers were shot down or burned to death, by the frontiersmen, or dragged themselves into the forest to die of their wounds. He could see many of the survivors return, and erect their wigwams amid the ashes of their former homes. He could see hundreds of warriors assemble here, to march against Colonel Bouquet, in the summer of 1763. He could see the Eighth Pennsylvania Regiment assemble here in the latter days of 1776. He could see Fort Armstrong erected, a short distance below the village, in the summer of 1779, and Colonel Daniel Brodhead's army march past the place, in the same summer, on its way to attack the Senecas and Munsees. He could see the Indians once more assemble here, to march against Hannastown, in the summer of 1782. He could see the Indian finally depart from this ancient seat, and float in his canoe down the "Ohio" of the Senecas, the "La Belle Riviere" of the French and "The Beautiful River" of the English—terms that mean the same—to the "Land of the Lost Ones." He could see the pioneers, with their rifles and axes, entering the valley and erecting their cabin homes. He could see the Kittanning of the white man rise where the Kittanning of the Indian had stood for so many years, in the valley of the beautiful and historic Allegheny. As he stood on the river hill and gazed into the valley below, the past rose before him, as a dream, and these things passed before him, as a panorama.

Captain Hugh Mercer

As was seen earlier in this chapter, Captain Hugh Mercer was wounded in the engagement at Kittanning. Unhappily he was persuaded by some of his men to leave the main party. These men were old traders, and they proposed to conduct Captain Mercer by a nearer route to the settlements than the Kittanning Indian Trail, by which the army of Colonel Armstrong had come to the famous Indian town. Presently Mercer's party fell in with the Indians with whom Lieutenant Hogg had the engagement in the morning, and some of the Captain's companions were killed. Mercer made his escape with two others. In a short time, he and these two halted in order to adjust the bandage on his arm. At this moment an Indian was seen approaching, whereupon Mercer's two companions, sprang upon the horse from which he had just alighted, and hurried away, abandoning him. He hastily concealed himself behind a log overgrown with weeds. The Indian approached to within a few feet of where he lay, when, seeing the other two hurrying away on horseback, he uttered the war-whoop, and ran after them.

The wounded captain soon crawled from his place of concealment, and descended into a plum-tree bottom, where he refreshed himself with the fruit and remained until night. Then he began his terrible journey over the mountains to the settlements, a journey which consumed an entire month, and during which he became so ravenously hungry that he killed and ate a rattle-snake raw. Reaching the west side of the Allegheny Mountain, he discovered a person whom he supposed to be an Indian. Both took to trees, and remained in this position a long time. At length Captain Mercer concluded to go forward and meet his enemy; but when he came near, he found the other to be one of his own men. The two then proceeded on over the mountain, so weak that they could scarcely walk. Near Frankstown, the soldier sank down with the expectation never more to rise. Captain Mercer then struggled about seven miles further, when he, too, lay down on the leaves, abandoning all hope of reaching the settlements. At this time, a band of Cherokees in the British service, coming from Fort Littleton on a scouting expedition, found the exhausted captain, and a little later, the soldier, and carried them safely to the fort on a bier of their own making. The Cherokees had taken fourteen scalps on this scouting expedition.

We shall meet Captain Mercer several places in this history. He became one of Washington's able generals in the Revolutionary War, and laid down his life on the bloody battlefield of Princeton that liberty might live. Mercersburg and Mercer County are named for him.

The Girtys

As stated earlier in this chapter, Thomas Girty, who was captured at Fort Granville, was one of the English prisoners recovered by Colonel Armstrong at the destruction of Kittanning. The family to which he belonged figured prominently in the Indian history of Pennsylvania, not as defenders of the Province but as allies of the hostile Indians.

Reference was made, in a former chapter, to the fact that Simon Girty, Sr., an Irish trader, was one of the squatters whom the Provincial Authorities compelled to remove, in 1750, from lands not yet purchased from the Indians, north of the Blue or Kittatinny Mountains. He was an Indian trader, and had settled on Sherman's Creek, in Perry County, about 1740. Here his son, Simon, who figured notoriously in the annals of border life, was born, January 16th, 1744. After the elder Girty was compelled to remove from Sherman's Creek, he settled on the east side of the Susquehanna River, near where the town of Halifax now stands. Here he was killed in a drunken brawl, it is said, by his wife's paramour, John Turner. Here his widow married John Turner, and soon thereafter they removed to the Buffalo Valley, Union County. About 1755, the family, consisting of Mr. and Mrs. Turner, their infant son, John Turner, Jr., and the four sons of Simon Girty, Sr.—Simon, James, George and Thomas—removed to the vicinity of Fort Granville. The whole family was captured at the destruction of the fort, by Captain Jacobs. John Turner, it will be recalled, was the person who opened the gates of the fort to the enemy, and was later tortured to death at Kittanning, in the presence of his wife, his son, John Turner, Jr., and the four sons of Simon Girty, the elder, all the family having been taken to Kittanning by their captors.*

Thomas Girty was the only member of the family liberated by Colonel John Armstrong, when his forces destroyed Kittanning. Mrs. Turner and her son, John, then a child less than three years of age, were taken to Fort Duquesne, where the child was baptized on August 18th, 1756, by the Reverend Baron, chaplain of the Roman Catholic chapel at the post. This John Turner was liberated by Colonel Bouquet in the autumn of 1764, and then joined his mother at Fort Pitt, to which place she seems to have made her escape. During the Revolutionary War, he fought on the American side, although his half-brothers, Simon, George and

*Theodore Roosevelt, in his "Winning of the West," erroneously says that Simon Girty, Sr., was tortured to death at Kittanning.

James Girty, early espoused the British cause. He died in Pittsburgh at an advanced age.

Simon, the most notorious of the Girty brothers, was adopted by the Senecas, and given the name of Katepacomen. He soon became in dress, language and habits a thorough Indian, and lived among the Indians continuously until Colonel Henry Bouquet led his army to the Muskingum in the autumn of 1764 and liberated over two hundred white captives. Among these was Simon Girty. Brought back to Fort Pitt, he took up his residence on a little run, emptying into the Allegheny from the west a few miles above Fort Pitt, and since known as Girty's Run. In Lord Dunmore's war of 1774, he, in company with Simon Kenton, served as a scout. He subsequently acted as an Indian agent, and became well acquainted with Colonel William Crawford, at whose cabin on the Youghiogheny, where Connellsville now stands, he was a frequent and welcome guest. On the outbreak of the Revolution, he was commissioned an officer of militia at Fort Pitt, but on March 28, 1778, deserted to the British, in company with Alexander McKee and Matthew Elliott.

The atrocities committed by Simon Girty after he deserted to the British fill many pages of border annals. His name became a terror in the frontier cabin, causing the mother's cheek to blanch and the children to tremble with fear. He fully earned the name given him by Heckewelder— the "White Savage." His brutality reached its climax when he viewed with apparent satisfaction the burning of his former friend, Colonel William Crawford, at the stake, in the summer of 1782, as will be related in a subsequent chapter. On one occassion he committed a hostile act against the Americans shortly after the Revolutionary War was proclaimed at an end. This was the capture of a lad, named John Burkhart, at the mouth of Nine Mile Run, near Pittsburgh, in May, 1783, by a war party of Indians led by him. The guns of Fort Pitt were firing at the very time of the boy's capture, on account of the reception of the news that Washington had discharged the American Army on April 19th, and announced that the long war was over. This fact was made known to Girty by the boy; yet he was carried to Detroit. However, he was well treated by Girty, and, in July, was permitted by Colonel De Peyster, then commandant at Detroit, to return to his friends.

In the defeat of General St. Clair's army in the autumn of 1791, as will be related in a subsequent chapter, the "White Savage" saw and knew General Richard Butler, who was writhing

According to Butterfield: Simon Girty, Sr. was killed by an Indian named "The Fish", who was later killed by John Turner; Simon, Jr., born in 1741, died, Feb. 18, 1818; James, born in 1743, died at Goshfield, Canada, Apr. 15, 1817; George, born in 1745, died near Ft. Wayne prior to 1812; Thomas, born in 1739, died in Pittsburgh, Nov. 3, 1820; Simon, Jr., James, George, Mrs. Turner and her son, John, delivered up at Fort Pitt, in 1759.

in the agony of his wounds. Girty told an Indian warrior that General Butler was a high officer, whereupon the Indian buried his tomahawk in the unfortunate General's skull, scalped him, took his heart out, and divided it into as many pieces as there were tribes in the battle in which St. Clair went down to overwhelming and inglorious defeat.

There is no doubt, however, that Simon Girty was blamed for many atrocities of which he was innocent, especially atrocities committed by his brothers George and James. At times, too, when sober, he was moved by considerations of humanity, as when he saved his friend, Simon Kenton, from death at the hands of the Indians, and when he caused Mrs. Thomas Cunningham, of West Virginia, to be returned to her husband, after her son had been tomahawked and scalped and her little daughter's brains dashed out against a tree, in her presence. Such occasional gleamings of his better nature stand out in strong relief against a career of outrage, blood and death.

After General Anthony Wayne defeated the western tribes at the battle of the Fallen Timbers in August, 1794, Simon Girty removed to Canada, where he settled on a small farm, near Malden, on the Detroit River and became the recipient of a British pension. Here he resided, undisturbed and almost blind, until the War of 1812. After the capture of the British fleet on Lake Erie by Commodore Perry, in this war, Girty followed the British in retreat, and remained away from home until the treaty of peace was signed. Then he returned to his farm, where he died in 1815—the passing of the most notorious renegade of the Pennsylvania, Kentucky and Ohio borders. Girty's Gap, or Girty's Notch, on the west side of the Susquehanna, a few miles below Liverpool, Perry County, is named for him. At this place the rocks of the precipitous river hill form almost a perfect Indian head, a wonderful likeness in stone of the primitive American race.

George Girty was adopted by the Delawares, and became a terror to the Pennsylvania and Ohio frontiers. As will be seen in a subsequent chapter, he was among the Indian forces which ambushed Colonel Lochry's troops in the summer of 1781.

James Girty was one of the messengers sent to the Shawnees, in the summer of 1778, in an effort to have this tribe join with the Delawares in an alliance with the Americans, at a treaty at Fort Pitt, in that year. He did not return from this mission, but deserted the Americans, was adopted by the Shawnees, and became an infamous and blood-thirsty raider of the Kentucky frontier, "not sparing even women and children from horrid tortures."

Simon, George and James Girty were underlings of Henry Hamilton, the British "Hair Buyer General," who was in command at Detroit during a large part of the Revolutionary War, and had charge of operations against the western frontier. Hamilton was so named by the Americans on account of his giving his Indian allies rewards for American scalps, even the scalps of women and children.

Thomas Girty was the best of the four brothers. He took no part in raids against the Americans, but served his Country loyally. For many years he made his home near Fort Pitt, and was living in Pittsburgh in May, 1782, at which time he joined with other inhabitants of the town in a petition to General William Irvine, asking that the General order the soldiers of Fort Pitt to discontinue their practice of "playing at long bullets" in the streets, and thus endangering the lives of the children of the petitioners. This petition was granted.

Some time prior to 1800, Thomas Girty took up a tract of four hundred acres of land, a few miles south of Prospect, Butler County. Some authorities say he lived here until his death, which, they say, occurred prior to 1803, while other authorities say he died in Pittsburgh, on November 3d, 1820. Whatever may be the fact as to the time of the death of Thomas Girty, a settler, named David Kerr, laid claim to the Girty land, and, one evening in 1803, came to the cabin when no one was there except Ann Girty, wife of Thomas, and fatally shot her. Kerr had come for the purpose of ejecting Mrs. Girty. During the argument, which took place between them, Mrs. Girty struck Kerr in the face with a clapboard with which she was raking the fire, whereupon he shot her in the breast with his pistol. She died of the wound several weeks later. Kerr was never brought to justice for his crime, on account of the stigma attaching to the Girty name, and, for the same reason, the body of poor Ann Girty was refused burial in the Mount Nebo Presbyterian cemetery near her home. She was laid to rest in the forest, where the author has often seen her grave. Yet, the Butler County settlers bore testimony to the fact that the family of Thomas Girty were good and peaceable neighbors. Thomas Girty, Jr., lived on the Butler County plantation for some years after his mother's death. On December 26th, 1807, he sold all his interest in the farm to Thomas Ferree, for a consideration of one hundred dollars, the instrument being recorded in the office of the recorder of deeds in and for Butler County, in deed book A, page 558.

CHAPTER XIV

Efforts for Peace in 1756

THE declaration of war against the Delawares and Shawnees was very distasteful to the Quaker members of the Provincial Assembly. They believed that these tribes would not have taken up arms against the Province without a reason. Furthermore, they believed that adequate efforts had not been made towards reconciliation before war was declared. Without going into details, we state that, a few days after war was declared, Israel Pemberton waited upon Governor Morris on behalf of numerous members of the Society of Friends, and, as a result, Canachquasy, or Captain New Castle, was sent to the Delawares and Shawnees of the Susquehanna with overtures of peace, while Scarouady was sent to the territory of the Six Nations and to Sir William Johnson to acquaint them with the efforts Pennsylvania was instituting to bring about peace with the Delawares and Shawnees. (Pa. Col. Rec., Vol. 7, pages 103 to 109.)

Canachquasy spent four days at Wyoming, and then went on to Tioga, an important town of the Six Nations, Nanticokes, and Munsee Clan of Delawares, situated on the site of Athens, Bradford County. It was the southern gateway to the country of the Iroquois, and all the great war paths and hunting trails from the South and Southwest centered there. He held conferences with the Indians of this place and the surrounding towns, and made known to them the Governor's message. These Indians agreed to lay aside the hatchet and enter into negotiations for peace; but they cautioned Canachquasy not to charge them with anything that may have been done by the Delawares of the Ohio and Allegheny Valleys under the influence of the French.

Canachquasy then returned to Philadelphia early in June, and laid his report before the Governor and Provincial Council. The Governor and Council, upon hearing the favorable report, drafted a proclamation for a suspension of hostilities with the enemy Indians of the Susquehanna Valley for a period of thirty days, and desired that a conference with them for the purpose of making peace, should be held at the earliest possible date. (Pa. Col. Rec., Vol. 7, pages 137 to 142).

Canachquasy then left once more for Tioga, bearing the Governor's message, advising the Susquehanna Indians that the Colony would agree to a truce of thirty days and that, as one of the conditions of making peace, the prisoners taken on both sides should be delivered up. Shortly after he left, messengers were sent to him by the Governor carrying a few additional instructions, which were delivered to him at Bethlehem. In the meantime, Sir William Johnson, of New York, was holding a peace conference with the Six Nations at Otseningo, at which the assembled sachems of the Iroquois decided that the Delawares were acting like drunken men, and sent deputies to order them to become sober and cease their warfare against the English. This conference was composed of only a portion of the Iroquois, and the Delawares replied very haughtily saying that they were no longer women but men. "We are determined," said they, "to cut off all the English except those that make their escape from us in ships."

After a dangerous journey over the mountains and through the wilderness, Canachquasy reached Tioga, held conferences with the great Delaware chieftain, Teedyuscung, and persuaded him to bury the hatchet,—a most remarkable victory.

First Conference with Teedyuscung

Canachquasy then returned to Philadelphia in the middle of July, 1756, and laid before the Governor and Provincial Council the results of his second mission to Tioga.

Immediately upon Canachquasy's return to Philadelphia from his second mission to Tioga, arrangements were made for a conference with Teedyuscung at Easton, which place Governor Morris with the Provincial Council, reached on July 24, 1756. The conference formally opened on July 28th, Conrad Weiser in the meantime having posted his troops in the vicinity of Easton. Teedyuscung and the fourteen other chiefs accompanying him were formally welcomed by Governor Morris. Teedyuscung made the following reply:

"Last spring you sent me a string [of wampum], and as soon as I heard the good words you sent, I was glad, and as you told us, we believed it came from your hearts. So we felt it in our hearts and received what you said with joy. The first messages you sent me came in the spring; they touched my heart; they gave me abundance of joy. You have kindled a council fire at Easton. I have been here several days smoking my pipe in patience, waiting to hear your good words. Abundant confusion has of late years been rife among the Indians, because of their loose ways of doing business. False leaders have deceived the people. It has bred quarrels and heart-burnings among my people.

"The Delaware is no longer the slave of the Six Nations. I, Teedyuscung, have been appointed King over the Five United Nations [meaning the three Clans of Delawares, the Shawnees and the Nanticokes], and representative of the Five Iroquois Nations. What I do here will be approved by all. This is a good day; whoever will make peace, let him lay hold of this belt, and the nations around shall see and know it. I desire to conduct myself according to your words, which I will perform to the utmost of my power. I wish the same good that possessed the good old man, William Penn, who was the friend to the Indian, may inspire the people of this Province at this time."

In the conferences that followed, the Governor insisted that, as a condition for peace, Teedyuscung and the Indians under his command should return all the prisoners that they had captured since taking up arms against the Colony; and Teedyuscung insisted that his people on the Susquehanna were not responsible for the actions of the Delawares and Shawnees on the Ohio. But, inasmuch as only a small delegation of chiefs had accompanied Teedyuscung to Easton, it was desired that he and Canachquasy should go back among the Indians, give the "Big Peace Halloo," and gather their followers together for a larger peace conference that would be more representative of the Indians, and to be held in the near future.

The Governor then gave Teedyuscung a present, informing him that a part of it "was given by the people called Quakers, who are descendants of those who first came over to this country with your old friend, William Penn, as a particular testimony of their regard and affection for the Indians, and their earnest desire to promote the good work of peace, in which we are now engaged."

This first peace conference with Teedyuscung, at Easton, closed on July 31st, 1756, the very day the Delaware chief, Captain Jacobs, attacked Fort Granville. A full account of the conference is found in Pa. Col. Rec., Vol. 7, pages 204 to 220.

After the conference, Teedyuscung and Canachquasy, as stated above, started to give the "Big Peace Halloo" among the hostile tribes, but Teedyuscung remained for a time at Fort Allen, where he secured liquor and remained intoxicated for a considerable time. Lieutenant Miller was in charge of the fort at this time, and Teedyuscung brought sixteen deer skins which he said he was going to present to the Governor "to make him a pair of gloves." Lieutenant Miller insisted that one skin was enough to make the Governor a pair of gloves, and after supplying Teedyuscung liberally with rum, he secured from him the entire sixteen deer skins for only three pounds. The sale was made while the chief was intoxicated, and afterwards he remained at the fort demanding more rum, which Miller supplied, Canachquasy in the meantime having gone away in disgust.

On August 21st, Teedyuscung and his retinue went to Bethlehem, where his wife, Elizabeth, and her three children desired to remain while the "King" went on an expedition to the Minisinks, for the purpose of putting a stop to some depredations which they were committing in New Jersey. Returning from this expedition, he went to Wyoming, where he sent word to Major Parsons at Easton requesting that his wife and children be sent to join him. Upon Parson's making known the King's desire, the wife determined to stay at Bethlehem. He then made frequent visits to this place, much to the annoyance of the Moravian missionaries.

When the Provincial Authorities learned of the cause of Teedyuscung's detention at Fort Allen, Lieutenant Miller was discharged, and Teedyuscung went to Wyoming, thence up the North Branch of the Susquehanna, persuading the Indians to lay down their arms, and to send deputies to a second conference to be held at Easton, in October. However, in the meantime, Governor William Denny, who succeeded Governor Morris in August, becoming suspicious of the chief's long delay at Fort Allen and being influenced, no doubt by the statements of many Indians on the border that Teedyuscung was not sincere in his peace professions, that he was a traitor, and that the Easton conference was but a ruse to gain time, sent Canachquasy secretly to New York to ascertain from the Six Nations whether or not they had deputized Teedyuscung to represent them in important treaties. Canachquasy returned, on October 24th, with the report that the Six Nations denied Teedyuscung's authority. Appearing before the Provincial Council, he gave the following report:

"I have but in part executed my commission, not having opportunity of having done it so fully as I wished. I met with Canyase, one of the principal counsellors of the Six Nations, a

Mohawk chief, who has a regard for Pennsylvania . . . I related to this chief very particularly the manner in which Teedyuscung spoke of himself and his commission and authority from the Six Nations at the treaty at Easton. I gave him a true notion of all he said on this head and how often he repeated it to the Governor, and then asked whether he knew anything of this matter. Canyase said he did; Teedyuscung did not speak the truth when he told the Governor he had a regular authority from the Six Nations to treat with Onas. Canyase then proceeded and said: 'Teedyuscung on behalf of the Delawares did apply to me as chief of the Six Nations. He and I had long discourses together and in these conversations, I told him that the Delawares were women and always treated as such by the Six Nations.' " (Pa. Col. Rec., Vol. 7, pages 296 to 298.)

Governor Denny endeavored to have Teedyuscung attend a conference in Philadelphia, in an effort to continue the peace work begun at the Easton Conference of July of that year. Teedyuscung sent the following reply by Conrad Weiser to Governor Denny's invitation: "Brother, you remember very well that in time of darkness and danger, I came in here at your invitation. At Easton, we kindled a small council fire . . . If you should put out this little fire, our enemies will call it only a jack lantern, kindled on purpose to deceive those who approach it. Brother, I think it by no means advisable to put out this little fire, but rather to put more sticks upon it, and I desire that you will come to it [at Easton] as soon as possible, bringing your old and wise men along with you, and we shall be very glad to see you here."

Second Conference with Teedyuscung

Upon Teedyuscung's refusal to go to Philadelphia, Governor Denny decided to meet the chief at Easton, where the second great conference with him and the Indians under his command opened on November 8, 1756. "The Governor marched from his lodgings to the place of conference, guarded by a party of Royal Americans on the front and on the flanks, and a detachment of Colonel Conrad Weiser's provincials in subdivisions in the rear, with colors flying, drums beating, and music playing, which order was always observed in going to the place of conference." Says Dr. George P. Donehoo, in his "Pennsylvania—A History":

"Teedyuscung opened the council with a speech and with all of the usual formalities of an Indian council. This Indian chief, called a 'King', was a most gifted orator and talented diplomat. His one most bitter enemy was his own vice of drunkenness which led to all of his troubles and to his death. The one marvel about him was that when he had been on a drunken spree all night and kept so by his enemies, he would appear the next day with a clear head, fully fit to deal with all of the complex problems which arose. His foes among the Indians and among the English kept him filled with rum in the hope that he could be rendered so drunk that he could not attend to his business. He would sleep out all night, under a shed, anywhere, in a drunken stupor, and appear the next day with a clear head and an eloquent tongue to 'fight for peace, at any price.' In his opening address, in referring to the tales which had been told about him he says: 'Many idle reports are spread by foolish and busy people; I agree with you that on both sides they ought to be no more regarded than the chirping of birds in the woods.' What great orator today could express himself more perfectly and beautifully?"

Teedyuscung Charges That Delawares Were Defrauded Out of Their Lands

Governor Denny in his reply to Teedyuscung's speech, asked him why the Delawares had gone to war against the English. Teedyuscung in his reply stated that great injustice had been done the Delawares in various land purchases. The Governor then asked him to be specific in his statements and point out what land sales, in his opinion, had been unjust. Then Teedyuscung stamped his foot upon the ground and made the following heated reply:

"I have not far to go for an instance; this very ground that is under me [striking it with his foot] was my land and inheritance, and is taken from me by fraud. When I say this ground, I mean all the land lying between Tohiccon Creek and Wyoming, on the River Susquehannah. I have not only been served so in this Government, but the same thing has been done to me as to several tracts in New Jersey over the River. When I have sold lands fairly, I look upon them to be really sold. A bargain is a bargain. Tho' I have sometimes had nothing for the lands I have sold but broken pipes or such triffles, yet when I have sold them, tho' for such triffles, I look upon the bargain to be good. Yet I think that I should not be ill used on this account by those very people who have had such an advantage in their purchases, nor be called a fool for it. Indians are not such fools as to bear this in their minds."

Governor Denny then asked him if he (Teedyuscung) had ever been dealt with in such a manner, and the chief replied:

"Yes, I have been served so in this Province; all the land extending from Tohiccon, over the great mountain, to Wyoming, has been taken from me by fraud; for when I agreed to sell the land to the old Proprietary, by the course of the River, the young Proprietaries came and got it run by a straight course by the compass, and by that means took in double the quantity intended to be sold. . . . I did not intend to speak thus, but I have done it at this time, at your request; not that I desire now you should purchase these lands, but that you should look into your own hearts, and consider what is right, and that do."

It is thus seen that Teedyuscung referred directly to the notorious Walking Purchase of 1737. Governor Denny then consulted Richard Peters and Conrad Weiser about the transactions complained of. Peters said that Teedyuscung's charges should be considered, inasmuch as they had been made before; but Weiser advised that none of the Indians attending Teedyuscung at this second Easton conference had ever owned any of the lands in question; that if any were living who had at one time owned the lands, they had long since removed to the valleys of the Ohio and Allegheny. Weiser further told the Governor that the land in question had been bought by the Proprietaries when John and Thomas Penn were in the Colony; that a line was soon after run by Indians and surveyors; and that, when a number of the chiefs of the Delawares complained about the Walking Purchase afterwards, the deeds were produced and the names of the grantors attached to them examined at the council held in Philadelphia, in 1742, at which council, after a long hearing, Canassatego as the speaker of the Six Nations declared that the deeds were correct, and ordered the Delawares to remove from the bounds of the purchase.

The Governor then advised Teedyuscung that the deeds to which he referred were in Philadelphia; that he would examine them upon his return to the city, and if any injustice had been done the Delawares, he would see that they should receive full satisfaction. Some days later, however, Governor Denny denied that any injustice had been done the Delawares by the Walking Purchase, but offered a very handsome present to make satisfaction for the injuries which they complained of. This present

Teedyuscung refused to receive; and the matter was then placed in charge of an investigating committee.

It was then decided that a general peace should be proclaimed, provided that the white prisoners were delivered up, and that the declaration of war and Scalp Act should not apply to any Indians who would promise to lay down their arms.

Teedyuscung then made the following promise in regard to the delivery of the captives:

"I will use my utmost endeavors to bring you down your prisoners. I have to request you that you would give liberty to all persons and friends to search into these matters; as we are all children of the Most High, we should endeavor to assist and make use of one another, and not only so, but from what I have heard, I believe there is a future state besides this flesh. Now I endeavour to act upon both these principles, and will, according to what I have promised, if the Great Spirit spare my life, come next spring with as great a force of Indians as I can get to your satisfaction."

At the close of the conference, Teedyuscung's delegation was given a present to the value of four hundred pounds, the Governor advising that the larger part of it was from the Quakers. Teedyuscung in his reply urged that the work of peace be continued.

The second peace conference with Teedyuscung, at Easton, closed on November 17th, 1756. In its minutes, recorded in Pa. Col. Rec., Vol. 7, pages 313 to 338, we read: "Teedyuscung showed great pleasure in his countenance, and took a kind leave of the Governor and all present."

Upon the close of the conference, Conrad Weiser, Joseph Pumpshire and the friendly Delaware chief, Moses Tatemy, accompanied Teedyuscung to Bethlehem, and then to Fort Allen, on his way back to his people. Says Weiser: "Teedyuscung, quite sober, parted with me with tears in his eyes, recommended Pumpshire to the Government of Pennsylvania, and desired me to stand a friend to the Indians, and give good advice, till every thing that was designed was brought about. Though he is a drunkard and a very irregular man, yet he is a man that can think well, and I believe him to be sincere in what he said." (Pa. Archives, Vol. 3, pages 67 and 68.)

About this time, Conrad Weiser had a conversation with Joseph Pumpshire and the friendly Delaware chief, Moses Tatemy, in which Tatemy informed him of the full speech Teedyuscung was to have made, but did not make, through fear of the Six

Nations' chiefs present at the treaty. The undelivered speech dealt, in part, with the occupation of the Wyoming Valley by the Connecticut settlers as being one of the causes of the hostility of the Indians.

Shortly after the Easton Conference of November, 1756, murders were committed below the Blue Mountains, which the Wyoming Delawares disavowed, and when the Governor sent Mr. Hill with a message to Teedyuscung, he was waylaid on his journey from Minisink, and murdered, it was claimed, by Iroquois. Heckewelder states that the Delawares assured him that many murders were committed by the Iroquois in order to "prevent the effects of the [Easton] treaty."

Subsequent peace conferences with Teedyuscung, during the years 1757 and 1758, will be described in later chapters of this history. The plan was first to work out peace with the Delawares and Shawnees on the Susquehanna, whose leader Teedyuscung claimed to be, and then to draw the Delawares and Shawnees of the Ohio and Allegheny away from the French interest. This latter was suggested by Teedyuscung and accomplished through the peace missions of the Moravian missionary, Christian Frederick Post, in the summer and autumn of 1758, as will be seen in a later chapter.

Obstacles in the Way of Peace

J. S. Walton, in his "Conrad Weiser and the Indian Policy of Colonial Pennsylvania," thus sets forth the obstacles which confronted Pennsylvania in her efforts to make peace with the hostile Delawares and Shawnees:

"The prospects of peace were growing more and more embarrassing. England, now that war was declared with France, sent Lord Loudon to America to take charge. Indian affairs were placed under the control of two men, Sir William Johnson for the northern, and Mr. Atkins for the southern colonies. Loudon's policy was to secure as many Indians as possible for allies, and with them strike the French. To this end Mr. Atkins secured the alliance of the Cherokee and other southern tribes. These were immediately added to the armies of Virginia and Western Pennsylvania. This act stirred the Northern Indians. The Iroquois and the Delawares declared that they could never fight on the same side with the despised Cherokees. This southern alliance meant northern revolt, and threatened to crush the peace negotiations at Easton. At this critical juncture, Lord Loudon, whose ignorance of the problem before him was equalled only by his contempt for provincialism, ordered the Governor of Pennsylvania to have nothing whatever to do with Indian affairs. Sir William Johnson, only, should control these things. Moreover, all efforts towards peace were advantages given to the enemy. Johnson, however was inclined towards peace, but he seriously complicated affairs in Pennsylvania by appointing George Croghan his sole deputy in the Province. Croghan and Weiser had quite different views upon Indian affairs. The Indians were quick to notice these changes. Jonathan, an old Mohawk chief, in conversation with Conrad Weiser said: 'Is it true that you are become a fallen tree, that you must no more engage in Indian affairs, neither as counsellor nor interpreter? What is the reason? Weiser replied, 'It is all too true. The King of Great Britain has appointed Warruychyockon [Sir William Johnson] to be manager of all Indian affairs that concern treaties of friendship, war, etc. And that accordingly the Great General (Lord Loudon) that came over the Great Waters, had in the name of the King ordered the Government of Pennsylvania to desist from holding treaties with the Indians, and the Government of Pennsylvania will obey the King's command, and consequently I, as the Government's servant, have nothing more to do with Indian affairs.' Jonathan and his companion replied in concert, 'Ha! Ha!' meaning 'Oh, sad.' The two Indians then whispered together a few minutes, during which Weiser politely withdrew into another room. When he returned Jonathan said, 'Comrade, I hear you have engaged on another bottom. You are made a captain of warriors and laid aside council affairs and turned soldier.'

"To this Weiser replied with some spirit, setting forth his reasons for self-defense, the bloody outrages of the Indians, the reception of the first peace messengers. 'You know,' said Weiser, 'that their lives were threatened. You know the insolent answer which came back that caused us to declare war. I was at Easton working for peace and if I had my wish there would be no war at all. . . . So, comrade, do not charge me with such a thing as that.' The Indians thanked Weiser for the explanation and went away satisfied. But at the same time Weiser was shorn of his power among the Indians. Making him commander of the Provincial forces robbed Pennsylvania of her most powerful advocate at the council fires of the Indians." (Pa. Col. Rec., Vol. 7, pages 491 and 492.)

To the above statements of Walton we would add that Croghan

and Weiser never did agree in the conduct of Indian affairs; that Croghan, on account of his long trading with the Delawares and Shawnees, was more of a friend of them than he was of the Six Nations; that Weiser, on account of his having lived among the Six Nations in his youth and having always been in close relations with their great chiefs, especially Shikellamy, was always on their side in any disputes with the Delawares and Shawnees; that now, since the chief Indian character in the peace measures, was Teedyuscung, a Delaware, Weiser's influence became less than that of Croghan; that the hatred of the Delawares, Shawnees and Six Nations for the Catawbas and Cherokees was too deep-seated to be wiped out by a few conferences; that these Southern tribes had been driven out of the Ohio Valley, generations before, by the Iroquois, Delawares and Shawnees, and ever since that time, not only the Iroquois, but also the Delawares and Shawnees had been sending war parties against the Catawbas and Cherokees—a warfare that the Iroquois said had existed "since the world began and would last forever;" and that the French took advantage of this age-long feud between the Northern and the Southern Indians, in telling the Delawares and Shawnees, when the Ohio Company began to open a road to the Ohio, that it was for the purpose of making a route over which the Cherokees and Catawbas could come to enter their former habitat and to kill them—a statement that the French repeated to the Delawares and Shawnees when Braddock was marching over the mountains against Fort Duquesne, in the summer of 1755, causing such fear to remain in the hearts of the Delawares as seriously to hinder peace negotiations, even the peace mission of Christian Frederick Post, in the autumn of 1758.

Death of Canachquasy

While attending the first conference with Teedyuscung, at Easton, Canachquasy had a presentiment of death—a presentiment soon to be fulfilled. Shortly after his appearance before the Provincial Council, on October 24th, when he gave a report of his mission to the Six Nations, he contracted small-pox, which was then raging in Philadelphia, and before the middle of November, this firm friend of the English, this great peace apostle among the Indians, was no more. At the closing session of the second conference with Teedyuscung, at Easton, Governor Denny informed the assembled Indians of the death of Canachquasy and several other friendly Indians who had recently died of small-pox, at Philadelphia. Said the Governor to Teedyuscung and the other chiefs: "I wipe away your tears; I take the grief from your hearts: I cover the graves; eternal rest with their spirits." Then Teedyuscung addressed the chiefs on this mournful occasion. They remained silent for some time. Then the oldest of them arose and pronounced a funeral oration, after which Teedyuscung again spoke, praising the efforts Canachquasy had made in promoting the good work of peace. Canachquasy's devotion to the cause of the English commands our great admiration and respect. He said he would die for the sons of Onas.

CHAPTER XV

Events of the Year 1757

ON January 13th, 1757, Governor William Denny issued a proclamation suspending hostilities with the Delawares and Shawnees on the Susquehanna for the period of fifty days. However, this proclamation did not prevent the soldiers and inhabitants of the Province from defending themselves, or from killing any Indians committing acts of hostility against any of the forts or against any of the inhabitants of Pennsylvania. (Pa. Col. Rec., Vol. 7, page 300.)

Lancaster Council of May, 1757

At about this time, as stated in a former chapter, Sir William Johnson, who had been put in charge of Indian affairs in the colonies, appointed George Croghan as his deputy in charge of Indian affairs in Pennsylvania. During the first few days of April, Croghan held a council with a large body of Delawares, Tuscaroras, Mohawks, Oneidas, Onondagas, Cayugas, Senecas and Nanticokes, at Harris' Ferry (Harrisburg). Rev. John Elder, Captain Thomas McKee, John Harris, Hugh Crawford and Joseph Armstrong also attended this council. Not being able to accomplish much at Harris' Ferry, Croghan urged the Indians to go to Philadelphia to hold a treaty. They declined to do this, but consented to go to Lancaster, to which place the council fire was removed on April 7th.

Teedyuscung, did not attend the Lancaster Council, being still among the Indians, working for peace. It was the desire of Johnson and Croghan that all friendly Indians should take up the hatchet in the English cause; but Teedyuscung opposed this, and contended that the friendly Indians should be asked no more than to remain neutral. While the delegation of chiefs was waiting near Lancaster for Teedyuscung, Governor Denny received orders from Lord Loudon not to take part in Indian treaties, and to forbid the Quakers from attending such treaties or contributing thereto in any manner. The Governor then declined to take part in the Lancaster treaty.

Says Walton: "Letters and petitions now poured in upon the Governor. William Masters and Joseph Galaway, of Lancaster, voiced the sentiment of that vicinity in a letter urging the Governor to come to Lancaster immediately, and use every possible means to ascertain the truth or falsity of Teedyuscung's charges. 'The Indians now present have plainly intimated that they are acquainted with the true cause of our Indian war.' The Friendly Society for the Promotion of Peace Among the Indians asked permission of the Governor to examine the minutes of the Provincial Council and the Proprietaries' deeds, in order to 'assist the Proprietaries in proving their innocence of Teedyuscung's charges.' The Governor positively refused to show them any papers. The Commissioners in charge of Indian affairs were also refused the same request. The Governor then lost his temper and charged the Quakers of Pennsylvania with meddling in affairs which did not concern them. The Assembly then sent a message to the Governor, denying that the people of the Province ever interfered with his majesty's prerogative of making peace and war . . . 'Their known duty and loyalty to his majesty, notwithstanding the pains taken to misrepresent their actions, forbids such an attempt. It is now clear by the inquiries made by your Honor, that the cause of the present Indian incursions in this Province, and the dreadful calamities many of the inhabitants have suffered, have arisen in a great measure from the exorbitant and unreasonable purchases made or supposed to have been made of the Indians, that the natives complain that there is not a country left to hunt or subsist in.' "

Governor Denny was compelled by pressure of the people to go to the Lancaster conference. He arrived there on May 11th. At this time, the Cherokees, who were serving in the army at Fort Loudon and Fort Cumberland, were particularly opposed to any peace with the Delawares. While the conferences were in progress at Lancaster, some Indian outrages occurred on the Swatara, so exasperating the people that they brought the mutilated body of a woman, whom the Indians had scalped, and left it on the court house steps, at Lancaster, as the silent witness, as they said, of the fruits of an Indian peace. All these matters, together with the absence of the great Teedyuscung, made it impossible to accomplish anything definite at Lancaster. George Croghan was anxious that the Western Indians be taken into a treaty of peace at Lancaster, and this question was therefore postponed on account of the absence of Teedyuscung.

While Teedyuscung did not attend the Lancaster treaty, he sent a message complaining bitterly of the Moravians at Bethlehem, as follows:

"Brothers, there is one thing that gives us a great deal of concern, which is our flesh and blood that live among you at Bethlehem and in the Jersies, being kept as if they were prisoners. We formally applied to the minister at Bethlehem [probably meaning Bishop Spangenberg] to let our people come back at times and hunt, which is the chief industry we follow to maintain our families; but that minister has not listened to what we said to him, and it is very hard that our people have not the liberty of coming back to the woods where game is plenty, and to see their friends. They have complained to us that they cannot hunt where they are. If they go to the woods and cut down a tree, they are abused for it, notwithstanding that very land we look upon to be our own; and we hope, brothers, that you will consider this matter and let our people come back into the woods, and visit their friends, and pass and repass, as brothers ought to do."

The Moravian missionaries resented this message of Teedyuscung, claiming that he well knew the sentiments of the Indian converts at Bethlehem, and that they were there of their own free will. The Colonial Government, however, paid no attention to the message.

The matter of the fraudulent land sales came up at this conference at Lancaster. One of the chiefs of the Six Nations, Little Abraham, a Mohawk, spoke as follows concerning the frauds upon the Delawares:

"They lived among you, brothers, but upon some difference between you and them, we [the Six Nations] thought proper to remove them, giving them lands to plant and hunt on at Wyoming and Juniata on Susquehanna. But you, covetous of land, made plantations there and spoiled their hunting grounds. They then complained to us, and we looked over those lands and found the complaints to be true . . . The French became acquainted with all the causes of complaint that the Delawares had against you; and as your people were daily increasing their settlements, by this means you drove them [the Delawares] back into the arms of the French, and they took the advantage of spiriting them up against you by telling them: 'Children, you see, and we have often told you, how the English, your brethren, did serve;

they plant all the country, and drive you back; so that in a little time you will have no land. It is not so with us. Though we built trading houses on your land, we do not plant it. We have our provisions from over the great waters.' "

The Six Nations' chiefs at this conference then advised that part of the lands of the Delawares be given back to them and promised to make both the Delawares and Shawnees return the captives. They further urged that another invitation be sent to Teedyuscung to come and bring some Senecas with him, in order that the land question might be fully settled. Governor Denny followed the suggestion of the chiefs of the Six Nations made at the Lancaster conference, and accordingly arranged for the third council or treaty at Easton, where the complaints of the Delawares might be more fully heard. This treaty we shall discuss later in this chapter.

Little Abraham also gave information as to the things that took place at the Indian council at Otseningo (Chenango), when the Delawares threw off the yoke of the Six Nations, and said: "We are men, and are determined not to be ruled any longer by you as Women; and we are determined to cut off all the English, except those that make their Escape from us in Ships."

While the Indians were encamped at Lancaster, Scarouady left with some Mohawk warriors to reconnoitre the wilderness in the vicinity of Fort Augusta and the region towards the Ohio. The old chief asked permission from Croghan to make this expedition, saying that he was apprehensive that the French and their Indian allies would make an attempt against this fort.

Some of the messengers, sent by Croghan to the Ohio, returned to Lancaster on May 9th. They had gone to Venango, Kuskuskies and other towns in the western part of the Province. They reported that the most of the Delawares who formerly lived at Kittanning, were living at Kuskuskies; that, at Venango, they were well received by the Delaware chief, Custaloga, at which place they found but fifteen Frenchmen at the French fort (Fort Machault); that the Delawares at Venango advised them that they would be very glad to enter into peace negotiations, but must first consult the Senecas; that the messengers then went to a town some miles from Venango where they consulted with the Seneca chief, Garistagee, who then and there advised the Venango Delawares not to accept Croghan's overtures, giving, as a reason, that the messengers had not brought "proper belts for this occasion," but further saying that, if Croghan would send "a proper belt with men wrought in it for the several tribes he wants to meet with, made of old council wampum, which is the custom of the Six Nations, I will go down with you and see him." The returned scouts and messengers further reported that they were sure the French intended to make an attack of importance against the English, but that they could not tell where this attack would take place. Then they gave the following information as to the activities of the Cherokees and Catawbas in behalf of the English:

"The Ohio Indians are much afraid of the Southern Indians, having been struck three times by them this spring—twice near Fort Duquesne and once at the Logs Town."

The Lancaster Council closed on May 22nd. During its sessions, many of the Indians contracted small-pox, and some of them died. For account of this council, the reader is referred to Pa. Col. Rec., Vol. 7, pages 510 to 551.

In the spring of 1757, a number of Cherokees and Catawbas came to Pennsylvania to assist the English. They were brought by Captain Paris, a trader among them. Reference has been made in a former chapter, to the fact that the presence of the Cherokees and Catawbas among the forces of the English hindered peace negotiations with the Delawares and Shawnees, their age-long enemies. From the time when the Ohio Company began to open a road to the Ohio, the French never ceased to tell the Delawares and Shawnees that the English were planning to cause the Catawbas and Cherokees to destroy these tribes. In 1756, the French were especially active in spreading this propaganda among the Delawares and Shawnees. John A. Long, who was captured near Cumberland, Maryland, in April of that year, and carried to the Indian town of Buccaloons, or Buckaloon, at the mouth of Brokenstraw Creek, Warren County, reported to Governor Dinwiddie, after his return to Fort Cumberland, in September (1756), that the Iroquois of Buckaloons had heard a report that the English had joined with the Cherokees and Catawbas. (Pa. Col. Rec. Vol. 7, page 289.) Furthermore, Croghan was distasteful to these southern tribes. (Pa. Col. Rec., Vol. 7, page 557.) All these things, added to the fact that Croghan and Weiser differed in their ideas as to the manner of conducting Indian affairs, threw many obstacles in the way of attaining peace with the Delawares and Shawnees.

The Cherokees and Catawbas acted principally as scouts. They were familiar with the Indian trails of Western Pennsylvania, from the long warfare they had carried on against the Iroquois, Shawnees and Delawares. Their principal base of operations in Pennsylvania were Forts Loudon and Littleton. On May 20th, 1757, a scouting party of five soldiers and fifteen Cherokees went out from Fort Cumberland, led by Lieutenant Baker. They went almost to the walls of Fort Duquesne, and had an engagement with some French and Indians within two miles of the fort, in which a number of scalps were taken and a French officer was captured. (Pa. Col. Rec., Vol. 7, page 603.)

Third Conference with Teedyuscung at Easton

The third council with Teedyuscung at Easton opened on July 21, 1757, and continued until August 7th. The friendly Shawnee chief, Paxinosa, was also present. There were almost endless discussions about Teedyuscung's having a secretary of his own, deeds, frauds, and other matters which had come before Indian councils for many years prior to this council. Finally, John Pumpshire was selected by Teedyuscung as his interpreter, and Charles Thomson, master of the Quaker school in Philadelphia, as his clerk. Thomson, in writing of this affair to Samuel Rhodes, says:

"I need not mention the importance of the business we are come about. The welfare of the Province and the lives of thousands depend upon it. That an affair of such weight should be transacted with soberness, all will allow; how, then, must it shock you to hear that pains seem to have been taken to make the King [Teedyuscung] drunk every night since the business began. The first two or three days were spent in deliberating whether the King should be allowed the privilege of a clerk. When he was resolute in asserting his right and would enter into no business without having a secretary of his own, they at last gave it up, and seem to have fallen on another scheme which is to unfit him to say anything worthy of being inscribed (?) by his secretary. On Saturday, under pretense of rejoicing for the victory gained by the King of Prussia and the arrival of the fleet, a bonfire was ordered to be made and liquor given to the Indians to induce them to dance. For fear they should get sober on Sunday and be fit next day to enter on business, under pretense that the Mohawks had requested it, another bonfire was ordered to be made, and more liquor given them. On Monday night the King was made drunk by Conrad Weiser, on Tuesday by G. Croghan; last night he was very drunk at Vernon's, and Vernon lays the blame on Comin and G. Croghan. He did not go to sleep last night. This morning he lay down under a shed about the break of day and slept a few hours. He is to speak this afternoon. He is to be sure in a fine capacity to do business. But thus we go on. I leave you to make reflections. I for my part wish myself at home."

Teedyuscung Renews Charge of Fraud

Teedyuscung entered this third Easton council with his mind made up not to reiterate the charge of fraud concerning the Walking Purchase, doubtless fearing the Six Nations. His advisors told him that he could afford to wait until peace was fully established, before asserting the Delaware rights to lands drained by the Delaware River. However, Governor Denny was determined to make the great chief deny that any fraud had been practiced upon the Delawares in land purchases. When pressed for the cause of the alienation of the Delawares, Teedyuscung unequivocally asserted that it was the land purchases. Said he:

"The complaint I made last fall I yet continue. I think some lands have been bought by the Proprietors or his agents from Indians who had not a right to sell . . . I think, also, when some lands have been sold to the Proprietors by Indians who had a right to sell to a certain place, whether that purchase was to be measured by miles or hours walk, that the Proprietors have contrary to agreement or bargain, taken in more lands than they ought to have done, and lands that belonged to others. I therefore now desire that you will produce the writings and deeds by which you hold the land, and let them be read in public, and examined, that it may be fully known from what Indians you have bought the lands you hold; and how far your purchases extend; that copies of the whole may be laid before King George, and published to all the Provinces under his Government. What is fairly bought and paid for I make no further demand about. But if any lands have been bought of Indians to whom these lands did not belong, and who had no right to sell them, I expect a satisfaction for those lands; and if the Proprietors have taken in more lands than they bought of true owners, I expect likewise to be paid for that."

Teedyuscung Requests Benefits of Civilization

Said Teedyuscung, further, at this conference: "We [the Delawares] intend to settle at Wyoming, and we want to have certain boundaries fixed between you and us, and a certain tract of land fixed which it shall not be lawful for us or our children ever to sell, nor for you or any of your children ever to buy . . . To build different houses from what we have done before, such as may last not only for a little time, but for our children after us; we desire you will assist us in making our settlements, and send us persons to instruct us in building houses and making such necessaries as shall be needed, and that persons be sent to instruct us in the Christian religion, and to instruct our children in reading and writing, and that a fair trade be established between us, and such persons appointed to conduct and manage these affairs as shall be agreeable to us."

Walton's Account of the Council

The remaining matters taken up at this great conference are thus succinctly set forth by J. S. Walton, in his "Conrad Weiser and the Indian Policy of Pennsylvania":

"Teedyuscung then asked that the territory of Wyoming be reserved to the Indians forever. That it might be surveyed and a deed given to the Indians, that they might have something to show when it became necessary to drive the white men away. After these charges [concerning fraudulent land purchases] were again made the Governor called Croghan and Weiser together to know what was the best thing to do. Each of these men with his large share of experience in Indian affairs agreed in the opinion that some outside influence had induced Teedyuscung to revive these charges. They also united in the opinion that the Indians merely wanted a glimpse of the old deeds, and would be satisfied with a cursory examination of the signatures.

"Upon these assertions the Governor and Council were induced to grant Teedyuscung's request and to show him the deeds of 1736 and 1737 from the Delawares, and of 1749 from the Iroquois. When the Governor applied to Mr. Peters for the papers and deeds they were again refused. Peters declared that he held them as a sacred trust from the Proprietors and would neither surrender them nor permit himself to be placed under oath and give testimony. These two things could only be done, he insisted, in the presence of Sir William Johnson, before whom as a final abritrator, the Proprietors desired that these charges should be laid. James Logan immediately opposed Richard Peters. He insisted that all deeds relating to lands which the Indians claimed were fraudulently purchased, should be shown. To refuse this would be unjust to the Indians and dangerous to the cause of peace. Logan explained that the Proprietary instructions should not be too literally construed and obeyed. The Indians were opposed to having their case settled before Sir William Johnson. After an animated discussion in council it was reluctantly agreed that the deeds should be shown. The Council only consented to this after Conrad Weiser had assured them that Teedyuscung did not insist upon seeing all the deeds, but only those pertaining to the back lands. R. Peters again protested, but was overruled. The deeds were laid on the table August 3, 1757.

"Charles Thomson, at Teedyuscung's request, copied these deeds. The chief said he would have preferred to have seen the deeds of confirmation given to Governor Keith in 1718, but the great work of peace was superior to the land dispute, and if the Proprietors would make satsfaction for the lands which had been fradulently secured, he would return the English prisoners held captive among the Indians. The peace belt was then grasped by the Governor and Teedyuscung, and the two years' struggle for peace was crowned with victory. After much feasting and dancing, drinking and burning of bonfires the treaty closed.

"Teedyuscung promised to fight for the English on condition that his men should not be commanded by white captains. The Governor and his party returned to Philadelphia, deeply worried over the publicity of the Indian charges of fraud which had occurred at the Easton conference. Peace to the Proprietors was dearly purchased, if the people of the Province were confirmed in their belief that the Indian outrages had been caused by fraud in land purchases."

For a full account of the third conference or treaty with Teedyuscung at Easton—a treaty of peace between Pennsylvania and the Delawares and Shawnees of the Susquehanna, leaving the Delawares and Shawnees of the Ohio and Allegheny yet to be won over from the French—the reader is referred to Pa. Col. Rec., Vol. 7, pages 649 to 714.

The council ended on Sunday, August 7th. Governor Denny then returned to Philadelphia realizing that two things were imperative. One was to disprove Teedyuscung's charge of fraud, in order to remove from the Proprietaries of the Colony the responsibility for the hostility of the Delawares and Shawnees; the other was to make peace with the Indians of the valleys of the Ohio and Allegheny, in order that the expedition of General Forbes, then planned, might be a success. The Governor was very apprehensive that, on account of the allegiance of the Western Indians with the French, the proposed expedition of General Forbes would meet with the same fate as the expedition of the ill-fated Braddock in the summer of 1755. Besides, unless the hostile Indians of the Ohio and Allegheny could be persuaded to sever their allegiance with the French, there was little chance of ending the barbarous raids which they were making on the frontier settlements. How these Western Indians were induced by the Moravian missionary, Christian Frederick Post, to sever their allegiance with the French, will be told in a subsequent chapter.

Chief Tatemy and his Son, William

Mention has been made, in a former chapter, that the Delaware chief, Tatemy, or Titami, after petitioning the Colonial Authorities, in November, 1742, and evidently obtaining the consent of the Iroquois, was permitted to reside on his tract of land, near Stockertown, Northampton County, after the other Delawares of the Munsee Clan had removed from the bounds of the Walking Purchase. This chief, who had been baptized by the missionary, Rev. David Brainerd, on July 21st, 1746, and given the name of Moses Fonday Tatemy, was closely associated with Teedyuscung in the attempt to win back the Delawares to friendly relations with the Province, and acted as interpreter at the various councils at Easton. He was also sent on important missions with Isaac Still and others, and interpreted at several conferences at Philadelphia. He died about 1761. A town in Northampton County perpetuates the name of this noted chief.

When Teedyuscung and his party of more than 200 Indians were on their way to the Easton Council of July and August, 1757, Tatemy's son, William, who had strayed from the main body, was mortally wounded by a fifteen year old Irish boy. This wanton act threatened to break up the peace negotiations, and it was feared that the Delawares, angered by the outrage, would take revenge. Teedyuscung demanded, at the council, that, if young Tatemy should die, the Irish boy who shot him, should be tried and punished, according to law, before a deputation of Indians. Governor Denny replied, expressing his sorrow to the father, and promised that the boy should be punished. Young Tatemy was taken to the house of a farmer, named John Jones, near Bethlehem, where he was attended by Dr. John Matthew Otto. However, in spite of all that medical skill could do for him, the unfortunate Indian, after suffering for more than a month, died on August 1st. The gentle Moravian missionaries soothed his dying hours with their kind ministrations. At Bethlehem, in the presence of more than 200 Indians, Rev. Jacob Rogers conducting the funeral services, the friendly young Delaware, with marble face upturned to the glorious summer sky, was laid away from sight until the heavens be no more.

We shall now narrate the principal atrocities, committed by the Delawares and Shawnees in 1757.

Atrocities in Monroe County

On March 25th, the Delawares made an incursion into Monroe County, killing Sergeant Leonard Den within two miles of Fort Dupui. This was followed by another on April 20th, spreading terror, devastation and death in this region. On this day, Andreas (Casper) Gundryman was killed within sight of Fort Hamilton, while bringing fire wood to his father's house, near the fort. Michael Roup, an inhabitant of Smithfield Township, Monroe County, made the following affidavit before William Parsons, at Easton, on April 24th, describing some of the murders committed during this incursion:

"That, on Friday morning last, John Lefever, passing the houses of Philip Bozart and this deponent [Roup] informed them that the Indians had murdered Casper Gundryman last Wednesday evening, whereupon this deponent went immediately to the house of Philip Bozart to consult what was best to be done, their houses being about half a mile apart. That they concluded it best for the neighbours to collect themselves together, as many as they could, in some one house. That he immediately returned home and loaded his wagon as fast as he could with his most valuable effects, which he carried to Bozart's house. That as soon as he unloaded his wagon, he drove to his son-in-law, Peter Soan's house, about two miles, and loaded as much of his effects as the time and hurry would admit, and took them also to Bozart's, where nine families were retired. That a great number of the inhabitants also retired to the houses of Conrad Bittenbender and John McDowell. That Bozart's house is seven miles from Fort Hamilton and twelve miles from Fort Norris. That yesterday morning, about nine o'clock, the said Peter Soan and Christian Klein with his daughter about thirteen years of age went from Bozart's house to the house of the said Klein and thence to Soan's house to look after their cattle and bring off more effects. That about half an hour after these three persons had gone from Bozart's house, a certain George Hartleib, who also fled with his family to Bozart's and who had been at his own house about a mile from Soan's to look after creatures and to bring away what he could, returned to Bozart's and reported that he had heard three guns fired very quickly one after another towards Soan's place, which made them all conclude that the above three persons were killed by the Indians. That the little company was afraid to venture to go and see what happened that day, as they had many women and children to take care of, who, if they had left, might have fallen an easy prey to the enemy. That this morning, nine men of the neighbourhood armed themselves as well as they could, and went towards Peter Soan's house, in order to discover what was become of the above three persons. That when they came within three hundred yards of the house, they found the bodies of the said Soan and Klein about twenty feet from each other, killed and scalped, but did not find Klein's daughter. Soan was killed by a bullet which entered the upper part of his back and came out at his breast. Klein was killed with their tomahawks. The nine men immediately returned to Bozart's and reported as above. That this deponent was not one of the nine, but that he remained at Bozart's with the women and children. That the rest of the people desired this deponent to come to Easton and acquaint the Justice with what had happened. That the nine men did not think it safe to bury the dead." (Pa. Col. Rec., Vol. 7, pages 492 to 494.)

On June 20th, 1757, George Ebert, who was captured in this same incursion, made an affidavit at Easton, in which he said that Conrad Bittenbender, Jacob Roth, and John Nolf were killed and Peter Sheaffer was captured in this incursion, adding that "they [the Indians] immediately set off; that on the evening of the second day they fell in with another Company of about Twenty-four Indians, who had Abraham Miller, with his Mother, and Adam Snell's Daughter, Prisoners; that on their way on this Side of Diahogo they saw Klein's Daughter, who had been taken Prisoner about a week before this deponent was taken; that a Day's Journey beyond Diahogo, they came to some French Indian Cabbins, where they saw another Prisoner, a girl about Eight or nine Years old, who told this deponent that her name was Catherine Yager, that her father was a Lock Smith and lived at Allemangle, and that she had been a Prisoner ever since

Christmas." Ebert also stated in his affidavit that the Indians killed Abraham Miller's mother when she became unable to travel further, on account of weakness, likewise Snell's daughter, "who had received a Wound in her Leg by a Fall when they first took her Prisoner." At the "French Indian Cabbins," both George Ebert, the deponent, and Abraham Miller made their escape. (Pa. Col. Rec., Vol. 7, pages 620 and 621.)

Shortly after the capture of George Ebert and the murder of Bittenbender, Roth and Nolf, the Indians killed a certain Mrs. Marshall near the same place. On June 23d, of this year (1757), a large body of Indians attacked and burned the home of Broadhead in sight of Fort Hamilton, killing and scalping a man named John Tidd. During the same month, also, Peter Geisinger was shot and scalped while plowing in his field between Fort Henry and Fort Northkill, and Adam Drum was killed in Allemangle.

Murder of John Spitler and Barnabas Tolon

On May 16th, John Spitler while fixing up a pair of bars on his farm a few miles from Stumpton, was shot and his body cruelly mangled. His body was buried in the graveyard at Hebron, near Lebanon. The following account of his murder and burial is contained in the records of the Hebron church:

"1757, May den 16, wurde Johannes Spitler, Jr. ohnweit von seinem Hause, an der Schwatara von moerderischen Indianern ueberfallen und ermordert. Er war im acht unddreisigsten Jahr seines Alters, und verwichenes Jahr im April, an der Schwatara aufgenommen. Seine uebelzugerichtette Leiche wurde den 17ten May hieher gebracht, und bei einer grossen Menge Leute begleitet auf unsern hiesigen Gottesacker beerdigt."

The following is the translation of the record:

"On the 16th of May, 1757, John Spitler, Jr. was fallen upon and murdered by savage Indians not far from his house on the Swatara. He was in the thirty-eighth year of his age, and had taken up his residence on the Swatara in April of the preceding year. His badly mangled body was brought here on the 17th of May, accompanied by a large concourse of people, and buried in the graveyard of this place."

The Lancaster Council, described earlier in this chapter, was in session at the time of these atrocities. In its minutes, under date of May 18th, we read: "This day four persons that were killed on the frontiers, in the settlement of Swatara, were brought to this town." (Pa. Col. Rec., Vol. 7, page 538.)

On May 22nd, Barnabus Tolon was killed and scalped in Hanover Township, Lebanon County. "We are," says the editor of the Pennsylvania *Gazette*, "well informed that 123 persons have been murdered and carried off from that part of Lancaster [Lebanon] County by Indians since the war commenced, and that lately three have been scalped and are yet living."

Other atrocities were committed in this neighborhood during the summer of 1757, thus referred to in the "Frontier Forts of Pennsylvania":

"A correspondent from this township Hanover of the Pennsylvania *Gazette*, says in its issue of May, 1757, that the house of Isaac Snevely was set on fire and entirely consumed, with eighteen horses and cows, and that, on May 17th, five men and a woman were killed and scalped about thirty miles from Lancaster. In another letter, dated August 11th, it is stated that, on Monday the 8th, George Mauerer was killed and scalped whilst cutting oats in George Scheffer's field."

Massacre on Quitapahilla Creek

"Londonderry Township (Lebanon County) being more towards the interior, was not so much exposed to the depredations of the savages as those on the northern frontiers. Nevertheless, in the more sparsely settled parts they committed various murders. June 19, 1757, nineteen persons were killed in a mill on the Quitapahilla Creek, and on the 9th of September, 1757, one boy and a girl were taken from Donegal Township, a few miles south of Derry. About the same time, one Danner and his son Christian, a lad of twelve years, had gone into the Conewago hills to cut down trees; after felling one, and while the father was cutting a log, he was shot and scalped by an Indian, and Christian, the son, taken captive into Canada, where he remained until the close of the war when he made his escape. Another young lad, named Steger, was surprised by three Indians and taken captive whilst cutting hoop-poles, but, fortunately, after remaining with the Indians some months made his escape."—(Frontier Forts of Pennsylvania.)

Murder of Adam Trump

On June 22nd occurred the murder of Adam Trump, in Albany Township, Berks County, thus referred to in a letter of James Read, from Reading, on June 25th:

"Last night Jacob Levan, Esq., of Maxatawney, came to see me and showed me a letter of the 22d inst. from Lieutenant Engel, dated in Allemangel, by which he advised Mr. Levan of the murder of one Adam Trump in Allemangel, by Indians, that evening, and that they had taken Trump's wife and his son, a lad nineteen years old, prisoners; but the woman escaped, though upon her flying, she was so closely pursued by one of the Indians, (of which there were seven) that he threw his tomahawk at her, and cut her badly in the neck, but 'tis hoped not dangerously. This murder happened in as great a thunderstorm as has happened for twenty years past; which extended itself over a great part of this and Northampton Counties. * * * *

"I had almost forgot to mention (but I am so hurried just now, 'tis no wonder), that the Indians after scalping Adam Trump left a knife, and a halbert, or a spear, fixed to a pole of four feet, in his body."

Other Atrocities East of the Susquehanna

About the middle of May, 1757, a boy was killed and scalped, and another who had small-pox was dangerously wounded, about one half mile from Fort Northkill. The Indians did not scalp the wounded boy for fear of infection. Four persons were killed and four captured near this fort, about October 1st, 1757.

On June 22nd, 1757, as already narrated, Peter Geisinger was killed and scalped by Indians in the vicinity of Fort Northkill. On the following day, a girl about fifteen years old, a daughter of Balser Smith, was captured by two Indians, near the same neighborhood. On June 29th, in the vicinity of this fort, Frederick Myers and his wife were killed and scalped. Three of Myers' children, a boy aged ten years, a girl aged eight years, and a boy aged six years were captured, while another child, aged one and one half years, was scalped, but was alive when some scouts from Fort Northkill found it late that afternoon. It was lying in a ditch crying, with the water just up to its mouth. ("Frontier Forts of Pennsylvania," Vol. 1, pages 108 and 110.)

The Pennsylvania *Gazette* of July, 1757, contains a letter written from Heidelberg, Berks County, on July 9th, as follows:

"Yesterday, about three o'clock in the afternoon, between Valentine Herchelroar's and Tobias Bickell's, four Indians killed two children. They, at the same time, scalped a young woman of about sixteen; but, with proper care, she is likely to live and do well.

"A woman was terribly cut with a tomahawk, but not scalped. Her life is despaired of. Three children were carried off prisoners. One Christian Schrenk's wife being among the rest, bravely defended herself and children for a while, wrestling the gun out of the Indian's hands, who assaulted her, also his tomahawk, and threw them away, and afterwards was obliged to save her own life. Two of her children were taken captive in the meantime. In this house were also twenty women and children who had fled from their own habitations to take shelter. The men belonging to them were about one half mile off, picking cherries. They came as quickly as possible, and went in pursuit of the Indians, but to no purpose. The Indians had concealed themselves."

Lieutenant Jacob Wetterhold, in a letter written from Lynn Township, Lehigh County, to Major William Parsons at Easton, on July 9th, 1757, describes an atrocity which took place that day in Lynn Township. This letter, recorded in Penna. Archives, Vol. 3, page 211, is quoted verbatim, except as to spelling:

"These are to acquaint you of a murder happened this day at the house of Adam Clauce, in said Township of Lynn, where three or four neighbors was cutting said man's corn; as they was eating their dinner, they were fell upon by a party of savages, Indians, and five of the whites took to their heels, two men, two women and one girl, and got safe out of their hands. Was killed and scalped, Martin Yager and his wife, and John Croushores, wife and one child, and the wife of Abraham Secles, and one child of one Adam Clouce, and the wife of John Croushore, and the wife of Abram Secles was scalped and is yet alive, but badly wounded, one shot through the side and the other in the thigh, and two children killed belonging to said Croushore, and one to said Secles, and one belonging to Philip Antone not scalped, and this was done at least three miles within the outside settlers and four miles from John Everett's, and Philip Antone's wife was one that took her Tilit [?], and came home and acquainted her husband, and he came and acquainted me, and I immediately went to the place with seven men, besides myself, and saw the murder, but the Indians was gone, and I directly pursued them about four miles and came up with them in the thick groves where we met with nine Indians, and one sprung behind a tree, and took sight at me, and I run direct at him, and another one flashed at me, and then both took to their heels, and I shot one through the body, as he fell on his face, but I loaded and after another that was leading a mare, and in the meantime he got up and ran away, and I fired one the other, and, I think, shot him."

Lieutenant Wetterhold's letter is not very clear as to the number killed by the Indians on this occasion. However, Conrad Weiser, writing Governor Denny, from Easton, on July 15th, mentions this atrocity, and says that ten were killed. (Penna. Archives, Vol. 3, page 218.)

Loudon says that, on August 27th, "one, Beatty, was killed in Paxton." On Sunday, August 21st, according to the Pennsylvania *Gazette* of September 1st, 1757, Indians burned the house and barn of Peter Semelcke, within two miles of Fort Lebanon, and carried off three of his children, Mr. Semelcke, his wife and one child being away from home at the time. About the same time Peter Wampler's four children were carried off from Lebanon Township, Lebanon County, as they were going to the meadow for a load of hay. About the same time, also, some settlers in Berne Township, Berks County, were murdered. On September 27th, four persons were killed and four captured near Fort Northkill. The Pennsylvania *Gazette* of October 27th says that, on October 17th, Alexander Watt and John McKennet were killed and scalped as they were cutting corn, near Fort Hunter, and that some soldiers of the Augusta Regiment, coming down from Fort Halifax, met the murderers and had a skirmish with them. On November 25th, Thomas Robinson and a son of Thomas Bell were killed, in the Swatara region. In August, John Winkelbach's two sons and Joseph Fischbach were fired upon while bringing in their cows at sunrise, in Lebanon County. Both Winkelbach boys were killed, and Fischbach was badly wounded. About the same time, Leonard Long's son was killed and scalped while plowing in his father's field, and Isaac Williams' wife was killed, both these murders taking place in Lebanon County.

The Mackey Atrocity

During one of the incursions into Dauphin County, in the summer of 1757, Elizabeth Dickey, her child, and the wife of Samuel Young were captured. On the same day a Mr. Barnett and a Mr. Mackey were at work on the former's farm near Manada Creek, when news reached them that their families were murdered in the block house nearby. They at once started for the scene of horror, but had not gone far until they were ambushed by a party of Indians who killed Mackey and severely wounded

Barnett who, nevertheless, was able to escape, owing to the swiftness of his horse. He concealed himself until the Indians left the neighborhood the next day, when he learned that his family was safe with the exception of his son, William, aged nine, whom the Indians had captured, together with Mackey's son about the same age. The Indians proceeded westward with the two little boys. Upon learning that one of the boys was the son of Mackey, whom they had just killed, they forced him to stretch his father's scalp. For a time, the little Mackey boy carried his father's scalp, which he would often stroke with his little hand, and say, "My father's pretty hair."

Mr. Barnett at length recovered from his wound. In the hope of recovering his son, he accompanied George Croghan to Fort Pitt, and attended the council which Croghan, Colonel Hugh Mercer, Captain William Trent, and Captain Thomas McKee held with the Shawnees, Delawares, and other Indians at that place on July 5th, 1759. One day during his stay at the fort, he wished to get a drink of water from Grant's Spring, above the fort, so named from the defeat of Major James Grant at that place in the preceding September. He had proceeded only a short distance, when something told him to turn back. At the same instant, he heard the report of a rifle, and looking towards the spring, saw the smoke of the rifle and an Indian scalping a soldier, who had gone to the spring for a drink.

Mr. Barnett returned home without recovering his son, but Croghan promised to use every endeavor to obtain the child. At length the boy was brought to Fort Pitt, but so great was his inclination to return to the Indians that it was necessary to guard him closely until there would be an opportunity to send him to his father. On one occasion, he jumped into a canoe, and was half way across the Allegheny River before he was observed. Quick pursuit followed; but he reached the other side and hid in the bushes, where it took a search of several hours to find him. Soon thereafter, he was sent to Carlisle, where the father received him with tears of joy, and took him home to the arms of the mother. During his captivity, the Indians frequently broke the ice on rivers and creeks, and dipped him in "to make him hardy." This treatment impaired his constitution. He sank into the grave in early manhood, leaving a wife and daughter. Shortly thereafter, the mother died. Then Mr. Barnett, the elder, removed to Allegheny County, where he died at the great age of eighty-two years. His dust reposes in the church yard of Lebanon, Mifflin Township, Allegheny County.

But, to return to the Mackey boy. The Indians gave this child to the French, and at the close of the French and Indian War, he passed into the hands of the English, was taken to England, and later, became a soldier in the British army, and was sent to America during the Revolutionary War. He procured a furlough, and sought out his widowed mother, who had mourned him as dead. As he stood before her in the strength of robust manhood, she was unable to see in him any trace of her long lost boy. "If you are my son," said she, "you have a mark upon your knee that I will know." He then exposed his knee to her view; whereupon she threw her arms around his neck in unrestrained joy. He never returned to the British army, but remained with his mother to the end of her days, often meeting William Barnett, and recounting with him their experiences while captives among the Indians.

Atrocities in Cumberland and Franklin Counties

Egle, in his "History of Pennsylvania," in the chapter on Cumberland County, relates the following atrocities that were perpetrated by the Indians, in this county, during the summer of 1757:

"In the spring and summer of 1757, the Indians invaded East Pennsboro. On May 13th, 1757, William Walker and another man were killed near McCormick's Fort, at Conodoguinet. In July of the same year, four persons were killed near Tobias Hendricks' . . . Companies of rangers scoured, in the summer of 1757, the country between the Conodoguinet Creek and the Blue Mountain, from the Susquehanna westward as far as Shippensburg, to route the savages who usually lurked in small parties, stealing through the woods and over fields to surprise laborers, to attack men, women and children in the 'light of day and dead of night,' murdered all indiscriminately whom they had surprised, fired houses and barns, abducted women and children. On July 18, 1757, six men were killed or taken away near Shippensburg, while reaping in John Cesney's field. The savages murdered John Kirkpatrick, Dennis Oneidan; captured John Cesney, three of his grandsons, and one of John Kirkpatrick's children. The day following, not far from Shippensburg, in Joseph Stevenson's harvest field, the savages butchered inhumanely Joseph Mitchell, James Mitchell, William Mitchell, John Finlay, Robert Stevenson, Andrew Enslow, John Wiley, Allen Henderson and William Gibson, carrying off Jane McCammon, Mary Minor, Janet Harper and a son of John Finlay. July 27, Mr. McKisson was wounded, and his son taken from the South Mountain. A letter, dated Carlisle, September 5, 1757, says three persons were killed by the Indians, six miles from Carlisle, and two persons about two miles from Silver's old place."

The list of those murdered in John Cesney's field is also given on page 219 of Vol. 3, of the Penna. Archives, where it is stated that the tragedy took place about seven miles from Shippensburg, and that, "these people refused to join with their neighbors who had a guard appointed them, because they couldn't have their fields reaped the first."

Says Egle, in his "History of Pennsylvania," in the chapter on Franklin County:

"The following are the names of persons killed and taken captive on the Conococheague: on the 23d of April, 1757, John Martin and William Blair were killed, and Patrick McClelland wounded, who died of his wounds, near Maxwell's Fort; May 12th John Martin and Andrew Paul, both old men, were captured; June 24th, Alexander Miller was killed and two of his daughters, from Conococheague; July 27th, Mr. McKisson was wounded, and his two sons were captured, at the South Mountain; August 15th, William Manson and his son were killed near Cross' Fort; September 26th, Robert Rush and John McCracken, with others, were killed and taken captive, near Chambersburg." It will be noted that Dr. Egle mentions Mr. McKisson in both the chapter on Cumberland County and the chapter on Franklin County.

Loudon, in his "Indian Narratives," gives a list of atrocities that took place in 1757, the list being compiled by John McCullough whose captivity we have narrated in a former chapter. The list includes many already narrated in this chapter, as well as the following:

"March 29th, the Indians took one person from the South Mountain. May 16th, eleven persons killed at Paxton, by the Indians. June 6th, two men killed and five taken, near Shippensburg. June 9th, four men killed in Sherman's Valley. June 17th, one man killed at Cuthbertson's Fort; four men shot at the Indian while scalping the man. June 24th, Alexander Miller killed and two of his daughters taken from Conococheague, and Gerhart Pendergras' daughters killed at Fort Littleton. (See Pa. Col.

Rec., Vol. 7, page 632.) July 2nd, one woman and four children taken from Trent's Gap; same day one, Springson, killed, near Logan's Mill, Conococheague. July 9th, Trooper Wilson's son killed at Antietam Creek. July 10th, ten soldiers killed at Clapham's Fort. August 19th, one man killed, near Harris Ferry. September 2nd, one man killed near Bigger's Gap, and one Indian killed. August 19th, fourteen people killed and taken from Mr. Cinky's congregation. On July 8th, two boys were taken from Cross' Fort in Conococheague."

One or more of the above murders probably took place within the limits of the state of Maryland.

The Eckerlin Tragedy

A few years prior to the French and Indian War, the three Eckerlin (Eckerling) brothers, Samuel, Israel and Gabriel, who were Pennsylvania-German mystics, settled near the mouth of a stream flowing into the Monongahela in the southeastern part of Green County, since known as Dunkard Creek from the fact that the Eckerlin brothers and their associates who formed the settlement, were German Baptists, or Dunkards. They had come from Ephrata, in Lancaster County. For several years the brothers lived in their new home in the western wilderness, in the midst of the Delaware Indians, and at peace with the world. Understanding the French language, they soon learned that the French were coming into the Ohio Valley and making preparations to assert their claim with force of arms; but the brothers gave no thought to the preparations for war on the part of the French, inasmuch as they (the brothers) felt that they were safe, being much beloved by the Indians. Samuel had a knowledge of medicine and surgery, and often ministered to his Indian neighbors in times of illness. On account of this, he was known as "Doctor Eckerlin." As the Indian troubles increased, the friendly Delawares advised them to remove to a safer position on the Cheat River, as their settlement near the mouth of Dunkard Creek was directly on the line of the old Catawba War Trail. Accordingly the brothers removed to a place since called Dunker's Bottom, near the mouth of the Cheat River, a few miles from their first settlement.

Late in August, 1757, Samuel started on one of his trading trips to Winchester, Virginia, after the harvest had been gathered. Upon his return, he was stopped at Port Pleasant, on the South

Branch, where he was accused of being a spy and in confederacy with the Indians. In vain he protested his innocence, and it was not until he appealed to the Governor that he was allowed to start on his homeward journey, accompanied by a squad of soldiers, who were ordered to follow him to his home on the Cheat River.

When Samuel and the soldiers were within a day's march of the Dunker settlement, a party of Indians led by a French priest, attacked the other brothers and their companions. Israel, who had absolute faith in divine protection, would neither defend himself nor attempt to escape, and he, Gabriel and a servant named Schilling were captured. The other members of the household were killed and scalped, and the cabins were pilfered and burned. The two brothers and Schilling were taken to Fort Duquesne, where the Indians scalped Gabriel. Schilling was kept by the Indians as their slave, while Gabriel and Israel were later taken to Montreal, and thence to Quebec. What eventually became of the two brothers, is not definitely known. One report says they were carried to France, where they died as prisoners, while another report says they died at sea.

It was not until seven years after their capture that definite rumors reached Ephrata as to the fate of the brothers. Samuel, who, upon his return to the settlement on the Cheat River, found the ashes of the cabins, the half-decaying bodies of the Dunkers, and the hoops on which their scalps had been dried, once wrote a letter of inquiry to Benjamin Franklin, who was then in France. This letter is among the Franklin correspondence now in the possession of the American Philosophical Society.

George Croghan, in the journal of his journey to Logstown, in the spring of 1751, says, under date of May 25th, that "a Dunkar from the Colony of Virginia came to the Logs Town, and requested Liberty of the Six Nation Chiefs to make [a settlement] on the River Yough-yo-gaine, a branch of Ohio." This Dunkar (Dunker) was doubtless Samuel Eckerlin. For the details of the Eckerlin tragedy, the reader is referred to Dr. Julius F. Sachse's "German Sectarians of Pennsylvania," also to Captain H. M. M. Richards' "Pennsylvania-Germans in the French and Indian War," Vol. XV of the Publications of the Pennsylvania-German Society.

Conclusion

The year 1757 was one full of horrors on the Pennsylvania frontier, yet it witnessed the bringing about of peace between the

Province and the Eastern Delawares and Shawnees. It also witnessed the recalling of Lord Loudon as commander-in-chief of the British forces in America and the appointment of Major-General James Abercrombie in his place. This change in supreme commanders was made by William Pitt soon after he assumed the office of Prime Minister of Great Britain; and, on December 30th, he wrote Governor Denny, giving him notice of the appointment of General Abercrombie. This letter Governor Denny received on March 7th, 1758.

In 1757, also, upon a report that French and Indians from the Ohio were on their way over the Indian trail along the West Branch of the Susquehanna to attack Fort Augusta, Colonel Burd sent a detachment under the command of Captain Patterson to scout as far as the town of Chinklacamoose (Clearfield). The detachment soon returned, having met with no Indians. Captain Patterson's men found Chinklacamoose burned and unoccupied. (Pa. Archives, Sec. Ser., Vol. 2, page 777).

During 1757, only fragmentary news was received from time to time from Indian scouts and captured hostile Indians as to the strength of the garrison at Fort Duquesne. One of these reports placed the strength of the garrison as only two hundred, during the first months of the year. (Pa. Archives, Vol. 3, page 147.) Another placed it as high as six hundred, in the month of June, Captain Lignery being the Commander. Other reports, coming from the Ohio and Allegheny during this year, were to the effect that many Shawnees in these valleys were moving to the mouth of the Scioto and that many Delawares were moving up the Allegheny towards the Seneca habitat: also that the Western Delawares would be willing to make peace with the English if the latter would send a sufficiently strong expedition to capture Fort Duquesne. The year, 1758, saw both these things accomplished.

CHAPTER XVI

Post's Peace Missions—Grand Council at Easton

(1758)

MAJOR-General James Abercrombie having been appointed commander-in-chief of all the British forces in America, three expeditions were planned for the year 1758. (1) Generals Amherst and Wolf were to join with Admiral Boscawen's fleet for the recapture of Louisburg. (2) General Abercrombie, with Lord Howe as real leader, was to move against Ticonderoga and Crown Point. (3) Brigadier-General John Forbes was placed in command of an expedition against Fort Duquesne. We shall not discuss the first two expeditions in this history, but shall treat the expedition of General Forbes in the following chapter. In the meantime, while Forbes' forces were assembling and later marching over the mountains against Fort Duquesne, other important events were taking place, which claim our attention in the present chapter.

Post's Missions to Teedyuscung

Teedyuscung came to Philadelphia on March 13th, 1758, and advised Governor Denny and the Provincial Council that, in compliance with his promise at the third Easton conference of July and August, 1757, he had given the "Big Peace Halloo," and had secured the alliance of eight nations of the Western Indians, who had taken hold of the peace belt, in addition of the ten for whom he had spoken at the Easton treaty. Among these eight nations were the Ottawas, Twightwees and Chippewas. The calumet which these new allies sent to Teedyuscung was smoked by Teedyuscung, the Governor, and members of the Provincial Council and Assembly during the councils which followed Teedyuscung's arrival.

During the conferences that attended the above visit of Teedyuscung to the Governor and Provincial Council, the old chief urged that the Provincial Authorities should not neglect the opportunity to do everything possible to strengthen the alliance with the eight western nations who had agreed to his peace proposal. He urged that a messenger should be sent to his friends on the Ohio, warning them to sever their allegiance with the French. He said: "I have received every encouragement from the Indian nations. Now, brother, press on with all your might in promoting the good work we are engaged in. Let us beg the God that made us to bless our endeavours, and I am sure if you assert yourselves, God will grant a blessing, and we shall live."

Governor Denny then, on March 24th, instructed Teedyuscung to see that the peace belt and calumet pipe were carried to the Western Indians, especially the Delawares and Shawnees on the Ohio. Teedyuscung then appointed five Indians, led by his son, Hans Jacob, to carry the peace message to the Ohio.

At this time, the Cherokees were coming to join the expedition of General Forbes against Fort Duquesne, much to the displeasure of the friendly Delawares and Shawnees; and Teedyuscung, during the above conferences, requested that a messenger be sent to stop these Southern Indians from coming further. (Pa. Col. Rec., Vol. 8, pages 29 to 56.) The friendly Shawnee chief, Paxinosa, of Wyoming, was especially wrought up over the presence of the Cherokees at Carlisle, Fort Littleton and other places, and threatened to leave Wyoming and join the French on the Ohio. Finally, on account of his fear of the Cherokees and Catawbas, he left for the Ohio early in May, saying he was going back to "Ohio where he was born."

Fearing that the peace efforts would be frustrated by the actions of the wise and able Paxinosa, the Governor and General Forbes decided to send the Moravian missionary, Christian Frederick Post, on a mission to Wyoming to explain the situation concerning the Cherokees, and to request the Indians on the Susquehanna to call all friendly Indians east of the mountains while the General advanced against Fort Duquesne. Post and Charles Thompson left Philadelphia on June 7th, and arrived at Bethlehem on the following day, having engaged the friendly Delaware chief, Moses Tatemy, and the Moravian Delaware, Isaac Still, on the way, to accompany them to Wyoming. At Bethlehem, they engaged three other friendly Indians to accompany them. From that place they went to the Nescopeck Mountains, about fifteen miles from Wyoming, where they met a party of nine Indians on their way to Bethlehem, who warned them not to go to Wyoming, as the woods were full of strange Indians. It was then decided to go back to the east side of the mountain, and to send two messengers forward to invite Teedyuscung to meet them. The next day Teedyuscung came from his residence at Wyoming. Post complained to him that the path to Wyoming was closed, and that it was his (Teedyuscung's) business to keep it open. The Delaware "King" replied that the road had been closed by the Six Nations, explaining that a war party of about two hundred Senecas had recently passed through several towns on the Susquehanna to attack some Virginians who had treacherously killed a party of Senecas three years previously, as they were going against the Catawbas.

Post gained much valuable information from Teedyuscung as to the situation among the Indians on the Ohio. The old chief told him that his son, Hans Jacob, one of the five messengers he had sent to carry the peace message to the Ohio, had killed a French soldier a short distance from Fort Duquesne; that the commander of this fort then called the Senecas of the Ohio together, and told them the Catawbas had killed the soldier, whereupon the Senecas told the commander that the Delawares committed this deed; and that a heated argument then took place between the commander and the Senecas, in which the leader of the Senecas told the commander that "the English are coming up, and as soon as they strike you on the one side, I will strike you on the other." Many other reports from the Ohio were made to Post by Teedyuscung tending to show that the time was ripe for authoritative peace overtures to be made by Pennsylvania to the Indian allies of the French on the Ohio. Post and Thompson then returned to Philadelphia, on June 16th, and delivered the report of their journey. (Pa. Archives, Vol. 3, pages 412 to 422.)

On June 20th, a peace message and accompanying belts from the Cherokees to the Eastern Delawares were delivered to Governor Denny. This message, coming from two of the principal chiefs of the Cherokees, assured the friendly Delawares that the Cherokees had no intention of harming the friendly Delawares or any other Indians in alliance with the English. It also contained the request that the Eastern Delawares should cause all friendly members of their tribe on the Ohio to come east of the mountains, so as not to be in danger of being harmed by the Cherokees in attacking the Indian allies of the French. (Pa. Col. Rec., Vol. 8, pages 135, 136.)

Governor Denny deemed the peace message from the Cherokees

so important that he decided to send the same at once to Teedyuscung at Wyoming. Post was the messenger selected for this purpose, who set out for Wyoming over the same course that he had recently traveled, at which place he arrived on June 27th, and delivered the message to Teedyuscung. At Wyoming, Post met a number of chiefs from the Allegheny, to whom he explained all about the peace measures that were under way. An old sachem from the Allegheny, named Katuaikund, upon hearing the good news, "lifting up his hands to heaven wished that God would have mercy upon them, and would help them to bring them and the English together again, and to establish an everlasting ground foundation for peace among them. He wished further that God would move the Governor and the people's hearts toward them in love, peace, and union. . . He said further that it would be well if the Governor sent somebody with them at their return home, for it would be of great consequence to them who lived above Allegheny to hear from the Governor's mind from their own mouths." At Wyoming, Post learned that the garrison at Fort Duquesne consisted of about eleven hundred French, almost starved, who would have abandoned the fort, had not the Mohawks sent them assistance, and that the commander had recently said that, "if the English come too strong upon me, I will leave." Two of the messengers who had come from the Allegheny with news concerning the situation of the French, were Keekyuscung and Pisquetomen, the latter a brother of Shingas and King Beaver. (Pa. Col. Rec., Vol. 8, pages 142 to 145.)

Post's First Mission to the Western Delawares

Post then returned to Fort Allen (Weissport) on June 30th accompanied by fifty Indians. After the Governor heard his report and had talked with Pisquetomen and Keekyuscung, it was decided to send these two Indians to the Ohio, in order to gain information as to the situation among the Indians there, and to advise them of the peace measures. Post was requested to accompany these messengers, and he agreed to do so, if Charles Thomson were permitted to go with him. The Governor replied that "he might take any other person." Post then left Philadelphia on July 15th, reaching Bethlehem on the 17th, at which place he made preparations for his journey to the Ohio. On the 19th he reached Fort Allen (Weissport), where Teedyuscung tried to dissuade him from going on his dangerous mission. Post says:

"He [Teedyuscung] was afraid I should never return, that the Indians would kill me." Post replied to Teedyuscung that he was obliged to go, even if he should lose his life. On the 22nd, when Post again prepared to set out, Teedyuscung again protested saying that he was afraid that the Indians would kill Post, or that the French would capture him. Post then made the final reply to Teedyuscung that he would go on this peace mission to the Ohio, even if he died in the undertaking, and that, if, unhappily, he should die before completing the mission, he hoped that his death would be the means of saving many hundreds of lives. Without further delay, he therefore set forth on his first mission to the Ohio, accompanied by Pisquetomen, Keekyuscung and Shamokin Daniel.

Before narrating Post's mission to the Western Delawares, we call attention, at this point, to the fact that no more suitable person could have been found in all the colonies for carrying the peace proposal to these Indians than the gentle and honest Moravian missionary. Weiser's influence was waning. He was an Iroquois at heart; Teedyuscung disliked him; he was a Colonel in the armed forces of the Province. Most of the Delawares and Shawnees disliked him. For these reasons, he was not the proper person to send on this important mission. Nor would George Croghan have been the proper person, at the time of which we are writing. He was a trader, bent on personal gain. But Post was not a military man. He had no selfish interest, and the Delawares knew this. Born in Germany, he came to America and labored as a Moravian missionary among the Delawares, being located for some time at Wyoming. He knew Shingas, King Beaver and all the important Delaware chiefs. The Delawares loved and trusted him. For years he had lived among them in all the intimacy of friends and companions. His first wife, Rachel, was a Delaware convert, whom he married in 1743, and who died at Bethlehem in 1747. In 1749, he chose as his second wife, Agnes, a dusky Daughter of the Delawares, who was baptized by Bishop Cammerhof on March 5th of that year and who died at Bethlehem in 1751. So that, in dealing with Post, the Delawares looked upon him as one of their own flesh and blood.

We shall now follow Post on his journey to the Western Delawares. He arrived at Fort Augusta at Sunbury, on July 25th, having passed many devastated and deserted plantations on the way. From this point, he followed the trail the Delawares used in their first migration from the region of Sunbury to the Allegheny, mentioned in Chapter II, as far as a point near the town of Punxsutawney in the southern part of Jefferson County. Here the trail branched, one branch leading in a north-western direction across Jefferson, Clarion and Venango Counties to Venango (Franklin), at which place he arrived on August 7th. The next morning, while hunting his horses, he passed within ten yards of Fort Machault. He then set out for Kuskuskies, but proceeded too far to the southward, and on the 10th, his party met a renegade English trader and an Indian, who told them they were then within twenty miles of Fort Duquesne. Thus having lost their way, they spent almost two days in trying to find the right trail to Kuskuskies. Reaching an Indian town on Conoqueness-ing Creek, about fifteen miles from Kuskuskies, Post sent Pisquetomen on ahead to let the chiefs know that he was coming with a message from the Governor and people of Pennsylvania and the King of England. Shortly after Pisquetomen left, Post met some Shawnees, who formerly lived at Wyoming. They recognized him and treated him very kindly.

Arriving at Kuskuskies that same day (August 12th), Post was kindly welcomed by King Beaver, and ten other chiefs saluted him. They had long conversations with Post around the council fire until midnight. Post was now among the leaders of the bloody raids into the Pennsylvania settlements—King Beaver, Keckenepaulin and Shingas, the last of whom was the terror of the frontier, for whose head Governor Denny, in 1756, set a price of two hundred pounds. Other chiefs with whom Post held councils at Kuskuskies until August 20th, were Delaware George, who was his former disciple at the Moravian mission, and Killbuck. He made known to all the chiefs the peace between Pennsylvania and the Eastern Delawares brought about at the treaty with Teedyuscung at Easton. After one of the councils, lasting far into the night, Delaware George was unable to sleep, so affected was he by the peace message of his former teacher and mentor. A French Captain and fifteen soldiers came to Kuskuskies to build houses for the Indians, and they used every art to get possession of Post, but to no avail. Even the bloody Shingas loved the gentle Moravian, and protected him.

On August 20th, Post, accompanied by twenty-five horsemen and fifteen footmen, went to Sauconk at the mouth of the Beaver. Here he was not well received, being surrounded by Indians with drawn knives. Finally recognizing a few and talking with them, their manner suddenly changed. Post went from here to Logstown, at which place he arrived on the evening of August 23d. Here he met many English captives, and was permitted to shake hands with them—a thing he was not permitted to do at Kuskuskies where he saw Marie le Roy and Barbara Leininger, as well as other English captives. Leaving Logstown on August 25th, Post's party arrived on the right bank of the Allegheny, just opposite Fort Duquesne, in the afternoon. Here King Beaver introduced him to the Indians who came over from the fort. All were glad to see him except "an Old deaf Onondaga Indian who rose up and signified his displeasure." He apologized, however, the next day, when some Delaware and Shawnee friends of Post gave him a roll of tobacco.

Post's situation was now most critical. French officers demanded that he be taken to the fort, but his Indian friends would "not suffer him to be blinded and carried into the Fort." The next day, the Indians told him the French had offered a reward for his scalp and that he should "not stir from the Fire." "Accordingly," he says in his journal, "I stuck constantly as close to the fire as if I had been charm'd there." The Indian to whom the French offered a reward for Post's scalp was Shamokin Daniel, one of his own party, and from this time on, Post had much trouble with this Delaware, to whom the French had given a string of wampum "to leave me there."

Here, on August 26th, on the bank of the Allegheny, under the guns of Fort Duquesne, in the presence of French officers, who, with paper and pen, took down every word he spoke, and in the presence of three hundred Indians—Delawares, Shawnees, Mingoes and Ottawas, — this heroic Knight of the Cross, Christian Frederick Post, delivered the peace message of the Governor of Pennsylvania and the King of England to the assembled warriors, and pleaded that they accept the message and withdraw from their allegiance with the French. After he ended his plea for peace, the French held a council with their most devoted Indian allies, at Fort Duquesne, and urged that, inasmuch as the Delawares accompanying Post were wavering in their allegiance and inclining to the English interest, they should all be killed, to which proposal the Ottawas objected and prevented its being carried into execution.

Realizing that it was too dangerous for Post to remain longer so near Fort Duquesne, a party of his Indian friends left with him for Sauconk before daylight, on August 27th, by a different trail than the one over which they had come. They passed through three Shawnee towns on the way, at all of which Post was well received, and arrived at Sauconk in the evening, where he was also gladly welcomed. In the Shawnee towns, Post saw many Indians he became acquainted with at Wyoming.

On August 28th, Post and a party of twenty set out from Sauconk for Kuskuskies. One of the party was Shingas. "On the road," says Post, "Shingas addressed himself to me, and asked if I did not think that, if he came to the English, they would hang him, as they had offered a great reward for his head. He spoke in a very soft and easy manner. I told him that was a great while ago; it was all forgotten and wiped clean away; that the English would receive him very kindly." At this point Shamokin Daniel interrupted, and told Shingas not to believe Post; that the English had hired hundreds of Cherokees to kill the Delawares; and that both he (Daniel) and Post had seen an Indian woman lying dead in the road, murdered by the Cherokees. "D—n you," said Daniel, "why do not you (the English) and the French fight on the sea? You come here only to cheat the poor Indians, and take their land from them." That night Post and his party arrived at Kuskuskies.

Post remained at Kuskuskies until September 7th, holding many councils with Shingas, King Beaver, Pisquetomen, Delaware George and other leaders of the Western Delawares. In these councils, Shingas told him that the English and French were fighting for lands that belonged to neither, but to the Indians, and that this fighting was taking place "in the Land that God has given us." Said this Delaware chief, in a speech as patriotic as ever fell from the lips of Daniel Webster:

"The English intend to destroy us, and take our lands, but the land is ours, and not theirs . . . It is you that have begun the war . . . We love you more than you love us; for, when we take any prisoners from you, we treat them as our own children. We are poor, and we cloathe them as well as we can, though you see our children are as naked as at the first. By this you may see that our hearts are better than yours. . . Why do not you and the French fight in the old country, and on the sea? Why do you come to fight on our land? . . . You want to take the land from us by force, and settle it. The white people think we have no brains in our heads."

Shingas and his associate chiefs "had brains in their heads." They saw through the schemes and plans of both the English and the French. Like all races, primitive and civilized, the Indians had their faults—faults that were increased by the white man's rum and vices—but no close student of Indian history will say that they did not have an intelligence far beyond that of other primitive races. Furthermore, no citizen of old Rome loved his country more than these children of the American forests loved the mountains, the valleys, the streams, the hunting grounds, for which they were fighting and dying—the beautiful and loved region which Shingas described as "the Land that God has given us."

From what Post told them and from what was promised in various conferences to be discussed in a subsequent chapter, the Western Delawares and Shawnees believed that, as soon as the English would succeed in driving the French from the Ohio and Allegheny valleys, they (the English) would withdraw east of the Allegheny Mountains and leave the western lands to the Indian. It was this understanding that caused Shingas, King Beaver, Delaware George and the other chiefs with whom Post held his conferences, to accept the peace message of which he was the bearer.

On September 3d, Post was given a peace belt of eight rows of wampum. It was delivered by King Beaver, Delaware George, Pisquetomen, John Hickman, Killbuck, Keckenepaulin and eight other chiefs, representing the three clans of the Delawares.

On September 4th, two hundred French and Indians came to Kuskuskies on their way to Fort Duquesne. They stayed all night. During the middle of the night, King Beaver's daughter died, "on which," says Post, "a great many guns were fired in the town."

Just before Post left, September 7th, King Beaver and Shingas, referring to the fact that Governor Denny and Teedyuscung had entrusted Post to their brother, Pisquetomen, addressed their brother as follows:

"Brother, you told us that the Governor of Philadelphia and Teedyuscung took this man out of their bosoms, and put him into your bosom, that you should bring him here; and you have brought him here to us; and now we give him into your bosom, to bring him to the same place again, before the Governor; but do not let him quite loose; we shall rejoice when we shall see him here again."

Post and his companions then hastened on their way over the mountains to Eastern Pennsylvania, bearing the peace belt of the Western Delawares. During the night of September 13th, at a point near Punxsutawney, rustling was heard in the bushes near their camp, whereupon Post's Indian companions kept watch, one after another, all the rest of the night. "In the morning," says Post, "I asked them what made them afraid. They said I knew nothing; the French had set a great price on my head; and they knew there was gone out a great scout to lie in wait for me."

Arriving at the Great Island (Lock Haven), on September 19th, Post met a war party of twenty Delawares and Mingoes, returning from the settlements with five prisoners and one scalp. Post informed them where he had been and what he had accomplished, whereupon the warriors said that, if they had known this, they would not have gone to war.

Post arrived at Fort Augusta on September 22nd. At Harris' Ferry, he sent Pisquetomen and Thomas Hickman, a friendly Delaware, on to Philadelphia to deliver the peace belt and message of the Western Delawares, while he went on to see General Forbes, who was then at Raystown (Bedford) with the main part of his army. (Thomas Hickman was brutally murdered by a white man, in the Tuscarora Valley, in 1761.) Pisquetomen and Thomas Hickman went to the "Grand Council," which convened at Easton, on October 8th, described later in this chapter, where the former delivered the peace belt and message, and where Governor Denny prepared a reply to the same, and directed Pisquetomen and Hickman to carry this reply back to the Western Delawares. Then, on October 22nd, just as Pisquetomen and Hickman were leaving, Post arrived at the Council with the news from General Forbes that twelve hundred French and two hundred Indians had attacked his advance guard at Loyalhanning (Ligonier), on October 12th. (Pa. Col. Rec., Vol. 8, pages 187, 188, 212.)

For Post's journal of his mission, see Pa. Archives, Vol. 3, pages 520 to 544.

Post's Second Mission to the Western Delawares

Governor Denny's message in reply to the message and peace belts brought by Post from the Western Delawares, contained assurance of pardon for past hostile acts of these Indians and their allies, upon their agreeing to withdraw from the French allegiance. It also contained a request that the chiefs of the Western Delawares come to Philadelphia for a conference with the Colonial Authorities.

As stated above, Pisquetomen and Thomas Hickman were ready to start from Easton with the Governor's message when Post arrived at the Grand Council at that place, on October 22nd. These messengers were to be accompanied by Togennontawly, a Cayuga chief, the youngest son of Shikellamy, Captain John Bull, William Hays and the Delaware, Isaac Still, the last being a Moravian convert—the first two being appointed by the Six Nations' chiefs and the rest by the Governor.

On October 25th, Post received orders from Governor Denny, at Easton, to go once more to Kuskuskies, carrying the Governor's reply. He left Easton that day, going to Bethlehem, where he prepared for his journey. On the 27th, he arrived at Reading, where he met Captain John Bull, William Hays and the above named Indians, who were to accompany him. At the house of Conrad Weiser, at Reading, he read the Governor's letter of instructions in which he was requested to go on this journey by the same route that the army of General Forbes was following, instead of the route he had followed on his first mission. Pisquetomen and the other Indians were at first unwilling to travel by the route followed by Forbes' army, as it led through the Scotch-Irish settlements in Cumberland and Franklin Counties, where so many atrocities had been committed since the beginning of the war. The Indians feared they might be harmed by the inhabitants of these counties, but finally gave their consent to travel by this route. The party arrived at Carlisle on the evening of October 29th, where the Indians spent the night in a house just outside Fort Lowther. The next day, the party arrived at Shippensburg, where all spent the night in Fort Morris.

While Post and his companions were passing Chambers' Fort, now Chambersburg, on October 31st, some Scotch-Irish settlers, recognizing the Indians, "exclaimed against them in a rash manner." Post had some difficulty in getting his Indian companions through this neighborhood, but reached Fort Littleton the next day, where he and his party remained until November 3d, when they set out for Raystown (Bedford), arriving there that night and remaining there until November 6th. On November 7th, they arrived at Loyalhanning (Ligonier), where they were received by General Forbes, who gave them a message and a belt of wampum for the Western Delawares.

On November 9th, Post and his party left Loyalhanning, escorted by one hundred troops under Captain John Haselet, and went to a fortified place ten miles west, still known as Breastwork Hill, in Unity Township, Westmoreland County, where they spent the night. The next day, after travelling about five miles, Captain Haselet and his company proceeded towards the Ohio by the old trading path, while Post and his party, accompanied by Lieutenant Hays and fourteen troops, went down the Loyalhanna to the Shawnee and Delaware town, called Keckenepaulin's Town, then deserted, located at the mouth of the Loyalhanna and just opposite the town of Saltsburg; thence to Kiskemeneco, or Kiskiminetas Town, also then deserted, located on the south bank of the Kiskiminetas River, about seven miles from its mouth, where they encamped the night of November 11th. Here Captain Hays and his party of fourteen men left Post's party. We shall learn the fate of Captain Hays presently. Leaving Kiskiminetas Town, Post arrived at the Allegheny River on the afternoon of November 12th, at that part of Chartier's Old Town on the east side of the river, the principal part of the town being on the west side. Here he spent the night in this deserted Shawnee town. "The wolves and owls made a great noise in the night," he said. Crossing the Allegheny the next day, Post and his party proceeded through the northern end of Allegheny County, the south-central part of Butler County, and into Lawrence County, to Kuskuskies, consisting, at that time, of four villages whose center was at or near the site of the present city of New Castle.

Post arrived at Kuskuskies on November 16th, where he found only two men, the rest of the warriors being away in the service of the French. On November 17th, Post held a conference with Delaware George, to whom he delivered the wampum and message sent by General Forbes. That evening the Delaware chief, Kechenepaulin, returned to Kuskuskies, and brought the sad news that his party of Indians had attacked the party of Lieutenant Hays, about twelve miles from Fort Duquesne, killing the Lieutenant and four of his soldiers and capturing five others, one of whom, Henry Osten, then at Sauconk, was to be burned at the stake. The Indians attacking Lieutenant Hays and his party, had first attacked the scouting parties of Colonel George Washington and Colonel Hugh Mercer, near Ligonier, on November 12th, and had been repulsed. An account of this skirmish will be given in the following chapter. Post at once sent an Indian to Sauconk with the message that the prisoner, Henry Osten, was one of the party guarding him on his mission of peace, whereupon the prisoner was not burned, but was sent to Kuskuskies, on November 20th, where he ran the gauntlet.

Post says, in his journal, under date of November 17th, that the warriors gave the following explanation as to how the attack on Captain Hays' party took place: That the Indians were on their way to see General Forbes and hold a conference with him, when some French with them "made a division among them;" that the Delaware chief, Kekeuscung, told the others that he would go on and meet the General, if the others would follow him; "but the others would not agree to it; and the French persuaded them to fall upon the English at Loyalhanning; they accordingly did, and as they were driven back, they fell in with that party that guided us, which they did not know. They seemed sorry for it."

The next three days filled the heart of Post with dread. The warriors who had been repulsed at Loyalhanning had returned, "possessed with a murdering spirit." They had a French captain with them, who endeavored to get possession of Post. Post and his companions were warned not to go from the house. Finally in conferences with the French captain, in which he endeavored to get the support of the Indians, they refused to accept his wampum belt, whereupon he "looked pale as death."

On November 22nd, Kittiuskund (Kekeuscung) returned to Kuskuskies with the information that General Forbes was only fifteen miles from Fort Duquesne, and that the French had taken the roofs off the buildings near the fort and placed them around it, so as to be able quickly to set the place on fire rather then let it fall into the hands of the English. On this day, also, some of the Indians told Post that Shamokin Daniel, who accompanied him on his former mission, "had fairly sold me to the French; and the French had been much displeased that the Indians brought me away."

Under date of November 24th, Post wrote in his journal: "We hanged out the English flag in spite of the French; on which our prisoners folded their hands, in hopes that their redemption was nigh; looking up to God, which melted my heart in tears, and prayers to God, to hear their prayers, and change the times, and the situation, which our prisoners are in, and under which they groan."

That day King Beaver returned to Kuskuskies and saluted the heroic peace messenger in a very friendly manner.

Shingas returned on November 25th, whereupon Post called

the chiefs and warriors together, told them of the Grand Council at Easton, delivered the peace belt and strings of wampum, and read the letter of General Forbes. Says Post: "The messages pleased and gave satisfaction to all the hearers except the French captain. He shook his head with bitter grief, and often changed his countenance." On that very day, as we shall see in the following chapter, the English flag was raised above the smouldering ruins of Fort Duquesne.

On November 28th, all the chiefs and warriors at Kuskuskies met in council to frame an answer to the letter of General Forbes and the peace belt and message from Governor Denny. Their deliberations lasted long into the night and the greater part of the next day. The matter that disturbed the chiefs was fear that the English would not withdraw east of the Allegheny Mountains after having driven the French from the valleys of the Ohio and Allegheny. Kittiuskund, one of the principal chiefs, secretly told Post this day:

"That all the nations had jointly agreed to defend their hunting place at Allegheny, and suffer nobody to settle there; and as these Indians are very much inclined to the English interest, so he begged us very much to tell the Governor, General, and all other people not to settle there. And if the English would draw back over the mountain, they would get all the other nations into their interest; but if they staid and settled there, all nations would be against them; and he was afraid it would be a great war, and never come to peace again."

As we have already pointed out and as we shall see further on in this chapter and a subsequent chapter, the reason why the Delawares and their allies, the Shawnees, accepted the peace messages of Governor Denny, carried over the mountains to them by the heroic Moravian missionary, was their belief and understanding that the English would withdraw from the valleys of the Ohio and Allegheny after they had driven the French from this region. We shall also see, in a subsequent chapter, that the failure of the English to keep their many promises to withdraw from this region after the expulsion of the French therefrom, was the prime cause of Pontiac's War—mis-named "Pontiac's Conspiracy."

On November 29th, Post and his party went to Sauconk, accompanied by twenty Indians, arriving there in the evening. Here they met George Croghan and Andrew Montour, who had come to that place from the ruins of Fort Duquesne. The next day Post read the messages of the Governor and General Forbes, this time in the presence of Croghan and Mountour, as well as Shingas, King Beaver and the other Delaware chiefs. Conferences were held here on December 1, at which the Delawares asked Post to come and live among them and to preach to them. On December 2nd, Post, his party, and many chiefs of the Delawares, left Sauconk, and travelled to within eight miles of the ruins of Fort Duquesne, which he now calls Pittsburgh, doubtless having been advised by Croghan of the new name given the place by General Forbes. On their way they passed through several deserted Shawnee towns as well as Logstown. He specifically describes Logstown as follows: "On the east end is a great piece of low land, where the old Logstown used to stand. In the new Logstown the French have built about thirty houses for the Indians. They have a large corn-field on the south side, where the corn stands ungathered."

On December 3d, Post's party reached the Allegheny, opposite Pittsburgh, but were unable to cross the river, being obliged to remain "on that island where I had kept council with the Indians, in the month of August last." This was Killbuck's or Smoky Island. While Post says in the journal of his first mission to the Ohio that the councils of August 26th, were held on the west bank of the Allegheny, it would seem from the above quoted statement in the journal of his second mission that these councils were held on Smoky Island.

Post and his party finally got across the Allegheny on December 4th. Arriving at the ruins of Fort Duquesne, Post learned from Mr. Hays that Colonel Henry Bouquet, whom Forbes had left in command, was much displeased with the answer that Shingas, King Beaver and the other Delaware chiefs had made to the letter of General Forbes—an answer in which they insisted that the English withdraw east of the Allegheny Mountains. Bouquet desired that the chiefs change their answer, but they declined to do so. That afternoon the Delaware chiefs held a council, in which King Beaver said: "We likewise join, and accept the peace offered to us; and we have already answered your messenger what we have to say to the General, that he should go back over the mountains; we have nothing to say to the contrary."

The events now being narrated have such an important bearing on more serious events to follow, when the warriors of Pontiac, Guyasuta and Custaloga rose in savage wrath to drive the English into the sea, that we shall let Post tell in his own words what happened after King Beaver made the statement, above quoted:

"Neither Mr. Croghan nor Andrew Montour would tell Colonel Bouquet the Indians' answer. Then Mr. Croghan, Colonel [John] Armstrong and Colonel Bouquet went into a tent by themselves, and I went upon my business. What they have further agreed to I do not know; but when they had done, I called King Beaver, Shingas and Kekeuscung, and said: 'Brethren, if you have any alteration to make, in answer to the General, concerning leaving this place, you will be pleased to let me know.' They said they would alter nothing. 'We have told them three times to leave the place, and go back; but they insist upon staying here; if, therefore, they will be destroyed by the French and Indians, we cannot help them."

Colonel Bouquet set out for Loyalhanning that day (December 5th.) Under date of December 6th, Post wrote the following in his journal:

"Mr. Croghan told me that the Indians had spoke, upon the same string that I had, to Colonel Bouquet, and altered their mind; and had agreed and desired that 200 men should stay at the fort. I refused to make any alteration in the answer to the General, till I myself did hear it of the Indians; at which Mr. Croghan grew very angry. I told him I had already spoke with the Indians; he said it was a d—d lie; and desired Mr. Hays to enquire of the Indians, and take down in writing what they said. Accordingly, he called them, and asked them if they had altered their speech or spoke to Colonel Bouquet on that string they gave me. Shingas and the other counsellor said they had spoken nothing to Colonel Bouquet on the string they gave me, but what was agreed between the Indians at Kushkushking [Kuskuskies.] They said Mr. Croghan and Henry [Andrew] Montour had not spoke and acted honestly and uprightly; they bid us not to alter the least, and said: 'We have told them three times to go back; but they will not go, insisting upon staying here. Now you will let the Governor, General, and all the people know that our desire is that they should go back, till the other nations have joined in the peace, and then they may come and build a trading house.' Then they repeated what they had said on the 5th instant."

Post left Pittsburgh on December 6th. He arrived at Loyalhanning on December the 8th. He remained here until December 27th, having given General Forbes a report of his mission, in the meantime. On December 14th, he had a long talk with the General, at Loyalhanning. General Forbes also set out from Loyalhanning on December 27th, Post accompanying him as far as Carlisle, at which place they arrived on January 7th, 1759. Post set out on foot from Carlisle, on January 8th, and arrived at Lancaster, on January 10th.

Thus ends the account of the historic missions of Christian Frederick Post to the Western Indians—missions whose importance it would indeed be difficult to overestimate. If Shingas and his associate chiefs had not welcomed the peace message of the gentle Moravian missionary, who can tell how different would have been the result? Would the Anglo-Saxon today have the ascendancy in the Western World? Would America be speaking English today? Logstown and Sauconk were filled with warriors, and in the villages in the valleys of the Tuscarawas and Muskingum were hundreds of others. One word from Shingas or King Beaver, and they would have arisen in savage wrath. But that word was not spoken, because Post, whom they loved and in whom they had confidence, held them silent and kept them from assisting the French, as the army of General Forbes marched over the mountains and through the wilderness to dislodge the French from the beautiful and fertile valleys of the Ohio and Allegheny, and to end the French and Indian War in Pennsylvania. Let us pay due tribute to the memory of Christian Frederick Post. Let us admire his sublime courage. At Pittsburgh, the "Gateway to the West," and at New Castle, there should be monuments proclaiming to future generations the deeds and worth of this honest, courageous and noble character of the early days of Pennsylvania. He was born in 1710, and died at Germantown, on April 29th, 1785. His dust reposes in the "Lower Graveyard" at Germantown.

Post's journal of his second mission to the Western Delawares is published in several historical works, among them being, Thwaites' "Early Western Travels," Vol. 1, pages 234 to 291. George Croghan's journal of November and December, 1758, found in Pa. Archives, Vol. 3, pages 560 to 565, is erroneously attributed to Post.

Kuskuskies

Kuskuskies, or Kuskuski, where Post held the momentous treaty with King Beaver, Shingas and their associate chiefs, was, at that time, a group of four Delaware towns whose center was, as has already been stated, at or near the site of the present city of New Castle, Lawrence County. In the journal of his first mission to this place, Post describes the Indian settlement as follows: "Cuskusking is divided into four towns, each at a distance from the others, and the whole consists of about ninety Houses and two hundred able Warriors."

Delawares of the Wolf and Turkey Clans took up their abode here at least as early as 1742, possibly soon after the founding of the Delaware town of Kittanning. Prior to the coming of the Delawares, however, the Senecas had a village, called Kuskuski, at the junction of the Mahoning and Shenango Rivers and another of the same name on the Shenango at the mouth of Neshannock Creek, both within the limits of the present city of New Castle.

Kuskuskies was a regional term, applied by the Delawares, not only to the four towns mentioned by Post, but to the territory for many miles along the Beaver, the Mahoning, the Shenango and the Neshannock, as General William Irvine pointed out in the report of his exploration of the Donation and Depreciation Lands in Western Pennsylvania, in 1785.

For a comprehensive sketch of Kuskuskies, see Dr. George P. Donehoo's "Indian Villages and Place Names in Pennsylvania," pages 85 to 87.

The Grand Council at Easton

While Christian Frederick Post was on his first mission to the Ohio Indians, Teedyuscung was persuading the Six Nations to send deputies to a fourth grand peace conference at Easton. His purpose was to draw all the Indians into an alliance with the English, and to secure a general and lasting peace. As a preliminary, he had induced the Minisink Indians and a number of Senecas to go to Philadelphia in August and hold a conference with the Governor.

The Grand Council at Easton, known as the Fourth Easton Council, opened on Sunday, October 8, 1758, with more than five hundred Indians in attendance, representing all the tribes of the Six Nations, the Delawares, Conoys, Tuteloes, and Nanticokes. Governor Denny, members of the Provincial Council and Assembly, Governor Bernard, of New Jersey, Commissioners for Indian affairs in New Jersey, Conrad Weiser, George Croghan, and a number of Quakers from Philadelphia, made up the attendance of the whites. Those who acted as interpreters were Conrad Weiser, Isaac Still, Moses Tatemy and Andrew Montour.

Three great land disputes came before this council. The first was the Albany purchase of 1754, which, as we have already seen, caused the Delawares of the West Branch of the Susquehanna and the valleys of the Ohio and Allegheny to go over to the French. To the credit of Conrad Weiser, it must be said that he had all along insisted that this was not a just purchase; that the Indians were deceived, and that the running of the lines had been greatly misrepresented. Furthermore, the Six Nations had declared to Sir William Johnson in 1755, that they would never consent to this sale, pointing out that the West Branch of the Susquehanna was held by them simply in trust as a hunting ground for their cousins, the Delawares. The matter was adjusted at this treaty by Governor Denny, on behalf of the Proprietaries, telling the Six Nations that Conrad Weiser and Richard Peters would deed back to them all of the Albany Purchase west of the summits of the Allegheny Mountains, if the Six Nations would confirm the residue of the purchase. This they agreed to, and the mutual releases were executed October 24th.

The second land dispute taken up at the Grand Council was the complaint of the Munsee Clan of Delawares (Munseys) that their lands in New Jersey had never been purchased. Governor Bernard, of New Jersey, when asked by the Munseys what he should pay for the New Jersey land, offered them eight hundred dollars, saying that it was a very extraordinary offer. The Munseys then asked the Iroquois deputies for their opinion as to the price. The Iroquois replied that the offer was fair and honorable; that if it were their own case, they would cheerfully accept it; but, as there were a great many of the Munseys to share in the purchase money, they would recommend that the Governor add two hundred dollars more. To this Governor Bernard agreed, and so this second great land dispute was settled.

The third land dispute to come before the Grand Council was the old complaints made by Teedyuscung concerning the Walking Purchase. The Six Nations had not met with the Delawares at any public treaty with Pennsylvania since the treaty of 1742, in which Canassatego, as the spokesman of the Six Nations, ordered the Delawares to remove from the bounds of the Walking Purchase. Three questions called for an answer at the Grand Council: (1) Was the Walking Purchase just? (2) Had the Six Nations any right to sell lands on the Delaware? (3) Were the Delawares subject to the Iroquois, or were they independent?

Before taking up the matter of the Walking Purchase, the Iroquois deputies concluded that the first thing to do was to humble Teedyuscung, and break down his influence and standing. The great Delaware had entered this council more humbly than he did the councils of 1756 and 1757, realizing that his bitter enemy, Nickas, a Mohawk chief, was in attendance. George Croghan's Mohawk wife was a daughter of Nickas, according to Charles Thompson and others.

Nickas began the attack on Teedyuscung, designed to break down his influence. Pointing to Teedyuscung, he spoke with great vigor and bitterness. Conrad Weiser was ordered to interpret Nickas' speech, but declined, and desired that Andrew Montour should do it. Weiser clearly saw that the interpretation of his speech would cause great discord, and he planned to have the interpretation postponed until the anger of the Iroquois had time to cool. He therefore advised that the speech be interpreted at a private conference, which was arranged to take place the next morning, October 14th. The next morning came; but there was no conference. Weiser had succeeded in causing more delay to avert the threatening storm. However, on the morning of the 15th, Nickas, at a private conference, said: "Who made Teedyuscung chief of the nations? If he be such a great man, we desire to know who made him so? Perhaps you have, and if this be the case, tell us so. It may be the French have made him so. We want to inquire and know where his greatness arose."

Nickas was followed by Tagashata, chief of the Senecas, who said: "We do not know who made Teedyuscung this great man over ten nations, and I want to know who made him so." Then Assarandonquas, chief of the Onondagas, said: "I never heard before now that Teedyuscung was such a great man, and much less can I tell who made him so. No such thing was ever said in our towns." Then Thomas King, in behalf of the Oneidas, Cayugas, Tuscaroras, Nanticokes, and Conoys, said: "I now tell you we, none of us, know who has made Teedyuscung such a great man. Perhaps the French have, or perhaps you have, or some among you, as you have different governments and are different people. We for our parts entirely disown that he has any authority over us, and we desire to know from whence he derives his authority."

The following day, October 16th, after Conrad Weiser had time to advise Governor Denny and Governor Bernard as to the proper reply to make to these speeches of the Iroquois deputies, Governor Denny advised them that he had never made Teedyuscung a great chief. He further told the deputies that, at the former Easton conferences, Teedyuscung had spoken of the Iroquois as his uncles and superiors; and Governor Bernard also denied making Teedyuscung a great chief, or king. Thus, the skillful guidance of Conrad Weiser, in delaying the outburst of Iroquois anger and in framing the proper speeches for the Governors, smoothed matters over, and prevented the cause of peace from suffering a serious setback.

After the apologies of Governor Denny and Governor Bernard, Teedyuscung arose to speak on his land claims. Said he:

"I did let you know formerly what my grievance was. I told you that from Tohiccon, as far as the Delawares owned, the Proprietaries had wronged me. Then you and I agreed that it should be laid before the King of England, and likewise you told me you would let me know as soon as ever he saw it. You would lay the matter before the King, for you said he was our Father, that he might see what was our differences; for as you and I could not decide it, let him do it. Now let us not alter what you and I have agreed. Now, let me know if King George has decided the matter between you and me. I don't pretend to mention any of my uncles' [Iroquois'] lands. I only mention what we, the Delawares, own, as far as the heads of Delaware. All the lands lying on the waters that fall into the Susquehanna belong to our uncles."

He then took another belt and turned to address the Iroquois, but these proud sachems had, during his speech to Governors Denny and Bernard, noiselessly left the room. Teedyuscung then declined to speak further. The next day, October 17th, the Indians spent in private conferences. On October 18th, after Governor Denny had had a private interview with the Six Nations Teedyuscung came to his headquarters, stating that the Delawares did not claim the land high up on the Delaware, as those belonged to their uncles, the Iroquois, but that the land which he did specifically complain about, was included in the Walking Purchase. Governor Denny avoided giving Teedyuscung a direct reply until he would lay the land dispute before the Six Nations' deputies.

He then explained to the deputies that Pennsylvania had bought land from them which the Delawares claimed, advising that this was a matter which should be settled among themselves. The Six Nations replied that they did not understand the Governor. They said that he had left matters in the dark; that they did not know what lands he meant; that if he meant the lands on the other side of the Blue Mountains, he knew that the Proprietaries had a deed for them (the Purchase of 1749), which ought to be produced and shown to them; that their deeds had their marks, and when they should see them, they would know their marks again. Conrad Weiser then brought the deed. The Iroquois examined it and said: "The land was ours and we can justify it."

Teedyuscung said no more at the Easton conference concerning the Walking Purchase, but he charged the Six Nations with selling his land at Wyoming to the Connecticut interests at the Albany treaty of 1754. In fact, one of the conditions upon which he was willing to make peace was that he and his Delawares be settled at Wyoming, and that a deed be given to them for these lands. Addressing the Iroquois deputies, he said:

"Uncles, you may remember that you placed us at Wyoming and Shamokin, places where Indians have lived before. Now, I hear since that you have sold that land to our brethren, the English, [meaning the Connecticut commissioners]. Let the matter now be cleared up in the presence of our brothers, the English. I sit here as a bird on a bough. I look about and do not know where to go. Let me therefore come down upon the ground and make that my own by a good deed, and I shall then have a home forever; for if you, my uncles, or I, die, our brethren, the English, will say they bought it from you, and so wrong my posterity out of it."

The Oneida chief, Thomas King, promised to lay Teedyuscung's request for the Wyoming lands before the great council of the Six Nations.

It is well to explain, at this point, that Connecticut's claim to the Wyoming Valley had another basis than the irregular purchase made by the Connecticut interests from the Mohawks at the Albany Treaty of 1754. The Wyoming lands were included in the grant of Charles I, of England, to the Plymouth Company, which, in 1631, conveyed them to Connecticut. Then this latter grant was confirmed by Royal Patent from Charles II, in 1662. By a confusing error, Charles II, in making the grant of what is now the State of Pennsylvania, to William Penn, in 1681, included the Wyoming lands in the same. This error caused a bitter controversy between Pennsylvania and Connecticut over the Wyoming lands for about a century.

The Grand Council ended on October 26th. Peace was secured, and through the efforts of Post, the Ohio Indians had been drawn away from the French. For a full account of the Grand Council at Easton, see Pa. Col. Rec., Vol. 8, pages 175 to 223.

While Governor Denny, Teedyuscung and Christian Frederick Post were working for peace and General Forbes was preparing to advance against Fort Duquesne, Indian outrages were committed, which we shall now narrate.

Mary Jemison, White Woman of Genessee

On April 5th, 1758, a band of Indians and Frenchmen from the Ohio attacked the home of Thomas Jemison, near the confluence of Sharp's Run and Conewago Creek in Adams County. On the morning of that day, Jemison's daughter, Mary, aged about fifteen, had returned from an errand to a neighbor's, and a man* took her horse to go to his house after a bag of grain. Her father was busy with chores about the house, her mother was getting breakfast, her two elder brothers were at the barn, while the smaller children of the family and a neighbor woman,† were in the house. Suddenly they were alarmed by the discharge of a number of guns. Opening the door they found the man and the horse lying dead. The Indians then captured Mr. Jemison, his wife, his children, Robert, Matthew, Betsy, and Mary, together with the neighbor woman and her three children, the two brothers in the barn making their escape. The attacking party consisted of six Indians and four Frenchmen. They set out with their prisoners in single file, using a whip when anyone lagged behind. At the end of the second day's march, Mary was separated from her parents. During the night her parents and all the other prisoners, except Mary and a neighbor boy, were cruelly put to death, and their bodies left in the swamps to be devoured by wild beasts. As an Indian took Mary and this little boy by the hand, to lead them from the rest of the prisoners, her mother exclaimed, "Don't cry, Mary—don't cry, my child. God will bless you! Farewell—farewell!" These were the last words she ever heard fall from the lips of her mother. During the next day's march, the unhappy girl had to watch the Indians scrape and dry the scalps of her parents, brothers, sisters, and neighbors. Her mother had an abundance of beautiful, red hair, and she could easily distinguish her scalp from the others,—a sight which remained with her to the end of her days. The neighbor boy was given to the French, and Mary given to two Shawnee squaws, and carried to the Shawnee towns on the Scioto. Here these squaws adopted her, replacing a brother who had been killed during the French and Indian War.

Mary was given the name of Deh-ge-wanus by the squaws, who

*Robert Buck. †Mrs. William Mann.

had lost a beloved brother who had fallen on the field of the slain; and according to Seaver, in his "Life of Mary Jemison," the name means, "a handsome girl," while, according to other authorities, it means "two falling voices" or "two females letting words fall." On the occasion of giving her the Indian name, the squaws, crying bitterly and shedding an abundance of tears, recited the virtues of their brother, ending with the following chant:

"Oh, helpless and wretched, our brother has gone. Well we remember his deeds. The deer he could take on the chase. The panther shrunk back at the sight of his strength. His enemies fell at his feet. He was brave and courageous in war. As the fawn, he was harmless; his friendship was ardent; his temper was gentle; his pity was great. Though he fell on the field of the slain, with glory he fell, and his spirit went up to the land of his fathers in war. Then why do we mourn? With transports of joy, they received him, and fed him, and clothed him, and welcomed him there. Oh, friends, he is happy; then dry up your tears. His spirit has seen our distress, and sent us a helper whom with pleasure we greet. Deh-ge-wanus has come: then let us receive her with joy. She is handsome and pleasant. Oh! she is our sister, and gladly we welcome her here. In the place of our brother she stands in our tribe. With care, we will guard her from trouble; and may she be happy till her spirit shall leave us."

In the autumn of 1759, she was taken to Fort Pitt, when the Shawnees and other western tribes went to that place to make peace with the English. She accompanied them with a light heart, as she believed she would soon be restored to her brothers who had made their escape when she was captured. The English at Fort Pitt asked her a number of questions concerning herself, which so alarmed her adopted Indian sisters that they hastily took her down the Ohio in a canoe. Afterwards she learned that some settlers had come to the fort to take her away, but could not find her.

She married two Indian chiefs of renown. The first was a Delaware named Sheninjee, of whom she spoke as "noble, large in stature, elegant in appearance, generous in conduct, courageous in war, a friend of peace, and a great lover of justice." To this husband she bore two children. The first died soon after birth, but the second, who was born in the fourth year of her captivity, she named in memory of her father, Thomas Jemison. Her first husband died while they were enroute with her child to her new home in the Genesee Valley in New York. Several years after the death of her first husband, she married Hiokatoo, also known as Gardow, by whom she had four daughters and two sons. This second husband was a cruel and vindictive warrior. He was a Seneca, and as early as 1731, was appointed a runner to collect an Iroquois army to go against the Cherokees and Catawbas of the South. The Iroquois army, after a fatiguing march, met its enemies in what was then called "the low, dark and bloody lands," near Clarksville, Montgomery County, Tennessee. In a two days' battle in which the Southern Indians lost twelve hundred warriors, the Iroquois were successful. At Braddock's defeat, he is said to have captured two white prisoners whom he burned to death in a fire of his own kindling. He took part in almost every engagement in the French and Indian War. As will be seen he commanded the Senecas at the capture of Fort Freeland, July 28th, 1779. Seaver, in his "Life of Mary Jemison," says that it was this chief who painted Doctor John Knight on the occasion of Colonel William Crawford's defeat and torture, in June, 1782. Altogether, according to Seaver, Hiokatoo was in seventeen campaigns. He ended his days in November, 1811, at the great age of more than one hundred years.

Two great sorrows came into Mary Jemison's life. The first was when her son, John killed his brother, Thomas, her comforter and namesake of her father. The second was when this same John a few years later killed his other brother, Jesse. Her grief became somewhat assuaged when John was murdered later in a drunken quarrel with two Indians.

Mary Jemison continued to live in the Gardeau Flats, New York, and upon the death of her second husband, she became possessed of a large tract of valuable land. She was naturalized April 19, 1817, and received a clear title to her land. In 1823, she sold a major portion of her holdings, reserving a tract two miles long and one mile wide.

This remarkable lady who preserved the sensibilities of a white woman amidst the surroundings of barbaric life, died September 19, 1833, at the age of ninety-one years, and was buried, with Christian rites, in the cemetery of the Seneca Mission on the Buffalo Creek Reservation, in New York. On March 17, 1874, her body was removed to the Indian Council House Grounds at Letchworth Park, where a beautiful bronze statue marks the grave of "The White Woman of the Genesee."

We close this sketch with the following appropriate quotation

STATUE OF MARY JEMISON

"The White Woman of the Genessee," erected near the Jesuit Mission in Buchanan Valley, Adams County, Pennsylvania.

from page 421 of the twenty-second edition of Seaver's "Life of Mary Jemison":

"From all history and tradition, it would appear that neither seduction, prostitution, nor rape, was known in the calendar of crimes of this rude, savage race, until the females were contaminated by the embrace of civilized men. And it is a remarkable fact that, among the great number of women and girls who have been taken prisoners by the Indians during the last two centuries, although they have often been tomahawked and scalped, their bodies ripped open while alive, and otherwise barbarously tortured, not a single instance is on record, or has ever found currency in the great stock of gossip and story which civilized society is so prone to circulate, that a female prisoner has ever been ill-treated, abused, or her modesty insulted, by an Indian, with reference to her sex."

Capture of the Family of Richard Bard (Baird)

On the morning of April 13th, 1758, the family of Richard Bard (Baird) was captured by a band of nineteen Delawares from the Ohio. The family resided near a place since known as Marshall's Mills, in Adams County. On their way to the Bard home, the Indians captured Samuel Hunter and Daniel McManiny, who were working in a field near the home; also a boy named William White, who was coming to a mill near Bard's home.

In the Bard home, at the time of the attack, were Richard Bard; his wife Katherine; his infant son, John; Frederick Ferrick, his servant, about fourteen years old; Hannah McBride, eleven years old; and Lieutenant Thomas Potter, a brother of General James Potter. One of the Indians attacked Lieutenant Potter with a cutlass, but he succeeded in wresting it from the savage. Mr. Bard seized a pistol and snapped it at the breast of one of the Indians, but it failed to fire. As there was no ammunition in the home, the occupants of the house, fearing a slaughter or being burned alive, surrendered, as the Indians promised no harm would be done to them. The savages then went into the field nearby, where they captured Samuel Hunter, Daniel McManiny, and a boy named William White, who was coming to a mill near the Bard home.

The Indians then secured the prisoners, plundered the house, and burned the mill. At a point about seventy rods from the home, contrary to their promises, they killed Lieutenant Potter, and having proceeded over the mountain for several miles, one of them sunk the spear of his tomahawk into the breast of the child, and scalped it. When they had proceeded with their prisoners past the fort into Path Valley, they encamped for the night. The next day they discovered a party of settlers in pursuit. They then hastened the pace of their prisoners under threat of tomahawking them. Reaching the top of Tuscarora Mountain, the party sat down to rest, and one of the Indians, without giving any warning whatever, buried his tomahawk in the head of Samuel Hunter, and scalped him. They then passed over Sidling Hill and the Allegheny Mountains by Blair's Gap, and encamped beyond Stony Creek. Here they painted Bard's head red on one side, indicating that a council had been held; that an equal number were for killing him and for saving his life, and that his fate would be determined in the next council.

Bard then determined to attempt his escape and, while assisting his wife in plucking a turkey, he told her of his intentions. Some of the Indians were asleep, and one was amusing the others by parading around in Mrs. Bard's gown. As this Indian was thus furnishing amusement for the others, Bard was sent to the spring for water, and made his escape. After having made an unsuccessful search for Bard, the party proceeded to Fort Duquesne and then to Kuskuskies, where Mrs. Bard, the two boys and the girl were compelled to run the gauntlet, and were beaten in a most inhuman manner. Here also Daniel McManiny was put to death by being tied to a post, scalped alive, and pierced through the body with a red-hotgun barrel.

Mrs. Bard was separated from the other prisoners, led from one Indian town to another, and finally adopted by two warriors, to take the place of a deceased sister. Finally she was taken to the headwaters of the Susquehanna, and during the journey, suffered greatly from fatigue and illness. She lay for two months, a blanket her only covering and boiled corn her only food. She remained in captivity two years and five months.

Mr. Bard, after having made his escape and after a terrible journey of nine days, during which his only food was a few buds and four snakes, finally reached Fort Littleton, Fulton County. After this, he wandered from place to place throughout the frontier, seeking information concerning his wife. After having made several perilous journeys to Fort Duquesne for the same purpose, and in which he narrowly escaped capture on several occasions, he finally learned that she was at Fort Augusta (Sunbury), where he redeemed her.

During Mrs. Bard's captivity, she was kindly treated by the warriors who had adopted her. Before the Bards left Fort Augusta, Mr. Bard requested one of his wife's adopted brothers to visit them at their home. This he did some time afterwards, when the Bards were living about ten miles from Chambersburg, remaining at the Bard home for some time; but finally he went one day to McCormack's Tavern, where he became intoxicated and got into a quarrel with a rough frontier character by the name of Newgen, who stabbed him dangerously in the neck. Newgen fled from the vicinity in order to escape the wrath of Bard's neighbors. The wounded Indian, however, recovered after being tenderly nursed by his adopted sister, Mrs. Bard. He then returned to his people, who put him to death on the pretext of having, as they claimed, joined the white people.

For account of the capture and escape of Richard Bard, see his affidavit in Pa. Archives, Vol. 3, pages 396 and 397.

Other Atrocities in 1758

Other atrocities than the attacks on the Jemison and Bard families, were committed in Eastern Pennsylvania in the month of April, 1758. A man, named Lebenguth, and his wife were killed in the Tulpehocken Valley. Also, at Northkill, Nicholas Geiger's wife and two children and Michael Ditzelar's wife were killed.

On May 21st, 1758, Joseph Gallady was killed by Indians, and his wife and one child were taken captive, in Franklin County. On June 18th, Adam Read wrote from his home on the Swatara to Edward Shippen that, as Leonard Long was riding along the road about a mile from Read's house, he was killed and scalped. Read and some other men found the body lying in the road bleeding, but could not track the murderers. The son of Jacob Snabele was murdered not far from Fort Henry, on June 19th. (Pa. Archives, Vol. 3, page 426.)

On the morning of June 19th, 1758, occurred the attack on the home of John Frantz, about six miles from Fort Henry, Berks County. Captain Christian Busse, in a letter written on the day of the event to Conrad Weiser, and recorded in Pa. Archives, Vol. 3, page 425, says that Mrs. Frantz and three children were captured. It seems, however, that before Mrs. Frantz was taken far, she was killed by her captors. The "Frontier Forts of Pennsylvania," following closely an account of the tragedy appearing in the Pennsylvania *Gazette* of June, 1758, contains the following in regard to this atrocity:

"At the time this murder was committed, Mr. Frantz was out at work. His neighbors, having heard the firing of guns by the Indians, immediately repaired to the house of Frantz. On their way they apprised him of the report. When they arrived at the house, they found Mrs. Frantz dead (having been killed by the Indians because she was rather infirm and sickly, and so unable to travel), and all the children gone. They then pursued the Indians some distance, but all in vain. The children were taken and kept captives for several years.

"A few years after this horrible affair, all of them, except one, the youngest, were exchanged. The oldest of them, a lad of twelve or thirteen years of age, at the time when captured, related the tragical scene of his mother being tomahawked and shamefully treated. Him they compelled to carry the youngest.

"The anxious father, having received two of his children as from the dead, still sighed for the one that was lost. Whenever he heard of children being exchanged, he mounted his horse to see whether, among the captured, was not his dear little one. On one occasion he paid a man forty pounds to restore his child, who had reported that he knew where it was. To another he paid a hundred dollars, and himself went to Canada in search of the lost one—but, to his sorrow, never could trace his child. A parent can realize his feelings—they cannot be described."

The Mohawks, being inclined to side with the French, formed a large party, in June, 1758, to attack the Minisink settlement in Monroe County. Teedyuscung endeavored to dissuade them, but was not entirely successful. Two men were killed and scalped and another wounded in the vicinity of Fort Hamilton. Also a fort, located at the upper end of the Minisink region, was captured. Samuel Dupui, in a letter written from Smithfield on the night of June 15th, says that this band of Indians consisted of about forty in number, and that the men of "that Garrison were Farmers, and were out on their plantations when the Indians fired on them and killed them, whereupon the Indians marched up to the Fort, and took all the women and children captive." Also, in August, 1758, a party of Mohawks and a French Captain reached Tioga with the intention of making war on the English. The friendly Delawares at that place persuaded some of the

Mohawks to turn back, but ten of them and the French Captain proceeded apparently in the direction of the Minisink region, whereupon Teedyuscung sent word to Governor Denny of this fact, and messengers were sent to warn the Minisink settlers. In his message, which was delivered on August 9th, by the friendly Delawares, Zacheus and Jonathan, Teedyuscung said: "I consider the English our Brethren, and we have but one Ear, one Mouth, one Eye; you may be sure I shall apprize them of every motion of the Enemy." (Penna. Archives, Vol. 3, pages 424 and 509.)

In fact, from the time Canachquasy persuaded him to "bury the hatchet," Teedyuscung worked steadfastly for peace, and insisted from time to time that a strong fort be built at Wyoming. However, he was unable to remain neutral, and he petitioned the Governor for reward on scalps, believing that if the white man could enjoy the profits of such a bounty, there was no reason why the Indians friendly to the Province should not come in for their share. He even sent friendly Indians to protect the frontiers. When Will Sock, a Conestoga, had been over the country carrying a French flag, and had murdered Chagrea and a German in Lancaster County, Teedyuscung took away the flag, sent it to Philadelphia, and gave him an English flag. In the meantime, also, he kept urging the Provincial authorities to build houses for the friendly Indians at Wyoming, in accordance with Pennsylvania's promise at the Easton conference of 1757 to enact a law which would settle the Wyoming lands upon him and his people forever.

Death of Scarouady

We are now ready to describe General Forbes' march against and capture of Fort Duquesne; but before doing so, we call attention to the fact that the summer of 1758 marked the passing of the wise and able Scarouady. The date of his death is not known, but it was prior to August 26th, 1758, on which day several Mohawks came to Philadelphia from the territory of the Six Nations, bringing with them Scarouady's wife and all her children. She presented Governor Denny with "her husband's calumet pipe, and desired that he and the Indians might smoke it together; she intended to have gone into the Cherokee country, but had altered her mind, and would stay here with her children." Probably the old chief lost his life in one of Johnson's expeditions in New York.

It is with sincere regret that we take leave of Scarouady, an admirable character, a forceful orator, the leading speaker at many important conferences, the wise counselor, the strong enemy of the French, the firm friend of the English. Far past the prime of life when he first appears upon the scene, his aged shoulders bore a mighty burden to the end of his eventful career.

CHAPTER XVII

General Forbes' Expedition Against Fort Duquesne

(1758)

AS stated at the beginning of Chapter XVI, when the powerful hand of William Pitt took hold of the helm of the British Ship of State, three expeditions were planned for gaining possession of the territory claimed by the French, in America, one of these expeditions being against Fort Duquesne. On the same day on which General Abercrombie was appointed to succeed Lord Loudon, as commander-in-chief of the British forces in America, Brigadier-General John Forbes was appointed commander of the Southern District, including Pennsylvania, Virginia Maryland and the Carolinas. A large volume could be written on General Forbes' expedition against Fort Duquesne, but, in the limits of this history, it is possible to give only the main facts.

In the first place, let us take a view of the forces making up the army of General Forbes. Probably as accurate a list of these forces as has ever been given is the following from Lowdermilk's "History of Cumberland":

Name of Corps	Field Officers	Co. Officers	Total	
Division of 1st Battalion of Royal Americans	1	12	363	
Highland, or 62d Regiment	3	37	998	1,267
Division of 62d Regiment	3	12	269	
1st Virginia Regiment	3	32	782	1,484
2nd Virginia Regiment	3	35	702	
3rd North Carolina Companies	1	10	141	
4th Maryland Companies	1	15	270	
1st Battalion Pennsylvania	3	41	755	
2nd Battalion Pennsylvania	3	40	666	2,192
3rd Battalion Pennsylvania	3	46	771	
Three Lower Counties (Delaware)	3	46	263	
Total			5,980	

Detachments on the frontiers of Pennsylvania and the road of communication:

	Major	Captains	Subalterns	Total
From the Pennsylvania Regiments	1	10	17	563
From North Carolina Regiments	1	3	61	624

As indicated in the list of Forbes' forces, part of his army was composed of "Royal Americans." This was the name given to a force to consist of four battalions of one thousand men each—a force neither strictly British nor strictly Colonial, the men being recruited in the Colonies and the officers being comissioned by the King of England. The men were composed largely of Pennsylvania-Germans and other non-English speaking inhabitants of the Colonies. The law creating this force provided that fifty of the commissioned officers might be chosen from among Protestant foreign officers of ability and experience.

At this point, it will be well to state a few facts about the most noted officer of the Royal Americans, Colonel Henry Bouquet, commander of the first battalion. He was born at Rolle, in the Canton of Vaud, Switzerland, about 1719. Having had much experience in the regiment of Constance and in the service of the King of Sardinia, in whose wars he distinguished himself, he, in 1748, entered the Swiss Guards as Lieutenant-Colonel. When war broke out between England and France, in 1754, he entered the service of the British, and was sent to America, where he became the most distinguished and successful soldier of foreign birth, in Indian warfare. In the latter part of 1757, he was in South Carolina with four companies of Royal Americans, and on February 14th, 1758, was ordered to New York by General Forbes, at which place he landed on April 15th, with four companies of his Royal Americans and some Virginia troops. He then came to Philadelphia, and at once took an active part in the preparations for the advance against Fort Duquesne. In fact, he led the advance, and, on account of the physical weakness of General Forbes, who became seriously ill upon his arrival at Philadelphia, in April, most of the work of carrying out his plans of campaign devolved upon Colonel Bouquet. Not only was Colonel Bouquet an able and energetic soldier, but he was a scholar, as well, speaking and writing good French, German and English. In fact, he wrote better English than most British officers of his time. He was fond of the society of men of science. At the close of the Pontiac and Guyasuta War, he was made Brigadier-General and commandant in the Southern Colonies of British America, leaving New York for Pensacola, on April 10th, 1765. His new honors were not long enjoyed, as he died of yellow fever at Pensacola, in the summer of 1765, "lamented by his friends and regretted universally." He sleeps in an unknown grave in the summer land of our country.

For this expedition, Pennsylvania equipped twenty-seven hundred troops, but some of the companies were assigned to garrisoning Fort Augusta and other posts. The three Pennsylvania battalions, called a regiment, set forth in the above list, had, as their general officers Brevet Lieutenant-Colonel Joseph Shippen; Commissary of the Musters and Paymaster, James Young; Surgeon, Dr. Bond; Chaplain, Rev. Thomas Barton; Wagon Master, Robert Irwin; and Deputy Wagon Master, Mordecai Thompson.

The first battalion was commanded by Lieutenant-Colonel John Armstrong, of Kittanning expedition fame. Under him were Lieutenant-Colonel Hance Hamilton; Major Jacob Orndt, who was assigned to garrison duty; Surgeon Blain; Chaplain, Rev. Charles Beatty; Adjutant, John Philip de Hass; and Quartermaster, Thomas Smallman. Among the Captains in this battalion were: Samuel Allen, James Potter, Jacob Snaidor, George Armstrong, Edward Ward, Robert Callender, John Nicholas Wetterhold, William Lyon, Patrick Davis, Charles Garraway, William Armstrong, Richard Walter, John McKnight and David Hunter.

The second battalion was commanded by Colonel James Burd. Under him were Lieutenant-Colonel Thomas Lloyd; Major David Jamison; Surgeon, John Morgan; Chaplain, Rev. John Steel; Adjutant, Jacob Kern; Quartermaster Asher Clayton; and Commissary Peter Bard. Among the Captains of the second battalion were: Christian Busse, Joseph Scott, Samuel J. Atlee, William Patterson, William Reynolds, Levi Trump, Jacob Morgan, Samuel Weiser (son of Conrad Weiser), Alexander McKee, John Byers, John Haslett, John Singleton and Robert Eastburn.

The third battalion was commanded by Colonel Hugh Mercer. Under him were Lieutenant-Colonel Patrick Work; Major George Armstrong; Surgeon, Robert Bines; Chaplain, Rev. Andrew Bay; Adjutant, James Ewing; Quartermaster, Thomas Hutchins; and Sergeant-Major Samuel Culbertson. Among the captains of the third battalion were: Robert Boyd, John Blackwood, James Sharp, Adam Read, Samuel Nelson, John Montgomery, George Aston, Charles McClung, Robert McPherson, Paul Jackson, John Bull, William Biles, Archibald McGrew, Thomas Hamilton, Ludowick Stone, John Clark, John Allison, Job Rushton, Thomas Smith, Alexander Graydon, James Hyndshaw, William Biles and Thomas Armour.

The list of the officers of these three Pennsylvania Battalions is found in Pa. Archives, Fifth Series, Vol. 1, pages 178 to 185.

The Southern troops were commanded by Colonel George Washington, Colonel Byrd, Colonel Stephens, Major Lewis and others. They assembled, first at Winchester, Virginia, and then at Cumberland, Maryland.

Like Braddock, General Forbes had Indian allies—Cherokees and Catawbas. Like Braddock, also, nearly all of his Indian allies left him before he came near Fort Duquesne. Edmund Atkins, who, as was seen in a former chapter, was superintendent of Indian affairs for the southern provinces, being a member of the Council in South Carolina, had succeeded in procuring the Cherokees and Catawbas. As Forbes was advancing towards Fort Duquesne, many of these Indians went to the Ohio above and below the fort, in order to "annoy the enemy, get intelligence, and bring away prisoners." By the middle of May there were more than seven hundred of these Southern Indians in Forbes' service. However, it was necessary to give them presents almost constantly to keep them scouting. Six thousand pounds were spent to keep them out scouting. They gradually left the service, sighing for their southern homes. When July came, they had all gone home except about two hundred. By the first of September, all were gone home except about eighty; and, on October 27th, General Forbes wrote from "Camp at Top of Alleganey Mountains": "The Cherokee and other Southern Indians who came last winter and so early in the Spring to join us, after having by every Art they were Masters off, gott everything they could expect from us, left us without any remorse when they found they were not likely to get any more presents for retaining them, so that I have now left with me above fifty, and am now on my march to the Ohio, as the season will not admitt of one Moment's delay."

The Route Followed by General Forbes

Having taken this brief view of the forces, white and red, making up General Forbes' expedition, we shall now take a view of the route over which his army advanced against Fort Duquesne. On March 28th, 1758, the General wrote Governor William Denny from New York, giving directions for raising troops in Pennsylvania, and also saying: "I propose assembling the Regular Troops and those of Pennsylvania, at Conegochie

[Conococheague—the mouth of the creek of this name at Williamsport, Maryland], about the 20th of April." (Pa. Col. Rec., Vol. 8, pages 59, 60.) In making the mouth of the Conococheague the rendezvous and base of supplies for the Pennsylvania forces, he did so at the suggestion of Sir John St. Clair, his Quartermaster-General, who had held this same position in Braddock's army, and no doubt expected that Forbes would advance against Fort Duquesne over the same road that Braddock used, making, like Braddock, Fort Cumberland the starting point.

Washington and the other Virginians took it for granted that the Braddock road would be followed by Forbes. However, before the campaign was far advanced, Colonel Bouquet, who, as we have seen, led the advance, hoped to find a better way over the mountains than the Braddock road, and General Forbes shared this hope. Bouquet carefully studied the reports of his scouts and became strongly of the opinion that the route to be followed should start at Fort Loudon, thence to Raystown (Bedford), thence to Loyalhanna (Ligonier), thence to Fort Duquesne; that Fort Loudon should be the real starting point of the expedition and base of supplies, and that the assembling place of the southern troops should be Bedford, where a stockade (Fort Bedford) had been erected by Colonel John Armstrong in 1756. The Pennsylvania officers agreed with Colonel Bouquet. Conferences were held between Bouquet and the Pennsylvania officers, on the one hand, and Washington and the Virginia officers, on the other. An animated controversy soon arose, and continued for many weeks. At one time during the controversy, it was proposed that Washington lead the southern troops over the Braddock road from Fort Cumberland and join the main army on the Monongahela, just before the attack on Fort Duquesne. This proposal was rejected after General Forbes received reports from Colonel Bouquet which set forth the investigations his scouts had made of both routes. From first to last Washington was in favor of the Braddock road. He wrote to Major Peter Halket, one of Forbes' aides:

"I am just returned from a conference held with Colonel Bouquet. I find him fixed—I think I may say unalterably fixed—to lead you a new way to the Ohio through a road every inch of which is to be cut at this advanced season, when we have scarcely time left to tread the beaten track universally confessed to be the best passage through the mountains. If Colonel Bouquet succeeds in this point with the General, all is lost! all is lost, indeed! our enterprise is ruined! and we shall be stopped at the Laurel Hill this winter; but not to gather laurels, except the kind which cover the mountains."

In pressing the claims of the Braddock road, Washington and the other Virginians pointed out that it was nineteen miles shorter than the proposed new road and that it would not require so much work and expense as cutting the new road, overlooking, seemingly, the fact that it was then grown up with sprouts and brush.

Virginia had made the first settlements (the Ohio Company's) in the valley of the Ohio; she had constructed the first road to the Ohio, the Nemacolon Indian trail, which the Ohio Company cleared and widened; she claimed the valley of the Ohio, which Pennsylvania also claimed. Therefore it is fair to assume that Virginia feared her claim to the Ohio Valley would be endangered if a new road, leading directly from the settled parts of Pennsylvania to the Ohio Valley, were opened. Such road would afford easy access to the Ohio Valley for the Pennsylvania traders. The Pennsylvania officers, in urging the claims of the proposed new road, pointed out that it would afford direct communication to the fertile farms of Eastern Pennsylvania, from which food and other supplies for the army could be obtained. They also called attention to the fact that, when Braddock was marching against Fort Duquesne, work was in progress of cutting a road from McDowell's Mill, in Franklin County, to join the Braddock road at Turkey Foot (Confluence), by which supplies, so sorely needed by Braddock's army, could be brought from Eastern Pennsylvania,—a road which Colonel James Burd had completed as far as the summit of the Allegheny Mountains, when Braddock's defeat put an end to its construction.

At length the recommendation of Colonel Bouquet and the Pennsylvania officers was adopted by General Forbes, and as we shall presently see, Bouquet began the work of cutting the new road. The course followed by Forbes' army followed very closely the course of the old Indian trail which ran through Bedford to the "Forks of the Ohio,"—a trail that had been used very much by the Shawnees and Delawares in their migration from the valley of the Susquehanna to the valleys of the Ohio and Allegheny. Christopher Gist had followed this trail from Bedford to the Ohio, in 1750, when exploring for the Ohio Company. The Lincoln Highway follows its general course over the mountains to Pittsburgh today.

The starting point of the "Forbes Road" was Fort Loudon. Part of its course from this place to Bedford was over the road Colonel Burd had cut from McDowell's Mill to the crest of the Allegheny Mountain, in 1755. It (the "Forbes Road") ran from Fort Loudon to Fort Littleton; thence to Sideling Hill; thence to the crossing of the Raystown Branch of the Juniata; thence through Everett to Bedford; thence to Wolfsburg and Schellsburg; thence through Edmund's Swamp; thence near Stoystown, Quemahoning and Jenner; thence over the Laurel Hills to Ligonier; thence over the Chestnut Ridge to Youngstown; thence past old Unity Church to Hannastown; thence across the headwaters of Brush Creek to Murraysville, not, however, passing through the battlefield of Bushy Run, as some historians have stated, but turning to the northwest about four miles east of the battlefield; thence (from Murraysville) to Shannopin's Town, now within the limits of Pittsburgh, on the east bank of the Allegheny, about two miles from its mouth.

The present "Forbes Street," in Pittsburgh, does not mark the course General Forbes followed. After reaching Shannopin's Town, located between the present Penn Avenue and the Allegheny River at about Thirtieth Street, the army advanced along the bank of this river, and not the Monongahela, to the French fort.

For an accurate account of the course of the "Forbes Road," especially its course through the city of Pittsburgh to Fort Duquesne, the reader is referred to Dr. George P. Donehoo's "Pennsylvania—A History," Vol. 2, pages 823, 824, 831 and 832.

The March Over the Mountains

Colonel Bouquet arrived at Bedford early in July, where he enlarged and strengthened the stockade already erected there, in 1756, (Fort Bedford), and constructed entrenchments and palisades. By the first of August, a large part of Bouquet's forces was at work cutting the new road through the mountain forests towards Ligonier. His total forces at that time were about seventeen hundred men. By the sixteenth of August, Bouquet's forces, woodcutters and troops, consisted of thirty-nine hundred men, including two Virginia companies; and fourteen hundred were employed at that time in cutting the new road towards Ligonier, which place they reached about September 1st. (Pa. Archives, Vol. 3, page 510.) The best information as to the time when Bouquet himself reached Ligonier is his letter of September 17th, in which he says: "The day on which I arrived at the camp, which was the 7th [of September], it was reported to me that we were surrounded by parties of Indians, several soldiers having been scalped or made prisoners." (Frontier Forts of Pennsylvania, Vol. 2, pages 254–255.) By that time, all his force had reached that place. Here, on the banks of the Loyalhanna, Bouquet erected Fort Ligonier. He also erected the fortificai on known as Breastwork Hill, on Nine Mile Run, in what is now Unity Township, Westmoreland County, about ten miles west of Ligonier.

The work of cutting, hewing and blasting the road over the main range of the Allegheny Mountains and, particularly, the parallel range of the Laurel Hills to the westward, was prodigious. In many places, the road was cut in the rock on the sides of steep declivities. As far as the eye could reach, the vast and primeval forest covered the mountain ranges and the valleys between. Forbes described the mountain region through which the road was cut as an "immense uninhabited wilderness, overgrown everywhere with trees and brushwood, so that nowhere can one see twenty yards." At the summit of the Allegheny Mountains, not far from the Wilderness Club House, one can see today the most perfectly preserved of the breastworks which Colonel Bouquet erected while cutting this wilderness and mountain road. The earthen embankments can be plainly traced. It was known as McLean's Redoubt.

Washington arrived at Bedford on September 16th, Lieutenant Colonel Stephen, with six companies of Virginia troops, having reached that place previously.

General Forbes arrived in Philadelphia in April, 1758. At the head of the British regulars, he marched from Philadelphia about the last of June to effect a union with the other troops at Bedford. Reaching Carlisle, he was detained for some time on account of his severe illness. In fact, on account of bodily weakness, he was carried in a hurdle between two horses all the way from Carlisle to Fort Duquesne and back to Philadelphia. He reached Bedford about the middle of September, where he met the southern troops under Washington. Forbes' rear division left Bedford on October 23d (Penna. Col. Rec., Vol. 8, pages 224–225); he and his advance troops reached Ligonier about November 1st; but his entire army did not arrive there until about a week later. Christian Frederick Post, an account of whose peace missions to the Western Delawares was given in Chapter XVI, says in his journal that he passed Forbes' artillery on Laurel Hill, on November 7th.

Grant's Defeat

The most disasterous event connected with General Forbes' advance against Fort Duquesne was the defeat of Major James Grant, of the Highlanders, where the Allegheny Court House now stands, in the city of Pittsburgh, on September 14th, 1758. Major Grant, with a force of thirty-seven officers and eight hundred and five privates, was sent from Ligonier by Bouquet to reconnoiter the fort and adjacent country. Grant had begged Bouquet for permission to make this expedition. Grant's instructions were not to approach too near the fort and not to attack it. The wilderness between Ligonier and Fort Duquesne was filled with Indians constantly watching the movements of Grant's little army; yet he succeeded in coming within sight of the fort without being discovered. Late at night he drew up his troops on the brow of the fatal hill in the city of Pittsburgh, which still bears his name.

Not having met with either French or Indians on the march, and believing from the stillness of the enemy's quarters that the forces in the fort were small, Grant at once determined to make an attack. Accordingly, two officers and fifty men were directed to approach the fort and fall upon the French and Indians that might be outside. They saw none and were not challenged by the sentinels; and as they returned, they set fire to a large storehouse, but the fire was extinguished. At the break of day, September 14th, Grant sent Major Andrew Lewis with two hundred regulars and Virginia volunteers to take a position about a half mile back, and lie in ambush where they had left their baggage. Four hundred men were posted along the hill facing the fort, while Captain McDonald's company, with drums beating and bagpipes playing, marched toward the fort in order to draw out the garrison. The music of the drums and bagpipes aroused the garrison from their slumber, and both the French and Indians sallied out in great numbers, the latter probably led by Guyasuta.

The British officers marshalled their men according to European tactics. Major Lewis, at the beginning of the attack, left Captain Bullitt, with fifty Virginians, to guard the baggage, and hastened with the main part of his men to the scene of action. Lewis engaged in a hand-to-hand struggle with an Indian warrior, whom he killed, but was compelled to surrender to a French officer.

The French and Indians separated into three divisions. The first two were sent under the cover of the banks of the Monongahela and Allegheny to surround the main body of Grant's troops, while the third was delayed awhile to give the others time, and then lined up before the fort as if exhibiting the whole strength of the garrison. This plan worked admirably. Captain McDonald was obliged to fall back on the main body, and at the same time, Grant found himself flanked by the detachments on both sides. A desperate struggle ensued. The Highlanders, exposed to the enemy's fire without cover, fell in great numbers. The provincials, concealing themselves among the trees, made a good defense for a while, but not being supported and being overpowered by numbers, were compelled to fall back. The result was that Grant's forces were overwhelmingly and ingloriously defeated. Many of his brave troops were driven into the Allegheny River and drowned. The total loss was two hundred and seventy killed, forty-two wounded, and a number taken prisoners. Among the latter were Major Grant, Major Lewis and about nineteen other officers. The French account says that five officers and one hundred men were captured and that the French loss was only eight killed and eight wounded.

Captain Bullitt rallied some of the fugitives, and, dispatching some of the most valuable baggage with the best horse, made a barricade of the wagons, behind which he posted his men. After having finished the plunder of the battlefield, the Indians hastened in pursuit of the fugitives. They attacked Bullitt's men, who opened a destructive fire upon them from behind the baggage wagons. This checked them for a time, but they soon came with greater numbers. Then Bullitt and his men held out the signal of surrender, and advanced as if to lay down their arms. When within eight yards of the Indians, Bullitt's men suddenly leveled their rifles, poured in a destructive fire, and charged with the bayonet. The Indians then fled in order to get reinforcements. Bullitt took advantage of this check to collect some of the wounded and fugitives, with whom he hastened back to the camp at Ligonier. The Highlanders and the Virginians were those who fought the best and suffered the most in this bloody engagement. Six officers and sixty-two privates of the Virginia forces lay dead on the field. The road back to Ligonier was strewn with the dead.

A boy twelve years of age, who had been two years a prisoner among the French and Indians, made his escape from Fort Duquesne, on November 2nd, then succeeded in reaching Forbes' army, and gave the information that five of the prisoners taken at Grant's defeat had been burned to death by the Indians on the parade ground at Fort Duquesne and that several others were tomahawked. (Pa. Archives, Vol. 12, page 428.) One of the Highlanders, after witnessing the burning of several of his companions, planned a stratagem to avoid his being tortured by fire. He told one of the Indians that he could make a concoction of the juices of herbs that, when applied to any part of the body, would render that part invulnerable. He begged for permission to prove the truth of his statement. Permission was granted. Then, gathering some leaves and roots of plants, he squeezed out their juices, smeared his neck with the same, lay down with his neck across a log, and asked a warrior to attempt to cut off his head with an axe. The warrior swung the axe with all his might, and the Highlander's head was severed from his body. Seeing the trick that had been played upon them, the Indians praised the cunning of the soldier.

Grant's expedition was a monstrous blunder. General Forbes, with the main body of the army was as far in the rear as Bedford, and neither he nor Colonel Bouquet had any definite knowledge of the strength of the French and Indians at Fort Duquesne. In view of these facts, it seems strange, indeed, that Colonel Bouquet permitted Grant to advance into a death trap. Grant himself showed utter lack of judgment in playing the bagpipes and beating the drums at daylight, which had only the effect of telling the enemy of his advance. Neither the French nor the Indians knew of Grant's presence until the music broke the stillness of the autumn morning. How Grant's conduct impressed the Indians was expressed by one of the Delaware chiefs, Tecaughretango, in a conversation with James Smith, at that time a captive among them. This chief told Smith that the Indians believed that Grant "had made too free with spiritous liquors during the night, and had become intoxicated about daylight."

For account of Major Grant's defeat, see "Frontier Forts of Pennsylvania," Vol. 2, pages 80 to 90, also 197, 198 and 262 to 264.

Attack on the Camp on the Loyalhanna

After Major Grant's defeat, many of the Delawares, Shawnees and Mingoes in alliance with the French left Fort Duquesne, and returned to their villages, laden with the spoils of the battlefield. It was the custom of the Indians to return home after a battle, whether successful or not. Furthermore, owing to the success of the first peace mission of Christian Frederick Post to the Western Delawares, they and their allies were becoming dissatisfied with the French.

Colonel James Smith, then a prisoner among the Delawares and adopted by them, says in his Narrative that, after Grant's defeat, the Indians held a council, and were divided in their opinions, some saying that Forbes would now retreat, and others saying that he would come on. Many of the Delawares then, according to Smith, went back to their villages, not wishing to be absent from their squaws and children at this season of the year. The French were thus practically deserted by the Indians. Yet, emboldened by the crushing defeat of Grant, Captain De Ligneris, then commandant of Fort Duquesne, sent about one thousand French and two hundred Indians to attack Colonel Bouquet's camp at Ligonier, hoping to compel Bouquet to retreat, as did Dunbar after the defeat of General Braddock. This force of French and Indians attacked Bouquet's camp on October 12th. The following letter, written at Ligonier, on October 14th, probably by Colonel James Burd, and found in Pa. Archives, Vol. 12, page 392, thus describes this attack:

"We were attacked by 1200 French and 200 Indians, commanded by M. de Vetri, on Thursday, 12th current, at 11 o'clock, A. M., with great fury until 3 P. M., when I had the great pleasure of seeing victory attend the British arms. The enemy attempted in the night to attack us a second time; but in return for their most melodious music, we gave them a number of shells, which soon made them retreat. Our loss on this occasion is only 62 men and 5 officers, killed, wounded and missing. The French were employed all night in carrying off their dead and wounded, and, I believe, carried off some of our dead in mistake."

On the day of the attack, Colonel James Burd was in command of the fort and camp at Ligonier, and Colonel Bouquet was back at Stony Creek, near Stoystown, with seven hundred men and a detachment of artillery. After the first repulse of the French and Indians, Colonel Burd wrote Colonel Bouquet an account of the engagement. (Pa. Archives, Vol. 12, page 392; Frontier Forts of Penna., Vol. 2, pages 199 to 204, also page 264.)

As stated earlier in this chapter, General Forbes arrived at Ligonier about November 1st, although it was about a week later that all his troops had assembled at that place. On account of his illness, he was not able to keep up with the army, although it pushed on by slow stages and very wisely established fortified magazines as it went. The General's purpose was to assemble all his army at the camp at Ligonier preparatory to making the final advance

Washington's Engagement Near Ligonier

On November 12th, Colonel George Washington was out with a scouting party which attacked a number of French and Indians about three miles from the camp at Ligonier, killing one and taking three prisoners—an Indian man, a squaw, and an Englishman, named Johnson, who had been captured by the Indians several years before, in Lancaster County. Colonel Hugh Mercer, hearing the firing, was sent with a party of Virginians to the assistance of Washington. Mercer's men approached in the dusk of the evening, and, seeing Washington's party, with the three Indians, about a fire from which they had driven the enemy, mistook them for the enemy. Washington's party also mistook Mercer's men for the enemy. Both parties fired on each other, killing a lieutenant and thirteen or fourteen privates.

Such is the account of the unfortunate event, as given in the Pennsylvania *Gazette*, November 30th, 1758. However, Washington, in his account of the engagement, says that, when it was learned at Ligonier that the French and Indians were within two miles of the camp, a party commanded by Colonel Mercer, of the Virginia Line, was sent to dislodge them; that soon hot firing was heard which seemed to approach the camp, making General Forbes believe that Mercer's party was yielding ground; and that Washington, with permission of the General, then called for volunteers, and marched at their head to sustain Colonel Mercer. Washington, led on by the firing until he came within less than half a mile, and it then ceasing, sent scouts to investigate and to communicate his approach to Colonel Mercer. In the meantime he cautiously advanced, and the intelligence of his coming was not fully disseminated among Colonel Mercer's men. Night was now settling down the forests of Westmoreland. Taking Washington's men for the enemy, who had retreated, and thinking that they (the enemy) were now approaching in another direction, Colonel Mercer's men commenced a heavy fire upon Washington's relief party, which, in turn, drew the fire of Washington's men in spite of the exertions of the officers in Washington's party, one of whom and several privates were killed and many wounded. In order that the terrible mistake might not result in more deaths, Washington rushed between the two parties, knocking up their presented muskets with his sword. Being thus between two fires, he was never in more imminent danger of death. (Frontier Forts of Penna., Vol. 2, pages 206 to 208 and authorities there referred to.)

As stated in Chapter XVI, the Indians who had been attacked and routed in this engagement, came upon the party of Lieutenant William Hays, who escorted Christian Frederick Post as far as Kiskiminetas Town, killing the Lieutenant and four of his men, and capturing five others.

Washington's skirmish, on November 12th, was the last clash of arms between the French and Indians on the one side and the British on the other, in the Ohio Valley during the French and Indian War. It will be remembered that Washington was a leading figure in the opening conflict in this war, the attack on Jumonville, May 28th, 1754.

Fort Duquesne Falls

Upon General Forbes' arrival at Bouquet's camp on the Loyalhanna, he decided to go into winter quarters there, as the season was advanced. At this time, the French at Fort Duquesne were in a desperate situation. Practically deserted by their Indian allies, who, as an additional reason for returning to their villages, were in genuine fear of the Virginia troops, the French suffered the loss of the Louisiana and Illinois militia, who left Fort Duquesne in November. Worse still, the supplies intended for Fort Duquesne, had been destroyed by Colonel Bradstreet at Fort Frontenac. For this reason De Ligneris, the commandant at Fort Duquesne, was compelled through fear of starvation to dismiss the greater part of his force. All these things, however, were unknown to General Forbes at the time he intended to go into winter quarters on the Loyalhanna. (Frontier Forts of Pa., Vol. 2, pages 91 to 94 and authorities there referred to.)

The Englishman, Johnson, captured on November 12th, gave General Forbes the following information relative to the situation of the French at Fort Duquesne:

"That the Canadians who had been with Mons. Vetri at Loyal-Hanning [the attack of October 12th] were all gone home; that

Two views of the monument located on the Butler-Evans City Road, at a point ten miles south of Butler and two miles north of Evans City, Butler County, Pa., marking the approximate spot where Major George Washington narrowly escaped death when he was fired upon by a hostile Indian, less than fifteen steps distant, on the evening of December 27th, 1753, as he and Christopher Gist were on their way back to Virginia from Washington's historic mission to Fort Le Boeuf (Waterford, Pa.).

This monument was erected during the summer of 1924, and was dedicated, July 3d, 1925.

For account of Washington's Mission, see pages 144 to 149. The account of the Indian's attempt to kill him is found on pages 148 and 149.

—*Photographs by* H. E. Ripper, Evans City, Pa.

the Ohio Indians had also returned to their several towns; that the attempt made by Vetri at Loyal Hanning was only to make us apprehend their strength at Fort Duquesne to be very great, whereas they were very weak there . . . and our army would certainly succeed." (Pa. Archives, Vol. 12, page 393.)

This information caused General Forbes to decide not to go into winter quarters on the Loyalhanna but to press on against Fort Duquesne at once. Accordingly, on November 13th, Colonel John Armstrong, who was next in command to Colonel Bouquet, was ordered to advance with one thousand men. Washington was then already in the advance with about fifteen hundred men, building a road towards the French fort, and had erected one or more redoubts near Hannastown. On November 17th, General Forbes left Loyalhanning with forty-three hundred effective men, without wagons or heavy baggage, leaving a garrison at Fort Ligonier. On this same day, Washington had advanced as far as Bushy Run, and, on the 18th, Colonel Armstrong had reached a point within seventeen miles of Fort Duquesne. On the 24th, the entire army was within twelve miles of the fort, being encamped a few miles west of Turtle Creek. While here, a report was brought by Indian scouts that the fort was on fire, and Captain Haslet was sent with a detachment to endeavor to extinguish the fire. At midnight, Forbes' pickets "heard a dull and heavy sound booming over the western woods." The magazine at the fort had blown up.

The entire army advanced early the next morning, November 25th, and took possession of the smouldering ruins of Fort Duquesne, the coveted goal of the British for more than four long and bloody years. The same day Delaware messengers arrived at Kuskuskies, with the joyful news to Christian Frederick Post that "the English had the field, and that the French had demolished and burnt the place entirely, and went off; that the commander is gone with two hundred men to Venango, and the rest gone down the river in battoes, to the lower Shawnee town; they were seen yesterday passing by Sawcung [Sauconk]."

It was a Pennsylvanian, Colonel John Armstrong, who raised the British flag over the smoking embers this great stronghold of the French in the valley of the Ohio. French dominion in this valley was forever at an end. The joy in the British army was unbounded. By order of General Forbes, November 26th was observed by the army as a day of thanksgiving to Almighty God for the success of the British arms, and the day following a grand celebration was held.

Says Bancroft: "As the banners of England floated over the waters, the place, at the suggestion of Forbes, was with one voice called Pittsburgh. It is the most enduring monument to William Pitt. America raised to his name statues that have been wrongfully broken, and granite piles of which not one stone remains upon another; but, long as the Monongahela and the Allegheny shall flow to form the Ohio, long as the English tongue shall be the language of freedom in the boundless valley which their waters traverse, his name shall stand inscribed on the gateway of the West."

Forbes' troops found many of the dead of Grant's defeat within a quarter of a mile of the fort. They also found a number of stakes driven into the ground on which were stuck the heads and kilts of the Highlanders, killed on that fateful September morning. Detachments then buried Grant's dead and the bones of those who were slain at Braddock's defeat over three years before. (Pa. Archives, Vol. 12, pages 428 to 431; Pa. Col. Rec., Vol. 8, pages 231 to 234.)

As stated in Chapter XVI, General Forbes left Pittsburgh on December 3d, and went to Fort Ligonier, where he remained, on account of illness, until December 27th. He reached Carlisle, on January 7th, 1759, and from there went on to Philadelphia, where he was welcomed with great enthusiasm and joy. Here this great Scotchman of iron will died on March 11th, and was buried in the chancel of Christ Church.

Colonel Bouquet, next in command to General Forbes, remained at Pittsburgh until December 5th, when he left for Fort Ligonier, as was also seen in Chapter XVI. Colonel Hugh Mercer, with two hundred men, was then left in command at Pittsburgh, and immediately commenced erecting palisades and temporary quarters. By January 8th, 1759, his force was increased to two hundred and eighty men.

Thus began the occupation of the Ohio and Allegheny by the English. General Forbes was succeeded by General John Stanwix on March 15th, 1759, who soon arranged to erect a permanent fortification near the site of the former Fort Duquesne—Fort Pitt. Stanwix arrived at Pittsburgh, in August, 1759, and, on September 3d, the work of erecting Fort Pitt was commenced. By December 8th, the work was well advanced, and a garrison was being formed of 300 Provincials, one half of whom were Pennsylvanians and the other half Virginians, and 400 of the first battalion of Royal Americans. General Stanwix remained at Fort Pitt until March 21st, 1760, but the fort was not finally completed until the summer of 1761, under Colonel Bouquet, although it was occupied early in 1760.

The French had not more than four or five hundred troops at Fort Duquesne at the time when they set fire to the works and fled. On abandoning the fort one part of the French garrison went down the Ohio to the Illinois country, one hundred went by land to Fort Presqu' Isle, and two hundred went up the Allegheny to Fort Machault (Venango), while the Indians scattered to their various towns on the Ohio, Beaver and Muskingum. Fort Machault was strengthened, and it was proposed to remain there and defend the place if attacked. In the summer of 1759, great apprehension was felt at the temporary Fort Pitt that the French would descend the Allegheny from Fort Machault, and capture the place. George Croghan wrote Governor Denny from Fort Pitt on July 15th, and Colonel Hugh Mercer wrote the Governor from the same place on July 17th, both stating that two Indian spies whom Croghan had sent to Venango to ascertain the truth of the rumor that the French and Indians were gathering at that place to descend upon Fort Pitt, had returned and reported that seven hundred French and upwards of one thousand Indians had assembled at Venango before the middle of July, and were ready to descend the Allegheny on the 13th, when messengers arrived, advising that the British were marching on Niagara, which intelligence caused the French to abandon the project against Fort Pitt, and hasten to the relief of Niagara. Both before and after the French abandoned Venango, bands of Indians, led by French Canadians, went from that place and other Indian towns on the Allegheny, and attacked convoys on the road to Fort Pitt. In Colonel Mercer's letter, written at Fort Pitt on July 17th, he tells Governor Denny of a recent attack on Fort Ligonier by a band of Indians from Venango. (Pa. Archives, Vol. 3, pages 671 and 674.)

General Robert Monckton succeeded General Stanwix at Fort Pitt, on June 29th, 1760. He immediately gave orders for the march of a large detachment to Presqu' Isle to take possession of the upper French posts and those along the frontier to Detroit and Mackinaw. This detachment consisted of four companies of the Royal Americans, under Colonel Bouquet, Captain McNeil's company of the Virginia Regiment, and Colonel Hugh

Mercer's five companies of the Pennsylvania Regiment, the Captains being Biddle, Anderson, Clapham, Atlee and Miles.

During the autumn of 1759, Fort Redstone, also called Fort Burd, was erected at Redstone (Brownsville), by Colonel James Burd. During the summer of 1760, the English took possession of the sites of Fort Le Boeuf (Waterford) and Fort Presqu' Isle (Erie), and erected Fort Venango, almost on the site of the former Fort Machault, at Franklin.

Return of the White Captives

In the meantime, George Croghan, Deputy Indian Agent of Sir William Johnson, was receiving many white captives, delivered to him at Fort Pitt by the Delawares and Shawnees. From June, 1759 to October, 1761, he secured the release of three hundred and thirty-eight captives, at Fort Pitt.

Early in February, 1762, Governor James Hamilton received a letter from Shingas and King Beaver, then living on the Tuscarawas, through their faithful friend, Christian Frederick Post, advising the Governor that they desired to hold a treaty with him the following spring.

The Colonial Authorities had made many efforts after Post's mission to the Western Indians in 1758, to induce Shingas and King Beaver to come to Philadelphia for a conference. Shingas had declined to come, fearing that the English would retaliate upon him for the terrible atrocities that he had committed upon the frontier settlements during the French and Indian War. Now, however, that peace was secure and the Indian raids upon the border had stopped, Shingas wanted to meet the Governor in conference.

In March, the Governor sent a reply to Shingas and Beaver through Post, inviting these two chiefs to come to Lancaster to hold a conference at that place, inasmuch as smallpox was raging in Philadelphia. Post was appointed as the guide and escort, not only for the two chiefs and their delegation of Indians, but also for the captives which were to be returned by the Indians from the villages on the Muskingum and Tuscarawas, as well as the villages on the Beaver and Ohio. King Beaver and other chiefs of the Western Delawares had already returned seventy-four captives to Fort Pitt. Post immediately went to the villages of Shingas and King Beaver on the Tuscarawas, and began preparations for the return of the remaining captives. Among them were: Philip Studebaker, captured in the Conococheague settlement, Mary Stroudman, captured in the same settlement; Elizabeth McAdam, John Lloyd and Eleanor Lancestoctes, captured in the Little Cove; and Dorothy Shobrian, captured in the Big Cove. (Pa. Col. Rec., Vol. 8, page 728.) Post was beset with many troubles. He had difficulty in getting Shingas and Beaver to return with him and also in keeping the captives from running away and returning to the Indian villages. He arrived at Lancaster on August 8th, with Shingas, King Beaver and the captives. Dr. George P. Donehoo, in his "Pennsylvania—A History" thus comments upon the reluctance of the white captives to return to the settlements:

"One of the most remarkable facts in the relation of the English with the Indians during this entire period is that these captives, whose parents or husbands or wives had been most cruelly killed and scalped by Indians, had to be guarded and oftentimes fettered in order to keep them from running back to the captivity from which they had been released. One explanation of this most peculiar condition has been attempted by some writers, who have dealt with the topic, saying that the captives were men and women of the lower sort, and had not been accustomed to anything different from that which had been their condition in the villages of their Indian masters. But this is an absolutely false statement. Some of them had been taken from the best class of frontier families. The great majority of them, as shown by their names, belonged to the hardy, religious Scotch-Irish families along the frontiers of Pennsylvania and Virginia, which furnished the leading men and women of the Colonial period. The only explanation is to be found in the statements made by the captives and by the Indians, that these adopted relations were treated with the utmost kindness and respect by their captors."

However, many captives, taken during the French and Indian War, were not released until Colonel Henry Bouquet made his expedition to the Muskingum and Tuscarawas in the late autumn of 1764. Others, those held by the Shawnees, were not delivered until the spring of 1765. These matters will be discussed in a subsequent chapter. However, at this point, we call attention to the fact that many prisoners never returned to the settlements, preferring to spend the remainder of their lives with the Indians.

Conclusion

General Forbes' victorious expedition closed the French and Indian War, in Pennsylvania. But the irresistible pressure on the lands the Delawares and Shawnees were occupying west of the Allegheny Mountains went on, notwithstanding the deeding back of these lands to the Indians at the Grand Council at Easton, in October, 1758. Numerous treaties and councils were held with the Delawares and Shawnees, at Fort Pitt, Philadelphia, and Lancaster during several years following the capture of Fort Duquesne—treaties in which the English promised these tribes that they would withdraw east of the Allegheny Mountains, and not invade the hunting grounds and homes of the Indians—promises which the English had no intention of keeping. The awful consequences that followed the breaking of these promises will be seen in our next chapter.

80657988R00234

Made in the USA
Middletown, DE
16 July 2018